GERSHWIN
HIS LIFE AND MUSIC

GERSHWIN

HIS LIFE AND MUSIC

by

Charles Schwartz

A DA CAPO PAPERBACK

Library of Congress Cataloging in Publication Data

Schwartz, Charles.
  Gershwin, his life and music.

  (A Da Capo paperback)
  Reprint of the ed. published by Bobbs-Merrill, Indiana-
polis.
  "Compositions by George Gershwin": p.
  Discography: p.
  Bibliography: p.
  1. Gershwin, George, 1898-1937. 2. Composers — United
States — Biography.
  [ML410.G288S33 1979]   780'.92'4 [B]   78-20838
  ISBN 0-306-80096-9

ISBN 0-306-80096-9
First Paperback Edition 1979

This Da Capo Press paperback edition of Gershwin: His Life and Music is an unabridged
republication of the first edition published by the Bobbs-Merrill Company in New York
and Indianapolis in 1973. It is reprinted by permission of the author.

Published by Da Capo Press, Inc.
A Subsidiary of Plenum Publishing Corporation
227 West 17th Street, New York, N.Y. 10011

To Red and Pick Heller with deep affection

ACKNOWLEDGMENTS

How can I thank *all* who were helpful in the writing of this book: those who suffered through interviews or masses of correspondence, or who gave encouragement, advice, and criticism, or who assisted in any of a variety of ways? But if the list is too long and cumbersome to do justice to all involved, I would still like to note my appreciation collectively for the help rendered.

On a personal basis, my gratitude goes to Dr. Victor Yellin, who first encouraged my Gershwin studies; to my family for their devotion and support; to Elissa Epel, for her many critical and invaluable comments on the manuscript; to Joseph Machlis, for his ever practical advice; to Charlotte Fisher, whose outstanding typing of the manuscript remains a source of wonder; to Dr. Patricia Nash, for her numerous helpful suggestions; to Frank Campbell, Chief of the Music Division of the New York Public Library, and his staff, and to Richard Jackson, head of the Americana Collection of that division, for their consistent courtesy; to Melvin Parks, Curator of the Theater and Music Collection of the Museum of the City of New York, and Charlotte LaRue and Maggie Blackmon, of the Museum staff, for their excellent cooperation; to Donald Madison, for helping to reproduce much of the Gershwin reference material in my files; to Ross Hastings, former music editor of Music Publishers Holding Corporation, for allowing me access to edited Gershwin manuscripts; to Harold Spivacke, former Chief of the Music Division of the Library of Congress, and his staff, for their kind assistance; to Frederick Freedman, for his bibliographic help; to Mrs. James C. Pressey, assistant archivist of the Metropolitan Opera Company, for her aid relating to the Metropolitan; to Walter Evans, of Warner Brothers Music, for information about Gershwin copyrights; to Walter Myers, my editor at the Bobbs-Merrill Company, for his strong support; and to Lee and Betty Lee Kolker, Dr. George Nash, Theodore and Renee Weiler, Morris Golde, and Berta Walker, for their continued interest in my efforts.

If this book reflects in even a small measure the cooperation, good will, and encouragement of the many who somehow had a hand in its completion, it is the better for it.

CONTENTS

AN APPRECIATION

$\mathcal{A}$LL CULTURAL DISCIPLINES are subject to the tyranny of fashion. Suddenly, it's all about Hume or Diderot or the Post Royal grammarians; suddenly Thomas Mann is out and Macaulay is in; Coleridge is down five and a half points. . . .

The world of music is not exempt from this epochal whimsicality. In fact it tends to be more fickle and volatile than even the brave new world of linguistics. I vividly remember causing a sensation as a Harvard undergraduate by announcing that I loved the music of Tchaikovsky. It was considered an outrageous heresy; Tchaikovsky was located one pigeon-hole beneath contempt at the time, as was Verdi. The fashion dictated pre-Beethoven and post-Wagner. Today, half a lifetime later, Verdi is musicologized as solemnly as is Monteverdi; Hindemith is unfashionable, Ravel grossly underrated. Alas, the musical marketplace.

One of the most egregious victims of this musical *haute-couture* in our century has been George Gershwin. The "higher criticism" does not permit that name to enter the category of significant composers. This is sad, because Gershwin was certainly one of the true authentic geniuses American music has produced. Time and history may even show him to be the truest and most authentic of his time and place.

It is sad, and yet understandable. Gershwin was, after all, a songwriter

—in his nature, his origin, his experience, and his craft. His songs have become part of our language, or the vernacular, if you will, and they are happily hummed and whistled by people the world over. He came from the wrong side of the tracks, grew up in the ambience of Tin Pan Alley, song-plugging, and musical near-illiteracy. His short life was one steady push to cross the tracks, both musically and socially—an effort guided and sustained by ambition and an enormous reservoir of sensibilities. This book traces that track-crossing, from songs to shows, from shows to real theater pieces *(works)* such as *Of Thee I Sing,* from structurally weak concert pieces like the *Rhapsody in Blue* through the *Concerto in F,* to the final amalgamation we see in *Porgy.* All these works are easily demolished by the higher criticism: the *Rhapsody* for example is a model of structural ineffi- ciency. It is episodic, loosely strung together by rather artificial transitions, modulatory devices, and second-hand cadenzas. But what's important is not what's wrong with the *Rhapsody,* but what's right with it. And what's right is that each of those inefficiently connected episodes is in itself melodically inspired, harmonically truthful, rhythmically authentic. Again we call upon that word; no less a master of form and structure than Arnold Schoenberg recognized the "authenticity" of Gershwin's music.

Gershwin's tragedy was not that he failed to cross the tracks, but rather that he did, and once there, in his new habitat, was deprived of the chance to plunge his roots firmly into the new soil. He was given only a little more than a decade to develop the fruits of this transplantation and died shock- ingly and maddeningly in his thirties, a few years older than Mozart was when he died. These two names may be felt to be an uncomfortable pairing, but they make a fascinating comparison. Both men were "naturals," each evolving a body of music that sprang like phenomena of nature from their respective soils, fertile and flourishing. But Mozart had no tracks to cross; his was one great continuing harvest from childhood to death. Gershwin, on the contrary, had to plough, sow, thresh and reap afresh over and over again. By the time of *Porgy* we sense an incipient Master. We can only speculate about what degree of mastery he might have attained if he had lived. The tragedy of his death-in-the-prime is a great one; but we only compound the tragedy if we persist in the "higher criticism" and ignore the radiant fact that Gershwin was, and remains, one of the greatest voices that ever rang out in the history of American urban culture.

Leonard Bernstein
Cambridge, Mass.
April 19, 1973

PROLOGUE

WHAT MAGIC IN the name of George Gershwin! It conjures up the roaring 1920s, Broadway glitter, extravagant parties, beautiful women. Hum a Gershwin tune anywhere from Boston to Bangkok and probably someone can finish the chorus. Gershwin may be gone but he is hardly forgotten.

At his death on July 11, 1937, shortly before his thirty-ninth birthday, "Mr. Music," as Gershwin was called, was already a towering figure in the music and entertainment world; a legend in his own lifetime. Born in Brooklyn of Russian-Jewish parents of modest means and raised on the lower East Side, Gershwin never finished high school. Yet he became famous, wealthy, and the intimate of many celebrities because of his talent. But to say that his is just another success story begs the question. Gershwin is a lot more than that. For he also symbolizes American opportunity, American drive and ingenuity, American music, and an image of an earlier America that is colorful, dynamic, and perhaps a little innocent.

Gershwin is probably better known now than ever before. Evidence of his growing popularity can be seen in the number of buildings and schools named after him; in the postage stamp issued in his honor; in the Hollywood movie of his life (the highly fictional *Rhapsody in Blue*); in the broad appeal of numerous television specials based on his tunes; and in the many all-Gershwin concerts that attract capacity audiences throughout the world.

As the hero of his own bigger-than-life drama, Gershwin has been the subject of numerous articles and biographies. Yet with all that has been written about him, there are many aspects of his life and work that are practically unknown. As a result of repeated stories about him, a "definitive", image of Gershwin as man and musician has been established, one that does not reflect the facts of the case. Complicating the matter further, key biographies of Gershwin have been written by his friends or members of his family. They are often not so accurate or so objective as one might wish.

This book has been written in the hope of bringing Gershwin's life and music into better focus.

Charles Schwartz

GERSHWIN
HIS LIFE AND MUSIC

Morris and Rose Gershwin at about the time they were
married. *(Jewish Daily Forward)*

FAMILY
BACKGROUND

ON SEPTEMBER 26, 1963, in honor of one of its most famous sons, by proclamation of Borough President Abe Stark, Brooklyn celebrated the sixty-fifth anniversary of George Gershwin's birth. For the occasion, a ceremony—amply covered by the press—took place at the composer's birthplace, a modest two-story brick house at 242 Snediker Avenue, between Sutter and Belmont Avenues, in the East New York section of the borough. As part of the ceremony a student chorus, appropriately from Brooklyn's George Gershwin Junior High School, serenaded the guests with Gershwin songs. Among the guests were Borough President Stark; Morton Gould, the composer; Irving Caesar, the lyricist; and Frances Godowsky and Arthur Gershwin, sister and younger brother of George. In honor of the event a bronze plaque contributed by ASCAP was unveiled at the house, identifying it as Gershwin's birthplace.

Gershwin's birthplace at 242 Snediker Avenue is now a two-family house. It stands surrounded by rows of buildings in which various racial and ethnic groups live side by side. Signs in Spanish, Hebrew, and English, reflecting this diversity, abound in the neighborhood. By contrast, when Gershwin's parents and their infant son Ira moved to rural Brooklyn from the crowded East Side of Manhattan before the turn of the century, their

3

one-family house was surrounded by trees. Grapes grew on a vine in the yard around the house, and there was open space suitable for children to play. But most of George's boyhood years were not spent in this bucolic setting, for by the time he was about three years of age the Gershwins had moved back to Manhattan, where George's father was employed. There, among the tenements, the noise, and the hustle and bustle of the lower East Side, George grew up.

Gershwin's name is listed on his birth certificate as "Jacob Gershwine." As is the custom in many Jewish homes, Gershwin was named after a deceased relative, in this case his grandfather, Jacob, on his father's side. The birth certificate also lists such information as his father's occupation ("leather worker"), his mother's maiden name ("Rosa [Rose] Brushkin [Bruskin]"), the parents' ages (the father was twenty-six, the mother twenty-two), and the number of previous children (one). The name Gershwine on the certificate apparently resulted from a misspelling by Dr. Ratner of 71 Belmont Avenue, who signed the document. Gershwin's family name was actually Gershvin, an Americanization adopted by his father, Morris (Moishe) Gershovitz,[1] shortly after his emigration to the United States from St. Petersburg in the early 1890s. As recorded, Jacob was Gershwin's legitimate first name, but it was as George that he was always known. George was not the only member of the family whose first name was changed: Ira's given name also underwent a similar metamorphosis. Invariably called "Izzy" by his friends and family, Ira had always assumed that his real name was Isidore. It was not until 1928, when he applied for a passport, that he discovered that he was listed as "Israel" on his birth certificate.

At any rate, George changed the spelling of his last name when he became a professional musician, though it is not clear when he first used the name Gershwin consistently, for other variants of the name—such as Wynn and Gerchwin—also turned up on occasion. What is clear, however, is that all of his published music, starting with the 1916 song "When You Want 'Em, You Can't Get 'Em, When You've Got 'Em, You Don't Want 'Em," with lyrics by Murray Roth, lists his name as Gershwin. With George setting the lead, the other members of his immediate family also took the name Gershwin.

The family's rather casual use of names was reflected in its offhand approach to other matters, too. For instance, distrustful of banks as a repository for their limited financial assets in the early years, the Gershwins instead pawned Rose's diamond ring when cash was needed, and there were many such occasions. Equally haphazard was the attention paid to formal Jewish religious practices. As a consequence, only Ira of the three boys had a *bar mitzvah*. Morris Gershwin, moreover, was continually changing occupations. Among the diverse businesses—none of which made him financially secure—that he owned or operated were these: bakeries, restaurants, a bookmaking establishment, Russian and Turkish baths, a summer hotel, a cigar store and pool parlor, and a rooming house. Because Morris liked to live within walking distance of his various business activities, the family was frequently moving. Before George had reached the age of eighteen, the Gershwins had lived in twenty-eight residences, twenty-five in Manhattan and three in Brooklyn (the Brooklyn residences included the house on Snediker Avenue and apartments in Coney Island during the summers of 1914 and 1915).

Morris Gershwin's limited success as an entrepreneur was undoubtedly a direct result of his personality, for he was a gentle, whimsical, and artless man, short and rotund, with little drive and possibly less business acumen. In print he was generally treated as an attractive but comical figure; his social obtuseness became a positive virtue. Actually, though amiable and good-natured, he was so exceedingly naïve he often said or did ludicrous and gauche things, even after the composer had become a world figure: dressing up and serving as an elevator operator for some of George's friends and associates for no apparent reason other than his love of uniforms and the childlike pleasure of running a simple mechanical contraption; or claiming to all who would listen that he was an opera authority, though he had little knowledge of the medium; or insisting on entertaining George's guests by putting tissue paper on a comb and humming tunes through the contrivance, with dreadful results. In many families a Morris Gershwin would unquestionably be considered a fool, with few if any redeeming social graces. One might question whether he would not have been viewed differently in published reports had he not fathered so famous a composer.

Most reports have not given a true indication of his extraordinary involvement in cardplaying and betting on horses. He loved to spend every spare moment in these pursuits, continuing the interest in gambling that he had acquired while still in Russia. With family management left to his wife, Morris Gershwin's role as a father figure was understandably negative and weak,[2] though his children were always warmly attached to him, perhaps for what he was not rather than for what he was. Morris's role as father was weakened further by the fact that Rose was usually the complainant in the frequent arguments that took place between them, particularly while their children were still young. But despite his weak position in the home and the fact that he never earned enough money in his entrepreneurial pursuits to qualify even remotely as well-to-do, Morris was

5

somehow able to provide for his family in a decent, though at times precarious, fashion. In later years Rose claimed that the family had always had a maid, even when living on the lower East Side.

As an offshoot of Morris's ingenuous personality, a considerable number of anecdotes have been widely circulated in which quixotic comments and malapropisms have been attributed to him. At one time, friends of the composer gave thought to the idea of gathering these *bons mots* into a book, but nothing came of this idea.

Possibly because of deficiencies in speaking and understanding English, Morris also frequently altered the composer's song titles or misinterpreted some of the words as well as the actual import and function of various Gershwin tunes. "Fascinating Rhythm," for instance, was referred to by Morris, accent and all, as "Fashion on the River." The love song "Embraceable You," from *Girl Crazy*, Morris mistakenly assumed to have been written about him because of the words in the refrain, "come to poppa—come to poppa—do"; in the presence of guests, he would often ask the composer to play the song "about me." The production number "I'll Build a Stairway to Paradise," which received spectacular treatment in *George White's Scandals of 1922* (dancers in black garb were highlighted against a white stairway), Morris considered a "war song," apparently because of the tune's persistent, almost marchlike beat.

Himself not religious, Morris Gershwin could point to a grandfather who had been a rabbi. Morris's father, however, had not followed a religious calling. Instead, he was a mechanic who had been drafted into the Russian artillery. Gershwin family rumor has alleged that while Morris's father was in the service he helped in some way to invent a gun used in the Czarist army, though the actual part he played in the invention has never been clearly delineated.[3]

While still in St. Petersburg, Morris knew Rose Bruskin and became strongly attracted to her. When Rose and her parents emigrated to the United States about 1891, Morris soon followed them, both because of his interest in Rose and because he faced the possibility of being drafted into the Russian army, like his father before him, if he remained at home.

In contrast to her husband, Rose Gershwin has usually been described as "level-headed." The daughter of a St. Petersburg furrier, she had been nurtured from childhood on commonsense business practices. It was she who assumed the responsibility for handling the uncertain finances of a burgeoning household that eventually included four children. (Ira preceded George on December 6, 1896; Arthur followed him on March 14, 1900; and Frances was born on December 6, 1906.) Under Rose's management, money that Morris would have frittered away if left to his own devices was set aside during those infrequent periods of plenty to help sustain the family during its more numerous lean times.

Rose's marriage to Morris, the ever-persistent suitor, took place in a lower East Side restaurant on July 21, 1895, approximately four years after the Bruskins, parents and daughter, had emigrated from Russia. It has been alleged in family circles that the wedding festivities lasted three days. A small, dark, plump, pretty girl when Morris first met her, Rose blossomed into a handsome woman who managed to dress stylishly even when she and her husband had little money. Despite a limited education and a broad Russian-Yiddish accent that always remained with her, Rose assumed surprisingly well the increased social responsibilities that went hand in hand with George's rising fame as a composer. As a matter of fact, she always seemed to welcome the opportunity for broadening her own and George's social horizons. Time and again, even after George had arrived as a composer, she would make suggestions to him concerning professional and social contacts she felt he should cultivate. Not inconsistent with Rose's suggestions, one finds that George throughout his professional career seemed to gravitate toward the famous, the wealthy, and the highly placed. He enjoyed being in their company and solicited their friendship. It is interesting that with the social élite, Gershwin often seemed more boyish and charming than usual and almost diffidently modest, a characteristic hardly in keeping with the ebullience and outward confidence generally associated with him.

Rose, like her husband, could not resist betting on horses. She and Morris not only placed bets with neighborhood bookmakers but also, from the earliest days of their marriage, rented a private limousine from time to time to attend the races, disregarding their chronic financial instability before George became famous. Again like Morris, Rose was an inveterate cardplayer. For many years, Saturday evenings at the Gershwin apartment were set aside for poker games with her friends. On weekdays Rose played cards as well. For a while she could be found almost every night backstage at the National Theater on Second Avenue—close to where the Gershwins then lived—playing cards with finesse with her Jewish actress friends there while carrying on small talk with ease and gusto. When occasion demanded it, Rose's language could be off-color and tough. Considering that she had not been a longtime resident of this country, one might speculate that her relatively sophisticated behavior in the urban New York setting stemmed from the fact that she had grown up in a major Russian city rather than one of the small country towns, the *shtetls,* of the Pale of Settlement—the vast ghetto for East European Jews in the latter part of the nineteenth century which included Byelorussia, Lithuania, the Ukraine, and a considerable portion of Poland.

The failing commonly ascribed to many Jewish mothers of being overprotective of their children did not apply to Rose Gershwin. Once her children had passed their infancy, she generally let them go their own ways with a minimum of maternal interference. As a result, the Gershwin children spent a good deal of time on the streets of the city and quickly learned to shift for themselves. While on the streets, George learned all about sex from his peers. He also became acquainted with brothels and apparently developed a fascination for purchased sex that remained with him all his life. At the height of his fame, for instance, with women literally throwing themselves at him—and George did not hesitate to take sexual advantage of favorable situations—he still frequented brothels with some regularity.

Despite her laissez-faire attitude toward her children, Rose Gershwin was a substantial mother figure in the household. Key family decisions were usually made by her. From childhood on, George confided in his mother, sought her advice, and followed her counseling when it was volunteered, things he could not have done with his father. It is not surprising, therefore, that when George at the age of fifteen wanted to leave school in order to take a job at Remick's as pianist and song plugger, he sought his mother's permission and approval, not his father's. All in all, Rose was much more of an influence on George than was his father, whose relationship with the composer, though warm, was much more casual.

After the death of Morris Gershwin on May 14, 1932, of leukemia,[4] George and his mother seemed to become closer to each other than ever before. The composer was a loving and dutiful son, considerate, generous, and respectful. Rose was frequently present as an honored guest at parties given by him or to which he had been invited. She could also be seen prominently seated at concerts in which he performed, a celebrity in her own right, pampered by friends and family and closely watched by Gershwin's admirers in the audience.

In 1931 Gershwin was quoted as saying of his mother, "She's what the mammy writers write about and what the mammy singers sing about. But they don't mean it, and I do." He also felt that he resembled his mother rather than his father in personality and general makeup. He considered himself and his mother to be of the same mold: "nervous, ambitious, purposeful." Contrary to these opinions by Gershwin, some studies of him written after his death have stated or implied that he never loved his mother, only his father. Rose Gershwin, in turn, has been depicted as an almost impossible woman, unhappy, self-centered and overly domineering, who did not get along well with George. One must, of course, question why this viewpoint, so different from those expressed by the composer, found support. But now with Gershwin and his mother both dead (Rose died of a heart attack on December 16, 1948, after several weeks of failing health), the answer may not be readily available. As a possible explanation for this altered image, it should be noted that there have been reports, never stated publicly, of strained relations which developed between Ira and his mother after George had died. As a result of these reputed differences, it is conceivable that Ira, as a major source of information about George's life, may have helped to influence, no matter how subtly or unconsciously, opinions about Rose Gershwin. As an indirect reinforcement of this hypothesis, one finds that Ira speaks of his father with warm affection in three humorous anecdotes in his 1959 book, *Lyrics on Several Occasions,* whereas his mother is not mentioned even once.[5]

Be that as it may, Ira, just as he was when the composer lived, continues to be closely associated with George's affairs. Not only does he spend a considerable amount of time maintaining his archives on the composer, he also oversees numerous personal and business matters relating to his brother.

The other living members of Gershwin's immediate family are Arthur and Frances. Married since 1930 to Leopold Godowsky, Jr., the son of the famous pianist, Frances is now the mother of four grown children. She and her husband—co-inventor, with Leopold Mannes, of the Kodachrome process used in color photography and a wealthy man through his own efforts—lead socially active lives, frequently shuttling between their Westport and Sutton Place homes. Frances has also found time to concentrate on painting, a medium in which she has shown considerable flair. As for Arthur, he is perhaps the least known of the Gershwin children. A musician by inclination, he has tried to emulate George by writing popular songs, but his efforts have never caught on with the public. Like his brother and sister, he receives a large annual income from the Gershwin estate that enables him to live in comfortable style.

In contrast to their parents, relatively poor and unknown Russian-Jewish immigrants, the Gershwin children are now wealthy and prestigious. This transformation can be attributed almost solely to George's success as a composer, though Ira of course has clearly established himself as a fine lyricist.[6] More than three decades after his death, George remains the dominant member of his family.

The lower East Side (Hester Street), where Gershwin grew
up about the turn of the century. (*The Byron Collection,
Museum of the City of New York*)

BOYHOOD YEARS

Gershwin's childhood in the New York ghetto resembled that of many other youngsters of working-class immigrant families. Like most of his peers, he had few toys to play with at home, because his parents had little money to spend on such luxuries. An outgoing, active child, he never cared much for reading books or other solitary intellectual pursuits; his play activities took place mainly on the East Side streets. There, among the noisy tenements, pushcarts, horse-drawn wagons, dogs and cats, and the endless stream of humanity, he participated in such sports as punchball, stickball, handball, baseball, foot races, jumping contests, wrestling, and hockey. He soon showed that he was athletically inclined by excelling in nearly all sports. He was especially adept at roller skating—so much so that he came to be considered roller-skating champion of a number of streets in which he played. "Follow the leader" and "Cat" were other outdoor favorites with Gershwin's set, while cardplaying, billiards, and pool were common indoor sports that boys such as he were generally expected to master by their adolescent years. Since many of these games were competitive, fighting among the participants was commonplace. He soon learned to handle himself with finesse in these situations. It has even been claimed that he went out of his way to provoke fights for the sheer physical excitement of thrashing others; his broken nose, evident in

11

numerous pictures of him as an adult, is a memento of these pugilistic adventures.

In contrast to his clear-cut demonstrations of interest in physical activity as a child, he revealed a scholastic deficiency that may possibly be attributed to the fact that for boys such as George any activity that smacked of intellectualism was deemed sissyish. Not only were his elementary school grades very poor, but he often misbehaved in class as well. He usually showed only a casual concern for homework assignments and also played hookey whenever he thought he could get away with it. As a result of his indiscretions at school, particularly at P.S. 20 in the heart of the lower East Side, his teachers often sent notes of complaint home, many of which never reached the hands of Rose or Morris Gershwin. Through ingenuity born of desperation, whenever possible Gershwin got neighbors to sign these notes instead of his parents. Ira also played a part in these deceptions. When the occasion demanded it, he would appear in school as the alleged substitute for his parents, thus placating George's irate teachers. Against this rough-and-tumble background, such ruses were taken for granted by George, as were his numerous petty thefts from neighborhood stores and street vendors. If he had been caught in some of these pilferings, his life might easily have taken a different turn.

Music had little meaning for Gershwin as a youngster, for he heard little of it and paid little attention to what he did hear: this included the sound of the organ-grinder's hand organ; the isolated scales, melodies, and chords coming from tenement windows as budding pianists and violinists practiced; the high-pitched, distorted music of the merry-go-round; the rather dull and unappealing songs that were presented in elementary school; and the few free concerts he attended when he was eight or so at the Educational Alliance on East Broadway. Apparently none of these experiences left much of a mark on him as a child. However, years later, after he had become established as a composer, looking back to these early days Gershwin claimed that when he was about six years old Anton Rubinstein's *Melody in F* had made a strong impression on him. According to Gershwin, "The peculiar jumps in the music held me rooted." He remembered that he first heard the piece played on a pianola as he stood barefoot and in overalls outside a penny arcade on One Hundred Twenty-fifth Street in Harlem. He also looked back fondly to his brief youthful encounters with ragtime and jazz while skating past Harlem nightclubs or standing in front of Coney Island cafés during the summer.

Gershwin subsequently claimed, too, that he was profoundly moved by Dvořák's *Humoresque* played at a school entertainment at P.S. 25 by a fellow student, an eight-year-old violin prodigy named Maxie Rosenzweig.

Gershwin's birthplace in Brooklyn.

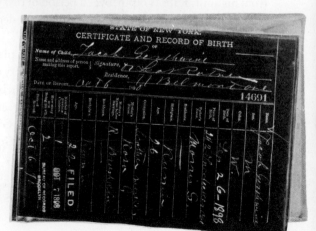

Gershwin's birth certificate, listing him as "Jacob Gershwine."

(The young talent eventually came to be known professionally as Max Rosen and had a brilliant career as a violin soloist; he died in 1956.) Gershwin, Maxie's senior by two years, did not actually attend the recital in the school's assembly hall. This did not prevent his hearing Maxie's sonorous violin playing, which carried beyond the confines of the hall. He was so excited by what he heard that he waited outside of school that afternoon in a pouring rain to meet Maxie. But he did not see him: the violinist had left by another exit. Not easily deterred, Gershwin found out where Maxie lived and, soaking wet, went to the boy's house, where he introduced himself as an admirer of the young virtuoso. Maxie was not home at the time to hear the words of praise. His family, however, were so impressed by Gershwin's adulation that they arranged a meeting for the two boys shortly afterward. He and Maxie soon became close friends: they shared secrets, wrote numerous letters to each other, though they did not live far apart, and engaged in wrestling bouts, with Gershwin—the elder, stronger, and more athletic of the two—invariably winning. They also discussed music. Here, Maxie's more sophisticated background proved helpful to the untrained Gershwin, who conceded that "Max opened the world of music to me." Under the influence of Maxie, he was even motivated to try his hand at playing simple tunes on a friend's piano. However, Maxie did not encourage Gershwin's faint hope of becoming a musician. In the bluntest way he advised Gershwin that he lacked musical aptitude.

Maxie's bleak prognosis apparently did not stop Gershwin from continuing occasional musical experiments at the keyboard of his friend's piano, and when the Gershwins in 1910 finally bought a secondhand upright on the installment plan, George astounded his family by his ability to play simple pieces he had taught himself. The Gershwins had actually bought the piano for Ira, who had been taking piano lessons sporadically from his aunt, Kate Wolpin, over a period of two years. But George soon had the piano entirely for his own use when Ira decided that his interests lay elsewhere than in a musical career.

Gershwin began his formal study of the piano with several neighborhood teachers, starting with a Miss Green at fifty cents a lesson and progressing to a Mr. Goldfarb, a Hungarian with an impressive mustache and a commanding presence, who charged a dollar and a half a lesson, a high price in those days. According to Gershwin, Goldfarb "played the piano with great gusto and a barrel of gestures." Goldfarb's method of piano teaching was novel, for he concentrated solely on having his pupils play excerpts from grand operas rather than exercises and the traditional repertoire. After six months with Goldfarb, he had advanced as far as the overture to *William Tell.*

P.S. 20, on Eldridge and Rivington Streets, the school that George and Ira attended. *(Courtesy Aaron Fishman)* Other famous alumni of this school include Edward G. Robinson (Emanuel Goldenberg), Paul Muni (Muni Weisenfreund), Harry Golden, and Irving Caesar.

Charles Hambitzer, Gershwin's first important music teacher.

Realizing that Goldfarb's approach to music was incompatible with his own instincts, Gershwin was amenable to the suggestion of a pianist friend, Jack Miller, whose playing he admired, that he see Miller's teacher, Charles Hambitzer. At the first meeting with Hambitzer, which probably took place sometime in 1912, Gershwin played the overture to *William Tell* as taught him by Goldfarb. Hambitzer listened quietly until George finished playing and then exploded. "Let's hunt out that guy," he sarcastically remarked, referring to Goldfarb and his teaching system, "and shoot him—and not with an apple on his head, either." As Gershwin soon found out, Hambitzer, a sensitive, dedicated musician, was a fine pianist and a talented composer of light music. He also had had extensive practical experience performing with orchestral and chamber ensembles; he was far and away the most musically skilled of the teachers Gershwin had encountered until then. Despite Gershwin's rough edges, Hambitzer was sufficiently impressed by the boy's musical potential to accept him readily as a pupil. Moreover, he refused to accept a fee for the lessons.

Gershwin's studies with Hambitzer were to prove a milestone in his life. Hambitzer not only improved Gershwin's piano technique, but he also stimulated his interest in the music of the masters, especially the works of Chopin, Liszt, and Debussy. Hambitzer helped, too, to focus his attention on the importance of harmony in musical composition. Though the composer never formally studied harmony with Hambitzer, the latter, as Gershwin put it, "made me harmony-conscious."

A born teacher, kind and yet forceful where the interests of his art were concerned, Hambitzer had the gift for bringing out the best in his pupils. He was an ideal instructor for Gershwin, who was so taken with Hambitzer that he made a point of extolling his teacher's notable qualities to his friends. Gershwin's enthusiasm apparently carried much conviction, for in no time at all he had recruited ten new students for Hambitzer.

Gershwin's high regard for his teacher was more than matched by Hambitzer's esteem for his pupil. In a letter to his sister Olive, written shortly after young Gershwin started studying with him, Hambitzer prophetically described him as a "pupil who will make his mark in music if anybody will." He added, "The boy is a genius, without doubt; he's just crazy about music and can't wait until it's time to take his lessons. No watching the clock for this boy. He wants to go in for this modern stuff, jazz and what not. But I'm not going to let him for a while. I'll see that he gets a firm foundation in the standard music first."

Under Hambitzer's guidance, Gershwin began to go to concerts quite regularly, certainly more frequently than ever before. Years later, Gershwin claimed that it was through these concerts that he acquired the "habit of

16

intensive listening." According to him: "I . . . listened so earnestly [at the concerts] that I became saturated with the music. . . . Then I went home and listened in memory. I sat at the piano and repeated the motifs."

In a gray ledger book that he used as a scrapbook, now at the Library of Congress, Gershwin pasted souvenirs of many of the musical events he attended while with Hambitzer. These included a concert on April 13, 1913, at the Waldorf-Astoria in which Hambitzer performed a movement from Anton Rubinstein's *Concerto in D Minor;* a concert that Maxie Rosenzweig gave at Cooper Union only five days later; and a concert by the Civic Orchestral Society of New York, conducted by Pierre Monteux. Also in his scrapbook, under the headings "Great Pianists of the Keyboard" and "Russian Musicians" (the headings are in Gershwin's youthful hand), are pictures of musicians clipped for the most part from *The Etude,* a popular music magazine. Inasmuch as the scrapbook was started as early as 1909 or 1910, before his studies with Hambitzer, many of the names it contains could hardly have been familiar ones to Gershwin; among the "Russian Musicians" in the scrapbook are such composers as Ilyinsky, Liapunov, and Sapelnikov. By virtue of the haphazard and indiscriminate manner in which it was put together, his scrapbook, if nothing else, clearly confirms that his interest in music began when he was relatively young.

Gershwin's familiarity with the traditional repertoire was of course strengthened by his concert attendance. Nonetheless, his preference for jazz and popular music, which Hambitzer had noted in his letter to his sister, soon proved to be the dominant element in shaping his career. By 1913, Gershwin had already written two songs, "Since I Found You" and "Ragging the Traumerei" (Leonard Praskins was lyricist for both songs), neither of which has been published. During the summer of that year, Gershwin also served as a pianist, performing popular pieces, at a summer resort in the Catskill Mountains at a salary of five dollars a week.[1] The following year, on Saturday evening, March 21, 1914, Gershwin appeared in public for the first time as both pianist and composer,[2] playing a tango of his own at a social given by the Finley Club, a literary group affiliated with City College of New York. Ira, then a student at the college (where he was known as "Isidore Gershvin"; he left school after several semesters and never received a degree), served on the entertainment committee of this group and was able to schedule Gershwin's piece for the event, which was held at the Christadora House, 147 Avenue B, on the lower East Side. Gershwin's unpublished tango was listed on the program for the social simply as "Piano Solo" by "George Gershvin." It followed two addresses by club members that opened the proceedings—a rather modest and inauspicious beginning for one who was to become world-famous as a composer.

17

The interest Gershwin showed in music never carried over to the classroom setting of New York City's public schools. On the basis of his poor record in the elementary grades, it soon became clear to his family, particularly to his mother, that he was not cut out to be a scholar. It was Rose's considered judgment that business training rather than an academic education would be in order for him. A musical career was ruled out too because of the difficulties involved in earning a livelihood in this most precarious of professions. Because he had shown a certain affinity for arithmetic, it was decided, not without deliberation, that he should prepare himself for the position of accountant. After all, it was argued, an accountant's life offered a reasonable amount of security, and maintaining and auditing business records was orderly and respectable. With this decision made, immediately after graduating from P.S. 25 in 1912, he enrolled in the High School of Commerce for training in accounting.

At Commerce, Gershwin did not neglect his music. He not only persisted in his piano studies but also performed from time to time in the morning assembly programs at school. Week by week, he continued to advance in music as a result of his interest and diligence. On the other hand, his scholastic record at Commerce showed no improvement over the one he had achieved in elementary school. As before, his marks were almost uniformly bad, and he gave no indication that his grades would improve in the future. It was soon apparent that the idea of becoming an accountant held no appeal for him.

Because an accountant's career now seemed unlikely, Rose Gershwin started to give thought to alternative professions for him. To her way of thinking, the fur business offered excellent possibilities. But before she could broach the subject, Gershwin asked her one day for permission to leave school in order to take a job as pianist and song plugger at Remick's, the music publishers. He informed her that through the good graces of Ben Bloom, a friend in the popular-music field, he had been introduced to Mose Gumble, manager at Remick's, and had been offered a job there at fifteen dollars a week. Rose, as was to be expected, considered him too young to leave school and was anything but receptive to the idea of his becoming a professional musician. Gershwin, however, was adamant in wanting to be a musician; no other career, he insisted, had any attraction for him. In the face of his sincerity and persistence, Rose relented and allowed him to accept the job. Thus, in May 1914, at the age of fifteen he left school to work at Remick's, where he had the distinction of being one of the youngest pianists employed in Tin Pan Alley.

With his job at Remick's, Gershwin entered on a full-time basis the professional world of music, where the demands and the commensurate financial and artistic rewards were greater than anything he had ever encountered. His childhood can be considered to have ended at this tender age with the start of his Tin Pan Alley affiliation. At Remick's, Gershwin left his boyhood years behind him as he became almost instantaneously a young adult competing in an adult's world.

Gershwin during his early days in Tin Pan Alley.

THE YOUNG
PROFESSIONAL

JEROME H. REMICK AND COMPANY began operation in Detroit as the firm of Whitney-Warner, music publishers. On the strength of a varied assortment of hit tunes, such as "Dance of the Brownies"; "Creole Belles," a cakewalk; and "Hiawatha," a pseudo-Indian number, the organization moved to New York shortly after the turn of the century. As Remick's, the company soon established itself as one of the most important publishers in Tin Pan Alley, the center for popular music in New York and the nation. Though it is not completely clear how Tin Pan Alley got its name, it has been suggested that the title may have been derived in the early 1900s from the tinny sounds that emanated from the pianos of publishers such as Remick's, purveyors of tunes for the masses. From the start Tin Pan Alley was invariably located near the panoply of theaters and music halls that constituted New York's key entertainment area. As these amusement places moved uptown from Fourteenth Street, Tin Pan Alley followed in their path.

When Gershwin began working for Remick's in 1914 the firm was located in a drab brownstone walk-up, similar to those of other publishers, on West Twenty-eighth Street between Broadway and Sixth Avenue. Twenty-eighth Street at the time was considered the heart of Tin Pan Alley. Most of the popular tunes of the country originated in the publishing houses there. Popular music to them was strictly a business—one with immense potential for rich rewards. For those publishers who were bright enough, forceful enough, and lucky enough to catch the public's fancy with a hit tune, thousands of dollars could be made almost overnight, mainly from the sale of sheet music.

In such a lucrative arena, competition was keen. It was crucial for the financial success of any song that it become widely known—the sooner the better. Radio, television, and the other present-day mass communications media did not exist in the early 1900s: other ways of reaching the song-buying public were used. Most often, publishers hired song salesmen or pluggers to help publicize and sell their tunes. To the pluggers fell the task of getting their companies' songs performed by singers, instrumentalists, vaudevillians, and other professionals at theaters, saloons, and restaurants. In order to achieve this goal, pluggers were not above resorting to questionable or less than honorable devices; for them the ends more than justified the means. A common practice for pluggers was the use of bribery for obtaining performances of their tunes. Less devious, perhaps, was their habit of mingling with audiences in theaters and elsewhere so they could clap loudly and shout approval when their songs were presented. Sometimes they would hire claques to do the same thing. Nothing was overlooked in the pluggers' attempts to draw attention to their songs. To succeed as a plugger, ingenuity and a lack of scruples were almost mandatory.

Gershwin entered the corrosive and blatantly aggressive world of the song plugger when he joined Remick's. Because of his youth and lack of experience, however, he usually was not entrusted by his employer with promotional schemes that required a great amount of guile. Instead, he spent most of his time in his cubicle—one of many on the premises for the pluggers. There, as a low-ranking musical salesman in the so-called professional department, he pounded the piano from eight to ten hours a day, playing Remick songs for all who would listen to them. Years later, looking back at this job, he recalled: "Every day at nine o'clock I was there at the piano, playing popular tunes for anybody who came along. Colored people used to come in and get me to play 'God Send You Back to Me' in seven keys. Chorus ladies used to breathe down my neck. Some of the customers treated one like dirt."

He had other duties besides playing piano in his cubicle. On orders from Mose Gumble, his manager, he visited vaudeville houses to check on whether Remick tunes were used in particular acts. At night, after his place of business had closed, Gershwin often accompanied a team of singers and dancers as they made the rounds of cafés and restaurants, publicizing

Remick songs. These duties or similar ones were not confined to New York City. As the occasion demanded it, he traveled out of town.

Offsetting the many less than desirable aspects of the popular-music field, Gershwin's stay at Remick's was of immeasurable benefit to him. In almost every way, his association with Remick's turned out to be sound on-the-job training for his future career. Starting as a tyro in a highly competitive field, he quickly became aware of the pitiless and often unscrupulous ways of Tin Pan Alley. He saw firsthand the behind-the-scenes machinations and the skulduggery involved in producing hit tunes. He became hardened to the mores of the trade. More importantly, his pianistic facility improved by leaps and bounds from playing hours on end, often under conditions that taxed his inventiveness to the fullest. Much of his progress as a pianist undoubtedly derived from his own curiosity, for he was constantly experimenting with new runs, chords, and modulations. He was never content to play Remick tunes, or any others, in standard fashion. His adventuresome approach to playing was a wholly pragmatic one. It was self-teaching in the finest sense, whether or not he was aware of it: the musical devices that worked, he held on to and used again; the rest he discarded. Gershwin's ability to transpose material at the piano also improved while at Remick's. Because he frequently had to play songs within the limited range of singers with inadequate vocal techniques, he had to perfect his ability to switch from key to key almost instantaneously in order not to strain the limited vocal talents of those he accompanied.

As Gershwin's playing ability increased, his reputation as a pianist increased accordingly. Soon he came to be regarded as possibly the finest pianist at Remick's. Many professionals—among them entertainers, songwriters, lyricists and fellow pluggers—sought him out in his cubicle to hear him play. By 1915, on the basis of his impressive skill as a performer, Gershwin was asked to make player-piano rolls for a modest fee—five dollars for one roll, twenty-five dollars for six—for which there was a substantial market. He was more than happy to record the rolls: it was a means of both broadening his professional experience and supplementing his meager salary at Remick's. (Besides recording piano rolls, Gershwin, early in his career, added to his income by playing at parties, nightclubs, and theaters.)

When he began making rolls, he traveled from his family's apartment to New Jersey on Saturdays for the recording sessions. Surprisingly, he did not record only in his own name. Perhaps to avoid giving the impression of a monopoly of the piano-roll market by one performer, he also used the unlikely pseudonyms of Fred Murtha, Bert Wynn, and James Baker. Whatever the reason for the pseudonyms, George recorded more than one hundred rolls[1] under various names from 1915 to around 1926 for the Universal Hand-Played, Metro-Art, Melodee, Perfection, Angelus, and Duo Art labels. Among these rolls were a number of pieces he had composed himself, including a piano version of the *Rhapsody in Blue*.

While at Remick's, Gershwin wrote numerous songs with the hope that his Tin Pan Alley connection would lead to their publication. It did not take him long, however, to realize that his aspirations as a composer were not necessarily helped by his job. When one of his songs was submitted to Remick's for consideration, it was rejected. In unequivocal terms he was told that he had been hired as a pianist and plugger, not as a songwriter. Conceivably someone less sure of himself might have been badly shaken by the rejection. But he hardly seemed to notice it. His characteristic self-confidence remained with him throughout his life. He continued to write songs as before and eagerly played them for all who would listen.

Many of the tunes that date from the Remick period were successfully revived by Gershwin some years later, for he always made a point of storing material for future use. "Nobody but You," for example, from *La La Lucille* (1919), was written while Gershwin was at Remick's. "Drifting Along with the Tide," heard in *George White's Scandals of 1921,* as well as "Some Rain Must Fall" and "Dancing Shoes," introduced in *A Dangerous Maid* (1921), also trace their genesis to his days as a plugger.

Gershwin frequented the National Theater on Second Avenue in his spare time as a means of learning as much as he could about the Yiddish musical theater, particularly the music of Joseph Rumshinsky—then installed at the National as composer and conductor—and the operettas of Abraham Goldfaden, an actor turned composer who died in 1908. (Some indication of Goldfaden's enormous popularity with the Jewish people can be deduced from reports that at his death hundreds of thousands of people followed his funeral procession through New York's streets.) Gershwin's interest in the Yiddish theater began about 1913 and continued through the first year or two of his employment at Remick's. His interest in this medium was not motivated by ethnic devotion, as neither he nor his family were involved with Jewish customs to any marked degree, but by practical considerations. Composing for the Yiddish theater offered a considerable amount of security, it paid well, and employment was steady. Yiddish musicals were extremely popular with the thousands of Jewish immigrants from Eastern Europe who had settled on the East Side at the turn of the century. Theaters such as the National, the Second Avenue theater, and the Public were filled night after night with eager audiences.

Gershwin's flirtation with Yiddish musical theater finally bore results.

Remick's, on West Twenty-eighth Street, at about the time Gershwin worked there. *(Museum of the City of New York)*

Gershwin during his early days in Tin Pan Alley.

Boris Thomashevsky, who tried to persuade Gershwin and Sholom Secunda to collaborate on a Yiddish operetta. *(Jewish Daily Forward)*

Sholom Secunda.

AGREEMENT made and entered into this thirtieth day
of October, 1929, by and between the METROPOLITAN OPERA COMPANY,
represented by its General Manager, Mr. Giulio Gatti-Casazza, of New
York, N.Y., party of the first part, and MR. GEORGE GERSHWIN, party
of the second part.

FIRST:-   The party of the second part agrees to compose the music
of a new opera, the libretto and title of which are to be known as
"DYBBUK", this opera to be ready for performance by April 1, 1931. The
party of the second part representing also the librettiest of this
opera, hereby grants to the party of the first part the exclusive rights
in all languages for the cities of New York, Brooklyn, Philadelphia,
Baltimore, Washington, Atlanta, and Cleveland of performing said opera
during the season of 1931-1932 or 1932-1933.

SECOND:-   The party of the first part agrees to pay to the party of
the second part the sum of Two Hundred Fifty ($250) Dollars for each
and every performance of said opera and further guarantees to give or
pay for not less than four (4) performances; this payment to include the
rights for the use of the material, of the libretto and the plot.

THIRD:-   The party of the second part agrees to furnish the
following material at the times specified hereinafter to the Metropolitan
Opera Company at the Metropolitan Opera House in New York City, as
follows:

a) The PIANO AND VOCAL SCORE on April 1, 1931;

b) The full orchestra score (Conductor's score) on April 1, 1931;

c) The chorus parts on April 1, 1931;

d) The orchestral parts for the full orchestra of the Metropolitan
    Opera Company by April 1, 1931.

FOURTH:-   The party of the second part agrees to supervise gratis
the work in connection with getting out the above mentioned material and
agrees to have the same done at the most reasonable figure for account
of the party of the first part, which agrees to pay for same. The

party of the second part agrees to correct the orchestral parts before
delivery of same for account of the party of the first part at the most
reasonable price.

FIFTH:-   The party of the second part agrees that after the material
has been copied, he personally will look over said material, in order to
correct not only the orchestral parts but also the conductor's score and
solo parts, before the time of delivery, as mentioned above.

SIXTH:-   It remains understood that the first performance on any
stage of this opera shall take place at the Metropolitan Opera House,
New York City.

SEVENTH:-   The party of the first part shall have the right to renew
this agreement upon the same terms and conditions for the following
seasons.

EIGHTH:-   It remains understood that the material enumerated in
paragraph "third" shall become the property of the party of the second
part at the expiration of this contract.

                              METROPOLITAN OPERA COMPANY

                              General Manager.

A c c e p t e d:

. . . .

A copy of the agreement Gershwin signed with the
Metropolitan Opera Company in 1929 for the production
of *The Dybbuk*. *(Courtesy Metropolitan Opera Company)*
Gershwin planned to incorporate Jewish music
into this opera.

In 1915 he was invited by Boris Thomashevsky, the impresario of the National, to collaborate on a Yiddish operetta with Sholom Secunda, four years his senior and a gifted musician steeped in the Jewish tradition. Thomashevsky reasoned that the combined efforts of two young and promising talents would almost automatically guarantee a fine musical. The idea, however, was rejected by Secunda for several reasons. First, Secunda considered Gershwin a primitive because he didn't read music very well; he still played the piano mainly by ear. Furthermore, Secunda had studied at the Institute of Musical Art—now the Juilliard School of Music—and preferred to associate with his equals in musical training. Also, Secunda had had a Yiddish tune published in 1914 called "Haym Zieser Haym" ("Home Sweet Home"), which Regina Prager, a famous Jewish singer, had performed extensively. Consequently, he considered it beneath his professional stature to collaborate with a young man whose background was not on a par with his own and who had no published works to his credit.

It is undoubtedly of little value to speculate on the path that Gershwin might have taken if the proposed Gershwin-Secunda collaboration had become a reality. Suffice it to say that Secunda, after rejecting Gershwin as a musical partner, went on to write innumerable scores for the Yiddish stage. In so doing, he clearly established himself as one of the foremost composers of Yiddish musicals. Gershwin, on the other hand, never wrote anything explicitly for the Yiddish theater. Except for his youthful nod in the direction of Second Avenue, he concentrated mainly on composing for Tin Pan Alley, the Broadway stage, and the concert hall. His music, perhaps more than that of any other composer of his generation, has come to be universally viewed as an indigenous American product. Contrary to this widely held opinion, a number of sources have claimed that Gershwin's work was influenced by Jewish music, though these supposed influences have generally not been spelled out.[2] In connection with these claims, it should be noted that Gershwin once planned to write a Jewish opera, *The Dybbuk*, for the Metropolitan Opera. He even signed a contract with the Metropolitan to that effect on October 30, 1929, at the behest of his friend Otto Kahn, the noted art patron and financier who was closely associated with the opera company. Gershwin's opera was to be based on the Yiddish play of the same title by S. A. Ansky, a pseudonym for the Polish-Jewish author Solomon Rappaport (1863–1920). In preparation for the opera, Gershwin went so far as to write some musical sketches, which unfortunately are not extant, and to consider studying Jewish music in Europe so as to lend authenticity to the work.[3] But Gershwin gave up the idea of writing *The Dybbuk* when he learned that the rights to the original play had been assigned to the Italian composer Lodovico Rocca.

When Gershwin abandoned the writing of *The Dybbuk*, a potentially valuable source of information dealing with his conscious handling of Jewish material was lost to the world. Without this opera to serve as a frame of reference, the presumed Jewish legacy in Gershwin's music must be sought in the body of his existing work. This is a problematic and speculative task at best, especially as one cannot ever be sure that he actually borrowed material from Jewish sources. He himself never spoke out on the matter. Yet in examining Gershwin's music, one finds that many of his melodies and motifs resemble Jewish prayer chants and secular pieces. As a matter of fact, one of Gershwin's most famous tunes, "'S Wonderful," seems to have been lifted bodily from "Noach's Teive" ("Noah's Ark"), a number in the Goldfaden operetta *Akeidas Izchok* ("The Sacrifice of Isaac").[4] Because of this apparent duality in Gershwin's musical style (that is, Second Avenue Yiddish combined with native American), the question of Jewishisms in his compositions deserves further consideration and will be examined in Appendix I.

By 1916, Gershwin could qualify at last as a professional composer. That year one of his songs, "When You Want 'Em, You Can't Get 'Em, When You've Got 'Em, You Don't Want 'Em," was published. Interestingly, Sophie Tucker, the renowned "red-hot mama," was helpful in bringing about publication of the tune. He had played the song for her one day. She had reacted favorably to it and recommended it to Harry von Tilzer, the publisher. As a result of her recommendation, Gershwin signed his first contract as a composer on March 1, 1916, with the Harry von Tilzer Publishing Company.[5] For his part in writing the lyrics, Murray Roth, a Tin Pan Alley acquaintance of Gershwin, accepted an advance of fifteen dollars from the publisher. Gershwin, however, waived an advance. He decided instead to wait for royalties, with the idea in mind of ultimately receiving a large lump sum. When a considerable length of time had passed and no royalties were forthcoming, he asked von Tilzer for some money for his song. In answer to his request, the publisher handed him five dollars. This was the first and only payment Gershwin received for the tune, which had little to commend it save its historic value as his first published piece.

Gershwin and Roth wrote another song that same year, "My Runaway Girl." With this second tune their collaboration ended. One day in youthful exuberance they started wrestling, apparently in wholly amicable fashion. Suddenly their jousting took a different turn, gradually increasing in intensity and animosity and ending with the two quite shaken up, their relationship severely strained. They never wrote a song together after that.

"My Runaway Girl," unlike the first Gershwin-Roth tune, was never

28

Excerpt from Goldfaden's "Noach's Teive"

Kum zu mir in teive a-rein,   kum a-rein,   kum a-rein.
(Come to me, in the ark,   come in,   come in.)

Excerpt from Gershwin's " 'S Wonderful"

'S won-der-ful! ——————— 'S mar-ve-lous! ———————

The close resemblance between the melody for
Goldfaden's "Noach's Teive" (top) and
that of " 'S Wonderful" (bottom) lends support
to the claim that the Yiddish musical theater
was a source for some of Gershwin's material.

Abraham Goldfaden, the dean
of American Yiddish musical theater.
(*Jewish Daily Forward*)

Left: Jerome Kern, one of Gershwin's important musical influences. *(Courtesy ASCAP)*

Bottom left: Sophie Tucker as a young "red-hot mama." Her recommendation helped Gershwin to get his first song published.

Bottom right: Vivienne Segal, an early champion of Gershwin's songs. *(Museum of the City of New York)*

published, but it had a part in advancing Gershwin's career. Confident that this song was suitable for a Shubert production, he played it for a Mr. Simmons of the Shubert office. Simmons liked it well enough to arrange for Sigmund Romberg, the Shuberts' chief composer, to hear it. After meeting with Gershwin, Romberg suggested that the two collaborate on some songs for his next Winter Garden musical, scheduled to open shortly afterward. He asked that Gershwin bring him appropriate material for the forthcoming show as quickly as possible. Overjoyed at the chance of being associated with a Broadway production, Gershwin brought a number of songs to Romberg over a period of a few weeks, hoping they would elicit his approval. From these, Romberg selected one song, "Making of a Girl," with lyrics by Harold Atteridge, and incorporated it into *The Passing Show of 1916* (which opened at the Winter Garden on June 22, 1916). For his efforts, Gershwin received credit as Romberg's collaborator in writing the tune—his second publication. He also realized slightly more than seven dollars in royalties the following January from Schirmer's, publisher of the song.

Remick's finally published a piece by Gershwin in 1917. It was "Rialto Ripples," a piano solo in ragtime style which he had written the previous year with a collaborator, Will Donaldson. Before the piece's publication, Gershwin had made a piano-roll recording of it which was released in September 1916 on the Universal Hand-Played label. Essentially an attempt to emulate the earlier and more famous ragtimes of Joseph Lamb, Ben Harney, and Scott Joplin, "Rialto Ripples" did not cause much of a to-do in either its piano-roll or its published version. But then his musical interests no longer revolved around Tin Pan Alley; rather, a career as a composer for the Broadway musical theater had slowly but surely become his preference and his goal. As he later claimed, "The popular-song racket began to get definitely on my nerves. Its tunes somehow began to offend me. Or perhaps my ears were becoming attuned to better harmonies." Obviously unhappy at Remick's, he left his job on March 17, 1917, after being with them for more than two years. In his own words: "Something was taking me away [from Remick's]. As I look back, it's very clear that I wanted to be closer to production-music—the kind Jerome Kern was writing."

It was at the wedding of his Aunt Kate that Gershwin heard renditions of "You're Here and I'm Here" and "They'll Never Believe Me" from *The Girl from Utah* and became attracted to Kern's show tunes. According to Gershwin, "Kern was the first composer who made me conscious that most popular music was of inferior quality and that musical-comedy music was made of better material."

With his job at Remick's behind him, Gershwin sought to enter the

31

musical-comedy field in emulation of Kern. The means by which that goal could be realized, however, were anything but clear to him. In a quandary, he visited the office of a good friend, Will Vodery (1885–1951), a Negro arranger, to solicit his advice. Vodery listened sympathetically to his story and promised to see what he could do. (Later he orchestrated Gershwin's 1921 one-act opera *Blue Monday Blues* and also worked as an arranger for some of Gershwin's shows.)

Through Vodery, Gershwin obtained a job as pianist at Fox's City Theater, a vaudeville house on Fourteenth Street. He was hired at a salary of twenty-five dollars a week to play during the supper show; that is, while the members of the orchestra had their dinner meal, Gershwin alone was to accompany the acts from the pit. His employment at the vaudeville house was spectacularly brief. While accompanying an act during his first evening at the theater, he missed some cues as he read a manuscript at sight. He found himself playing one thing while the chorus girls on stage were singing another. The comedian in the act, sensing his predicament, took advantage of the situation and began to deride his piano playing. Embarrassed and angered by this ridicule and by jeers and laughter from the audience he quit the job immediately after the performance was over, without bothering to collect his pay for the day.

Sometime in July, not long after this fiasco, Gershwin's luck took a turn for the better when he began employment as rehearsal pianist for *Miss 1917*, a musical with a score by Victor Herbert and Jerome Kern. His salary had now risen to thirty-five dollars a week. But more important than salary, this job enabled him to see at close range the backstage workings of Broadway musical comedy. With this job, he also came in contact with his idol, Kern, the illustrious Herbert, and such other notables as Florenz Ziegfeld, P. G. Wodehouse, Vivienne Segal, and Lew Fields.

Gershwin's rehearsals with the chorus, ensemble, and principals and his impromptu concerts to entertain the staff during their leisure moments were carried off with such skill and aplomb that he was retained on the company payroll at his regular salary even after the musical opened at the Century Theater on November 5, 1917. During the musical's short run of forty-eight performances, Gershwin, among his other duties, served as accompanist for Sunday evening concerts at the Century. These started on November 11 and featured principals from the *Miss 1917* cast. At the November 25 concert, Vivienne Segal, a star of the show, sang two of George's songs: "There's More to the Kiss Than the X-X-X" and "You-oo Just You" (Irving Caesar was the lyricist for both songs). Miss Segal, one of the earliest devotees of Gershwin's music, sang the tunes with so much grace and style that a representative of Remick's in attendance at the concert was persuaded to consider "You-oo Just You" for publication; the song was subsequently published by them in 1918. Also present at the concert was Harry Askins, manager for *Miss 1917*. Askins had already been won over by Gershwin by the job he had done as pianist for the company. On hearing the two songs, Askins was still further impressed by Gershwin and took it upon himself to commend him to Max Dreyfus, head of T. B. Harms, probably the most important publishing company in Tin Pan Alley.[6] Askins's praise of Gershwin was not overlooked by Dreyfus.

Dreyfus was always seeking new talent. But more than that, he had an extraordinary gift for recognizing potentially outstanding composers early in their careers, among them Jerome Kern, Richard Rodgers, Sigmund Romberg, Vincent Youmans, Cole Porter, and Kurt Weill.[7] Dreyfus's sound judgment and foresight in selecting composers may have derived from the fact that he himself was a talented musician. His composition "Cupid's Garden," written under the pseudonym of Max Eugene, was frequently performed in theaters at the turn of the century. Born in Germany in 1874, Dreyfus had a long and close connection with Tin Pan Alley—first as arranger, song plugger, pianist, and composer, and then as publishing executive—which began when he was a young man and lasted until his death on May 12, 1964, at the age of ninety.[8]

Not long after Askins had brought Gershwin to the attention of Dreyfus, a meeting was arranged between the two. After speaking with Gershwin and hearing samples of his work in the early part of February 1918, Dreyfus made an unusual offer. He proposed that Harms pay Gershwin thirty-five dollars a week. There would be no set duties for him, such as plugging or pounding a piano in a cubicle. He had only to continue to write songs and to submit them to Harms for consideration. For each song published, he would be entitled to royalties—three cents for each copy of sheet music sold. This arrangement would even allow him to supplement his income through outside work as a pianist. Under the circumstances, he eagerly agreed to join the staff of Harms, but not before he had fulfilled an earlier commitment to tour the Keith theater chain as accompanist to Louise Dresser, a song stylist of national repute.

Beginning in New York, Miss Dresser and Gershwin went on to Keith theaters in Boston and Baltimore and concluded their tour in Washington, D.C., during the week of March 4, 1918. The tour was eminently successful for both of them; they enjoyed working together and their act was well received. Moreover, Gershwin's association with Miss Dresser was especially valuable in making him aware of the subtle tricks of showmanship which help to win audiences.

Prior to his affiliation with Harms, Gershwin had also been offered a job as musical secretary to Irving Berlin, putting to paper the tunes Berlin picked out on the piano and harmonizing them. Gershwin's facility at the piano, combined with the ease with which he embellished everything he performed, made him a natural for the job. He was greatly flattered by the offer, inasmuch as Berlin happened to be one of his favorite composers (Gershwin particularly liked "Alexander's Ragtime Band"). But after thinking it over, they both decided it would probably be best if Gershwin continued to try to make a career as a composer. A job as musical secretary, even for a Berlin, they agreed, held limited promise for the future and might have a stifling effect on his musical ambitions.

Under Dreyfus's benevolent patronage, Gershwin slowly forged ahead, but he was not above accepting employment as a rehearsal pianist for musicals. In the spring and summer of 1918, for instance, he served as pianist for *Rock-a-Bye Baby* (music by Jerome Kern) as well as for the *Ziegfeld Follies of 1918* (music by Louis A. Hirsch). He also found time to learn to play the saxophone. In anticipation of being drafted into the army, with World War I still raging, he practiced the saxophone so that he might qualify for an assignment in a military band, thus possibly avoiding the risk of serving in the infantry; the armistice of November 11, 1918, ended his concern with the matter. Of most immediate interest to him, however, was the publication by Harms—now his exclusive publisher—in September 1918 of their first Gershwin song: "Some Wonderful Sort of Someone," with lyrics by Schuyler Greene. This marked the start of a long line of Gershwin tunes that Harms published, many of which proved to be immensely profitable for both the publisher and the composer.

Shortly after the publication of "Some Wonderful Sort of Someone," Gershwin learned that the tune had been chosen by the celebrated Nora Bayes, of vaudeville and musical comedy fame, for her new show *Ladies First* (originally titled *Look Who's Here*), a farce on women in politics. Though the writing of the complete score for this musical had been assigned to A. Baldwin Sloane, Miss Bayes (née Dora Goldberg) wanted to interpolate Gershwin's song into the second act as part of a series of solo numbers she planned to do. She also hired Gershwin to serve as her accompanist during a six-week tour of the show preceding its Broadway opening.

As her accompanist, Gershwin found Nora Bayes to be a difficult, abrasive personality. She seldom had a kind word to say to him. He was often the target of reprimands by the tempestuous Miss Bayes, who complained continually that his accompaniments interfered with her singing style. Yet if we are to take the word of one eyewitness, Oscar Levant, his playing actually enhanced Nora Bayes's singing. When he was only twelve, and

34

wholly unfamiliar with Gershwin, Levant had attended a performance of *Ladies First* in Pittsburgh.[9] Years later, in his book *A Smattering of Ignorance,* Levant recollected that in the second act Nora Bayes took the center of the stage. Alone with her pianist, she performed her specialty numbers as all other stage action stopped. Levant recalled his first impression of Gershwin as accompanist in the following manner: "I had never heard such fresh, brisk, unstudied, completely free and inventive playing—all within a consistent frame that set off her [Nora Bayes's] singing perfectly."

Perhaps in retribution for her many unkind remarks to him, Gershwin had the last word in an incident that brought about the parting of their ways. One day Miss Bayes suggested that he change the ending of one of his songs for her. To her chagrin, he would not comply with her suggestion. Refusing to accept defeat lightly, Miss Bayes reminded him that even established composers such as Kern and Berlin would gladly make similar changes to suit her if they had been asked. He still would not budge, declining to consider her request further.

During his tour with Miss Bayes, another of his songs, "The Real American Folk Song" was added to the show. The lyricist, Arthur Francis, was actually Ira Gershwin using a pseudonym that combined the names of his younger brother, Arthur, and his sister, Frances. This piece was the first songwriting collaboration by George and Ira ever performed. Aside from the song's historical significance, its text clearly portends Ira's gift for writing lyrics, as evidenced by the refrain:

> The real American folk song is a rag—
> A mental jag—
> A rhythmic tonic for the chronic blues.
> The critics called it a joke song, but now
> They've changed their tune and they like it somehow.
> For it's inoculated
> With a syncopated
> Sort of meter,
> Sweeter
> Than a classic strain;
> Boy! You can't remain
> Still and quiet—
> For it's a riot!
> The real American folk song
> Is like a Fountain of Youth:
> You taste, and it elates you,
> And then invigorates you.
> The real American folk song—
> IS A RAG!

Ira has given this explanation for his use of the pseudonym: "When I first went into the lyric business, I adopted the name Arthur Francis . . . so that I shouldn't be suspected of trying to work my way into the game on the strength of my brother George's reputation." Explicit in Ira's statement is the fact that George, young as he was, had already made a sizable name for himself as pianist and composer. Ira, on the other hand, had not made much progress as a writer; his most important claim to literary distinction was the publication of a short story, "The Shrine" (under still another pseudonym, Bruskin Gershwin), in the February 1918 issue of the H. L. Mencken–George Jean Nathan magazine *Smart Set,* for which he received one dollar as full payment.[10] In order to support himself, Ira was still floundering around in a variety of odd jobs (cashier for a carnival; desk clerk at the Turkish baths run by his father; helper in a photographer's darkroom; assistant in the receiving section of Altman's department store; and the nonsalaried reviewer of vaudeville for the New York *Clipper*). Because of his uncertain status as a writer, Ira welcomed all signs of appreciation and encouragement. He was therefore very pleased when "The Real American Folk Song," after being tried out on Miss Bayes's tour, was retained in the show when *Ladies First* opened in New York on October 24, 1918, at the Broadhurst Theater. Shortly after the opening, however, the song was dropped from the show. Ira earned nothing for his lyrics, although, as he later noted, he "would gladly have paid for the honor" of being represented on Broadway. After its excision from the show, the song lay dormant for over forty years. Finally in 1959 it was published.

Neither did George benefit financially from the inclusion of his music in *Ladies First*. He soon learned that as a rule only the composer credited with writing the complete score for a musical stood a chance of making any appreciable amount of money for his work. This point was emphasized by him in a letter he wrote to a friend while touring with Miss Bayes's show. Gershwin reported that A. Baldwin Sloane, the composer on record for *Ladies First,* had told him he had received four hundred dollars in royalties —based on three percent of the gross receipts—when the show played in Trenton and Pittsburgh. Gershwin's parenthetical comment was, "Why didn't I write the show and let him interpolate?" Then he added: "Seriously, I am thinking of writing a show. . . . I am getting confidence and encouragement from this show and from B. Sloane and his royalties. I'm going to make an attempt when I reach New York."

Not one to waste time, Gershwin was represented on Broadway by a complete musical score the following year, only seven months after *Ladies First* had started its run in New York. But in 1918, he had had to content himself with having his songs interpolated into other composers' musicals. Such a musical was *Hitchy-Koo of 1918*. It opened at the Globe Theater on June 6, 1918, with Adele Rowland, star of the show, singing Gershwin's "You-oo Just You," one of the two Gershwin tunes performed by Vivienne Segal at a *Miss 1917* Sunday concert the previous November.

Besides *Ladies First* and *Hitchy-Koo of 1918,* he was associated with a third musical in 1918, *Half Past Eight*. It was produced by a young promoter named Perkins, who had had little show-business experience before mounting this revue. He had originally come to Dreyfus with some musical material he had brought from Paris. He was in need of a composer for additional songs for a revue he was planning. Did Dreyfus have any suggestions? Dreyfus, always on the lookout for shows Gershwin might do, recommended him and even volunteered to give Perkins an advance toward the revue and to pay for the orchestrations as well.

Under the impetus of Dreyfus's generous offer, Perkins went ahead with plans for producing the revue. Before long, he met with Gershwin, who proceeded to write five songs for the show to Perkins's lyrics (Ira assisted the promoter to some extent with the texts); four of the tunes were used in the show though none was published. In recruiting the cast, the fast-talking, glib Perkins persuaded Joe Cook, the comedian renowned for his inconsequential patter, to appear in the show along with his troupe. He also gathered a twenty-five-piece black band from the Clef Club, a bicycle act, and a few other assorted attractions. With a small cast in hand and no chorus Perkins started rehearsals for the show.

On Monday, December 9, 1918, *Half Past Eight* opened at the Empire Theater in Syracuse, New York, to a sold-out house; a local organization had paid eight hundred dollars for all the seats in the theater. The air of expectation and excitement in the audience before the curtain went up was soon dispelled. Most of the attractions in the revue were not of top caliber, and the show itself was not long enough for an evening's entertainment by usual standards. Starting at eight-forty-five, the first act was over by nine-thirty. After a half-hour intermission, the second act got under way and ended at a quarter to eleven. Typical, too, of the shoddy way in which Perkins had put his revue together was his having advertised that the show contained a Broadway chorus, though actually it had none. To simulate a chorus Perkins had followed a suggestion made by Gershwin. For the opening-night finale, Perkins sent the comedians in his company out on stage dressed in colorful Chinese pajamas with instructions to hold large umbrellas in front of their faces so that they might appear to be a line of chorus girls. The idea backfired when three of the cheap umbrellas did not open, revealing the true sex of the chorus line. When the final curtain came down, the show was greeted with vociferous hisses and boos from the audience.

Understandably, the show was castigated in the local paper the following day. By Wednesday's matinee, box-office sales were virtually nonexistent, and backstage rumors were rampant that the cast would not receive paychecks at the end of the week. To compound difficulties for the producer, one of the acts refused to take part in Wednesday's matinee unless they received their salary. In desperation, Perkins came to Gershwin and asked him to play some of his tunes in place of the missing act. Gershwin obligingly went on stage and improvised a medley of his pieces. On completing his performance, he was received in stony silence by the small audience. But they could hardly have reacted otherwise. Gershwin and his tunes, after all, were still unknown quantities to them. This was one of the few instances when his piano playing had little effect on an audience.

The revue's fate was all too clear. By Friday night the show had given its last performance. Fortunately Gershwin managed to get his fare back to New York. He never received another cent for his part in this flop.

The travails that Gershwin suffered as a result of his association with *Half Past Eight* or the personal insults he endured while on tour with Nora Bayes's *Ladies First* were not especially unusual for a young professional trying to make his mark in Tin Pan Alley and the Broadway musical theater. Wisely, he did not place undue emphasis on them. He preferred to look at the brighter side of things. He was young, talented, confident of his ability, and ambitious. It was clear to him from the beginning that a fortune could be made in the popular-music field. He desperately wanted to reap the rewards of glamor, excitement, fame, and worldly possessions that went with success in this field. He was prepared to put up with temporary obstacles and discomfitures in order to reach his long-range goal: to become a successful composer. With this goal uppermost in his mind, Gershwin soon became inured to the difficulties inherent in the professional world of popular music. He realized that the popular-music business, like the many sports he had learned as a child, was a hard and tough game in which the fittest often had the best chance of winning. As in sports, in the music field it was important to try to keep ahead of the competition. So he played and sang his tunes endlessly to all comers in the hope of selling them. In a sense, he was still a plugger, but now the wares were his own. Performances of his pieces soon became as natural to him as breathing. Moreover, he performed with such exuberance he was actually his own best salesman. If only in terms of sheer physical stamina, Gershwin had a decided edge on his competitors. By dint of persistence, coupled with an apparent love and enthusiasm for his chosen profession, it was inevitable that he would move forward. With hindsight, it is clear that it was merely a question of time before he would burst forth on the world as a figure of consequence. When he did emerge from the shadows, he was loved and rewarded by the public to an extent that far exceeded his wildest expectations. For he did not become simply a celebrated composer. Rather, he developed into a truly outstanding phenomenon of his time.

Emil Mosbacher, shown with Gershwin in Havana in 1932.

ONWARD AND UPWARD

$\mathbb{G}$ERSHWIN'S DRIVE TO write a complete score for a Broadway musical finally succeeded when, on May 26, 1919, the bedroom farce *La La Lucille* opened at the Henry Miller Theater—the first musical to appear there—with all of the songs by Gershwin. Thanks to this show, he could now qualify as a full-fledged Broadway composer. As an added pleasure for him, *La La Lucille* was relatively well received by the press, with some opening-night reviewers such as Burns Mantle in the New York *Evening Mail* considering it the best of the summer productions on Broadway at the time.

In keeping with warm-weather fare, the book for *La La Lucille,* written by Fred Jackson, was very light. It concerned the plight of a dentist, John Smith, who finds himself heir to two million dollars left him by his late aunt, provided—according to the terms of her will—he divorce his pretty wife, Lucille. The aunt, an eccentric Boston dowager, had strongly disapproved of Lucille, who had been associated with the stage before her marriage. To get around the terms of the will, John and Lucille decide to engineer a divorce based on adultery, in compliance with New York state law of the time, and then remarry. Two of the three acts of this musical take place in the bedrooms of the Hotel Philadelphia in the "Windy City," where the Smiths have come for John to be compromised by Fanny, a janitor's frowzy and comical wife, whom the couple have selected as the "adulteress." After numerous complications and embarrassments for all the principals, the "late" aunt, very much alive, suddenly appears before the final curtain. It turns out that her will had been contrived as a joke on her nephew to test his love for his wife.

Using the lyrics of Arthur Jackson and B. G. "Buddy" De Sylva, Gershwin came up with a highly respectable score for *La La Lucille*. The song that attracted the most favorable reactions from the press and the public was the cryptically titled "Tee-Oodle-Um-Bum-Bo." Winningly sung by Janet Velie, who played Lucille, it invariably brought down the house, but it soon faded from the scene after the show had completed its run of 104 performances.[1] "Nobody But You" originally written during Gershwin's stay at Remick's but resurrected for this musical, also turned out to be an audience favorite. Among Gershwin's other tunes in *La La Lucille* were "The Ten Commandments of Love" borrowed from *Half Past Eight,* the Perkins fiasco of the previous year, and "There's More to the Kiss Than the X-X-X," lyrics by Irving Caesar, taken from an earlier 1919 musical, *Good Morning, Judge* (Vivienne Segal had introduced this tune in 1917 at the Sunday evening concerts given by the cast of *Miss 1917*).

Gershwin had been asked by Alex A. Aarons, the show's twenty-nine-year-old producer, to write the *La La Lucille* score. Aarons had sufficient faith in Gershwin's talent to overlook his still limited Broadway experience. Though *La La Lucille* represented Aaron's first Broadway production—he then earned his living from retailing men's clothes—he had been exposed to every facet of show business from his earliest years. His father was Alfred E. Aarons, a noted theatrical manager and producer as well as a composer of more than modest success; for example, he had written the score for *Mam'zelle 'Awkins,* a big Broadway hit musical of the early 1900s that he had also produced.[2] The senior Aarons, a shrewd and tough businessman, had served for many years as manager for Klaw and Erlanger, internationally famous theatrical producers, and is credited with being the originator of large-scale theatrical bookings for road shows. As a producer, young Aarons combined his father's business acumen with taste and a genuine love for the theater, attributes that more than made up for his lack of impresario experience at the time he produced *La La Lucille*. He was also rather adventuresome, gambling as he did on a young talent such as Gershwin rather than inviting a more established composer to write the score; it has been reported that Aarons turned down his father's suggestion that Victor Herbert write the music. But then, a more famous composer would have undoubtedly made greater financial demands on Aarons—who as a fledgling producer had relatively limited funds at his disposal—than someone like Gershwin, still eagerly trying to make a name for himself on Broadway and prepared to work for little or almost nothing to advance his career.

With *La La Lucille,* Gershwin and Aarons began a fruitful association that lasted until 1933. For Aarons not only put on Gershwin's *Tell Me More* in 1925 but, in partnership with Vinton Freedley, also produced *Lady, Be Good* (1924), *Tip-Toes* (1925), *Oh, Kay!* (1926), *Funny Face* (1927), *Treasure Girl* (1928), *Girl Crazy* (1930), and finally *Pardon My English* (1933)—all with Gershwin scores. Together, Aarons and Freedley were Gershwin's most important producers until the dissolution of their partnership in 1933 after *Pardon My English.*[3]

Except for *La La Lucille,* Gershwin continued during 1919 to be represented on Broadway only by interpolated songs. Such 1919 shows as the previously mentioned *Good Morning, Judge,*[4] as well as *The Lady in Red*[5] and the *Morris Gest Midnight Whirl*[6]—competent productions all, but hardly outstanding—incorporated Gershwin songs. Though none of his tunes in these shows became big hits, the cumulative effect of having them used on Broadway was unquestionably beneficial to him, for his name became better known with each passing month.

That year Gershwin wrote a patriotic anthem, "O Land of Mine, America," with lyrics by Michael E. O'Rourke (a pseudonym for Herbert Reynolds, a lyricist for Jerome Kern), and submitted it anonymously in an anthem contest sponsored by the New York *American,* for which a $5,000 prize was offered. Unfortunately, Gershwin's entry—judged by a jury consisting of Irving Berlin, John McCormack, John Golden, John Philip Sousa, and Josef Stransky—did not win. It received an honorable mention, however, in the March 2, 1919, issue of the *American* and was awarded a consolation prize of fifty dollars.

In 1919, too, he tried his hand at writing a movement for string quartet, an early indication of his interest in creating music for the concert hall as well as for Broadway. Commonly known as *Lullaby,** this brief movement consists mainly of a principal theme repeated in episodic fashion with little development. It not only is naïve in form and content but also shows little awareness of string writing: it could easily have been written for any number of other instrumental combinations. As a matter of fact, the principal theme of *Lullaby* was later incorporated into an equally unsuccessful quasi-operatic work in one act—Gershwin's 1922 jazzy *Blue Monday Blues.* Of little intrinsic musical value, *Lullaby* remained an oddity through the years, usually hidden away on the composer's shelf. Save for occasional per-

---

* Gershwin originally misspelled the title as "Lulluby." The piano sketch for the work, now at the Library of Congress, is so spelled.

formances at parties by string-quartet friends, *Lullaby* did not receive a public performance until 1963, when Larry Adler, the harmonica virtuoso, played it at Scotland's Edinburgh Festival in an adaptation for harmonica and string quartet. *Lullaby* finally received its first public performance in its original version on October 19, 1967, when no less a group than the Juilliard String Quartet played it in Washington, D.C., presumably more as a Gershwin memento than for its musical qualities. The Juilliard Quartet gave the first New York performance of *Lullaby* as well. They played it on April 14, 1968, at a Sunday brunch concert series at the Hotel Pierre. At about the same time in 1968, *Lullaby* was published—forty-nine years after it was written.[7]

In 1919 Gershwin also wrote "Swanee," the song that was to become his first smash hit. The idea for "Swanee" was arrived at in brilliant fashion by Gershwin and his lyricist, Irving Caesar. Why not write a one-step in the style of "Hindustan," the song rage of the time, and cash in on some of its popularity? they reasoned. But instead of a foreign locale, why not an American one, specifically the Deep South of Stephen Foster's "Swanee River," everybody's favorite? With their title borrowed in part from Foster and their overall objective clearly in mind, Gershwin and Caesar began work on "Swanee" one evening in the Gershwins' apartment in Washington Heights. While Caesar sang lustily and Gershwin pounded out the tune on the living room piano, the song practically wrote itself,[8] despite some caustic comments from the perennial poker players in the Gershwins' adjoining dining room, who complained at first that all the noise interfered with their card game. However, they were soon won over to the tune when Morris Gershwin joined in by accompanying George and Caesar on his "instrument," the kazoo-like comb with a tissue wrapped around it. The poker game even stopped briefly while the cardplayers cheered the performers on.

There was little or no cheering from the public when "Swanee" received its first hearing. The occasion was the opening of a major Broadway movie house, the Capitol Theater, on October 24, 1919. In honor of the opening, an elaborate stage show, *Capitol Revue,* produced by Ned Wayburn, was presented as an added attraction along with the feature film. Besides "Swanee," the revue incorporated another song by Gershwin, "Come to the Moon," lyrics by Lou Paley and Ned Wayburn. Though neither song made much of a dent on the audience, "Swanee," at least, received fairly lavish stage treatment by Wayburn, consisting of a chiaroscuro setting of chorus girls dancing with lights on their slippers against a darkened stage background.

"Swanee" might have remained permanently in oblivion had not

Top left: Louise Dresser. Gershwin served as her accompanist for a tour of Keith theaters in 1918. *(Museum of the City of New York)*

Top right: Nora Bayes, the volatile star of *Ladies First. (Museum of the City of New York)*

Right: Max Dreyfus, the publishing wizard of Tin Pan Alley who put Gershwin on the payroll of Harms as a "house" composer. *(Courtesy Chappell Music)*

Gershwin had the good fortune to play the tune for Al Jolson at a party not long after *Capitol Revue* had run its course. The experienced, show-hardened Jolson was immediately won over to the song. When he later interpolated "Swanee" into his own show, *Sinbad,* running at the Winter Garden Theater, the tune caught on at once. For when Jolson cried out for the Southland and his "Mammy," his cry seemed to pierce the theater-goer's heart. Jolson wasted little time in putting the tune on wax. On January 8, 1920, he recorded "Swanee" for Columbia Records (record number A–2884). In short order hundreds of thousands of records of "Swanee" were sold in this country and abroad, and sheet-music sales skyrocketed in similar fashion.[9] "Swanee" did so well that Jolson subsequently interpolated still another Gershwin tune into *Sinbad.* It was "Dixie Rose," lyrics by Caesar and B. G. De Sylva. This tune, however, never really caught on, even when its title was changed to "Swanee Rose" in an attempt to capital-ize on the fame of "Swanee."

Although he was a well-established stage personality before "Swanee," Jolson's image as an entertainer became more sharply focused than ever before because of the tune; when you thought of one, you invariably thought of the other. Gershwin and Caesar also benefited from their crea-tion. In about a year's time they had each earned approximately ten thou-sand dollars in royalties, a fortune in those days. Besides their newly acquired wealth, they each secured a firmer footing on the precarious ladder of Broadway success as a result of the popularity of "Swanee."

As Gershwin moved forward in his professional life, his circle of friends widened. With each passing year not only did he come to know an ever larger number of actors, producers, directors, singers, dancers, and other Broadway professionals, but he also became friendly with many people of all types, backgrounds, and personal convictions outside of the theater. His basic nucleus of friends, however, consisted of devoted ad-mirers for whom he could do no wrong. These included Herman Paley, a Tin Pan Alley composer of some training who had studied music briefly with the famous Edward MacDowell, Hambitzer, and others; his brother Lou, an English teacher and lyricist;[10] George Pallay, Lou's cousin; and Emily Strunsky, Lou's attractive fiancée and the daughter of a well-to-do intellectual Greenwich Village family. When Emily—of whom Gershwin was particularly fond—and Lou married in 1920, their apartment at 18 West Eighth Street in the Village became a meeting place for their many friends, especially on Saturday evenings. Animated discussions about music, books, painting, the theater and other arts, and politics regularly took place. Gershwin quickly became the center of attention at these get-togethers because of his rising fame as a composer and his extraordinary facility at the piano; everything stopped when Gershwin started playing and singing.[11] Gershwin's talent was a great source of satisfaction to the Paleys and many of their friends who, like them, were charming, bright, and sophisticated but often lacking in these special qualities that Gershwin so evidently possessed. Through him they vicariously savored the satisfaction that went with public recognition and appreciation of an unusual talent. Every advance in his career became almost a personal advance for themselves; so involved were they with him they almost lived their lives through his. As tribute to their devotion to Gershwin, a number of them have since derived a small measure of fame based almost solely on their friendship with him.

Ira, too, was a beneficiary of the gatherings at the Paley home. While visiting them one day with George, Ira was introduced to Emily's vivacious sister, Leonore. From this very casual initial meeting a warm relationship gradually developed over a period of years between the shy and diffident Ira and the outgoing, bustling Leonore, culminating in their marriage on September 14, 1926. This union of apparent personality opposites has proved to be an enduring and convincingly successful, though childless, one. Undoubtedly a contributing factor to their marital constancy has been their devotion to George, while he lived and after his death.

Another of Gershwin's friends who was particularly helpful to him early in his career was Jules Glaenzer. The two first met in 1921. An executive of Cartier's, the jewelers and silversmiths, and a dapper and convivial man about town, Glaenzer played an important part in expanding Gershwin's social world by introducing him to numerous celebrities who attended the elegant parties held regularly at his fashionable East Side home. Glaenzer collected celebrities the way others collected great works of art. His guest lists were broad in scope and catholic in choice and included luminaries from the social, theatrical, musical, sports, artistic, and political worlds. (Many of Glaenzer's celebrity friends bought their jewelry and other valuables from him; he often mixed business with pleasure.) At his parties could be found such international celebrities as Douglas Fairbanks, Jack Dempsey, Charles Chaplin, Lord and Lady Mountbatten, Noël Coward, Jascha Heifetz, Fanny Brice, Maurice Chevalier, Gertrude Lawrence, and Fred and Adele Astaire. A dated and signature-filled guest book, meticulously maintained by Glaenzer through the years, attests to the many notables who graced his household at one time or another.

Through Glaenzer, Gershwin not only came to meet many notables but was also initiated into sophisticated modes of social behavior. For when Glaenzer met him, Gershwin was quite gauche in social deportment and seemed to be more at home in a darkened poolroom playing pool with his cronies than in a brilliantly lit living room filled with people of style and achievement. Glaenzer was particularly taken aback by Gershwin's ever-present cigar that jutted from his mouth; at first George did not even bother to take the cigar out of his mouth when he was introduced to women. Glaenzer was also distressed by his disconcerting habit of wolfing down his food, as though he hadn't eaten for months, as well as by his injudicious mixing of alcoholic drinks, with no apparent awareness of the consequences. As for his clothes, Glaenzer found them to be neat and comfortable but somewhat loud and lacking in style; he was definitely not a fashion plate in the early days.[12]

Under Glaenzer's tutelage, Gershwin quickly discarded the more obnoxious personal habits brought to his attention and in short order acquired a veneer of social respectability that would have gladdened the heart of even the most demanding host. From a talent born of a constant and pressing search for worldly success, he made the necessary adjustments in his etiquette and was soon able to handle himself with apparent poise and confidence at parties of all kinds. He began to welcome soirées, particularly when given by the social élite, and attended more and more of them with each passing month. His dress, too, benefited from Glaenzer's advice and eventually—especially as his fame reached worldwide proportions—became, in Glaenzer's words, "very *soigné*."

Early in his career Gershwin also established a reputation that was to remain with him for the rest of his life, that of a "ladies' man." This reputation derived mainly from his being frequently seen in the company of pretty women. Many of them were statuesque, busty, show-business types. Understandably, his work brought him into contact with numerous showgirls, actresses, singers, and dancers. But whether or not they were from the theater, he had little difficulty attracting pretty women, for he had more than his share of manly sex appeal. He was dark, with soulful, puppylike eyes that seemed trustful; almost handsome, slim, yet well built, and sufficiently tall to make a positive impression (he was about five feet ten inches tall). Besides, he was an up-and-coming composer of musicals who also played his own pieces on the piano like a demon. Gershwin, for his part, seemed to thrive on adulation of the women and readily took advantage of the large supply of females nearly always at his disposal. Often he would be seen with a different woman every night at various parties and social gatherings. On the basis of this impressive turnover, a virtually inexhaustible supply of female companions, he soon came to be regarded as a veritable Don Juan by nearly all who knew him. His subsequent romantic involvement—aired with relish in the press—with such internationally

An announcement for the *Morris Gest Midnight Whirl,* a 1919 girlie revue that featured six of Gershwin's tunes.
(Museum of the City of New York)

Bottom left: B. G. "Buddy" De Sylva, the co-lyricist for *La La Lucille. (Courtesy ASCAP)* He collaborated with Gershwin on numerous songs and also wrote the libretto for *Blue Monday Blues,* a one-act "opera" Gershwin composed in 1922.

Bottom center: Irving Caesar, Gershwin's lyricist for "Swanee" and other tunes.
(Courtesy ASCAP)

Bottom right: Al Jolson in blackface. His rendition of "Swanee" made it a hit.

Above: A page from Glaenzer's guest book dated April 27, 1923, signed by Gershwin shortly before he left Paris after an exciting stay there that included a visit to a Parisian brothel. Note Gershwin's comments.

Right: The opening page of Jules Glaenzer's guest book. The book contains the signatures of many of the celebrities who attended his parties.

Below: Jules Glaenzer, an important social contact for Gershwin.

famous and glamorous movie stars as Simone Simon and Paulette Goddard only tended further to solidify his renown, especially among his peers, as one of nature's great gifts to womankind.

Despite his reputation as a romantic figure, Gershwin often used women at least as much to impress friends with his successful liaisons as to satisfy his romantic needs.[13] A story that inadvertently points up this fact has been told by Bennett Cerf. It concerns an incident that took place in 1932 when Cerf and Gershwin were in Havana together. Cerf recalls that Gershwin "reserved one unpublished little waltz tune for affairs of the heart. 'You're the kind of girl who makes me feel like composing a song,' he would tell the enraptured lady of the moment, and lead her off to his suite. We would follow on tiptoe to hear him compose the familiar tune for her. 'It will be dedicated to you,' he would conclude soulfully."[14]

A somewhat different story that demonstrates still another aspect of Gershwin's relations with women has been told by Jules Glaenzer. In April 1923 Gershwin and B. G. "Buddy" De Sylva were guests at Glaenzer's Paris home at 5 rue Malakoff. One evening, Glaenzer escorted his guests around town, where they made the rounds of the more interesting night spots and restaurants, savoring fully the sights and sounds of this extraordinary city during springtime. To cap their evening's activities, Glaenzer had arranged in advance for the three of them to visit a fancy Parisian brothel noted for its beautiful women. As part of the arrangement, the madam had agreed to allow Glaenzer and De Sylva to secretly observe Gershwin from peepholes in another room. Aware of Gershwin's reputation with the ladies, the voyeurs Glaenzer and De Sylva were not prepared for what followed. Though they had not necessarily expected a virtuoso performance—considering the surroundings and circumstances—they were amazed when Gershwin showed almost no sophistication in the art of love. He seemed neither to enjoy nor to desire the experience and dispensed entirely with foreplay. Instead, he completed the sexual act quickly, in an almost mechanical way, despite the fact that his bed companion was a lusty, attractive French courtesan with all the wiles of her profession at her command. When Glaenzer and De Sylva met with him afterward, their stupefaction was heightened by Gershwin's boastful claim regarding his sexual vitality with the courtesan as well as his prowess as a lover. Of course they did not challenge his boast or admit their prank to him.

Irrespective of the limited sophistication shown by Gershwin in the Paris brothel, his general confidence in his sexual prowess seemed to increase with the passage of time. This seeming confidence was undoubtedly aided by the fact that more and more women literally threw themselves at him as his fame and fortune grew ever larger. With democratic promiscuity,

Gershwin had affairs with untold numbers of women ranging from show-girls to socialites, though most of these liaisons can be described as temporary at best. As his sexual adventures increased in number, Gershwin was emboldened to invite women whom he hardly knew but who struck his fancy to sleep with him. Often he did not hesitate to make such proposals in the most inappropriate of social circumstances. One such instance occurred one evening at the theater. On being introduced to an attractive, virginal young thing about to be married and her fiancé, Gershwin took her aside and insisted that she sleep with him in advance of her nuptial night; after all, the famous George Gershwin was offering her a privilege denied to most women. The young thing, of course, turned him down, shocked by his request.

Surprisingly, with his broad range of amateur sexual adventures, Gershwin still frequented brothels. Sex, it would seem, whether of the free or paid variety, was practically an obsession with him. It was something he craved and could almost never get enough of. His sexual appetite was immense by nearly any standard. However, considering that he could have had all the free sex he wanted—probably more than he could possibly have handled—one must reasonably ask why he needed recourse to brothels. In attempting to answer that question, one unfortunately has little to go on. For Gershwin understandably never discussed the matter openly. He may not himself have been fully aware of the reasons for his action. One might speculate that he sought the brothel when he wanted to avoid "human" entanglements and to concentrate solely on his own needs—a place where he could seek surcease from the pressures of day-to-day activities in his hectic career and satisfy his sexual needs without becoming involved in the affairs of others.

Consistent with this viewpoint is the story told by Emil Mosbacher,[15] a long-standing friend of Gershwin. In December 1933 he and Gershwin briefly visited the Charleston, South Carolina, home of DuBose Heyward, the librettist for *Porgy and Bess,* so that Gershwin and Heyward could discuss plans for their forthcoming opera. Despite the many details that had to be worked out between him and Heyward and their overall excitement at the potentially immense artistic importance of their project, Gershwin still found it necessary to visit a Charleston brothel. Apparently, through sex almost divorced from humanity, he could relax there. Whatever his motives, Gershwin's brothel experiences obviously had a tonic effect on him.

Another facet of his personality that manifested itself early in his life was his ever-continuing desire—more aptly, perhaps, his compulsion—to study with musicians of stature. The restlessness he had exhibited as a child by changing piano teachers until he found a Charles Hambitzer to satisfy his needs showed itself again when he became a young professional. But by then his musical needs had changed. For after studying piano with Hambitzer on and off for a number of years—it is not exactly clear when the lessons stopped, though they probably ended considerably before Hambitzer's death in 1918—Gershwin apparently felt quite comfortable with his piano playing; that is, his playing ability was sufficient for his requirements. As a matter of fact, Hambitzer can be considered his last piano teacher of any consequence. Except for an occasional piano lesson later in his life from such teachers as Herman Wasserman and Ernest Hutchenson—the latter a distinguished pianist and friend of Gershwin who became president of the Juilliard School of Music in 1937—Gershwin essentially went his own way as pianist after leaving Hambitzer. But while Hambitzer proved invaluable as a piano teacher to the boy Gershwin, he did not fulfill his need for a broader knowledge of the theoretical aspects of music as he advanced in his art, notwithstanding Gershwin's claim (noted earlier) that Hambitzer had made him "harmony-conscious." The truth of the matter is that Gershwin did not learn very much harmony from Hambitzer. Nor, for that matter, did he learn much harmony from a number of other teachers with whom he studied after Hambitzer. In this regard, Isaac Goldberg stated in his 1931 biography of Gershwin that Gershwin knew "as much harmony as could be found in a ten-cent manual"[16] at the time he wrote the *Rhapsody in Blue* in 1924. Gershwin himself said that many of the chords he used in his works "were set down without any particular attention to their theoretical structure. When my critics tell me that now and then I betray a structural weakness, they are not telling me anything I don't know."[17]

In retrospect, it is clear that Gershwin's lack of knowledge of harmony and other technical aspects of music was not the fault of the numerous teachers with whom he eventually studied. He never approached the study of music with the kind of dedication that was expected of the best music students. For Gershwin was never prepared to extend himself fully in his studies. Rather, it appears that he artlessly, or perhaps lazily, assumed that he could pick up musical skills and knowledge almost by osmosis, simply by association with top professionals instead of through the effort that extensive study requires.[18] In this respect, his approach to the study of music was not inconsistent with his approach to improvising at the piano, which he often did for his own pleasure for hours on end. Whether at home or in the midst of noisy parties, he could usually be found at the piano, endlessly playing his own tunes and improvising on them for his own amusement. Though his improvisations frequently produced impressive results, they were essentially instinctive acts, with music literally pouring out of his fingertips and with minimal intellectual considerations involved. Yet most of his compositions were derived from such improvisations. According to Oscar Levant, every time Gershwin "sat down [at the piano] just to amuse himself something came of it. Actually this is how he got most of his ideas—just by playing. He enjoyed writing so much, because in a sense it was play for him—the thing he liked to do more than anything else."[19]

Notwithstanding Gershwin's enormous facility at improvising, there were many gaps in his musicianship besides his limited knowledge of harmony. His music-reading ability, for example, was never more than barely adequate, and he had only a limited knowledge of such theoretical aspects of music as counterpoint and orchestration. In an attempt to overcome some of his many shortcomings as a musician, he studied with a number of teachers over the years, usually for a short period of time with each one. These included Artur Bodanzky, Edward Kilenyi, Rubin Goldmark, Henry Cowell, Wallingford Riegger, and Joseph Schillinger. Moreover, at one time or another, Gershwin expressed an interest in studying with Edgard Varèse, Ernest Bloch, Maurice Ravel, Nadia Boulanger, Arnold Schoenberg, and Ernst Toch, among others, but never managed to do so for a variety of reasons. For instance, Bloch was director of the Cleveland Institute of Music when Gershwin considered studying with him in 1922, but he soon dropped this idea, inasmuch as he did not want to leave the New York scene, where he had his social, familial and professional roots, to go to Cleveland, Bloch or no. Varèse, for his part, gently turned down Gershwin's inquiry regarding possible study with him (about 1920) because of their clearly divergent artistic goals. Nothing came of Gershwin's apparent wish to study with Maurice Ravel and Nadia Boulanger, either, for reasons that will be touched on later. His plans for studying with either Schoenberg or Toch while in Hollywood in 1936 and 1937 unfortunately did not materialize.

Among the well-known musicians Gershwin did study with was conductor Artur Bodanzky (1877–1939), who was closely associated with the Metropolitan Opera for many years. Gershwin had gone to Bodanzky at the suggestion of Max Dreyfus in order to improve his musicianship. The exact dates of his work with Bodanzky are not known. What is known, however, is that his lessons with Bodanzky were terminated very quickly because in the opinion of the conductor Gershwin did not have the capacity for the formal study of music.[20] Implicit in Bodanzky's conclusion is the presumption that Gershwin could not apply himself with diligence to his lessons, nor could he meet the required standards of musicianship.

54

A considerably more favorable opinion of Gershwin as a student has been given by Edward Kilenyi, a Hungarian-born conductor, arranger, and composer,[21] with whom George studied harmony and theory intermittently between 1919 and 1921.[22] In 1950, long after Gershwin's death, Kilenyi claimed that Gershwin's lessons with him "systematically cover[ed]" the "harmonies used by Haydn, Wagner, Richard Strauss, Rachmaninoff, and others."[23] Kilenyi's overstated claim, made perhaps as a self-serving attempt to elevate the importance of his teaching role on the composer, is not supported by the evidence. Copies of Gershwin's harmony exercises with Kilenyi are still in existence. The manuscripts of these exercises, in Gershwin's own hand, are now at the Library of Congress. Dated by the composer, they run from August 1919 to September 28, 1921, and reveal that his harmony lessons with Kilenyi were of the most elementary kind—essentially limited to simple diatonic harmony, including secondary dominants. They in no way suggest, as Kilenyi's claim implies, that Gershwin had any substantial experience with the intricacies of late nineteenth-century chromatic harmony. As further refutation of Kilenyi's claim, Gershwin himself admitted that his knowledge of harmony, even late in his life, was rather rudimentary.

In 1923 Gershwin studied very briefly with still another teacher, Rubin Goldmark, the well-known American pianist and composer who was the nephew of the even better-known Austro-Hungarian composer Karl Goldmark of *Rustic Wedding* fame. Rubin, also a teacher of Aaron Copland, became head of the composition department of the Juilliard School of Music in 1924 and remained there, teaching numerous budding American composers until his death in 1936. Since Gershwin had a total of only three lessons with Goldmark, a strict pedagogue of the old school, that teacher's influence on the composer was negligible. Goldmark's lack of impact on Gershwin was due at least as much to Gershwin's customary casual approach to the study of music as to anything else, for he would not devote very much time to the harmony exercises suggested by Goldmark in advance of his lessons and would usually wait until the very last moment to complete something to show him. As a consequence of this lackadaisical attitude, Gershwin found himself in a dilemma shortly before one of his lessons—possibly his last—with Goldmark. He had not prepared anything for his meeting with his teacher and was at a loss to know how to handle the situation. At the last moment he decided to show Goldmark his movement for string quartet, *Lullaby*, written several years earlier, and pass it off as one of his recent endeavors.[24] After looking at the quartet and being pleasantly surprised at what he saw, Goldmark is purported to have praised Gershwin by telling him, "It's plainly to be seen that you have already learned a great deal of harmony from me!" This comment, quoted in a number of Gershwin sources[25] as a humorous example of Goldmark's pomposity and lack of insight, was obviously spread by Gershwin, since he alone stood to gain from its being aired; it gave indirect proof of Gershwin's innate musical gifts even without benefit of a Goldmark, while boosting the composer's musical self-esteem at the expense of his teacher. This remark, moreover, evidently served as a rationale to convince Gershwin to end his lessons with Goldmark. After all, why should he study with the strict, old-fashioned, and easily fooled Goldmark, when he could do better on his own? Whatever his reasons for leaving Goldmark, he demonstrated once more in this instance his inability to extend himself in his musical education.

In his subsequent lessons with such well-known American composers as Wallingford Riegger—for a brief period in the 1920s[26]—and Henry Cowell—starting in 1927 and lasting intermittently for about two years[27]—Gershwin, again, never really subjected himself to the rigorous training and discipline required for a complete technical mastery of his art. Even his lessons in theory, composition, and orchestration with Joseph Schillinger, which lasted for about four years beginning in 1932[28]—longer than his studies with any of his other music teachers—were in a sense makeshift measures, generally subordinate to Gershwin's lucrative assignments for Broadway and Hollywood.

Though Gershwin might be characterized as an indifferent music student—self-indulgent, dilettantish, often casual and uncertain in his musical approach, and at times inept—he was, from the very beginning, a veritable human dynamo in pursuing his tunesmith career. Here, he was inevitably self-assured and professional, deliberate, knowledgeable of his medium, and frequently far sighted in his plans. He kept his eyes and ears open and was constantly on the alert for any and all contacts that would help him move forward in his field. One of those who came to his attention was George White, a Broadway dancer who had gravitated toward producing musicals. On June 2, 1919, White had managed to get on the boards his own *George White's Scandals of 1919,* a spectacular revue of sorts featuring pretty girls and costumes. *Scandals of 1919* represented White's attempt to cut in on the lucrative market for such revues which the *Ziegfeld Follies* had virtually cornered. Though the 1919 *Scandals* did not fare very well with the press or the public and came off second best in comparison with Ziegfeld, it marked the start of annual *Scandals* by White.

Early in 1920 Gershwin made a point of visiting White in Detroit, where the producer was staying, with the idea of selling him on the possibility of his writing the score for the next *Scandals.*[29] White needed little

Artur Bodanzky, conductor. *(Courtesy Metropolitan Opera Company)* Gershwin studied with him very briefly.

Edward Kilenyi, with whom Gershwin studied between 1919 and 1921.

Rubin Goldmark. *(Courtesy Juilliard School of Music)* Gershwin had several lessons with him in 1923.

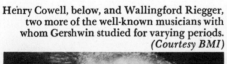

Henry Cowell, below, and Wallingford Riegger, two more of the well-known musicians with whom Gershwin studied for varying periods. *(Courtesy BMI)*

Joseph Schillinger, shown with a
Rhythmicon, an electronic instrument
capable of producing a variety of
rhythms. Gershwin studied with
Schillinger for approximately
four years, starting in 1932.

Top right: A page from the program
for George White's *Scandals of.1921*
for which Gershwin wrote
the music.

Right: Ann Pennington, the star
of *Scandals of 1921*. (*Museum of
the City of New York*)

persuasion. He had not been too happy with the score by Richard Whiting for the 1910 *Scandals* and attributed much of the lack of success of this revue to the music. Besides, he was familiar with Gershwin's ever-rising reputation in the theater. He decided that the composer would be the right man for the job.

White's confidence in him was definitely not misplaced, judged by Gershwin's long association with the *Scandals*. In addition to writing the music for White's 1920 revue, he went on to write the scores for four more annual *Scandals*—a total of five shows between 1920 and 1924. His long tenure with the *Scandals* was aided by White's zealous determination to make his revue an annual event. It was a matter of ego and personal pride for him to keep his "namesake" alive. He doggedly spared no effort to keep his *Scandals* on the boards while strengthening his reputation as a rival of Ziegfeld's. Somehow, White kept his *Scandals* going year after year until 1939, with some annual gaps here and there, and the momentum of his efforts helped not only his cause but Gershwin's; White's revues, after all, gave the composer a showcase for his talent for half a decade. For his part, Gershwin served White's purposes equally well; their relationship can thus be easily considered a marriage of convenience. Not only did Gershwin write highly serviceable scores for White's *Scandals,* but—and this factor was at least as important to the producer—he also worked very cheaply; White paid him only a small weekly salary during the run of the show, supplemented by royalties that Gershwin received from the revues' published tunes.

The weekly salary Gershwin received from White was modest by nearly any standard. It started at fifty dollars[30] for the 1920 *Scandals* and slowly worked itself up to $125 for White's 1924 revue. Nor did Gershwin make very much money at the time from royalties from the publication of *Scandals* tunes; among the few exceptions were the more than $3,000 he earned from "I'll Build a Stairway to Paradise" (lyrics by De Sylva and Arthur Francis), used in the 1922 *Scandals;* and, even more financially rewarding, the very popular "Somebody Loves Me" (lyrics by De Sylva and Ballard MacDonald), from the *Scandals of 1924.* However, the experience and publicity resulting from his association with the *Scandals* were more important than money. He eagerly welcomed the opportunity in his early days to work in the theater at almost any salary in order to solidify his reputation on Broadway. When he left the *Scandals* after his five-year affiliation, he was better known and could command considerably higher fees for his scores than when he began writing for White. It was because of these higher fees that he finally broke with White. When he found that he could make more money composing scores for other producers, he simply quit the *Scandals.*

He felt no particular obligation to continue working for White at bargain prices when he could do better elsewhere, especially after he had reached the point where he no longer benefited from an association with the *Scandals*.

Ira contributed to the *Scandals* as co-lyricist with De Sylva for one song, "I'll Build a Stairway to Paradise," the hit of White's 1922 revue. The song was really a reworking by De Sylva, along with George and Ira, of "A New Step Every Day," a tune the brothers Gershwin had written in advance of the 1922 *Scandals*. On De Sylva's advice, one line from the earlier tune, "I'll build a staircase to Paradise," with a slight change—"staircase" to "stairway"—became the title of the revised song. It also became the focal point of an elaborate production number devised by White for the first-act finale. In writing his various *Scandals* scores, Gershwin worked with a number of lyricists. These included E. Ray Goetz and Arthur Jackson as well as the previously mentioned Buddy De Sylva, Ballard MacDonald, and Arthur Francis (i.e., Ira).

Besides introducing "Stairway to Paradise" to the public, the 1922 *Scandals* proved memorable for Gershwin for a number of other reasons. To begin with, this revue brought him into close contact with Paul Whiteman of "King of Jazz" fame, who later helped to bring *Rhapsody in Blue* to the attention of the world. Since Whiteman and his ensemble, the Palais Royal orchestra, were then featured in the *Scandals*, it was almost inevitable that he and Gershwin would become friends.

The *Scandals of 1922* also marked the first time that Gershwin tried his hand at writing an opera. His one-act, jazzy *Blue Monday Blues*, better known simply as *Blue Monday*, was an offshoot of White's 1922 revue. The idea for writing a Negro opera set in Harlem, the basis for *Blue Monday*, came from the bright and clever De Sylva, who also wrote the libretto.* After selling Gershwin on the opera project, he and the composer then slowly won over White with their planned twenty-five-minute jazz opus on Harlem life. The opera promised to mix jazz with a look at true-to-life Negro characters, presumably sure-fire ingredients for box-office success. When White agreed to include *Blue Monday* in the 1922 *Scandals*, the two collaborators began work immediately on the project. Working almost continuously day and night, they finished their brainchild in five days.

Despite the enthusiastic zeal of the contributors and the feverish pitch at which *Blue Monday* was written, the collaboration turned out abysmally

* De Sylva, born in New York on January 27, 1895, had the ingenuity not only to make a fortune writing lyrics with some of America's top songwriters, but also to become a script writer and director in Hollywood, where as executive producer he ran Paramount Pictures from 1941 to 1944. He died in California on July 11, 1950.

poor; the opera was a total failure. Not the least of the blame must be placed on De Sylva's naïve and trite libretto. Concerned mainly with three Harlemites—Vi; her lover Joe, a gambler; and Tom, an entertainer and Joe's rival for Vi—De Sylva's libretto captured little of the feeling or pulse of life in New York's black ghetto; the locale of the opera centered around a Harlem café at 135th Street and Lenox Avenue. In essence the story was soap opera of the shallowest kind, akin in its way to the worst of nineteenth-century Italian *verismo*: Vi shoots Joe at the instigation of Tom in the belief that Joe is leaving town to see another woman, when all he intended to do was to visit his old mammy in Georgia; Joe had withheld that information from Vi so as not to be considered a "momma's [mammy's] boy."

Gershwin's music compounded the problem of the libretto. It consisted mainly of feeble popular songs held together by dull, jazzlike recitatives and never really came alive. As a matter of fact, one of the key tunes of the score, "Has Anyone Seen Joe?" (also known by such titles as "Has One of You Seen Joe?" and "Has Anyone Seen My Joe?"), taken from Gershwin's *Lullaby* for string quartet, was not any more successful in its new setting than it had been in its original medium.

Another contributing cause for the failure of *Blue Monday* was the production itself, which drew on white actors in laughable blackface for the leading roles. This absurd treatment of an opera with pretensions of realism was too much to take for one reviewer, Charles Darnton. In his review which appeared in the *World* after *Blue Monday* had opened at Broadway's Globe Theater on August 28, 1922, as part of the *Scandals of 1922*, Darnton commented that the opera was "the most dismal, stupid, and incredible blackface sketch that has probably ever been perpetrated. In it," Darnton added sourly, "a dusky soprano finally killed her gambling man. She should have shot all her associates the moment they appeared and then turned the pistol on herself." Since there were few publicly stated opinions by critics or others to counter Darnton's effectively, the audience reaction had been very poor, and since White himself now had reservations about the efficacy of *Blue Monday* as revue material, the producer quickly withdrew the opera from the *Scandals* the day after it opened. It was White's judgment that the opera's morbid plot threw off the pacing of the entire revue and also went counter to the general emphasis of the *Scandals* on light-hearted fare geared for mass-audience appeal. *Blue Monday* promised box-office disaster to the producer; at best it would be a heavy burden on the *Scandals* if it remained in the show, and White understandably would have none of it.

Paul Whiteman, who conducted his orchestra for the premiere of *Blue Monday* (in an orchestration by Will Vodery, the Negro arranger and

61

friend of Gershwin), was apparently more kindly disposed to the work, judging by his performance of it several years later. For in a Carnegie Hall program on December 29, 1925, Whiteman led his group in a concert performance of the work, reorchestrated by Ferde Grofé and retitled *135th Street*. Whiteman's decision to present the work again, but this time under his own auspices, may have been prompted by Gershwin's fame, which had reached fantastic proportions by the end of 1925, his name having become a household word as a result of all the kudos he had received earlier from the *Rhapsody in Blue*. This practically guaranteed a sold-out house. But no matter what Whiteman's motives were for scheduling the opera again, and one cannot discount Whiteman's entrepreneurial rather than artistic instincts in making his decision, it did not come off any better the second time than the first, despite the filled house highly partial to the composer.

As in the first performance, white actors were featured: Blossom Seeley portrayed Vi, Jack McGowan played Tom, and Charles Hart was Joe, while Benny Fields, Francis Howard, and Austin Young had subsidiary parts. In this concert version no scenery was used except for a few props to suggest a Harlem nightclub, and the actors played their roles while standing in front of Whiteman's orchestra. Unlike the first performance in 1922, however, there were some passable reviews in the press, including one from music critic Olin Downes of the *New York Times* which stated that the opera contained "not only some good melodies, but certain genuinely dramatic passages." But despite Downes's sentiments and some additional though infrequent performances of the opera over the years, it has never caught on.[31] The reason for this may be gleaned from the comments made by Jack Gould, television editor of the *Times,* after a performance of the opera on the *Omnibus* television program on March 29, 1953. Writing in the *Times* the following day, Gould complained that "the work proved most ordinary and pedestrian. . . . [It] lacks any real motivation and does not seem to move in any clear-cut direction."

An unfortunate additional consequence of Gershwin's association with the 1922 *Scandals* was of a physical rather than of a musical nature. He developed a chronic digestive debility at about that time, which he attributed to the tensions built up during the New Haven tryouts of *Blue Monday*. Because of constipation and occasional stomach cramps that resulted from his much publicized "composer's stomach," Gershwin came to watch his diet with a diligence often bordering on the fanatic. To help overcome his digestive difficulties and to relieve his acute dietary anxieties, his meals became models of blandness and frugality. Such simple foods as toast, cereal, cooked fruits, sour cream, and zwieback became staples of his diet; only infrequently would he indulge himself in rich pastries, spicy dishes, and other "forbidden" foods. Some of these bland foods had been prescribed as part of an antacid diet by his doctor, A. L. Garbat, who treated Gershwin over much of his adult life. Gershwin nevertheless felt free to experiment with foods and diets on his own when he thought they would help his condition. According to Dr. Garbat, whenever Gershwin learned of a diet "that 'cured' a difficulty . . . he would try it."[32] Among the foods he added to his regular staples in his periodic dietary experiments were agar, lemon juice in hot water, and yeast. Unfortunately, none of these fad-diet attempts had any long-range effects in curing his symptoms, which remained with him until he died. Since his digestive infirmities apparently did not result from poor diet, considering all the care he lavished on it and the overall good health with which he was blessed most of his life, perhaps the cause was psychological.

While Gershwin was working for White's *Scandals* between 1920 and 1924, he kept his hand in other Broadway productions as well. During 1920, for example, his tunes, all competent though hardly world-shaking, were interpolated into these Broadway musicals: *Ed Wynn's Carnival, Broadway Brevities of 1920,* and *The Sweetheart Shop.*[33]

Another 1920 show, *Dere Mabel,* which closed out of town in the early part of the year, also made use of a tune by Gershwin, "We're Pals," with lyrics by Irving Caesar. Though *Dere Mabel* because of its early demise had little effect on Gershwin's career, it was the source of an incident that deserves brief mention. After starting its out-of-town tryouts at the Academy of Music in Baltimore on February 2, 1920, *Dere Mabel* went on to play a series of one-nighters in various cities. When the company arrived at Wilmington, Delaware, on February 12, the show's conductor became ill. As a last-minute substitute for him a member of the cast, Vinton Freedley—the same Freedley who with Alex Aarons produced *Lady, Be Good* in 1924 and other important Gershwin musicals—conducted the orchestra while another actor replaced him in his role as Jack Wing in *Dere Mable.* Freedley's talents as a conductor received favorable comment in a review of the musical which appeared the next day in Wilmington's *News Morning.* According to the reviewer, Freedley "conducted the performance with the skill and ease of a veteran."

In the following year, 1921, Gershwin contributed songs to Ed Wynn's successful musical *The Perfect Fool,* which opened at the George M. Cohan Theater on November 7, as well as to the unsuccessful *A Dangerous Maid,* which never reached Broadway. The latter show, whose cast included Vivienne Segal and the peripatetic Vinton Freedley, began its out-of-town tryouts in Atlantic City on March 21, 1921, and closed in Pittsburgh some five weeks later despite such attractive tunes as Gershwin's "Dancing Shoes" and "The Simple Life," with lyrics by Arthur Francis. Never one to waste material, Gershwin, several years after *A Dangerous Maid* had folded, took one of its tunes that had not been used, "The Sirens," and after some revision incorporated it into his 1924 musical *The Primrose* under the title "Four Little Sirens."

With his career in the ascendancy, it is not surprising that his Broadway activities increased in tempo in 1922. Besides the *Scandals*,[34] his music was heard in such Broadway productions as *The French Doll, For Goodness Sake, Spice of 1922,* and *Our Nell.* Though none of these shows had more than a moderate success on Broadway, they all played a part in keeping his name in the limelight. Moreover, one of his best-known tunes of that year, "Do It Again" (lyrics by De Sylva), derived its popularity from one of these productions: *The French Doll,* which opened at the Lyceum Theatre on February 20 and ran for 120 performances. As sung by Irene Bordoni, the French "doll" of the show, "Do It Again" had a naughty, insouciant quality that titillated the public's fancy.

The same night that *The French Doll* opened, *For Goodness Sake* began its run at the Lyric Theater. Produced by Alex Aarons and starring Fred and Adele Astaire, then still only a young and promising dance team,[35] *For Goodness Sake* had two interpolated songs by Gershwin, "Someone" and "Tra-La-La,"[36] both with lyrics by Arthur Francis; Ira, with the same pseudonym, also served as co-lyricist with Arthur Jackson for another of the show's tunes, "French Pastry Walk," the music for which was written by William "Bill" Daly and Paul Lannin, who are credited with the score for the production. Under the impetus of the brilliant Astaires, *For Goodness Sake* eked out a three-month run of 103 performances. Transferred to the London stage by Aarons some two years later and retitled *Stop Flirting,* this same musical with the Astaires still in it was one of London's smash hits. Perhaps more important than any box-office triumph, this show helped to cement a close working relationship between the Astaires and the Gershwins that was to prove to be felicitous for their careers. One of the big musical hits of 1924, *Lady, Be Good,* and the eminently successful *Funny Face* of 1927—both with music by George and lyrics by Ira and featuring the Astaires—are cases in point.

The last of Gershwin's 1922 productions to open on Broadway was *Our Nell.* Originally titled *Hayseed* and described in its promotional material as a "musical mellow drayma," *Our Nell* opened at the Nora Bayes Theater on December 4. As its title and publicity might indicate, *Our Nell* tried to combine the rustic country flavor of an earlier day with the

64

Paul Whiteman, seated, in a 1925 meeting with (from the left) Ferde Grofé, Deems Taylor, Blossom Seeley, and Gershwin. The meeting was in connection with Whiteman's performance in 1925 of Gershwin's *135th Street*, originally called *Blue Monday Blues*. On the same program, Whiteman conducted Deems Taylor's *Circus Days*.

Irene Bordoni, the "doll" of *The French Doll*. *(Museum of the City of New York)* She sang "Do It Again" with appropriate suggestiveness.

Bill Daly, in a pencil drawing by Gershwin. *(Museum of the City of New York)*

farcical approach of typical villain-heroine fare. To lyrics by Brian Hooker, who shared in the writing of the book, its score was fashioned by Bill Daly and Gershwin, working separately and in tandem; each wrote individual tunes: for example, Gershwin's "By and By" and "Walking Home with Angeline"; and also collaborated on others, such as their "Innocent Ingenue Baby." Though their individual and collaborative efforts produced no major hits, they found they enjoyed working together and soon became intimate friends. They remained so until Daly's death on December 4, 1936, at the age of forty-nine. In a letter to George Pallay dated August 15, 1931, Gershwin said of Daly: "I believe I have told you about Bill being probably my best friend."

Older than Gershwin by some eleven years, a graduate of Harvard, and a musician of impressive technical equipment and experience, whether as orchestrator, conductor, or composer, Daly made a marked impression on the younger man by reason of his age, background, musicianship, and personality. Daly, in turn, responded favorably to Gershwin and everything he represented. In many ways they were opposites. Gershwin was the former lower East Side boy who had come far quickly and was ready to take on the world. He was earthy and direct, outwardly dynamic, relatively well groomed and dapper, swarthy in appearance because of a heavy beard that required shaving at least twice daily, and quick in movement and speech. Daly, on the other hand, was the Harvard gentleman: circumspect, leisurely in gait, spectacled and shy, tall and lanky, fair-complexioned with unruly hair, and he was usually casually attired with clothes that bordered on the shabby.

Aside from their mutual esteem, respect, and admiration, Daly over the years came to be an important influence on Gershwin and his work because of his close association as friend and confidant, as well as conductor and arranger of Gershwin's music. He also served as his adviser-teacher. Because of Daly's musical expertise, Gershwin regularly went over many technical aspects of his symphonic compositions with him as they were being written and came to depend on him for advice, especially in orchestration. Such was their relationship that, when Gershwin hired an orchestra at his own expense for a trial run-through at the Globe Theater of his second orchestral work, *Concerto in F*, shortly before rehearsals began for its world premiere at Carnegie Hall on December 3, 1925, Daly was present to conduct and to assist Gershwin in evaluating the composition. Walter Damrosch was there, too, for he was to conduct the premiere of the piece. A number of revisions as we shall see were made in the *Concerto* as a result of this tryout. Daly undoubtedly had a hand in these revisions. All in all, from 1922 on, Daly unquestionably played a major role in

Gershwin's musical life, although it is difficult to determine with accuracy the scope of his influence. One can safely say, however, that Daly's influence on Gershwin, evolving as it did from a warm personal relationship between the two men, covered a broad and varied spectrum.

By the end of 1922 it was clear to nearly all who knew him that Gershwin, barely twenty-four, was a young tunesmith of exceptional talent. In approximately eight short years, from the time he had started working at Remick's in 1914, he had made remarkable strides in his career. From the Tin Pan Alley novice, he had become the experienced Broadway professional, yet he had made this enormous transition with relative ease. To be sure, the full potential of his success in the musical theater had yet to be realized—since by 1922 he had not yet written a smash Broadway musical —but it seemed enormous, considering his tender age and the impressive theatrical experience he had already accumulated.

By the end of 1922, too, there were unmistakable signs that he was not limiting his musical sights to Tin Pan Alley and Broadway musical comedy. If only on the basis of his composing a movement for string quartet in 1919 and a one-act jazz opera in 1922, Gershwin gave concrete, though not necessarily artistically impressive, evidence of his desire to expand his activities to the concert hall and possibly the opera house as well. Moreover, his recurring wish to study various technical aspects of music with teachers of distinction was still another indication of his desire to broaden his musical horizons.

Certain characteristics of Gershwin's personality had also become manifest by that time. His persistent concern with diet and his digestive debility; his enjoyment of the company of pretty women and his courting of the reputation of "ladies' man"; his immense sexual appetite and his need for the paid prostitute; his inability to extend himself fully in developing his musical skills; his interest in meeting and mingling with the social élite; his relish of night life and parties; his love of improvising at the piano, whether at home alone or at parties; his tremendous drive and vitality, particularly where the interests of his career were concerned; his great confidence in himself as a tunesmith—these were traits that can be traced to his early years. Whether judged by these traits or by his remarkable career advance from lowly song plugger to Broadway musical-comedy veteran, Gershwin by 1922 was an uncommon young man, someone who would make his mark in the world.

Paul Whiteman and his orchestra.

JAZZ AND THE
CONCERT HALL

$\mathbb{G}$ERSHWIN MADE HIS first trip abroad in the early part of 1923 to write the score for *The Rainbow,* a London revue. Even before he had set foot in London, his name was known to a large body of the public there because of Jolson's recording of "Swanee." In order to induce Gershwin to lend his name for its potential box-office appeal to *The Rainbow,* the English producers of the revue had guaranteed him a fee of $1,500 plus round-trip boat passage in addition to the usual royalties that he would get from the revue's published songs—a decided improvement over the salary he had received from White for the various *Scandals.*

Despite his unfamiliarity with the *modus operandi* of the London musical theater, Gershwin quickly completed the score, with lyrics by Clifford Grey, for *The Rainbow.* Opening at London's Empire Theatre on April 3, 1923, the revue got off to an incredibly bad start when its leading comedian, bitter because his part had been drastically cut during rehearsals, stepped out of character in the last-act finale and, approaching the footlights, angrily complained that English performers were not receiving their due. American actors, he shouted, were being favored over English ones in this revue. He was abruptly pulled off the stage at the height of his excoriation of favoritism toward Americans, but the damage had been

69

done. The following day this incident received much attention in the British press along with generally caustic criticism of the revue.

Gershwin's score for *The Rainbow* did not help to strengthen the revue. His songs for it are generally considered to be among the poorest he ever wrote. Even the inclusion of the attractive "Innocent Lonesome Blue Baby," a reworking of "Innocent Ingenue Baby" from *Our Nell*, could not overcome the pedestrian quality of much of the score. Since the whole production of *The Rainbow* was afflicted with a torpor that spells disaster at the box office, it was inevitable that the revue close shortly after opening. On his return to this country after the *Rainbow* debacle, Gershwin could not say he had added to his laurels abroad.

Nor could he claim that his Broadway affiliations during 1923 added exceptional luster to his reputation, either. Except for *Our Nell*, which had opened at the end of 1922 and had run until the early part of 1923, and the *Scandals*, Gershwin was represented on Broadway that year only by interpolated songs, none of them outstanding hits. These songs were used in Sigmund Romberg's *The Dancing Girl, Little Miss Bluebeard* which featured Irene Bordoni, and *Nifties of 1923*. Probably the best known of the songs for these productions was "I Won't Say I Will But I Won't Say I Won't," lyrics by De Sylva and Arthur Francis. When Miss Bordoni sang it in *Little Miss Bluebeard* with her coy Gallic insinuations, it evoked the kind of naughty flavor found in Gershwin's "Do It Again" from *The French Doll* of the previous year. As an adjunct to his musical comedy chores in 1923, Gershwin, to his brother's lyrics, also wrote "The Sunshine Trail," a tune that accompanied a similarly titled silent film by Thomas H. Ince. Though of little intrinsic significance, this tune has the distinction of being the first film "score" by the Gershwins.

Gershwin's most outstanding success in 1923 took place not in a Broadway theater but in a concert hall. The occasion was a recital on Thursday evening, November 1, 1923, at New York's prestigious Aeolian Hall by Eva Gauthier, a fine Canadian soprano. Trained for an opera career at the Paris Conservatory and in Berlin, Miss Gauthier ultimately came to concentrate on solo recitals in which she often performed contemporary music; Ravel and Stravinsky were particular favorites of hers. For her Aeolian Hall recital, Miss Gauthier tried a novel approach in programming. Billing her concert, quite inaccurately it should be noted, as a "Recital of Ancient and Modern Music for Voice," Miss Gauthier scheduled five groups of art songs ranging in style and period from those of England's William Byrd and Henry Purcell (the "ancients"?) to those of such internationally diverse twentieth-century figures as Arthur Bliss, Béla Bartók, Arnold Schoenberg, Darius Milhaud, and Paul Hindemith. She also included in her program a sixth group, consisting of popular American songs: Irving Berlin's "Alexander's Ragtime Band," Jerome Kern's "The Siren's Song," Walter Donaldson's "Carolina in the Morning," and Gershwin's "I'll Build a Stairway to Paradise," "Innocent Ingenue Baby," "Swanee" and, as an encore, "Do It Again." Consistent with the broad stylistic diversity of her songs—art contrasting with popular—Miss Gauthier used two accompanists in her program: Gershwin accompanied her in the popular pieces; for all others, Max Jaffee served as pianist.

Unquestionably, this commingling of art songs and popular songs was an ingenious idea on Miss Gauthier's part, for it gave her recital a novel dimension that a more conventional program would have lacked. For in 1923, with jazz a relatively new and exciting phenomenon, all works that smacked of jazz, no matter how tame and conventional they were, when heard in the context of the concert hall almost automatically took on an aura of contemporaneousness and creative boldness they did not necessarily have. When viewed in this light, it is not surprising that the popular songs in the concert, aided by Gershwin's imaginative piano playing, which added an improvised, quasi-jazz flavor to them, came off as the hits of the recital. As both pianist and composer Gershwin was the hero of the evening, as evidenced by the thunderous ovation he received.

Gershwin was singled out for praise by the press as well. Deems Taylor, one of those won over by the concert, reported in the *World* that the popular songs, Gershwin's included, "stood up amazingly well, not only as entertainment but as music." Commenting further, Taylor noted that Gershwin did "mysterious and fascinating rhythmic and contrapuntal stunts with the accompaniment" while playing from the sheet music whose gaudy multicolored covers added a distinctly irreverent touch to the formal elegance of the concert hall. When the Gauthier recital was repeated in Boston the following January, it was the same story. Writing in that city's *Evening Transcript* of January 30, 1924, Henry Taylor Parker also spoke highly of Gershwin as composer and pianist. In the latter capacity, Parker felt, his playing "diversified [the songs] with cross rhythms; wove them into a pliant and outspringing counterpoint; set in pauses and accents; sustained cadences; gave character to the measures." As composer, Parker predicted, Gershwin represented "the beginning of the age of sophisticated jazz."

With such plaudits as Taylor's and Parker's to his credit, combined with the overall attention he got in the press and the favorable reception accorded him by the audience, it seems clear that Gershwin was the main beneficiary of Miss Gauthier's recital. Furthermore, the timely inclusion of "jazz" in her program had given the concert a special significance it would not have had otherwise. Instead of being just a good concert—imaginative,

71

professional in execution, one of a number given yearly—the Gauthier recital had turned out to be an exceptional musical *event*. Because of this timeliness, Gershwin benefited simply from his association with such an event. For all these reasons, the Gauthier recital has come to represent still another milestone, one of a long list in Gershwin's dramatic and speedy climb to the top.

In 1938, almost two decades after this recital, after she had stopped singing in public,[1] Miss Gauthier claimed she had assisted Gershwin's career in at least one more way: by playing a part in the genesis of *Rhapsody in Blue*.[2] According to Miss Gauthier, Paul Whiteman was motivated to give his now-historic 1924 concert at Aeolian Hall, where the *Rhapsody* was introduced to the world, while he was present at her recital. In Miss Gauthier's words, Whiteman "decided there and then that he too could give an Aeolian Hall concert with his band, and . . . ask[ed] George to write him something for his orchestra, with a piano part that George might play."[3] Save for her statement, made years after the fact, there is little to substantiate this claim; certainly, however, Whiteman and Gershwin would have to have been influenced by the success of the Gauthier recital *after* it had occurred. There is always the suspicion, applicable to many others who knew Gershwin, that she had elevated the importance of her role in relation to the composer.

Still less credible is her allegation made in 1955 that her 1923 recital "established jazz as a genuinely American musical contribution."[4] After all, the popular songs on her program, though given a modicum of jazz flavor by Gershwin's performance at the piano, bore on their own only a tangential relationship to jazz. Jazz, moreover, had come to be accepted as a peculiarly American phenomenon well before the Gauthier recital. By the middle of the second decade of this century it had been acknowledged, if only by the cognoscenti, that jazz was the distinct product of and had evolved from the black man in America and that those responsible for the development of the unique nationalistic qualities of jazz were, obviously, the musicians themselves, preponderantly black, who had performed it over the years.

Although the origins of jazz may have been black, the distillation of its essence to a broad public, mainly middle class and white, was brought about in the 1920s largely by such non-black musical entrepreneurs as Paul Whiteman and others of his ilk. What they had to offer the public as "jazz" was slickly and skillfully orchestrated, but it was really only a bland version of the real thing, especially when compared with the playing of Fletcher Henderson's band at the Roseland Ballroom during the 1920s or Louis Armstrong's recordings with his Hot Five and Hot Seven during the same period. Yet the white musicians got away with it and made a lot of money from their music to boot. Paul Whiteman, through the efforts of his press agents and aided by a willing press and gullible public, came to be known in the 1920s as the "King of Jazz" even though, as John Wilson, jazz critic of the *New York Times*, has stated, "he was not really a king of jazz and he knew it; his relationship to jazz was more talk than fact."[5] In Wilson's opinion Whiteman's orchestra "played very little jazz."[6]

Paul Whiteman, born in 1890 in Denver, where his father supervised music in the public schools, started studying the violin at the age of seven. He later switched to the viola, the instrument he subsequently played as a member of the Denver Symphony and the San Francisco People's Symphony. During World War I, he served a hitch in the Navy and as a yeoman led a Navy band at Bear's Island, California, in 1917 and 1918. After the war, in 1919, he formed a dance band which featured orchestrated "jazz," one of America's first bands to do so. While performing at the Hotel Alexandria in Los Angeles, Whiteman and his group achieved prominence when they became a favorite of the movie-colony set. Any evening at the Alexandria one might find Charles Chaplin or Douglas Fairbanks and other film celebrities dancing side by side with the "common folk" to the strains of Whiteman's band.

A key element in the success of the band at the time was the brilliant arranging of Ferde Grofé, a former violist with the Los Angeles Symphony and a jack-of-all-trades musician, capable of playing nearly every instrument in Whiteman's ensemble and giving a good account of himself while doing so. After joining Whiteman's band at the Alexandria in 1920 as pianist and arranger, a noticeable improvement in the group's arrangements could be heard. Dispensing with the "busy," contrapuntal mixture of instruments common to most dance bands at the time, Grofé instead put great emphasis on a simple, homophonic texture for the orchestra, one in which the melody, clearly delineated, would be given to various solo instruments supported by sustained chords in the background. By cleverly varying solo and ensemble instruments to produce novel colors and effects—a muted trumpet here, a sliding trombone there, a saxophone trill on top, a booming bass-drum thud below—and by adding a lightly supportive rhythmic obbligato in the piano, banjo, bass and drums, Grofé came up with a sound that was eminently danceable and pleasant to listen to, but hardly jazz. His arrangement of "Whispering," written shortly after he joined Whiteman, demonstrated these principles. It was recorded on August 23, 1920, and sold in the millions.[7]

The recognition Whiteman and his group received at the Alexandria paved the way for a New York engagement. This followed in 1920 when Whiteman's band, after a brief stay at the Ambassador Hotel in Atlantic

City, settled at the Palais Royal, a large dance emporium on Broadway and Forty-eighth Street. With a New York base of operations to help promote himself, his band, and the "jazz" they played, it did not take long for Whiteman to achieve international acclaim and in so doing become recognized as the messiah of the new jazz everyone was talking about, though few knew what it really was. There are even those who believe that Whiteman brought the Jazz Age to New York with the start of his Palais Royal engagement. Whiteman was soon signed for records by the Victor Talking Machine Company; he was featured in White's 1922 *Scandals;* he played abroad— leaving New York on March 3, 1923, on the *S.S. President Harding* for an engagement at London's Hippodrome—to great acclaim; and on and on.

Returning to the Palais Royal after his highly publicized stay abroad, Whiteman, riding high on the crest of the wave of jazz's popularity and now widely recognized as the "monarch" of its world, set his sights on a musical venture that was to be the most important one in his career. Assessing that "the common people of America [were] taking all the jazz they could get and mad to get more, yet not having the courage to admit that they took it seriously,[8] Whiteman decided to do something about it. He would present "jazz" not in its more usual setting, the dance hall or nightclub, but in the venerable setting of the concert hall. Only in the concert hall, Whiteman claimed, could he show "that jazz was beginning a new movement in the world's art of music" and that it "had come to stay and deserved recognition."[9] For this avowed purpose, Whiteman chose Aeolian Hall as the appropriate setting. Here in the halls of one of New York's leading concert auditoriums, Whiteman and his band, almost like brave, hardy, and incorruptible warriors of yore going forth to do battle with the Philistines of the world, planned by their efforts to give "jazz" its due.

Notwithstanding Whiteman's stated purpose, surely as skilled a musical entrepreneur as he, thoroughly familiar with the ramifications of publicity, knew that the Aeolian Hall concert promised to get more than its share of attention from the communications media of the day because of its novelty. The projected event had all the built-in ingredients—new jazz crying for respectability while breaking down the stuffy, outworn concert-hall traditions of the past—to pique the interest of the publicity mills of the world, continually faced with the task of grinding out news and always welcoming novel events to talk about.[10]

Well before the actual event, Whiteman had discussed with Gershwin in general terms his plans for a "jazz" concert. He made clear he wanted Gershwin to write a work for piano and orchestra for the occasion and to appear as piano soloist in the piece as well. Gershwin, flattered by the invita-

AEOLIAN HALL

34 West 43rd Street

Thursday Evening

NOVEMBER 1st

Nineteen twenty-three
at 8.15 P. M.

RECITAL OF ANCIENT AND
MODERN MUSIC FOR VOICE
by

EVA
GAUTHIER

MAX JAFFE, At the Piano.

I

ANCIENT
a. Dolente Immagine (Romanza da) ....Vincenzo Bellini
b. La Lusinga (Arietta da) ....Gio. B. Perucchini
c. When I have often heard ... . ⎱ Henry Purcell
d. Hark! Hark! the Echoing Air "The Fairy Queen".... ⎰
   Author of words unknown

II

MODERN HUNGARIAN AND GERMAN
a. Two Folk and Two Modern Hungarian Songs..............Bela Bartok
b. Auf der Treppe sitzen meine Orchen................ ⎱ Paul Hindemith
c. Durch die Abendlichen Gärten .... ⎰
   Poems by Christian Morgenstern & Herrian Schilling

III

AMERICAN
a. The Siren's song (P. G. Woodhouse)..........................Jerome Kern
b. Everybody step (Irving Berlin)..................................Irving Berlin
c. Innocent ingenue baby (Brian Hooker)............. ⎱ George Gershwin
d. Stairway to paradise... ⎰
   (words by B. G. De Silva & Arthur Francis)
e. Swanee (I. Caesar) ....George Gershwin
   GEORGE GERSHWIN AT THE PIANO.

IV

AUSTRIAN
Lied der Waldtaube (aus "Gurrelieder").................. Arnold Schönberg
(J. B Jacobson)
Pianoforte arrangement by Alban Berg

V

BRITISH
THE BALLADS OF THE FOUR SEASONS
Spring - Summer - Autumn - Winter (New)...... ......Arthur Bliss
Words by Li-Po

VI

FRENCH
a. Chant de la Nourrice (Poemes Juifs)..............1916 Darius Milhaud
b. L'Alouette (Du Baras) .....(New)...........................Maurice Delage
c. 2 Chansons Espagnols......(New)........................... ⎫
d. Sur les murs de Salamanca .... ⎬ Swan Hennessy
e. Mon voisin est don Henriques (New)................... ⎭

Tickets 75c., $1.00, $1.50, $2.00. Boxes $15.00 Plus 10% War Tax.
On Sale at Aeolian Hall Box Office.

Management: WOLFSOHN MUSICAL BUREAU, INC.

Victor Records.   Steinway Piano Used

Eva Gauthier's announcement of her "Recital of Ancient and Modern Music for Voice." In the actual concert, Miss Gauthier included in her "American" group Irving Berlin's "Alexander's Ragtime Band" (rather than "Everybody Step"), Walter Donaldson's "Carolina in the Morning," and, as an encore, Gershwin's "Do It Again."

tion and welcoming the opportunity to be featured as piano soloist in an extended work for orchestra that he had written, readily agreed to Whiteman's proposal, though not without some trepidation about his ability to realize a large-scale work of this kind. Since there was then no specific date decided on for the concert, and since he was, as usual, busily involved with his career as Broadway tunesmith, Gershwin did not start writing the piece immediately, but rather gave thought to it from time to time as he improvised at the piano, jotting down a number of ideas as they came to him at odd moments.

The piece might never have taken concrete shape had not Gershwin's attention been drawn to a brief, unsigned news report in the *New York Tribune*[11] of January 4, 1924. While playing billiards with Buddy De Sylva at a Broadway billiard parlor late in the evening on January 3, Gershwin was interrupted in his game by Ira, who showed him a news report in the following morning's *Tribune* which stated that George Gershwin was "at work on a jazz concerto" for a concert Paul Whiteman planned to give on Tuesday afternoon, the following February 12. The news item, obviously the handiwork of a press agent given to grandiose and questionable pronouncements, or possibly even of Whiteman himself, reported that a distinguished panel of musicians—Sergei Rachmaninoff, Jascha Heifetz, Efrem Zimbalist, and Alma Gluck, *all either Russian- or Rumanian-born* —would "pass on 'What Is American Music' " at the Whiteman concert. Also stated among other things was that Irving Berlin, whose lack of even the most rudimentary musical training was widely known, was writing a "syncopated tone poem" for the program. (Not surprisingly, at the concert itself, instead of the "syncopated tone poem," the Whiteman band played Grofé arrangements of three popular Berlin tunes: "Alexander's Ragtime Band," "A Pretty Girl Is Like a Melody" and "Orange Blossoms in California.")

Spurred on by the news of Whiteman's imminent concert a little more than a month away, Gershwin decided to begin work as soon as he could. He was aided in his decision by a generous offer from Whiteman to have Ferde Grofé orchestrate the piece as Gershwin wrote it. This would not only speed up the realization of the work in orchestral terms—an important factor in view of the limited time at hand—but, at least as crucial, Grofé was unquestionably the best man for the job and knew from firsthand experience the full capabilities of the Whiteman ensemble. Another important consideration that helped Gershwin reach his decision was his fond remembrance of the Gauthier recital.

Despite a heavy schedule—involved mainly with putting the finishing touches on the score, to lyrics by De Sylva, for the musical *Sweet Little*

Devil,[12] which was due to open at New York's Astor Theater on January 21—he began composing his new piece in earnest on January 7. That date, "January 7, 1924," is inscribed on the opening page of the manuscript for the piece he had decided to title *Rhapsody in Blue*[13] "for jazz band and piano." He had originally considered writing simply an extended blues for orchestra. After mulling it over, he had opted instead for writing a piece wholly free in form; and to Gershwin that meant a "rhapsody." As he explained it:

> There had been so much chatter about the limitations of jazz, not to speak of the manifest misunderstandings of its function. Jazz, they said, had to be in strict time. It had to cling to dance rhythms. I resolved, if possible, to kill that misconception with one sturdy blow. Inspired by this aim, I set to work composing with unwonted rapidity. No set plan was in my mind—no structure to which my music would conform. The rhapsody, as you see, began as a purpose, not a plan.[14]

In similarly graphic language, Gershwin claimed that the overall outline of the *Rhapsody* took shape in his mind while he was traveling by train to Boston for the out-of-town tryout of *Sweet Little Devil* shortly before he began the main draft of the work on January 7, 1924:

> At this stage of the piece I was summoned to Boston for the premiere of *Sweet Little Devil*. I had already done some work on the rhapsody. It was on the train, with its steely rhythms, its rattle-ty bang that is often so stimulating to a composer. . . . I frequently hear music in the very heart of noise. And there I suddenly heard—and even saw on paper—the complete construction of the rhapsody, from beginning to end. No new themes came to me, but I worked on the thematic material already in mind and tried to conceive the composition as a whole. I heard it as a sort of musical kaleidoscope of America—of our vast melting pot, of our unduplicated national pep, of our blues, our metropolitan madness. By the time I reached Boston I had a definite *plot* of the piece, as distinguished from its actual substance.

Committed as he was to Whiteman's concert and the completion of his piece in time for rehearsals, he had no alternative but to work at full speed, doggedly pushing ahead without sparing himself. Calling on every physical and mental resource at his command while working from a battered upright piano in the back room of the Gershwin apartment on Amsterdam Avenue and One Hundred Tenth Street, where he still lived with his parents, two brothers and a sister, he sketched out his composition in what was essentially a two-piano version of the piece: one piano represented the solo part; the second piano, the orchestra. He finished the sketch of the *Rhapsody* about three weeks after he started, on January 25 or thereabouts (the exact date is open to speculation, because he left no completion date on his manuscript). Despite the great speed at which he worked, his manuscript is written very legibly, with few erasures and revisions or other signs of haste, and contains some tentative instrumental suggestions in the orchestral part. It is not always clear, however, whether these instrumental indications were made by Gershwin or Grofé, who orchestrated directly from the composer's sketch. Some of these suggestions appear to be in Grofé's hand, while others seem to be Gershwin's. Inasmuch as many of these instrumental suggestions were ultimately disregarded by Grofé in fleshing out Gershwin's sketch in orchestral terms, too much emphasis should not be placed on their importance in relation to the finished product performed at Whiteman's concert.

Grofé's scoring of the *Rhapsody* took ten days and was completed on February 4, 1924, the date listed on his original score.[15] During the time he was orchestrating the piece, Grofé would visit the Gershwin apartment daily to pick up pages of the manuscript and to convey his orchestration ideas to Gershwin, who listened to them eagerly, very much in awe of Grofé's skill as an arranger.[16] These visits were extremely pleasant ones for Grofé. He was especially won over by the warm hospitality of Gershwin's parents and the plentiful supply of Mrs. Gershwin's Russian tea.

Grofé's orchestration, written in a remarkably secure hand considering the deadline he had to meet, made knowing use of the virtuoso capabilities of Whiteman's musicians, many of whom could play several instruments. The names of key Whiteman instrumentalists are scrawled on Grofé's score. Because of his considerable experience as arranger for Whiteman, Grofé could indulge himself in the luxury of keeping specific players in mind while scoring the piece, something denied many orchestrators. Among the names Grofé wrote in his score are "Ross" (Ross Gorman, B-flat clarinet, also doubling on bass clarinet, oboe, E-flat soprano and alto saxophones), "Don" (Don Clark, E-flat alto saxophone, also doubling on B-flat soprano and E-flat baritone saxophones), "Busse" (Henry Busse, trumpet), and "Roy" (Roy Maxon, trombone). Grofé's score calls for Ross Gorman and Don Clark to play their assortment of wind instruments and for the other instrumentalists to play the following: B-flat tenor saxophone (doubling on B-flat soprano saxophone), two French horns in F, two B-flat trumpets, two trombones, tuba (doubling on contrabass), timpani, percussion, banjo, celesta, piano, and eight violins divided into two groups; all in addition to the solo piano.[17]

Despite the proven talents of Grofé as orchestrator and the general acknowledgment of the important part he played in the success of the *Rhapsody,* a number of authors—*after* the *Rhapsody* had achieved prominence—have questioned whether Gershwin really had need of Grofé's

Committee Will Decide "What Is American Music"

Among the members of the committee of Judges who will pass on "What Is American Music?" at the Paul Whiteman concert to be given at Aeolian Hall, Tuesday afternoon, February 12, will be Serge Rachmaninoff, Jascha Heifetz, Efrem Zimbalist and Alma Gluck.

Leonard Leibling, editor of "The Musical Courier," will be chairman of the critics' committee, which is to be composed of the leading musical critics of the United States.

This question of "just what is American music?" has aroused a tremendous interest in music circles and Mr. Whiteman is receiving every phase of manuscript, from blues to symphonies.

George Gershwin is at work on a jazz concerto, Irving Berlin is writing a syncopated tone poem and Victor Herbert is working on an American suite.

PAUL WHITEMAN

:: AND HIS ::

PALAIS ROYAL ORCHESTRA

WILL OFFER

An Experiment in Modern Music

ASSISTED BY

ZEZ CONFREY and GEORGE GERSHWIN

New Typically American Compositions by VICTOR HERBERT, IRVING BERLIN and GEORGE GERSHWIN will be played for the first time.

AEOLIAN CONCERT HALL

ENTRANCE AND BOX OFFICE   34 WEST 43rd STREET

Tuesday, February 12, 1924

Lincoln's Birthday, at 3 P.M.
Tickets on Sale Now: *From 55c to $2.20*

Victor Records Exclusively
Chickering Pianos   Buescher Band Instruments

Top left: The *New York Tribune* news item of January 4, 1924, telling of Paul Whiteman's planned concert at Aeolian Hall the following February 12 and of the "committee of judges who will pass on 'What Is American Music?' " for the concert.

Top right: Paul Whiteman's billboard announcement of "An Experiment in Modern Music."

Aeolian Hall

Tuesday Afternoon, February 12, 1924, at 3 P. M.

PAUL WHITEMAN
AND HIS
Palais Royal Orchestra
ASSISTED BY
ZEZ CONFREY
AND
GEORGE GERSHWIN

PROGRAM
PART I

1. True Form of Jazz
   a. Ten Years Ago—"Livery Stable Blues"....*La Rocca*
   b. With Modern Embellishment—"Mama Loves Papa"
   Baer
2. Comedy Selections
   a. Origin of "Yes, We Have No Bananas".....*Silver*
   b. Instrumental Comedy—"So This Is Venice"..*Thomas*
   (Featuring Ross Gorman)
   (Adapted from "The Carnival of Venice")
3. Contrast—Legitimate Scoring vs. Jazzing
   a. Selection in True Form—"Whispering"..*Schonberger*
   b. Same Selection with Jazz Treatment

Program continued on next page

PROGRAM—*Continued*

4. Recent Compositions with Modern Score
   a. "Limehouse Blues"..........................*Braham*
   b. "I Love You"..................................*Archer*
   c. "Raggedy Ann"..................................*Kern*
5. Zez Confrey—(Piano)
   a. Medley Popular Airs
   b. "Kitten on the Keys".......................*Confrey*
   c. "Ice Cream and Art"
   d. "Nickel in the Slot"........................*Confrey*
   Accompanied by the Orchestra
6. Flavoring a Selection with Borrowed Themes
   "Russian Rose"...................................*Groff*
   (Based on "The Volga Boat Song")
7. Semi-Symphonic Arrangement of Popular Melodies
   Consisting of
   "Alexander's Rag-Time Band"..........
   "A Pretty Girl Is Like a Melody"...... } ....*Berlin*
   "Orange Blossoms in California"......

PART II

1. A Suite of Serenades ....*Herbert*
   a. Spanish   c. Cuban
   b. Chinese   d. Oriental
2. Adaptation of Standard Selections to Dance Rhythm
   a. "Pale Moon".....................................*Logan*
   b. "To a Wild Rose"............................*McDowell*
   c. "Chansonette"..................................*Friml*
3. George Gershwin—(Piano)
   "A Rhapsody in Blue"..........................*Gershwin*
   Accompanied by the Orchestra
4. In the Field of Classics ·
   "Pomp and Circumstance" ....*Elgar*
   Chickering Piano Used

Paul Whiteman's program for the Aeolian Hall concert.

services.[18] These writers have stated or implied that Gershwin could have done the job himself, especially if he had had enough time, without a limiting deadline hovering over him. Some of his exercises with Kilenyi have been cited as evidence of Gershwin's early orchestration skill, as have the tentative instrumental indications found in his manuscript sketch for the *Rhapsody*. As further support of the hypothesis that Gershwin could have orchestrated the *Rhapsody,* it has been pointed out that he did his own scoring for all his orchestral works written after the *Rhapsody,* including the opera *Porgy and Bess.* Why not then the earlier piece as well?

The allegation that Gershwin could have orchestrated the *Rhapsody* for the reasons given is strongly refuted by objective evidence. Of the approximately thirty pages of exercises which he did with Kilenyi,[19] only a few pages have some remote bearing on orchestration; most of the pages are exercises concerned with the use of simple diatonic harmony. One exercise, dated September 15, 1921, for example, deals with clarinet writing. Except for the fact that this rather inconsequential exercise reflects some interest on Gershwin's part in the clarinet and that it also contains a scalar run that—stretching a point—bears at best an oblique resemblance to the opening clarinet solo in the *Rhapsody,* there is little in it to indicate that he could have orchestrated the work. Another page, dated simply "August 1919," shows two simple but incomplete measures, written on two staves and labeled "String Quartette." It can be considered some indication of Gershwin's awareness of string-quartet writing, nothing more. On another page, undated, one finds four inconclusive measures that were apparently written for strings also. In every instance, however, Gershwin's exercises with Kilenyi show little or no proof that he could have tackled the complexities of orchestrating the *Rhapsody* and come up with anything resembling an adequate job.

As for the assertion that the tentative instrumental suggestions in Gershwin's manuscript for the *Rhapsody* give evidence of his capabilities for orchestrating the work, that, too, is an idle claim. For, as already noted, not only is it uncertain whether these instrumental indications were Gershwin's or Grofé's, but many of them were subsequently ignored by Grofé in his actual orchestration. In the final analysis, it was Grofé, not Gershwin, who determined which instruments were used in the score. For example, on page six of Gershwin's sketch, "clarinet, cello [and] violin" are called for as ensemble instruments to be played in conjunction with the solo piano. In Grofé's orchestration (page seven), however, bass clarinet and alto and tenor saxophones are used instead. Grofé made a number of other changes in Gershwin's sketch in translating it into orchestral terms. In some instances Grofé revised Gershwin's chordal spacing, part-leading, octave placement, and even rhythm. This is not to imply that Grofé did not follow Gershwin's manuscript closely; he did. But he also had the responsibility for making the *Rhapsody* as effective as possible in its orchestral dressing. His revisions are more than justified on professional grounds.

Finally, the claim that Gershwin could have orchestrated the *Rhapsody* because he orchestrated all his symphonic pieces that followed does not hold water either. It is true, of course, that he assumed the responsibility for orchestrating all his later symphonic works. But it is also true that as late as 1935 he sought the help of Joseph Schillinger in orchestrating *Porgy and Bess*. There is every reason to believe, moreover, that, besides Schillinger, Gershwin welcomed the help of others, especially Bill Daly, in scoring his orchestral pieces. On that basis, one could hardly assume that he could have orchestrated the *Rhapsody* for Whiteman's band with little or no experience as orchestrator to his credit at the time. As added evidence for this conclusion, one might also take into account the opinion of Ferde Grofé, who worked so closely with him in getting the *Rhapsody* ready for the concert. In no uncertain terms, Grofé has stated that Gershwin "could not orchestrate"[20] at the time the *Rhapsody* was written.

Another area of misinformation relating to the *Rhapsody* concerns the solo clarinet's glissando, or "slide," in the opening measure of the piece, where the instrument slowly ascends upward in pitch with a jazz-like piercing "wail." Gershwin has generally been given credit for creating this brilliant opening, one of the most readily identifiable features of the *Rhapsody*, which sets the tone for the entire composition. It has been claimed that he conceived the glissando as it now stands at the time he wrote his sketch for the *Rhapsody*, or possibly even before. This is not the case. He had originally written a seventeen-note scalar run for the solo clarinet in his sketch, with each note clearly delineated in the upward climb and with *no* glissando or "slide" indicated between any of the notes—in other words, no "wail" as we now know it. In orchestrating the piece, Grofé followed Gershwin's sketch and also wrote the opening clarinet run as a clear-cut seventeen-note scale pattern. It was not until rehearsals of the *Rhapsody* began that the glissando accidentally came into being. According to Grofé, who of course was present at rehearsals, the opening clarinet passage at first was played "straight," as written, by Ross Gorman, Whiteman's virtuoso solo clarinetist and an incredible performer on other wind instruments as well. Then, states Grofé, as a joke on Gershwin and to enliven the often-fatiguing rehearsals, Gorman played the opening measure with a noticeable glissando, "stretching" the notes out and adding what he considered a jazzy, humorous touch to the passage. Reacting favorably to Gorman's whimsy, Gershwin asked him to perform the opening measure that way at the forthcoming

The opening page of Gershwin's manuscript for the *Rhapsody in Blue*. No glissando is indicated in the first measure. Following Gershwin's intentions, Grofé's original orchestration of the *Rhapsody* also does not specify a glissando.

concert and to add as much of a "wail" as possible to the upper notes of the clarinet run. Gorman even experimented before the concert with various reeds until he found the one that gave him the most "wailing" sound. Fully prepared for this particular effect by the time of Whiteman's concert, Gorman stunned the audience with his opening "wail." This plaintive but jazz-like cry, instrumental yet human-voiced in sound, unquestionably paved the way for the smashing success of the *Rhapsody* in its entirety. Since Whiteman's Aeolian Hall event, the clarinet glissando has come to be an expected feature of the *Rhapsody* and is always performed that way; clarinetists throughout the world, even those with limited or no jazz experience, play the passage with a jazzy "wail." The glissando effect, moreover, is now *always* specified in published orchestral scores of the *Rhapsody*.[21]

Shortly after it was orchestrated, rehearsals of the *Rhapsody* got under way at the Palais Royal. Rehearsals were held mornings before noon, when Whiteman and his band were free of their customary evening chores, playing until the early hours chorus after chorus of rhythmically provocative tunes that were geared to set feet in motion and fill the dance floor with swaying bodies. The Palais Royal looked out of character in daytime, with tables and chairs askew, the air putrid and stale, and the usually brilliant, sparkling dance-hall decorations, which coruscated at night like so many precious jewels, now cheap and gaudy in the morning sun that streamed through the long tawdry window drapes. Scrubwomen, standing with mops in hand or kneeling, went stoically about their business of cleaning up the previous night's debris. In this drab setting, Whiteman's band gathered for rehearsals, just as soon as they could drag themselves out of bed. Dressed casually, with sleeves rolled up and shirt collars open, and with many seated on large heavily ornamented chairs that were normally set aside for the exclusive use of Palais Royal dance patrons, they tore into the music placed before them with gusto and, considering the time of day, enormous good will. With Gershwin, also casually dressed, at the piano and Whiteman —all 300 pounds of him, wearing a sweater or an open, snappy vest— directing the ensemble from a small podium, the preparation of the *Rhapsody* moved inexorably ahead despite some occasional rough going because of the band's lack of familiarity with the music. All involved— soloist, conductor, and bandsmen—gave the rehearsals their all. It was as though they could sense they were preparing for a historic occasion and wanted to make certain they would do justice to it.

During the five days that the *Rhapsody* was rehearsed, Whiteman made it a point to invite many of New York's musical figures and others in the world of the arts to attend the rehearsals, not only to acquaint them with the music but also, as good public-relations strategy, to try to motivate them to publicize the forthcoming concert by writing and talking about it. As another public-relations stratagem, Whiteman took his guests to luncheon after the rehearsals to discuss the music with them very informally and, at the same time, try his best to convince them—and Whiteman could be most persuasive—of the merits of his undertaking. Whiteman's guests at these sessions included the music critics William J. Henderson, Leonard Liebling, Henry Osborne Osgood, and Pitts Sanborn, as well as Walter Damrosch and Victor Herbert and the writers Gilbert Seldes and Carl Van Vechten.

Whiteman assembled an impressive roster of patrons whose names and position lent great prestige to the event even before a note had been played. Appealing to their sense of progress in art, as a "serious" concert of "jazz" compositions promised to be a highly progressive and artistic undertaking for the time, Whiteman got musicians of such caliber as Leopold Godowsky, Fritz Kreisler, Sergei Rachmaninoff, Josef Stransky, Walter Damrosch, Jascha Heifetz, Moriz Rosenthal, Leopold Stokowski, John McCormack, Amelita Galli-Curci, Mary Garden, and Alma Gluck to agree to be patrons; as well as the writers Fannie Hurst, Heywood Broun, O. O. McIntyre, Karl Kitchin, Frank Crowninshield, Gilbert Seldes, S. Jay Kaufman, and Carl Van Vechten. Otto Kahn, the financier-music patron, and Jules Glaenzer also consented to be concert sponsors. On receiving their acceptances, Whiteman, understandably ecstatic over his exceptional good fortune at being able to recruit these prestigious figures as patrons, has admitted that he "pore[d] over the list [of patrons] the way one does over a new picture of one's self, scanning it again and again for the mere pleasure of looking."[22] Whiteman had unquestionably scored a major coup in the music world by the size and artistic depth of the patron list for his concert.

Whiteman called his concert "An Experiment in Modern Music." Both in the advance press releases for the event and in the program notes for the concert itself, a key phrase in keeping with Whiteman's concert label was conspicuously used: "The experiment is to be purely educational." This pose was maintained throughout the concert's elaborately printed program booklet, with its explanatory notes by Gilbert Seldes and Hugh C. Ernst, for which Whiteman had spent $900, an extravagant sum in those days. The program notes extolled Whiteman for his part in "the music of today" and included these opening remarks by Mr. Ernst:

> The experiment is to be purely educational. Mr. Whiteman intends to point out, with the assistance of his orchestra and associates, the

tremendous strides which have been made in popular music from the day of the discordant Jazz, which sprung into existence about ten years ago from nowhere in particular, to the really melodious music of today, which—for no good reason—is still called Jazz.

The program Whiteman actually devised for his "Experiment in Modern Music" was not very experimental or modern, no matter what he or his spokesmen claimed. It consisted mainly of a mélange of skillful arrangements by Grofé of popular tunes by such established "modern" composers as Jerome Kern, Irving Berlin, Zez Confrey, and Rudolf Friml, with Confrey and Gershwin adding an extra visual and personal fillip to the musical fare by serving as piano soloists for their own works. At Whiteman's bidding, Victor Herbert contributed a new composition, *A Suite of Serenades,* containing four movements in "Spanish," "Chinese," "Cuban," and "Oriental" styles respectively—a compendium of many of the musical clichés that have come to be associated with these nationalities. Together, Herbert's *Serenades* and Gershwin's *Rhapsody* constituted the only new works in this "modern" music concert. Also heard was an arrangement of Edward MacDowell's sentimental *To a Wild Rose,* while the "field of the classics"—the descriptive phrase used in the program—was represented by nothing more formidable than the perennial march favorite of school assembly programs, Elgar's *Pomp and Circumstance, No. 1,* which concluded the concert. Long by nearly any standard, the program was divided into eleven segments totaling some twenty-odd selections. It was obviously geared to show off Whiteman's band, with its numerous instrumental combinations, performing what was essentially a potpourri of popular tunes in a pseudo-jazz style. As Whiteman planned it, the program was quite clearly meant to have something in it for nearly everyone.

To assure that the various pieces on the program would be well performed and presented, Whiteman, without stinting on expenses, enlarged his regular Palais Royal orchestra of nine men to twenty-three. Whiteman was equally generous in giving away tickets to the concert to important figures, particularly distinguished musicians, including many of his patrons, whose presence lent stature to his "experiment." Thus a Fritz Kreisler, Sergei Rachmaninoff, Leopold Stokowski, Jascha Heifetz, Mary Garden, Walter Damrosch, Fannie Hurst, or John Philip Sousa, as well as other notables, could be seen in the audience. Interspersed among them were those of lesser distinction, many of whom had had to pay for their tickets: Tin Pan Alley song pluggers, lyricists and tunesmiths; Palais Royal regulars; Broadway hoofers and vaudevillians; and a good sampling of the hoi polloi drawn to Aeolian Hall by all the hoopla that had surrounded the event. This strange mixture of humanity, the élite contrasting with the lowly, filled the hall to the rafters and took up all the standing room permitted by the Fire Department that Lincoln's Day afternoon in 1924.

Much has been made of Whiteman's great financial loss in mounting the concert. He has been praised for his altruism because, in putting on his "educational experiment," he lost seven thousand dollars on an investment of eleven thousand dollars; he realized only four thousand dollars from ticket sales.[23] Yet it would seem to be rather obvious that Whiteman had not expected to show a profit or of even meeting his expenses when he undertook the concert. One has only to consider the many free tickets he gave away for status purposes, the pre-concert lunches he gave for critics and others in important positions, the fancy concert booklet he had had printed with its built-in propaganda, the advance promotion and press-agentry in which he had indulged himself, and the extra-large orchestra he had insisted on using—all expensive items—to realize that Whiteman had certainly been prepared to lose money on his undertaking, *but for sound business reasons.* Indeed, in large part because of the attention given his Aeolian Hall event, Whiteman earned six hundred eighty thousand dollars the following year and subsequently amassed a fortune. During his heyday as band leader, Whiteman had fifty bands operating under his name; he appeared in the movies in *The King of Jazz, Thanks a Million, Strike Up the Band, Atlantic City* and *Rhapsody in Blue;* he conducted symphony orchestras; he had his own radio program; he performed on television. All this, even though "as a conductor, [he] was somewhat less than dynamic" and his musicianship was such that he "could tell very little about a composition from reading it."[24] On the podium, Whiteman has been described as "looking like a Dutch miller, [as] he flicked a small baton, twitched an elbow or crooked an eyebrow. Virtually his only consistent movement was to wag his head to the band's rhythms."[25] Whiteman is an excellent example of a musician who made an international reputation, and a fortune to match, on limited musical talent but with considerable entrepreneurial acumen. Prior to his death on December 29, 1967, at the age of seventy-seven, Whiteman could look back on a life rich in success. His greatest triumph, however, was undoubtedly his Aeolian Hall concert of 1924, where he emerged as a hero of the arts, an altruistic educator, a music modernist, and a leader of jazz—none of which was really true.[26]

As Whiteman's long Aeolian Hall program progressed, many in the audience became restive. What had promised to be a concert of great innovation and excitement had turned out, instead, to be a conventional one, bordering on the dull. It was not enough that Whiteman featured various soloists and instrumental combinations brilliantly performing pieces such as "Mama Loves Papa," "Yes, We Have No Bananas," and "Kitten on the Keys." The program itself had little of intrinsic musical interest to sustain an audience's attention. Before long, many of the pieces had begun to sound alike. The crowded hall, moreover, began to become uncomfortably warm; people were starting to leave.

At about the point when the concert seemed to have reached bottom and more and more people were eyeing the exits, the *Rhapsody* was scheduled to begin; it was next to last on the program. Suddenly Gershwin appeared on stage, strode quickly and confidently to the piano, and sat down. He and Whiteman exchanged knowing glances. They had had sufficient rehearsals to know what to expect from each other as well as from members of the band. Despite a sense of urgency in the air—the concert until then had not really gotten off the ground, and the program was now practically over—all seemed in readiness for the *Rhapsody*. Whiteman gave a downbeat and Gorman began his clarinet solo. At the sound of the clarinet, with its opening "wail," the audience became as if transfixed. Jolted by the exuberant, unexpected beginning, they were rooted in their seats, their ennui and restlessness disappearing as if by magic. As the work gained in momentum, with Gershwin's hands flying over the keyboard and his body undulating in a natural counterpoint to his arm movements, a hushed expectancy came over those in the hall. The audience seemed to react as one person to the sounds from the stage and the sight of the soloist, conductor, and ensemble performing as if their very lives depended on it. It was unmistakably clear as the *Rhapsody* continued that it was generating a vitality and cohesiveness that are only too infrequently encountered in creative works. The *Rhapsody* seemed to have something pertinent to say and was saying it forcefully and directly, with personality and conviction.

When the *Rhapsody* ended, there were several seconds of silence and then all hell broke loose. A crescendo of tumultuous applause and enthusiastic cries swept the house. Henry Botkin, the artist and a cousin of Gershwin, vividly remembers that all around him "members of the audience, including Victor Herbert, were standing and clapping and cheering wildly in their enthusiasm for the composer and his piece." Gershwin was recalled to the stage again and again in response to the vociferous outcries of pleasure that greeted him and his work. In their enthusiasm for the *Rhapsody*, many in the hall quickly forgot their disenchantment with the earlier part of Whiteman's "experiment." Gershwin had saved the day.

As in the Gauthier recital, Gershwin, as pianist and composer, emerged as a hero, not only for the audience, but for many reviewers as well. Olin Downes in the *Times*, one of those favorably impressed by the *Rhapsody*, found that Gershwin had "expressed himself in a significant, and on the whole, highly original manner" despite a certain amount of "technical immaturity." For Downes, "the audience was stirred, and many a hardened concertgoer excited with the sensation of a new talent finding its voice." In indirect tribute to Grofé's orchestration, Downes noted that the musical material of the *Rhapsody* was "often ingeniously metamorphosed by devices of . . . instrumentation."[27] The *Sun*'s Gilbert W. Gabriel, in praise of the work, thought that "the title of *Rhapsody* was a just one" and that "the beginning and ending of it were stunning; the beginning, particularly, with a . . . drunken whoop of an introduction which had the audience rocking." In Gabriel's opinion, the *Rhapsody* "was the day's most pressing contribution. Mr. Gershwin has an irrepressible pack of talents, and there is this element of inevitability about his piece." Another enthusiast, William J. Henderson of the *Herald*, felt that the *Rhapsody* was "highly ingenious" and that Gershwin's "piano playing was not the least important feature of the work." Without mentioning Grofé by name, Henderson praised his contribution by innuendo when he cited the *Rhapsody* as an example of "a really skillful piece of orchestration." Deems Taylor, too, had some favorable words to say about the *Rhapsody* and its orchestration. Writing in the *World*, Taylor described the *Rhapsody* as "genuine jazz music, not only in its scoring but in its idiom," and added that it "hinted at something new, something that had not hitherto been said in music." In Taylor's estimation, "Mr. Gershwin will bear watching; he may yet bring jazz out of the kitchen." Henry Osborne Osgood, editor of *Musical America*, still another of those won over by the *Rhapsody*, believed the piece was better than either Stravinsky's *Sacre du Printemps* or Honegger's *Pacific 231*.[28]

At the other end of the critical spectrum was the review of the *Rhapsody* by Lawrence Gilman of the *Tribune*. Leading the opposition, as it were, by virtue of his position as chief music reviewer for the *Tribune*, Gilman voiced strong reservations about the quality of the *Rhapsody* as a whole, while praising its orchestration and its rhythms. "Recall the most ambitious piece on yesterday's program," he wrote, "and weep over the lifelessness of its melody and harmony, so derivative, so stale, so inexpressive. And then recall, for contrast, the rich inventiveness of the rhythms, the saliency and vividness of the orchestral color." For Gilman, the *Rhapsody*, as well as other works on the program, contained "trite and feeble and conventional . . . tunes . . . [and] sentimental and vapid . . . harmonic treatment."

Though the reviews of the *Rhapsody* covered a wide variety of opinion, ranging from the highly favorable to the downright hostile, like Gilman's, they nearly all affirmed, either directly or through implication, that

Gershwin was a composer of talent whose future work would be awaited with interest. A good deal of the credit for all the attention, both favorable and unfavorable, that the work generated must be placed on the outstanding performance that the *Rhapsody* received, especially Gershwin's playing of the long cadenza, when only he alone was heard in dramatic relief, his fingers covering the keyboard in a display of pianistic pyrotechnics. For greater effect, Gershwin had decided in advance of the concert that he would improvise the cadenza, even though he had written it out in his manuscript sketch for the piece.[29] Evidently he wanted to be free to make changes in the cadenza as the mood seized him so as to strengthen the musical and visual impression he made on the audience. To accommodate him, and with such an improvisation in mind, Grofé placed an empty page in his score instead of writing out the cadenza. It was put there for Whiteman's benefit. On the top of the page, Grofé wrote, "wait for nod [from Gershwin]," to alert Whiteman to cue the band for its entrance following the piano cadenza, after Gershwin had given the appropriate nod.

Whiteman quickly took advantage of all the publicity engendered by the concert and scheduled a repetition of his "experiment" several weeks later, on March 7, at Aeolian Hall and then again on April 21 at Carnegie Hall, with the latter concert also doubling as a benefit for the American Academy in Rome. To satisfy the ever-growing interest in the *Rhapsody,* Whiteman and his band, with Gershwin as soloist, also recorded the piece for Victor on June 10, four short months after its first performance. The famous Victor record 55225–A, now an invaluable collectors' item, resulted. In response to later public demand, Whiteman and Gershwin recorded the work again, on April 21, 1927,[30] using a new electrical sound process that had been developed. These are but two of the great number of recordings of the *Rhapsody* that have been made through the years and continue to be made by ensemble after ensemble and myriad soloists.

The financial rewards of the *Rhapsody* exceeded Gershwin's wildest dreams, for in the decade following its first performance, he earned more than a quarter of a million dollars from records and from the publication and rental of the music, as well as from various subsidiary rights connected with the piece. Just for allowing the use of the *Rhapsody* in the 1930 movie *The King of Jazz,* starring Paul Whiteman, he received $50,000; for appearing as soloist in the work with Whiteman's band at the Roxy Theater for two weeks in May 1930, he was paid $10,000. There has been no letup in the performances of the *Rhapsody,* and this has kept the money pouring in—first for Gershwin and then, after his death, for his estate. Among other things, the *Rhapsody* has been adapted for the dance—in versions ranging from solo tap dance to sumptuous ballet treatment; lyrics have been written

A page from the *New York Times* of February 13, 1924, containing Olin Downes's review of the *Rhapsody in Blue* as well as a listing of theatrical, musical, and film offerings available in New York at the time.

for it; and transcriptions of the piece have been made for a varied assortment of solo instruments and ensembles, including solo piano, two pianos, chorus, harmonica, violin and piano, violin and orchestra, and so on. One of the few instances where a transcription of the *Rhapsody* was *not* permitted occurred in 1949 when the famous Charlie Barnet band was enjoined by Harms, the publisher of the score, from playing its arrangement of the piece. In a statement calling attention to the "desecration and distortion" of the work as a result of Barnet's jazz version of it, Harms's attorney insisted that the band's "unauthorized arrangement" be withdrawn and discontinued because "the *Rhapsody* is something sacred, spiritually and financially."[31]

Though the *Rhapsody* has been performed more frequently than any other comparable contemporary work, reservations about the piece continue to appear in print, alluding to its flaws in construction and Gershwin's borrowings—whether conscious or not—of stylistic traits from such composers as Liszt, Chopin, Tchaikovsky, Debussy, and others. Yet if it is not a completely integrated work, the *Rhapsody* contains enough individuality to be readily identifiable as Gershwin, from the opening clarinet trill to the closing chords. Gershwin's tunes in particular, so well proportioned and inevitable-sounding, stand out; audiences invariably leave the concert hall singing, whistling, or humming them. With its clear-cut personality and tunefulness, the *Rhapsody* is a masterpiece of a kind, idiomatic and distinct, flawed though it may be with all sorts of technical immaturities, including a lack of musical development in the best sense. Generally speaking, as a substitute for the development of his material, Gershwin relied instead on much literal repetition, a few changes in tempo and numerous changes in key signature—nineteen in all—thrown in for variety's sake.[32] Interestingly enough, side by side with various musical ineptitudes, one finds evidence of motif transformation in the *Rhapsody* that is surprisingly sophisticated. As a matter of fact, there is a common relationship between the first fourteen measures of the *Rhapsody* and various important themes of the piece which becomes noticeable on close examination.[33] Inasmuch as Gershwin had limited technical experience in writing large-scale compositions prior to the *Rhapsody*, one can only assume that these evidences of relatively sophisticated musical treatment were wholly instinctive on his part.

Gershwin himself has admitted structural deficiencies in the *Rhapsody*, though defending its overall musical flow. Not inconsistent with his opinion of the *Rhapsody* are the mixed critical reactions to the piece that have persisted through the years. They are as prevalent today as when the *Rhapsody* was first heard. If anything, it has become fashionable in some circles to denigrate the *Rhapsody* just because of its popularity. One of those who

91

has cast an affirmative vote for the *Rhapsody* is Virgil Thomson. He has described the *Rhapsody* as "the most successful orchestral piece ever launched by an American composer. . . . It is a thoroughly professional job executed by a man who knew how to put over a direct musical idea and who had a direct musical idea to put over."[34] Thomson adds, however, "Rhapsodies . . . are not a very difficult formula, if one can think up enough tunes."[35] Leonard Bernstein, commenting further on the work, has conceded the merits of Gershwin's tunes but questions the construction of the *Rhapsody*. In Bernstein's opinion,

> The *Rhapsody* is not a composition at all. It's a string of separate paragraphs stuck together—with a thin paste of flour and water. Composing is a very different thing from writing tunes, after all. I find that the themes, or tunes, or whatever you want to call them, in the *Rhapsody* are terrific—inspired, God-given. . . . They are perfectly harmonized, ideally proportioned, songful, clear, rich, moving. The rhythms are always right. The "quality" is always there, just as it is in his best show-tunes. . . . I don't think there has been such an inspired melodist on this earth since Tchaikovsky. . . . But if you want to speak of a *composer*, that's another matter. Your *Rhapsody in Blue* is not a real composition in the sense that whatever happens in it must seem inevitable, or even pretty inevitable. You can cut out parts of it without affecting the whole in any way except to make it shorter. You can remove any of these stuck-together sections and the piece still goes on as bravely as before. You can even interchange these sections with one another and no harm done. You can make cuts within a section, or add new cadenzas, or play it with any combination of instruments or on the piano alone; it can be a five-minute piece or a six-minute piece or a twelve-minute piece. And in fact all these things are being done to it every day. It's still the *Rhapsody in Blue*.[36]

The *Rhapsody*, as it is now usually performed, is quite different from the work originally heard. To begin with, Gershwin wisely cut forty-eight measures from the score after the first performance to eliminate some musical excesses. Forty-four of the measures were eliminated from piano solos in various parts of the work,[37] while four measures of little importance were eliminated from the orchestral fabric.[38] Furthermore, Grofé reorchestrated the work in 1926 and 1942, each time for a larger orchestra. His 1942 orchestration for symphony orchestra is the one now commonly used and is available in published form. The full orchestral sound of this version understandably gives the work a different, possibly more mellow quality than was found—for better or worse—in the original score for "jazz" band, with its unmistakable brashness and period flavor of the 1920s.

Before the *Rhapsody* had appeared on the scene, a number of "art" composers had already tried their hand at writing works that incorporated "jazz" elements. Igor Stravinsky's *Ragtime for Eleven Instruments* and his *Piano-Rag Music* as well as Darius Milhaud's *Le Boeuf sur le toit* and *La Création du monde* are examples of compositions in this genre that antedate the *Rhapsody*. One finds "jazz" elements, too, in such pre-*Rhapsody* works as Erik Satie's *Parade*, Claude Debussy's "Golliwog's Cakewalk" from his *Children's Corner*, John Alden Carpenter's *Concertino* and his *Krazy Kat*, and *The Banjo* by the mid-nineteenth-century American composer Louis Moreau Gottschalk, whose pieces often reflect his New Orleans birth and upbringing by their surprising "jazziness." But before Gershwin had shown that it could be done, none of these composers, or any others for that matter, had come up with a "jazz" work that caught the public's fancy the way the *Rhapsody* did; unquestionably, the tremendous amount of publicity that has always surrounded the *Rhapsody* played a part in whetting the public's interest in it and gave it a certain advantage over the other pieces. Following in the footsteps of the *Rhapsody*, however, numerous works combining popular or "jazz" elements with more traditional approaches began to appear with increasing regularity in concert halls and opera houses throughout the world. There seemed to be a market for such works, and more and more composers wrote music to fulfill this demand. John Alden Carpenter's *Skyscrapers*, Aaron Copland's *Concerto for Piano and Orchestra*, Ernst Krenek's *Jonny spielt auf*, Paul Hindemith's *Neues vom Tage*, Maurice Ravel's *Piano Concerto in D for the Left Hand* and his *Piano Concerto in G*, and Kurt Weill's *Mahagonny* and *Die Dreigroschenoper* are but a few of the better-known compositions in this vein that were written, both in the United States and abroad, within the next decade or so after the *Rhapsody*.

As evidenced by its popularity, it is safe to say that the personal quality found in the *Rhapsody* evokes a sympathetic response in others. Since the *Rhapsody* obviously was not created in a vacuum, one can only conclude that the personality inherent in the work evolved from Gershwin's special background as a person and a musician. He grew up in the streets of New York City and knew and spoke the language of the common man. Moreover, his tunesmith experience in Tin Pan Alley and on Broadway, where he had to communicate in musical terms with a broad public, was in a sense a continuation of his childhood days on the lower East Side. As a tunesmith, just as in the streets of New York that he knew so well, Gershwin also had the common touch. His music was couched in a language that the "ordinary" man could respond to. It said what it had to say directly, simply, and in earthy, vivid terms indigenous to America. Furthermore, whether writing for a Broadway show or composing the *Rhapsody* and his other orchestral works, he spoke essentially the same musical language. One might even consider his symphonic works to be simply extensions of his scores for musical comedy. In each instance, the tunes are the *thing*. Thus technical considerations are less important in his orchestral pieces than are the attractiveness and memorableness of his melodies. One might even go so far as to generalize and say that where these works contain melodies that are especially tuneful, as in the *Rhapsody,* and the *Concerto in F* and *An American in Paris,* which followed, they have become major successes despite numerous technical flaws in each composition; to his credit, fewer technical flaws are to be found in each of these succeeding works. On the other hand, where his symphonic pieces contain melodies that are not particularly distinct and tuneful, as is the case with the *Second Rhapsody for Piano and Orchestra,* the *Cuban Overture,* and *"I Got Rhythm" Variations,* they have not done so well with the public even though these later orchestral works are more advanced, technically speaking, than the earlier, more popular ones. As for *Porgy and Bess,* his acknowledged *chef d'oeuvre,* it has the distinction not only of abounding in memorable melodies but also of showing technical improvements over the orchestral works that preceded it.

The accessibility, then, of the *Rhapsody* for the "ordinary" man, one not musically educated or sophisticated, has played a major part in its success. Audiences by the thousands, furthermore, have not only reacted favorably to what they have heard but also assumed, perhaps quite rightly, that on listening to the *Rhapsody* they were the recipients of "culture." Concert-hall music over the years, after all, has come to symbolize "culture," and the *Rhapsody,* from its first performance on, has usually been performed in concert halls, frequently by distinguished orchestras and soloists. Thus, for many, the listening experience associated with the *Rhapsody,* besides being a decidedly pleasant one, has come to represent a relatively painless way of absorbing "culture," a factor that cannot be overlooked in explaining the popularity of the *Rhapsody.* The "culture" inherent in the *Rhapsody,* of course, is more in keeping with Tin Pan Alley, Broadway, and the Jazz Age of the 1920s than with traditional art music in which the works of acknowledged European masters are emphasized. Simply by virtue of its uniqueness and popularity, the *Rhapsody* has helped to break down some of the stultifying traditions associated with the concert hall and, in so doing, has been responsible for attracting new audiences to concert halls.

It might also be properly said that with the *Rhapsody,* American music had come of age in the concert hall. Certainly, at the very least, the *Rhapsody* did its part to establish American music as a viable commodity and prepared the way for the broad acceptance of the works of other American composers who came after Gershwin. On the international level, too, the *Rhapsody* has stimulated composers of all nations to write music for the concert halls and opera houses of the world utilizing popular elements. When one considers that, prior to writing the *Rhapsody*, Gershwin's professional musical experience had been limited mainly to Tin Pan Alley and Broadway, it is all the more amazing that this work has had such an impact on the concert repertoire of the world. Indeed, the *Rhapsody* was, and remains, one of the wonders of its time.

Gershwin playing for Walter Damrosch, circa 1925.
(Courtesy New York Philharmonic)

SUCCESS PERSONIFIED

AGAIN IN 1924, as he had the previous year, Gershwin visited England to write the score for a musical. The show was *Primrose*. But unlike the dismal reception accorded *The Rainbow Revue* in 1923, *Primrose* was greeted enthusiastically when it opened at London's Winter Garden on September 11, 1924. Its success was aided by a lively book by Guy Bolton and George Grossmith which spewed forth a mishmash of zany commentaries ranging from the topical to the historical, including an indelicate reference to Mary, Queen of Scots, and the loss of her head at the chopping block. As an added bonus for theatergoers, it featured two of London's stars, Heather Thatcher and comedian Leslie Henson. Gershwin's tunes helped matters as well. To lyrics by Desmond Carter and Ira Gershwin,[1] George created a score that caught much of the grace and spirit of Gilbert and Sullivan, so much so that English audiences accepted the music as their very own. As a matter of fact, London ticket agencies, sensing a triumph and anticipating a deluge at the box office, purchased thousands of dollars' worth of tickets for *Primrose* almost immediately after the opening-night curtain went up. Their foresight paid off, for Londoners flocked in droves to see the show everyone seemed to be talking about. In keeping with the show's popularity, a vocal score of *Primrose* was soon published, the first of such publications for Gershwin musicals.[2] Despite this distinction, none of the individual tunes in the musical became big hits, though collectively they hit their mark. *Primrose* was also the first musical for which Gershwin reputedly orchestrated some of his tunes,[3] presumably to gain some experience in transferring the sounds he produced at the piano to the orchestra.

Returning to New York in a state of exhilaration and triumph, with the success of *Primrose* a soothing balm for his previous London failure, Gershwin hardly paused to take a breath before he was off and running. He did not believe in resting idly on his laurels; that would have gone against his nature. Thus, hardly had his ship from England docked than he was caught up in the hubbub of what had become for him his normal life-style: although first and foremost he concerned himself with writing music, he did not neglect frequent partygoing, his circle of friends, numerous business appointments, meetings with the press, and so forth. Besides coping with all the varied social and nonmusical demands made on his time when he returned home, he also immersed himself in preparations for his next show, the Alex Aarons–Vinton Freedley production of *Lady, Be Good,* for which he and Ira had been commissioned to write the score, their first complete one together.

In readying *Lady, Be Good* for the stage, the newly formed producing partnership of Aarons and Freedley—they had put on only one show as a team before this, Cosmo Hamilton's *The New Poor*—recruited an impressive array of talent in addition to the Gershwins and planned their production with infinite care; obviously they were on their mettle for a show so crucial to their young partnership. Their *Lady, Be Good* could boast of a delightful book by Guy Bolton and Fred Thompson, a fine cast headed by Fred and Adele Astaire, Walter Catlett, and Cliff Edwards, and imaginative scenery by Norman Bel Geddes. As a special treat for their audience, Aarons and Freedley hired the two-piano team of Phil Ohman and Victor Arden to add an extra musical dimension to the pit orchestra conducted by Paul Lannin; the sparkling and effervescent sounds of the two pianos so delighted Gershwin that he insisted on having Ohman and Arden play in subsequent shows of his, including *Tip-Toes, Oh, Kay!, Funny Face,* and *Treasure Girl.*

Fred Astaire and his sister Adele played a brother-and-sister dancing team in *Lady, Be Good,* Dick and Susan Trevors. Down on their luck and unable to pay their rent, the Trevors are ejected into the street with all their belongings at the beginning of the show. The main focus of the musical then becomes their attempts to overcome their straitened circumstances and better themselves. One solution for their predicament lies in Dick's playing up to a rich girl, purely for her money. Another is for Susan—

Black-Eyed Susan was the original working title of the show—to impersonate a Mexican widow in order to gain an inheritance. Neither of these plans bears fruit, but the Trevors happily resolve their difficulties by the final curtain amidst lots of singing and dancing. In addition to the brilliant Astaires, performing their roles with youthful verve and élan, all in the cast played their hearts out. Especially notable were Walter Catlett as a sly, roguish lawyer, J. Watterson Watkins, and Cliff Edwards as the amiable, likable Ukelele Ike—the name by which he came to be known to the public for his ukelele playing and singing. Both Catlett and Edwards kept the show moving with their fine contributions in specialty spots.

There was hardly a dull moment in the show, and Gershwin's tunes aided by fine renditions helped to keep the momentum going: the title song "Oh, Lady, Be Good!" as sung by Walter Catlett to a bevy of flappers; "Fascinating Rhythm," as performed by the Astaires; "Little Jazz Band," as played and sung by Cliff Edwards; and "The Half of It, Dearie, Blues," as done by Fred Astaire and Kathlene Martin, were but some of the show stoppers that made up the score. As usual, some of the tunes for *Lady, Be Good* were created specifically for it, while others had been written earlier and then shaped to meet the needs of the show. For instance, the irrepressible "Fascinating Rhythm," an extraordinary example of displaced and unexpected rhythms,[4] was begun by Gershwin while he was still in England writing the score for *Primrose*. He played eight measures of the unfinished and untitled tune to Alex Aarons, who was then in London, too. The producer liked what he heard and asked Gershwin to be sure to include the song in his next Aarons show. He obliged. He finished "Fascinating Rhythm" when he returned to New York and incorporated it, as requested, into the show that became *Lady, Be Good*.

Unlike "Fascinating Rhythm," his famous "The Man I Love" did not fare well in *Lady, Be Good*. Written in advance of the show, sometime in the spring of 1924, the melody started out at first as the introductory verse of another song. Gershwin, however, quickly saw the melody's potential as the focal point of a new song, and so he made it the chorus of the tune as we now know it. When *Lady, Be Good* started its trial run in Philadelphia on November 17, 1924, "The Man I Love" was part of its score. Adele Astaire was assigned to sing it. And sing it she did, with great charm, sweetness, and simplicity. Yet the audience was not exactly overwhelmed by the song, to judge by their polite applause. In the context of the slam-bang pacing of the production, "The Man I Love" seemed out of place and not very effective, no matter how sincere the rendition. Besides, the show was then a little long and the song only accentuated that unfavorable aspect of the production. It was therefore decided to withdraw the song after a week in

Philadelphia. It never appeared in the show when *Lady, Be Good* opened on Broadway.

Ironically, though "The Man I Love" did not survive the test of *Lady, Be Good,* it helped to get the show on the boards. As is customary in the theater, Aarons and Freedley approached potential investors to help finance the musical before it went into production. Among those contacted was multimillionaire Otto Kahn, who was always favorably disposed to Gershwin; there are even reports that he once hoped Gershwin would marry his daughter. Kahn listened sympathetically to the producers as they spoke glowingly of the many virtues of the show, including its fine cast and the score by Gershwin, but he declined to invest. There was no need for his investment, Kahn explained. With all the talent associated with *Lady, Be Good,* its success seemed assured. Financial backing, he felt, would surely be raised, even without him. Nonetheless, when it was mentioned to him that "The Man I Love," which Gershwin had played for him at a party at an earlier date[5] with great effect, would be in the show, Kahn reversed himself and wrote out a check for $10,000 in support of the production.

"The Man I Love" was subsequently considered for two other Gershwin shows as well, but never made the grade again for one reason or another. For example, Gershwin resurrected the song for the 1927 version of *Strike Up the Band*—the more successful second version of this musical was given on Broadway in 1930—but the show closed during its Philadelphia tryout, with "The Man I Love" in it. The tune was then earmarked for Marilyn Miller, possibly Broadway's biggest musical star at the time, who was to appear in Ziegfeld's 1928 production of *Rosalie,* with a score by both Romberg and Gershwin. Once more the tune did not get very far. Evidently Miss Miller did not find it suitable and soon lost interest in it; the song never got into the show.

Looking back, it is not too difficult to see why "The Man I Love" in its early days could not find a place for itself in Broadway musicals. Its subject matter, a woman yearning for her dream man, was perhaps too intimate and personal an expression for musical comedy of the time. The song did not readily conform to the larger-than-life projection required of most show tunes to reach the top balcony of the theater. Gershwin himself, in explaining the problems inherent in the song, conceded it was not a production number and did not easily lend itself to action or movement on the stage. He also felt that most audiences had difficulty remembering its melody.

Despite these reasons for its early nonacceptance, or possibly *because* of them, "The Man I Love" still caught on, but in a most unusual way. One of the song's earliest admirers was Lady Mountbatten, whom Gershwin had come to know along with her husband, during the course of his social rounds. Intrigued by the song, Lady Mountbatten asked Gershwin for an autographed copy of it while in New York one day, not long after "The Man I Love" had been dropped from *Lady, Be Good*. Gershwin, flattered by her request, willingly obliged. Returning to England with the copy, Lady Mountbatten brought it to the attention of the Berkeley Square Orchestra, her favorite dance band. They soon made an arrangement of it and started playing it with increasing regularity. Other London bands followed suit, pirating the tune from the Berkeley Square group since there was then no published version of the song in England. As the tune caught on, jazz bands in Paris also began to play it. Slowly the song made some inroads in the United States when Americans on hearing it abroad began to ask bands to play it on their return home. But more important for the tune's success was the intensive promotional campaign started in 1928 by Max Dreyfus to make it better known. To help publisher Dreyfus finance this promotion, George and Ira gladly agreed to cut their sheet-music royalties from "The Man I Love"; instead of the usual three cents, they consented to two cents a copy each. So effective was Dreyfus's promotion that in six months' time several recordings of the tune had been made and about 100,000 copies of sheet music sold. The song was further helped when Helen Morgan, the famous torch singer, and then other chanteuses of the tears-in-the-eyes-and-voice school adopted "The Man I Love" as their own. Over the years, innumerable recordings and performances attest to its well-entrenched popularity, a vivid contrast to its slow start.

With "The Man I Love" dropped in Philadelphia and a few slight changes made in the production during its tryout, *Lady, Be Good* opened in New York on December 1, 1924, at the Liberty Theater to a warm welcome. It soon became Gershwin's first smash musical-comedy hit. Before long, tunes from the show such as "Fascinating Rhythm" and "Oh, Lady, Be Good!" seemed to be heard everywhere and Gershwin's name along with them. Coming on top of the acclaim of the *Rhapsody* in the early part of the year, *Lady, Be Good* only reinforced all the good things that had been said about his music up to then—that it was fresh and very tuneful. He had unquestionably arrived with this show. For Ira, too, the show had great import. His fine lyrics for his brother's songs, with their own distinct brand of New Yorkese, clearly showed he had now come into his own. From this show on, Ira wrote the lyrics for nearly all George's tunes. Together or separately, the brothers helped to keep the Gershwin name almost constantly in the world's spotlight.

Lady, Be Good, during its run of 184 performances on Broadway, also helped to solidify the Astaires' reputation as a leading dancing-and-singing team. When Aarons and Freedley brought *Lady, Be Good* to England in the early part of 1926, the Astaires sparkled there as well. After the addition of a prologue, a two-week tryout in Liverpool (tryouts, common in America, were not customary in England; shows usually opened "cold"), a few changes in dialogue, and some minor adjustments in the production to make it conform to England's slower stage pacing, *Lady, Be Good* and the Astaires with it became the talk of London shortly after opening at the Empire Theatre there. Undoubtedly because of the success of *Lady, Be Good* in London, Aarons and Freedley were motivated to bring other Gershwin shows to England after they had played on Broadway. This was a policy they later followed for *Tip-Toes, Oh, Kay!*, and *Funny Face.*

In comparison with *Lady, Be Good,* Gershwin's other 1924 Broadway productions, *Sweet Little Devil* and White's *Scandals,* came off decidedly second best, but each had some merit. The four-month run of *Sweet Little Devil* on Broadway was less notable for Gershwin's score or its book by Frank Mandel and Laurence Schwab than for its star, Constance Binney. She had returned to Broadway from Hollywood, with much attendant publicity, for this production. Her fine performance combined with her name value gave *Sweet Little Devil* a vitality and a more glamorous sheen than it actually merited. Certainly Gershwin's tunes, merely competent for the most part, did not do very much for the show; an exception might be the humorous "Mah-Jongg," which saw extra duty when it was used again in the 1924 *Scandals.* As for the *Scandals* of that year, it was up to White's usual standards: highly professional, glossy, and filled with beautiful girls stunningly gowned. It opened at the Apollo Theater on June 30, 1924, not long after *Sweet Little Devil* had closed. Gershwin's score for the revue was distinctly below par and quite mediocre, except for "Somebody Loves Me." By its perennial popularity, this tune has served as an enduring memento of Gershwin's five-year affiliation with White, which ended with the 1924 revue. This association was renewed on a rather limited basis several years later when White incorporated *Rhapsody in Blue* into the first-act finale of his 1927 *Scandals.*

With numerous musical successes under his belt and a long string of shows to his credit, Gershwin's style of living, on the rise ever since he first became a professional tunesmith, underwent a noticeable change for the better by 1925. Although this change was reflected by the clothes he wore, the parties he attended and gave, and the multitude of famous and wealthy people he came to know, his new life-style was perhaps best epitomized by the large, five-story town house at 316 West One Hundred Third Street, between West End Avenue and Riverside Drive that he and his family bought that year and into which they moved from their apartment on

Fred and Adele Astaire, the stars of *Lady, Be Good,* in a scene from an earlier musical *(For Goodness Sake)*

Ernest Hutchenson. *(Courtesy Juilliard School of Music)* He invited Gershwin to Chautauqua during the summer of 1925 so that he could work on the *Concerto in F* without interruption.

Amsterdam Avenue and One Hundred Tenth Street. In a neighborhood filled with impressive, meticulously maintained homes, close by Riverside Drive, the Gershwin's handsome gray-stone house stood out by the elegance of its architecture, which featured an elaborate, sturdy overhang surrounding the second floor and a recessed upper floor hidden by grillwork.[6] Inside the house, each of the floors contained spacious, airy rooms. As an added luxury, the floors were connected by a self-service elevator, a particular source of satisfaction to Gershwin's father, who enjoyed pressing its buttons and riding up and down in it. The purchase of the house was made possible by the substantial income George received from *Lady, Be Good* and other productions, individual songs, and the *Rhapsody*, though Ira, too, was earning more money than ever before; as lyricist for *Lady, Be Good* alone, Ira earned approximately $300 weekly during the run of the show. Since George still lived with his family, as did Ira, the Gershwins' living style changed along with the composer's. To be sure, the close-knit Gershwins had seemingly always maintained a semblance of middle-class respectability. From George's boyhood days on, the Gershwins outwardly never seemed to be wanting, despite some rough periods of financial uncertainty. But by 1925, thanks to George's ever-increasing fame and fortune, the Gershwins, without undue pretense, could afford to live in a style expected of their newfound financial and social position. The elegant house on One Hundred Third Street symbolized their changed status as well as George's.

The entire fifth floor of the house was set aside for George's use and included his study. Lining the walls of the study were autographed pictures of famous people he knew. Here, among souvenirs of his career, his Steinway grand, the caricatures of great composers drawn for him by Will Cotton, and his music, George worked. The third and fourth floors contained the sleeping quarters for the rest of the family, with the fourth floor assigned to Ira and his wife, Leonore, after their marriage in 1926. On the second floor were the living and dining rooms, and on the first could be found a billiard room.

The highly gregarious Gershwins, as had been their habit even before they had the new house, often had many people around them. Their home was seldom quiet; it bubbled over with the laughter, talk, and cries made by them and their relatives, personal friends and neighbors, and even total strangers. Informality was stressed in the Gershwin household. According to one account of the Gershwin ménage, when "you rang the front door bell, a terrier yelped, a maid, neither prompt nor neat, answered, or his [George's] mother or his sister Frances. . . . Once his sister hollered up the stairs, 'I've got to have the money for my dancing lessons!' "[7] Another

104

colorful description of the house has been given by S. N. Behrman, who relates:

> I hadn't seen the Gershwins in a long time and I telephoned to ask if it would be convenient for me to call. It was a sweltering night in September and I arrived at the house about nine o'clock. For a long time I rang the doorbell but got no answer. Through the screened, curtained door-window I could see figures moving inside, and I kept ringing impatiently. No answer. Finally I pushed the door open and walked in. Three or four young men I had never seen before were sitting around the hall smoking. Off the hall was a small reception-room which had been converted into a billiard-room. I peered in—there was a game in progress but I knew none of the players. I asked for George, or his brother Ira. No one bothered to reply, but one of the young men made a terse gesture in the direction of the upper stories. I went up one flight and there I found a new group. One of them I vaguely remembered from 110th Street and I asked him where George and Ira were. He said he thought they were upstairs. On the third floor I found Arthur, the youngest brother, who had just come in and didn't know who was in the house, but on the fourth I got an answer to my—by this time agonized—cry. I heard Ira's voice inviting me up to the fifth. . . . "Who under the sun," I asked, "are those fellows playing billiards on the first floor?"
>
> Ira looked almost guilty. "To tell the truth," he said, "I don't know!"
>
> "But you must," I insisted. "They looked perfectly at home."
>
> "I really don't," he said. "There's a bunch of fellows from down the street who've taken to dropping in here every night for a game. I think they're friends of Arthur's. But I don't know who they are."
>
> "Where," I demanded sternly, "is George?"
>
> "He's taken his old rooms in the hotel around the corner. He says he's got to have a little privacy."[8]

The hotel to which Ira referred was the relatively new and attractive Whitehall, built in 1923, on One Hundredth Street and Broadway, several blocks from the Gershwins' home. It was to the Whitehall, where he rented a couple of rooms, that George would go for privacy when the house on One Hundred Third Street became too crowded and noisy for him to compose. At the Whitehall George worked on among other things his scores for the 1925 productions *Tip-Toes* and *Song of the Flame,* as well as his second orchestral piece, the *Concerto in F.*

The fortuitous circumstances surrounding the writing of the *Rhapsody in Blue* were conspicuously absent for the *Concerto in F.* This piece was commissioned by the venerable Symphony Society of New York in the spring of 1925, approximately eight months in advance of a specified concert date, for the New York Symphony Orchestra, which the Symphony Society sponsored. On the recommendation of Walter Damrosch, conductor of the New York Symphony, Harry Harkness Flagler, president of the Symphony Society, commissioned the concerto from Gershwin.[9] On April 17, 1925, before he had written a note of the concerto, Gershwin signed contracts with the Symphony Society in which he agreed to appear in seven concerts with the New York Symphony between December 3, 1925, and January 16, 1926, as soloist in the projected work, then titled *New York Concerto*. His fees as soloist were spelled out in the contracts.[10] For the first two performances of the concerto at Carnegie Hall on December 3 and 4, he was to receive a total of $500. Thereafter, he was to be paid $300 per concert for playing with the orchestra in Washington, D.C., on December 8; in Baltimore on December 9; in Philadelphia on December 10; and in Brooklyn on January 16. But contrary to the signed agreement, he actually performed as soloist in only six concerts; a seventh, a Sunday afternoon program, never took place.[11]

Gershwin's confidence in himself was such that, after accepting the commission to write a concerto, he reputedly first had to find out what a "concerto" was.[12] He also had to buy a text on orchestration—it was Cecil Forsyth's famous *Orchestration,* a tool of many music students since its first printing in 1914—to know how to write for the instruments of the orchestra. Gershwin's limited musical training had hardly prepared him for writing a concerto, despite the experience he had garnered composing the *Rhapsody.* Nevertheless, his musical instincts still enabled him to come up with a work that at least fit the title of "concerto." Doing what came naturally for him, he created his own personal version of a concerto, though hardly one that would conform to textbook models.[13]

Despite his contractual commitment to the concerto, Gershwin did not begin work on the piece at once. As usual, he had several musical chores that required his attention. Of immediate concern to him at the time was the score for *Tell Me More,*[14] a musical with a cliché-ridden plot about a heroine who portrays a shopgirl to conceal her true identity. Produced by Alex Aarons, this show opened at the Gaiety Theater on April 13, 1925, and closed after only thirty-two performances. With the possible exception of the title tune and "Why Do I Love You?" Gershwin's score to lyrics by Ira and Buddy De Sylva was so commonplace it could hardly be expected to save the production; the "hit" of *Tell Me More* was not one of Gershwin's tunes but a parody of the traditional Italian folk-tune, retitled "O So La Mi," sung by comedian Lou Holtz.

The musical was then moved to London in an attempt to make up for its Broadway failure. Gershwin went along to help resuscitate the show for English audiences as well as to write some new tunes to lyrics by Desmond Carter. The move proved to be a judicious one, for *Tell Me More,* with English favorites Heather Thatcher and Leslie Henson in the cast, had a long run in London after opening on May 26.

While in London with *Tell Me More,* Gershwin began sketching ideas for the concerto. By the time he left for New York in early June, he had sketched a number of themes and had made a tentative start on the work. He continued his sketching on his return home and had sufficient musical material at hand to be able to play themes from the projected concerto for Edwin Knopf, of the publishing family, while visiting him at his home on West Fifty-fifth Street on July 18, 1925. He began the actual writing of the concerto on July 22. On dining at Carl Van Vechten's apartment on July 24, Gershwin could report that he had begun the concerto two days earlier and had completed five pages of the work.[15]

Once he began writing the concerto seriously, the work moved speedily along. Generally speaking, he composed quickly and almost effortlessly at the piano, with ideas taking shape and following one another in steady profusion. This was true as well for the concerto. In keeping with its original title, *New York Concerto,* much of it was written close to Gershwin's home base in Manhattan, either at the Whitehall Hotel or at his study on One Hundred Third Street. However, he also worked on the piece in Chautauqua, in upstate New York, from the end of July through most of August. To ensure that he would be able to work for long stretches without interruption, and as a change of scenery, he had accepted the invitation of Ernest Hutchenson to come to Chautauqua, where Hutchenson held master piano classes during the summer months. In an isolated studio there, Gershwin worked steadily each day on the concerto, breaking his isolation from time to time to play some of his pieces for Hutchenson's students, many of whom were in awe of him, the world-famous celebrity, even though he wasn't very much older than they were. Gershwin, in turn, was greatly impressed with the talent of these hardworking, well-trained pianists and went out of his way to be friendly and easygoing in their presence.

He made a good impression on them, as he did on many others. Whether dealing with the press, professional associates of one kind or another, including the piano students at Chautauqua, or the general public, Gershwin usually acted in likable fashion. All things considered, his good public image certainly helped his career. Consistent with the attractive side of his personality shown at Chautauqua has been Isaac Goldberg's description of him. He characterized Gershwin as being "simple . . . unaffected . . . modest and as charming a youth [he was thirty-three when this

107

statement appeared in print] as one would desire to meet,"[16] though "not a shrinking violet."[17] On the other hand, Gershwin's good friend Oscar Levant has admitted in his humorous way that there existed another, less pleasing facet to his character:

> An evening with Gershwin was a Gershwin evening. There were recurrent, lengthy references to his piano playing, his composing, his conducting, his painting—marcato monologues in alla breve which George's audiences absorbed with the fascinating attentiveness of a Storm-trooper listening to one of Hitler's well-modulated firehouse chats.[18]

In keeping with this report of Gershwin's self-adulation, it is generally conceded that he monopolized the piano at the parties he attended.[19] True, he was invited to many parties at which it was *expected* he would play; it was a social coup, after all, for a host to have the famous Gershwin perform. But the fact remains that he played and sang for hours on end at parties and apparently always enjoyed doing it; he has even admitted he didn't have a good time otherwise.[20] This aspect of Gershwin's character, however, was less noticeable at the start of his career. Jules Glaenzer, for instance, recalls that when Gershwin first attended parties at his home he would usually play the piano only after other well-known musical personalities— such as Zez Confrey, the composer of "Kitten on the Keys"—had played first. As Gershwin gained in fame and prestige, this diffidence disappeared at Glaenzer's and other parties.

Levant has told an amusing story that indirectly helps to substantiate Glaenzer's observation. At a party for Gershwin in Hollywood in 1936, after dinner the composer went

> to the piano where [he] launched into a résumé of his music, old and new. Among the guests were Alexander Steinert, a Prix de Rome winner who had done considerable valuable work in the preparation of the chorus for *Porgy* and also conducted its road tour. In sheer politeness George finally suggested that Steinert play something of his own, in the confident belief that the surroundings and his own abashment would dissuade him. However, Steinert responded with the whole of a piano concerto by himself, which George slightly resented as an excess of acquiescence.[21]

Along with evidences of egocentricity away from the public spotlight, Gershwin could also be testy and unpredictable. Rouben Mamoulian, who directed the first performance of *Porgy and Bess,* tells of the time he and Gershwin

> were having lunch at Lindy's after a morning's rehearsal [of *Porgy and Bess*] which George had attended. As we sat there I started, for some

Oscar Levant
at the piano.

The beginning of the third
movement of the *Concerto in F,*
in a published version for
solo piano, closely resembles
an unfinished piano "prelude"
by Gershwin dated
"January 1925."

III

unknown reason, humming an air, out of Rimski-Korsakov. George stopped eating, turned to me with a very shocked expression on his face and said, "Rouben, I think this is terrible! You have been rehearsing my music and here you are humming some Russian melodies. Why do you do that?" At first, I thought George was joking, but then I saw the hurt look in his eyes and knew he was in dead earnest. So I said, "George, I am very sorry. I don't know why I did it." The lunch went on, but George didn't touch his food for quite a while, looking very depressed. Then suddenly his face lighted up with a smile, he turned to me and said with a triumphant ring in his voice: "I know why you were humming that Russian music." "Why?" I asked. "Because my parents were Russian," he said.[22]

Self-centered though he unquestionably was, Gershwin's behavior was frequently tinged with an artlessness and naïveté that was appealing in so talented a person. Like a child, he could laugh spontaneously at some silly remarks or acts that amused him, no matter how many times they were repeated. At such times he seemed wholly without guile and as innocent as a newborn babe. In his ingenuous moments, Gershwin was not unlike his father riding up and down an elevator as if it were a toy. Nevertheless, it is clear that he was not the "simple," "unaffected," and "modest" man Goldberg described. Nor would one expect him to be. He was capable of making such boastful statements as, "I am history"; or, "I am a better melodist than Schubert"; or, "I am going to write the greatest fugue ever." Furthermore, he was usually so concerned and involved with his work and himself that he was not a "listener" by any stretch of the imagination. He was not really interested in what others had to say if it had no direct relation to him in some way. He was happiest and functioned best when he was discussing his own work and activities or when he was performing his own music.

As he did for the *Rhapsody,* Gershwin sketched the concerto in what might be considered a two-piano version, with one piano representing the solo part and the other the orchestra. Moreover, as was also true for the *Rhapsody,* some suggestions for instrumentation are included in the initial draft of the concerto, though much of the sketch does not specify the instruments to be used or otherwise reveal the full extent of his orchestration plans. The sketch was probably finished by late September or early October of 1925, but the exact date of completion is speculative since it is not in Gershwin's manuscript.[23] He indicated in his sketch only that the first movement was written in "July 1925," the second in "August-September 1925," and the finale in "September 1925"—nothing more definite than that. During September, presumably while still working on the finale, Gershwin, with Bill Daly at a second piano, tried out the first two movements for a number of friends to get their reactions. As for the actual time spent in orchestrating the piece, that is not a certainty either. The orchestration was undoubtedly started after he had finished sketching the three movements and was done between early October and November 10, 1925. The latter date appears at the end of his orchestration manuscript.[24]

Though Gershwin did most if not all of the sketching of the concerto at the piano, he apparently conceptualized the broad plan of the piece away from the piano. On a work sheet for the concerto, obviously prepared before or shortly after he started sketching the piece, he outlined a succinct general plan for the three movements of the composition along with some references to the "development" of his material.[25] The overall plan of the concerto was indicated by George in this laconic manner for each of the numbered movements:

1. Rhythm
2. Melody [Blues]
3. More Rhythm

This estimate of the way he conceived the piece is not inconsistent with his own comments about his work habits:

> In composing we combine what we know of music with what we feel. I see a piece of music in the form of a design. With a melody one can take in the whole design in one look; with a larger composition, like a concerto, it is necessary to take it piece by piece and then construct it so much longer. . . .
>
> Composing at the piano is not a good practice. But I started that way and it has become a habit. However, it is possible to give the mind free rein and use the piano only to try what you can hear mentally. . . . The actual composition must be done in the brain.[26]

In writing the concerto, Gershwin also made use of his practice, one he frequently followed as a tunesmith, of drawing on material he had created earlier, possibly in another context. Just as the theme from his *Lullaby* for string quartet became an "aria" in his one-act opera *Blue Monday,* and tunes from some of his musical comedies were often incorporated with or without revision into other stage productions, so the opening of the third movement of the concerto came from another source. That source was an unpublished and unfinished piano sketch, one of a series of piano "Preludes" he had worked on over a period of several years. This particular sketch, sixteen measures long and dated "January 1925," with some minor changes in meter and rhythm, became the important opening theme of the concerto's finale. For a close replica of this "Prelude," one has only to look at the start of the third movement of the concerto in its published version for solo piano.

111

Unlike the relatively small "jazz" ensemble used in Grofé's 1924 orchestration of the *Rhapsody,* Gershwin's concerto score called for a symphony orchestra with these instruments in addition to the solo piano: piccolo, two flutes, two oboes, English horn, two B-flat clarinets, bass clarinet, two bassoons, four French horns, three B-flat trumpets, three trombones, tuba, timpani, percussion, and strings. Judging from the completed score, in Gershwin's hand, the concerto is rather well orchestrated. The clarity of the handwriting, moreover, suggests that he was obviously quite careful in working on the score. Actually, before tackling the job of orchestrating the concerto, he did some preliminary scoring of the work, eight pages of which are extant.[27] After some correction of instrumentation and accents, possibly at the behest of Bill Daly, the preliminary orchestration apparently served as the basis for the final score.

Even though the completed scores of all of Gershwin's orchestral pieces written after the *Rhapsody* including the concerto are in his hand, there is a good chance that they were orchestrated with some help. In all probability he had samples of his orchestration for the concerto and other works checked and then incorporated suggested improvements into the final scores as we now find them. The orchestrated score for *Porgy and Bess* is a case in point. All three acts of the opera, beautifully written and well orchestrated, are in Gershwin's hand. Solely on the basis of the finished product one would assume that he had not been helped in any way. Yet there is evidence that he was aided in his orchestration of the opera by Joseph Schillinger. According to Vernon Duke, he and George, as well as Ira and his wife, Leonore, and Moss Hart, all shared a house on Fire Island during the summer of 1935. All summer long, Duke claims, Gershwin saw Schillinger three times weekly for help in orchestrating the opera.[28] This claim is supported by a letter, dated May 16, 1935, which Gershwin sent to Schillinger. In it he wrote:

> I have finished the music for the opera [*Porgy and Bess*] and also the orchestrations of the first act and am now working on the second act scoring, but it goes slowly.
> Would like to see you one of these days and perhaps continue to take some lessons as I am planning to stay in New York all summer.

Though one might easily infer from this letter that Gershwin sought Schillinger's help in orchestrating *Porgy and Bess,* presumably the second and third acts of the opera if not the first act too, there is nothing in the finished score that would substantiate that inference. Any and all help Gershwin recieved from Schillinger was embodied in the score for *Porgy and Bess* as it stands. Without the benefit of the specific musical material relating to the opera that he showed Schillinger for him to pass on—and

112

this material may be destroyed or lost by now—one can only speculate on the amount of help he got for *Porgy and Bess*.[29] Schillinger himself, after Gershwin's death, alleged that he supervised the entire writing of the opera over a period of a year and a half, with Gershwin taking lessons from him three times weekly.[30] In defense of his brother and in answer to such a claim, Ira stated in 1944 that "lessons like these [that Gershwin took with Schillinger] unquestionably broaden musical horizons, but they don't inspire an opera like *Porgy*."[31] Conflicts of opinion such as that between Ira Gershwin and Joseph Schillinger only heighten speculation on the amount of assistance George obtained, especially in orchestration, for his large-scale works, the concerto included.

Not long after the concerto's orchestration had been finished, Gershwin had a run-through of the work, now titled simply *Concerto in F*,[32] at the Globe Theater, for which he hired an orchestra at his own expense. Bill Daly conducted the orchestra of sixty musicians, while Gershwin performed the solo piano part. Also present at the hearing was Walter Damrosch. Though admittedly delighted by what he heard,[33] Gershwin consented to have a number of extensive cuts made in the work. For instance, passages of forty-four and fourteen measures respectively were cut in the first movement; thirty measures were eliminated in the second movement; and, in the finale, the piano was given a solo passage originally played by the ensemble, sixteen measures cut from a canonic section, a measure of silence added, and a measure in triple meter changed to three in quadruple meter.[34] Some further revisions, mostly of a minor kind, were also made at the tryout.[35] But whether major or minor, these revisions strengthened the *Concerto*, mainly by eliminating superfluous material. Nevertheless, it is conjectural who initiated these changes. Because of Gershwin's general lack of expertise in the symphonic field, one might readily speculate that Daly and Damrosch, each with extensive orchestral experience, were in a stronger position to suggest revisions in the *Concerto* than Gershwin, though he as the composer understandably has received credit for the end result.[36]

With the tryout of the *Concerto* behind him, Gershwin turned his attention to rehearsal preparations for the work's premiere at Carnegie Hall on the afternoon of December 3, 1925 by the New York Symphony. In contrast to the dance-hall atmosphere of the Palais Royal, where the *Rhapsody in Blue* was prepared by Whiteman and his ensemble, the *Concerto* was rehearsed at venerable Carnegie Hall itself. There on the broad stage, where Tchaikovsky had conducted in 1891 at the opening of the hall and scores of the world's finest musicians had performed since, Gershwin, Damrosch, and the members of the orchestra gathered one

113

morning to rehearse. Henry Osborne Osgood, who had been present during Whiteman's rehearsals of the *Rhapsody* at the Palais Royal, found the Carnegie Hall setting, despite its hallowed tradition and its air of genteel respectability, as depressing as the inelegant, tawdry dance hall. Carnegie Hall in the morning, for Osgood, was oppressively dark, except for the light shining

> upon the orchestra on its high stage. The audience . . . for the most part . . . was made up of gentle, gray-haired ladies, longtime subscribers of the New York Symphony who los[t] no opportunity, even mornings, to sit at the feet of their beloved conductor. Walter Damrosch rehearsed a dull Glazunov symphony for nearly an hour and then at intermission came down and shook hands with the gentle old ladies and smiled at them.[37]

Things took a turn for the better for the more adventuresome in the hall when the orchestra started rehearsing Gershwin's *Concerto,* with its youthful vitality and propulsive drive. Coming as it did on the heels of the stuffy Glazunov symphony, the *Concerto* in comparison seemed to burst with a volcano of energy. Staid Carnegie Hall rocked as perhaps never before to an explosion of jazz-oriented sounds that roared forth from the orchestra. For the more conservative elements present, such as Damrosch's group of admiring ladies, what they heard must have seemed almost disreputable and heretical; possibly only their supreme faith in the judgment of their idol and master kept them from questioning his association with such musical shenanigans. Gershwin sat at the piano, giving impetus to the work by the dynamism of his playing and intensity of expression; in contrast a briar pipe rested casually between his lips, though at times it appeared to point menacingly at those members of the orchestra whose playing was too stiff. In this setting, the *Concerto* began to take shape. As Gershwin's jazz-inflected solos hit their mark, time and again, with the impact of a boxing champion pummeling a clumsy opponent, the men in the orchestra—many of whom were at first insufferably rigid and inflexible in their playing, the result no doubt of years of exposure to "tradition" and other forms of musical brainwashing—began to loosen up. After a while the stolid New York Symphony sounded as though many of its members had played in jazz ensembles all their lives. Like hypnotized followers at a revival meeting working themselves up to a frenzy at the exhortation of their leader, the orchestra's men began to let themselves go and swing with the music as they followed Gershwin's lead.

When the afternoon of December 3, 1925, rolled around, Carnegie Hall was filled to capacity for the premiere of the *Concerto,* despite a heavy rain that had fallen that day. Similar to Whiteman's Lincoln Day concert of the year before, there was a motley mixture of people in the hall to hear Gershwin's latest orchestral piece, with the wealthy and famous rubbing elbows with the lowly and nondescript. As with Whiteman, Gershwin gave a good account of himself at the piano. Gershwin could do no wrong from the moment he came on stage, walking briskly and confidently to the piano, without any sign of nervousness. If his "composer's stomach" was bothering him, he didn't show it. He made a stunning impact on the audience, aided by an aura of "star" quality that seemed to surround him. From the opening boom of the timpani to the closing chords of the full orchestra and piano, all eyes were on Gershwin. He was up to the occasion. His cheeks flushed with the excitement of the moment and his eyes flashing, he dominated the piano like a colossus. His hands were all over the keyboard as he pulled a phantasmagoric array of sounds from the piano with a Herculean ease that added to the general effect. Again and again, he left the audience almost limp and breathless with the visual and musical vibrancy of his performance.

Nearly all in the hall cheered mightily for their hero when he had finished. The piece had obviously hit home, and the audience responded with bravos. Many of the music critics in the audience, however, were not so easily impressed. For Pitts Sanborn and Olin Downes, the *Concerto* was less successful than the *Rhapsody*. William J. Henderson, too, had reservations about the piece, though he found it "interesting and individual." To Lawrence Gilman's ears, the *Concerto* was "conventional, trite, . . . a little dull." On the other hand, Samuel Chotzinoff, in the *World,* liked what he heard. In his judgment, Gershwin's originality more than made up for his musical shortcomings. "Of all those writing the music of today . . . he alone actually expresses us," Chotzinoff stated firmly.

Despite the fine reception given the *Concerto* by the audience and some favorable but mixed comments from the music critics, the piece, unlike the *Rhapsody,* did not become an overwhelming success at once. It took time and work on Gershwin's part for the piece to catch on. Undoubtedly one reason for this delay was that Damrosch and his orchestra, even with all the attention they drew to the *Concerto* and themselves, did not generate so much publicity for their efforts as had Whiteman's earlier event. Damrosch and his group, after all, represented the Establishment, whereas Whiteman and his "jazz" band had evoked the spirit of the *avant garde* in their "Experiment in Modern Music"; the *Rhapsody* benefited immeasurably from its association with the newness implicit in the "experiment." The *Concerto* probably also lagged behind the *Rhapsody* in initial popularity because it was Gershwin's second orchestral work. Inasmuch as he had already shown in the *Rhapsody* that he could write a large-scale piece, there was less inherent novelty in the *Concerto* than in the earlier composition. Whatever the reasons for its relatively slow start, the *Concerto* has become a fixture in the orchestral repertoire. It is one of the most frequently performed piano concertos written in this century.

The overall form of the *Concerto* as already noted does not follow textbook models. Gershwin did not have the training or the experience, or perhaps the inclination, to write a piece that conformed to classical tradition. Instead he came up with his own concept of a concerto. In many ways his second orchestral work resembles the first, although it is in three movements rather than one. It has many of the characteristics of a free-flowing rhapsody—a musical approach that evidently came naturally to him with his strong and spontaneous melodic gift. As in the *Rhapsody*, there is much repetition of material and limited development inconsistent with the quality of his rather sophisticated motif transformation. Like the *Rhapsody*, too, the *Concerto* drew strongly on "jazz" elements and the musical language of Tin Pan Alley and Broadway. But of the two works, the *Concerto* has greater structural strength. For instance, repetition of material is often less literal in the *Concerto*, and there is more notice-able use of counterpoint—including a brief, four-part free canon in the finale—than in the earlier piece. Also, the forms of the individual move-ments of the *Concerto* are more clear-cut and logically planned than one might expect on the basis of the *Rhapsody*. The first movement bears a vague resemblance to sonata form; Gershwin himself described it as being "in sonata form, but—."[38] The second movement, in turn, is a somewhat extended three-part song form, while the finale is an approximation of a rondo.

Gershwin described the three movements of the *Concerto* this way:

> The first movement employs the Charleston rhythm. It is quick and pulsating, representing the young enthusiastic spirit of American life. It begins with a rhythmic motif given out by the kettledrums, supported by other percussion instruments, and with a Charleston motif introduced by . . . horns, clarinet[s] . . . [and] violas [plus cellos and trombones]. The principal theme is announced by the bassoon. Later, a second theme is introduced by the piano.
>
> The second movement has a poetic nocturnal atmosphere which has come to be referred to as the American blues, but in a purer form than that in which they are usually treated.
>
> The final movement reverts to the style of the first. It is an orgy of rhythms, starting violently and keeping to the same pace throughout.[39]

Considerations of form and other technical matters aside, the end result in the *Concerto* as in the *Rhapsody* is pure Gershwin. Like the

116

Rhapsody, too, the *Concerto* somehow captured much of the essence of the time in which it was written. For in its special hybrid way—a mixture of New York musical vernacular and the concert hall—the *Concerto* evokes the spirit of the Jazz Age, with its speakeasies, raccoon coats, Stutz roadsters, the Charleston, whiskey flasks, and other razzle-dazzle features of the 1920s.

Consistent, too, with its time, was the metaphoric description of Gershwin and the *Concerto* made by Walter Damrosch at the premiere of the piece. Though his glowing and fanciful words in their praise leave him open to charges of favoritism because of his part in commissioning the work,[40] Damrosch's statement vividly underscores the composer's contribution:

> Lady Jazz, adorned with her intriguing rhythms, has danced her way around the world. . . . But for all her travels and her sweeping popularity, she has encountered no knight who could lift her to a level that would enable her to be received as a respectable member in musical circles. George Gershwin seems to have accomplished this miracle. He has done it boldly by dressing this extremely independent and up-to-date young lady in the classic garb of a concerto. Yet he has not detracted one whit from her fascinating personality. He is the prince who has taken Cinderella by the hand and openly proclaimed her a princess to the astonished world.

Even with such an encomium by Damrosch, it took more than two years after its Carnegie Hall premiere for the *Concerto* to be performed in Europe. It was finally played abroad for the first time on May 29, 1928, when Dimitri Tiomkin, now better known as a composer of Hollywood film scores, appeared as piano soloist in the work under the direction of Vladimir Golschmann at Paris's Théâtre National de l'Opéra.[41] In spite of the delay the *Concerto* encountered in being played outside the United States, the Paris performance by Tiomkin and Golschmann was a foretaste of the groundswell of interest that gradually built up for the piece and eventually made it a world favorite. But, then, nearly everything Gershwin did in music apparently turned out well for him. Whether writing for the concert hall or the musical theater, he was the veritable personification of success. The case of the *Concerto* is but one of a long line of examples that help to point up this fact.

Gershwin, with his ever-present cigar, working at the piano.
(Photograph by Edward Steichen, Collection of the Museum of Modern Art)

THE PERENNIAL
TROUBADOUR

THE YEAR 1925 closed in a blaze of glory for Gershwin. Along with the premiere of the *Concerto*, December of that year witnessed in quick succession the Broadway openings of *Tip-Toes* and *Song of the Flame*, both with Gershwin scores, and Whiteman's concert rendition at Carnegie Hall of Gershwin's *135th Street*, formerly *Blue Monday*. Within a three-day period, his work dominated New York's theatrical and musical scene. On December 28 *Tip-Toes*, produced by Aarons and Freedley, opened at the Liberty Theater to general acclaim. This was followed on December 29 by Whiteman's performance of *135th Street* to a packed house that cheered the composer. At the Forty-fourth Street Theater the next night, December 30, the Arthur Hammerstein production of *Song of the Flame* started its long run.

Not ones to tamper with a successful formula, Aarons and Freedley once again called on Guy Bolton and Fred Thompson, the authors of the previous year's smash, *Lady, Be Good,* to write the book for *Tip-Toes*. The plot concerned a vaudeville trio, the Kayes, made up of Tip-Toes Kaye, a diminutive but lovely dancer, played by tiny Queenie Smith; and her two uncles, Hen and Al Kaye, performed by Harry Watson, Jr., and Andrew Tombes. Out of money and stranded in Palm Beach, the Kayes try to pass themselves off as members of high society in an attempt to advance their

119

fortunes. Through their machinations, Tip-Toes meets and has a romance with Steve, a young multimillionaire glue tycoon, played by Allen Kearns. What had started out as calculated chicanery by the Kayes takes a somewhat different but predictable turn when Tip-Toes finds that she is really in love with Steve and he with her. "True love conquers all" at the final curtain, as Steve ultimately realizes that Tip-Toes loves him for what he is rather than for his money—or glue—alone.

Gershwin's score for *Tip-Toes* compared favorably with that for *Lady, Be Good*. To Ira's keenly honed, trenchant lyrics, George responded with such audience-pleasers as the capitvating "These Charming People," in which the Kayes in trio make known their plans for social climbing; the poignant "Looking for a Boy," sung by Tip-Toes; the rhythmically senti-mental "That Certain Feeling," a duet for the lovers; and the bright and lively ensemble number, "Sweet and Low-Down," which, in novel fashion, made use of a corps of kazoos in the production. If the score for *Tip-Toes* produced no hits comparable to those in *Lady, Be Good*, it was no less ef-fective than Gershwin's music for the earlier show.[1]

The music Gershwin put together for *Song of the Flame* was another matter. With Herbert Stothart as his composing partner, Gershwin's score smacked less of Gershwin than it did of bad Viennese operetta, but in a pseudo-Russian style. The mock-Slavic characteristics in the score evolved largely from the book by Otto Harbach and Oscar Hammerstein II—both of whom also wrote the lyrics—which concerned a peasant revolt in Im-perial Russia led by a young noblewoman, though watered down to a typical boy-meets-girl routine. But what it lacked in originality the produc-tion made up in lavishness. Besides a large cast, there were many costumes, elaborate sets, a slew of dancers, and even a Russian chorus. Yet the show did not jell as an entity. It was neither Cossack Russian nor Broadway Viennese. The score reflected this ambiguity, from the title song to such tunes as "Vodka" and the "Cossack Love Song" (also known as "Don't Forget Me"). But if *Song of the Flame* was not all of a piece, it did well at the box office. It ran for 219 performances, 25 more than the clearly more sophisticated and delightful *Tip-Toes*.

In contrast to the whirlwind pace of the closing days of 1925 when Gershwin's name and music seemed to be constantly in the news, the early part of the year started somewhat tentatively for him with the premiere on February 8 of his brief *Short Story* for violin and piano. It was played at the University Club of New York by the eminent violinist Samuel Dushkin, who along with Gershwin arranged the work from two unpublished short piano pieces by the composer called "Novelettes."[2] The two "Novelettes" of *Short Story*—one, untitled but dated August 30, 1923, is rather slow and deliberate; the other, more rhythmically incisive, is undated but titled "Novelette in Fourths"—like *Lullaby* and *Blue Monday,* represent early attempts by Gershwin at "serious" composition.[3] Separately, these "Novelettes" are not very distinguished, nor has their lack of distinction been improved or camouflaged by being grafted together. As a curiosity, *Short Story* has its pleasant moments, but it misses as a work of art. Though published, it has never established itself in the violin and piano literature.[4] When Gershwin, in 1926, incorporated the "Novelettes" of *Short Story* into a series of piano preludes performed as part of a program given by the singer Marguerite d'Alvarez, the two did not make much headway as piano pieces, either. Conversely, three of the other preludes played in Miss d'Alvarez's program have become famous repertory pieces under their collective title *Preludes for Piano.*

Gershwin's ingenuity in compiling an impressive list of compositions —orchestral pieces, piano preludes, opera, innumerable tunes and scores for various productions, even the unsuccessful *Lullaby* and *Short Story*— despite limited formal education, musical or otherwise, gives credence to a description of his learning ability made by Kay Swift, who knew him intimately for a number of years: "Anything he wanted to learn, he hit with a terrific sock. He just tore into it."[5] Mainly through a degree of inquisitiveness and applied diligence, the earmarks of probably the finest type of self-education, Gershwin was able to absorb sufficient information and skills to meet many of his professional and social needs. But it is one thing to be able to assimilate enough know-how for specific practical purposes, and still another to have an intellectual bent; the two are not the same or necessarily reconcilable. Gershwin, though dynamic, intuitive, sensible, engaging, and curious enough where his self-interests were concerned, was anything but an intellectual. He even exhibited a certain disdain for cultural refinement and an anti-intellectuality that was surprising for one engaged in creative pursuits, at least in the circles he often traveled in. For instance, those things of the mind that he could not understand through common sense were often suspect to him. Nor was he especially sympathetic to far-out music, art and literature; if they were not reasonably accessible to him, he questioned their validity. He also boasted on occasions that he never had time to read books because of his ever-busy musical schedule. In view of this sentiment on his part, many who knew him were amazed when at the peak of his career he was quoted in an advertisement as saying, "I am never bored by a Borzoi book."[6] A common retort of his friends on seeing the advertisement was: "Obviously he couldn't be bored with books, he *never* reads any."

Gershwin's intrinsic lack of broad-based knowledge was perhaps most noticeable when in the company of highly cultured people capable of discussing a variety of subjects on a convincing level of intellectuality. At such times Gershwin—assuming that he was not comfortably and safely ensconced at the piano playing and singing—would remain relatively silent during the often brilliant and animated discussions that inevitably followed, apparently intimidated by the company he was in and feeling himself out of his depth. His silence in such circumstances was indeed a saving grace.

On the other hand, Gershwin was completely at ease when talking about himself and his work. He could also hold his own in general conversations of a less-than-lofty nature when he was in groups with whom he could readily identify, such as fellow tunesmiths, lyricists, actors, singers, dancers; and those connected with Tin Pan Alley, theater, or the movies. Then he was his normal self, free to say what was on his mind and to speak out when the spirit moved him. Gershwin was equally at home in athletics and physical activities of all kinds. He was lean and well-muscled and partial to exercise, both for its own sake as well as for body conditioning. His athletic build was a particular source of pride to him and, like many other egocentric males vain of their bodies, would often flex his muscles in front of a mirror—especially if he thought he wasn't being watched—as though to reassure himself that his fine physique was really his. When he could walk or run, rather than ride, he would do so for the physical benefits involved and would make it a point to exercise regularly by hitting a punching bag, doing sit-ups and push-ups, using the medicine ball, or working out with weights. He was nearly always brimming over with energy, much of it nervous energy, judging by his quick movements and rapid speech, and exercise was an indispensable way for him to let off steam.[7] Moreover, from childhood on, he had always loved games, particularly those which made physical demands on him. The fine coordination he had shown as a youngster in his play carried over to his adult years, except that now the games or sports he took part in were more in keeping with his age and position in life. Instead of the jumping contests, foot races, and games of "Cat" he played as a child, golf, tennis, horseback riding and skiing became great favorites. But no matter what sport he participated in, whether Ping-Pong, swimming, or baseball—though he limited his baseball playing when he became a celebrity for fear of injuring his valuable piano-playing hands—he took to it like a duck to water. The quick, almost automatic reflexes that he demonstrated again and again in his improvisations at the piano also were evident in sports.

He was an excellent dancer, too, supple and graceful. At parties, when he could be dragged away from the piano, he kept up with the best of them on the dance floor. When the mood hit him, he could dance for hours on end, becoming more alive and vigorous as the night wore on. Gershwin was essentially a night person. He seemed to be at his most alert then and often composed after staying out much of the night. Seldom did he get to bed before dawn, rising at noon or later as befitting one in the theatrical profession. To make up for lack of sleep, he sneaked in some naps in the late afternoon or before dinner.

Gershwin's rugged, ruddy masculinity and general dynamism undoubtedly enhanced his appearance. Many even considered him a decidedly handsome man, despite his broken boxer's nose and less-than-perfect features. Others, less favorably impressed by his looks, were disquieted by an apparent sneer on his face in repose, the natural result of his bone conformation. This sneer was accentuated by a low-slung Neanderthal jaw and protruding, heavy lower lip that turned up at the corners in a cynically cryptic expression—a kind of half smile—round the mouth, from which jutted, like the phallic symbol of a warrior's lance ready to do battle, Gershwin's ever-present cigar.[8] Also unattractive was his nervous habit, particularly noticeable under stress, of simultaneously twisting his neck and stretching out his jaw with a grimace, as though trying to bring to the surface some hidden demon within him by peristaltic means. When asked about these jerky tic-like movements, he came up with some physiological mumbo jumbo, not inconsistent with his self-devised fad-diets, as explanation. He had dry neck bones, he claimed. He "lubricated" them, he maintained, by twisting and stretching his neck and jaw the way others crack their fingers and knuckles.

Gershwin's stated opinions on other matters were sometimes equally unconvincing. He did not always see cause and effect in his reasoning and jumped to conclusions much too quickly and easily. He was not above assuming an authoritative air on subjects outside his ken, a practice all too frequently indulged in by numerous outstanding people in all fields of endeavor who start believing all the good things said about them, including press-agent fabrications, and soon begin to consider themselves almost omnipotent in areas of specialization other than their own—like the famous actor who pontificates on political matters with conviction, if little insight; or the brilliant athlete who discourses on the state of world economy with similarly limited perspective. (Nowadays, of course, many who fit this description are seen and heard regularly on television talk shows.) For instance, in an essay, "The Composer in the Machine Age," written in 1930, Gershwin tackled a number of topics. On medicine and music he had this to say: "Music sets up a certain vibration which unquestionably results in a physical reaction. Eventually the proper vibration for every

Vernon Duke. *(Courtesy ASCAP)* He spent the summer of 1935 at Fire Island with Gershwin and claims that he saw Joseph Schillinger three times weekly for help in orchestrating *Porgy and Bess* during that period.

GEORGE GERSHWIN
132 EAST 72nd STREET
NEW YORK, NEW YORK

16 May 1935

Dear Joseph:

I've been wanting to write you for some time since I came back from Florida but so many things are happening that it's difficult to write a letter these days.

I have finished the music for the opera and also the orchestrations of the first act and am now working on the second act scoring, but it goes slowly.

Would like to see you one of these days and perhaps continue to take some lessons as I am planning to stay in New York all summer. I would like to clear up the amount outstanding on the organ loan and perhaps we could work this out in lessons.

Am leaving town today and will be back Monday. I will call you then.

Sincerely,

George Gershwin

Mr. Joseph Shillinger
315 East 68th Street
New York, New York

A letter from Gershwin to Schillinger in which he expresses interest in taking "some lessons" during the summer of 1935.

Gershwin with Bill Daly, discussing Gershwin's music.

person will be found and utilized." Speaking about the appreciation of music, he asserted: "People in the underworld, dope fiends and gun men, invariably are music lovers and, if not, they are affected by it." On the subject of Franz Schubert, Gershwin—turned music historian and prognosticator—volunteered:

> Schubert could not make any money because he did not have an opportunity through the means of distribution of his day to reach the public. He died at the age of thirty-one and had a certain reputation. If he had lived to be fifty or sixty, unquestionably he would have obtained recognition in his own day. If he were living today, he would be well-off and comfortable.

Of composers in general, Gershwin said: "Not many composers have ideas. Far more of them know how to use strange instruments which do not require ideas." Commenting on the effect of radio and the phonograph on the composer's lot, Gershwin stated categorically: "In the past, composers have starved because of lack of performance, lack of being heard. That is impossible today." About jazz, he voiced this notion: "Unquestionably folk songs are being written and have been written which contain enduring elements of jazz. To be sure, that is only an element; it is not the whole. An entire composition written in jazz could not live." So much for Gershwin's conclusions, sense of logic and apodictic reasoning.

His simplistic thinking can also be seen in a letter he sent to Joseph Schillinger on October 13, 1936, pertaining to the study of composition. At that late date, when he was already an international musical figure whose every word was watched with interest, Gershwin naïvely wrote to Schillinger from Hollywood, where he was then living, to say: "I've been considering doing some studying with either Schoenberg or Toch. I haven't gotten down to making the decision yet. . . . I'm very anxious to begin thinking about a symphonic composition, either for orchestra and piano or orchestra alone." Since Arnold Schoenberg and Ernst Toch were at almost opposite aesthetic and stylistic poles as composers and musical theoreticians, the lumping together of their names as possible teachers only points up Gershwin's lack of judgment in this matter, as in others. In his bitingly humorous, sarcastically tinged reply to Gershwin, Schillinger said:

> If I were you, I would study with Schoenberg *and* with Toch. Why not find out what the well reputed composers have to say on the subject. I think it would be a good idea to work with Schoenberg on four-part fugues and to let Toch supervise your prospective symphonic compositions.

Gershwin's correspondence with Schillinger about lessons with Schoenberg or Toch is one of the least known of the various stories dealing with his interest in studying with celebrated musicians. One of the best known, widely quoted during Gershwin's lifetime, concerned him and Igor Stravinsky. As Stravinsky has told it:

> Gershwin is supposed to have come to me in Paris and to have asked me how much I would charge to give him lessons. I am then supposed to have asked how much he earned, and after he had supposedly said $100,000 a year, my supposed reply was, "Then I should take lessons from you."[9]

Of this supposed incident, Stravinsky has stated emphatically: "[This] popular story . . . is . . . untrue." Adding: "A nice story but I heard it about myself from Ravel before I met Gershwin."[10]

There are a number of versions of another famous anecdote in which it is alleged that Gershwin discussed with Maurice Ravel the possibility of studying with the French master. In one of the versions, it is reported that when Gershwin met Ravel for the first time at a party in honor of the French composer's fifty-third birthday, given by Eva Gauthier in her New York apartment on March 7, 1928, he "took the opportunity to ask if he might become Ravel's pupil, but Ravel declined, insisting that George was perfectly fine the way he was."[11] In still another account, David Ewen claims that after Gershwin met the Frenchman at Miss Gauthier's, their "contact . . . was renewed . . . at other New York parties, including one at Jules Glaenzer's."[12] (Actually, Gershwin never saw Ravel at Glaenzer's.[13]) Subsequently, states Ewen, when George visited Paris later in 1928 and

> called on Ravel at his home in France he came as a friend. . . . When Gershwin suggested studying with him, Ravel replied, "Why should you be a second-rate Ravel when you can be a first-rate Gershwin?"[14]

An additional variant of this anecdote has been told by Nicholas Slonimsky, who relates that in 1928

> Gershwin was in Paris. He met Ravel and spoke to him about the possibility of studying with him. Ravel facetiously inquired about Gershwin's annual earnings, for he was well aware of Gershwin's fame. Upon being informed, Ravel suggested that he and not Gershwin would profit by a special seminar on how to make money with music.[15]

In an attempt to arrive at a reasonably conclusive version of the Gershwin-Ravel story, this writer questioned Slonimsky about the source of his information for the anecdote. In reply, Slonimsky admitted that his "story had several loose points and cannot be verified," but noted that he had obtained his "version . . . from Gershwin's sister [Frances] who in turn

RKO STUDIOS INC.

780 GOWER STREET, LOS ANGELES, CALIF.

October 13, 1936

Dear Joseph,

I understand you are back from what must have been a wonderful vacation in the Canadian Rockies. Did you take some marvelous pictures? I wish I could see them.

We've been doing some work on the new Fred Astaire picture, but in true Hollywood fashion the script is not ready yet and so far no real pressure has been put upon us. I think we have some pretty good tunes -- let's hope the public thinks so!

I see a great deal of Oscar Levant and Ed Powell and we speak of you quite often. In fact, there must be at least a half dozen of your former pupils out here. Maybe one of these days you will decide to come, too.

I've been considering doing some studying with either Schoenberg or Toch. I haven't gotten down to making the decision yet, but it might be a good idea for me to keep working a little.

I'm very anxious to begin thinking about a symphonic composition, either for orchestra and piano or orchestra alone. I'm leaning towards the idea of a bright overture. It would make me very happy to write a new symphonic work to be played sometime late this winter, or next summer.

I would appreciate a line from you, letting me know how you are and what your fertile brain is thinking of these days.

With all my best wishes,

Sincerely,

George Gershwin

Mr. Joseph Shillinger
315 East 68th Street
New York City

A letter from Gershwin to Schillinger expressing interest in studying with either Schoenberg or Toch.

Gershwin met Maurice Ravel for the first time at a party given by Eva Gauthier on March 7, 1928, to celebrate Ravel's fifty-third birthday. Ravel and Miss Gauthier are shown seated at the piano. Gershwin is at the far right.

had [received] it from George Gershwin himself."[16] Ewen, when questioned by this writer, also claimed that his account of the anecdote emanated from "George himself, who," it was stressed, "never made up stories."[17] From these replies, it would appear that the different versions of the Gershwin-Ravel anecdote probably all originated from one and the same source. For as he had done earlier with Goldmark—spreading a story in which he built himself up at the expense of his teacher—Gershwin evidently colored the reportage of his contact with Ravel so as to heighten his sense of importance, irrespective of what had actually taken place. In all likelihood he did the same thing with the Stravinsky anecdote; certainly he never made any attempt to disclaim its authenticity, even though the story made the rounds while he lived. Considering Gershwin's known egocentricity, such actions would presumably not be inconsistent with his personality. In any event, everything seems to point to Gershwin as the key figure responsible for disseminating the different versions of the Gershwin-Ravel story, none of which can be considered definitive.

In similar manner, Gershwin was clearly the initiator of the inaccurate but prevalent version of a story dealing with his attempt to study with Nadia Boulanger, the renowned teacher of many of America's outstanding contemporary composers, including Aaron Copland, Virgil Thomson and Walter Piston, all of whom went to Paris as young men to study with this remarkable woman. It has been alleged that while Gershwin was in Paris in 1928 he sought out Nadia Boulanger in order to study with her, "only to be refused . . . because she felt there was nothing she could teach him."[18] On the basis of such a claim, one might reasonably assume that Gershwin was too far advanced in his craft to benefit from study with her. That was definitely not the case. Though Mlle. Boulanger has never discussed this matter in public—in keeping with this policy she declined to comment on the incident in a letter to this writer, save to say that Gershwin's death "destroyed the . . . value my remarks may have had"—she has made it known to a number of her students that reports of her contact with the composer were not accurate. She did not accept Gershwin as a student because she was not sure he could handle an extensive amount of formal study. The reasoning behind her decision was that "it is never wise to enter a tunnel unless there is a good chance of coming out on the other side."[19] Gershwin, of course, was not privy to these personal reflections on her part, for, outwardly, Mlle. Boulanger encouraged George to write music in the way that was most natural for him and to stick to the type of composition he could handle best. In view of Gershwin's egocentricity and his decidedly favorable interpretation of Mlle. Boulanger's encouragement of his work, it was perhaps inevitable that the Gershwin-Boulanger episode be inaccurately reported, especially since the composer—not Nadia Boulanger—was the basic source for the story.

Shortly after the flurry of musical activities in December had brought 1925 to a sparkling close, Gershwin left for England to help prepare *Lady, Be Good* for its London premiere. By now, he felt very comfortable in London and enjoyed his visits there. His reputation in England, always good, had taken a noticeable upturn with the popularity of *Primrose*.

As a further boon for his ego, nearly every move of Gershwin's, as in New York, was reported in detail in the English press, where his name was frequently linked with important figures in London's social, business, theatrical and social worlds. (In general, wherever he went, columnists and reporters lavished attention on him; he seemed to be their fair-haired boy.) Exciting luminary that he was, it was inevitable that Gershwin would become the darling of Mayfair's social set. They came to lionize him as an American Liszt, romantic and daring, and swamped him with invitations, most of which he accepted, to attend Londons most glittering parties. Practically every night Gershwin would be at one party or another, performing at the piano for roomfuls of attentive guests who could not get enough of him. During his rounds of partygoing, Gershwin came to know well many of England's élite, including the Mountbattens and Prince George of England, who in 1924 had given the composer a signed photograph of himself. Addressed to Gershwin, it was signed simply "From George." Gershwin treasured this photograph and displayed it prominently among his mementos.

Accustomed by this time to being fawned upon and treated with the deference reserved for major celebrities, Gershwin now played to the hilt the part of the famous composer and came to accept the many favors showered upon him with the equanimity of one to the manor born. In the past, for whatever the reason, he had always found it difficult to be prompt for appointments. But now, perhaps fully aware of his own importance, he was often cavalier about not being on time, particularly when he felt he could get away with it. Gershwin now also dressed the role of an international figure. His suits were meticulously tailored in Savile Row, and the accessories that went with them were no less impeccable. Consistent, too, with the image of success that he projected, Gershwin lived in elegant quarters in Pall Mall, often filled with people bidding for his attention. Except for the change in locale, his life in London was as hectic and as brimming with excitement as in New York.

In adapting *Lady, Be Good* for the English stage, Gershwin added several songs to the original Broadway score. Cannily exploiting the Charleston craze that was still in vogue, he, with Desmond Carter as lyricist, wrote "I'd Rather Charleston" for the vivacious Astaires. Also with Desmond Carter, he wrote "Buy a Little Button from Us." As another addition to the score, he reached back to his early days, interpolating a tune first heard in *Lady in Red* of 1919: "Something About Love," lyrics by Lou Paley. Complementing Gershwin's score were the deft production touches devised by Aarons and Freedley for the English public. Somewhat softer around the edges and with a more leisurely pace than its American counterpart, *Lady, Be Good,* London style, endeared itself almost immediately to English audiences. Gershwin's happy stay in London was made even more joyful by the show's brilliant triumph.

By the time he returned to New York at the end of April 1926, he had already begun thinking of his next show, *Oh, Kay!,*[20] another Aarons and Freedley production, which was to star Gertrude Lawrence. Gershwin had come to know Miss Lawrence in 1924 when she made her Broadway debut in *Charlot Andre's Revue,* a well-received English import that helped to establish her in this country. He was taken with her and she with him; they each admired the other's talent. During Gershwin's stay in England for *Lady, Be Good* the two became warm friends. When she was approached by Aarons and Freedley to star in *Oh, Kay!* she jumped at the opportunity, reputedly turning down an offer from Ziegfeld for a Broadway show under his auspices.

Stimulated by the idea of writing for Miss Lawrence, Gershwin created a score for *Oh, Kay!* that was exceptional even by Gershwin standards, aided by a Ira's pithy lyrics that were models of ingenuity, humanity, and wit, combining repetition of words and phrases, unexpected shifts of emphasis, topical references, metaphor, alliteration, New York vulgarisms, singability, and a high degree of polish into an artistic whole. "Do, Do, Do" from the *Oh, Kay!* score possibly epitomizes the Gershwins at their best. The opening lines of the chorus set the tone for the song:

> Do, do, do what you've done, done, done before, baby.
> Do, do, do what I do, do, do adore, baby.

The inventive repetition of Ira's "do, do, do" and "done, done, done" are appropriately matched by George's music. So firmly united are the two, it is almost impossible to think of one without the other. As in all prime Gershwin songs, one remembers not only the melody for "Do, Do, Do," but the words that go with it. Yet so attuned were the Gershwins to working together, they were able to complete the chorus for this gem, words and music, in half an hour, possibly less. In reminiscing about the tune, Ira relates:

130

An hour or so before dinner one evening at our house on 103rd Street I told George that maybe we could do something with the sounds of "do, do" and "done, done." We went up to his studio on the top floor and in half an hour wrote the refrain of the song. (I am certain of the time it took because just as we started to work, my bride-to-be telephoned that she *could* make it for dinner with us; and when she arrived, taxiing in half an hour—less, she says—from Eighth Street, we were able to play her a complete refrain.)[21]

Felicitous and memorable too were such other delights in the score as "Someone to Watch Over Me," a meditative solo by Miss Lawrence tenderly sung to a small rag doll; the exuberantly rhythmic ensemble number "Clap Yo' Hands"—the actual phrase is "clap-a yo' hands," not "clap yo' hands" as the title would suggest—as well as "Fidgety Feet," "Maybe," "The Woman's Touch," and "Dear Little Girl."[22] Though Ira, of course, is the lyricist of record for *Oh, Kay!*, he was assisted in writing the lyrics in part by Howard Dietz, for while working with George on the score, Ira suffered an attack of appendicitis. After an emergency appendectomy, Ira was hospitalized for six weeks—this was before antibiotics hastened recovery— and unable to work on the lyrics. Pressed for time to meet the rehearsal deadline, Ira accepted Dietz's offer to help him with the lyrics. The two collaborated on the lyrics for the title tune and "Heaven on Earth," with Dietz helpful on a few of the other songs as well, especially "Someone to Watch Over Me." As first conceived by George at the piano, without title or lyrics, this tune was jazzy and fast, more suitable as a singing-dancing production number. When Gershwin slowed it down one day, he and Ira realized that it came off best as a warm and pensive song rather than a bright, rhythmic one. On hearing it in this slow version, Dietz suggested some possible titles for it, one of which was "Someone to Watch Over Me." Drawing on that title, Ira then went on to write the lyrics for the tune as they now exist.

The book for *Oh, Kay!*, a charming, comical trifle co-authored by Guy Bolton and P. G. Wodehouse, dealt with a financially pressed English duke and his sister, Kay, who use their yacht to bring bootlegged liquor into the United States during Prohibition. On the lam from prohibition agents, Kay disguised as a housemaid, takes a job in the sumptuous home of wealthy playboy Jimmy Winter, whose cellar unknown to him is the secret storage place for the bootlegged liquor. Overseer of the illegal booty is Shorty McGee, employed as Jimmy's butler but actually in cahoots with Kay and her brother. In an unlikely plot, studded with droll lines and implausible incidents, the nefarious but bumbling schemings of the would-be bootleggers had a refreshing madness about it that more than compensated for the overly pat conclusion which saw Kay and Jimmy deeply in love and the happy resolution of all their problems. Gertrude Lawrence as Kay, Oscar Shaw as Jimmy, and Victor Moore with his sad voice and helpless looks incongruously cast as Shorty McGee were the mainstays of a brilliant company that made *Oh, Kay!* an incomparable evening in the theater. From its tryouts in Philadelphia, starting on October 18, to its opening night at Broadway's Imperial on November 8, *Oh, Kay!* met with an enthusiastic response and compiled an impressive New York run of 256 performances. In the words of Brooks Atkinson, *Oh, Kay!* was an "excellent blending of all the creative arts of musical entertainment."

An artistic and financial success, *Oh, Kay!* demonstrated anew that Gershwin's glowing reputation in the theater was a deserved one. In a field where musical formulas are all too frequently the rule rather than the exception, George, especially in conjunction with Ira, had the uncanny knack for coming up with the fresh and the novel. To be sure, his ballads were appropriate for their time and genre. But they also added something new to what was usually expected of Broadway musical-comedy material by their often uncommon rhythmic, melodic, and harmonic turns as well as wonderfully creative lyrics. Almost like an alchemist transmuting iron ore into precious metal, Gershwin took the hackneyed musical ingredients of Broadway and shaped them into songful treasures; the best of his tunes transcended their original function and period and ultimately became classics. Moreover, he had a showman's instincts for what would work on the stage—there have even been reports that he had always harbored a secret ambition to be an actor—and his music bore witness to that gift. Just as he could, and often did, underline a phrase from his tunes with telling effectiveness simply by a gesture of his hands or an appropriate facial expression as he sang and played at parties,[23] so, too, he remained the composer-performer when writing for the theater, but with this difference: his songs were now performed by others than himself. Like the troubadours of old who so effectively sang their songs of chivalric love and gallantry, Gershwin was probably one of the finest interpreters of his own songs, despite a small, untrained voice more suitable for the intimacy of the drawing room than for the stage. Yet whether performing at parties or being represented on stage by actors singing his songs, Gershwin was the perennial troubadour. He loved performing for others, and his music for the theater can be thought of as merely a transference of this love to a related medium, with actors rather than himself singing his tunes. Like the best of troubadour art, his songs empathize with each of the characters he wrote for on stage: the ingenue, the romantic male lead, or any of a variety of different roles. In a way, his tunes for musical comedy were really written with himself in mind, no matter whom the parts called for; that is, songs that *he* could play and sing. Certainly his scores reflected this personal involvement. He could write a delicate, tender solo or a bombastic, show-stopping ensemble finale with equal artistic perspicacity. Like all expressive art, Gershwin's songs could evoke a spectrum of emotions. Their surface characteristics might be light-years apart—lonely uncertainty voiced alongside outgoing brashness—but they nearly all seemed to come from his heart. Somehow his songs captured this elusive quality in a way that distinguished them from his run-of-the-mill competition. The durability of so much of Gershwin's work for the theater is a testament to this quality.

A self-caricature of Gershwin made in 1931. *(Museum of the City of New York)*

COLLECTOR AND PAINTER

MAINLY BECAUSE OF his stay in England in 1926, Gershwin did not write a complete score for any other Broadway show save *Oh, Kay!* that year. He and Ira contributed a song, however, to a diverting review, *Americana,* which opened at the Belmont Theater on July 26. The tune, "That Lost Barber Shop Chord," was a droll mixture of the old and the new. On one hand, it was a novel, delightful spoof of an almost inviolate American tradition, barber-shop quartets, as it told the story of a fantastic chord "lost" by four singing barbers in Harlem. It looked back for inspiration to two musical chestnuts: "That Lost Chord," the famous setting of the Adelaide Proctor poem by Sir Arthur Sullivan (the composing partner of Sir William Gilbert), and "Play that Barber Shop Chord," a popular ragtime tune, 1910 vintage. As a matter of fact, the title "That Lost Barber Shop Chord" was concocted by the Gershwins as an amalgam of the titles of these two oldtime hits. On the other hand, "That Lost Barber Shop Chord" received fresh, satiric treatment in *Americana.* Instead of the usual quartet of colorfully dressed and mustachioed white barbers from middle America of the 1890s singing out in close harmony, "That Lost Barber Shop Chord" was performed by a black group, the Pan-American Quartet plus Louis Lazarin as soloist, in a stage setting that simulated a Harlem barber shop. Apparently the combination of the tune, lyrics, and title with this different treatment—quasi-Harlem black rather than "traditional" lily white—made some of the reviewers sit up and take notice, for "That Lost Barber Shop Chord" elicited some surprisingly favorable reviews in the press following the opening of *Americana*. Charles Pike Sawyer of the *Post,* for example, considered "That Lost Barber Shop Chord" "Gershwin at his best, which is saying a lot," while Stephen Rathbun of the *Sun* found it "the high mark" of the revue. Notwithstanding such praise and the exposure the tune got during the run of *Americana* (224 performances), "That Lost Barber Shop Chord" became an unknown quantity almost as soon as the revue closed. As Ira ruefully admitted in 1959, the tune "got lost pronto 11:15 P.M. closing night of *Americana*. . . . I haven't heard the song sung anywhere in over thirty years."[1]

Besides George's and Ira's association with *Americana* (Ira was also the lyricist for two other songs in the revue, "Blowin' the Blues Away" and "Sunny Disposish," both with music by Philip Charig), the revue was memorable as the launching ground for Helen Morgan's meteoric rise as torch singer.[2] In *Americana,* Miss Morgan's throaty, doleful voice and softly curvaceous looks, so easily capable of being lost or dissipated on the broad apron of a stage, were winningly projected and enhanced by having her sing atop a piano for the first time. The almost casual delivery of her material from the piano gave her a rapport with her audience that a less intimate presentation lacked; she seemingly embraced the audience with her purring, sexy languorousness and lovingly drew them to her. This technique worked beautifully for her. It set her apart from other singers and made her someone to remember. Singing on the piano, usually an upright, soon became her trademark as she went on to bigger and better things, including the role of Julie in Jerome Kern's *Show Boat* of 1927.

Another event of more than passing interest for Gershwin in 1926 took place in the closing days of the year. Less than a month after the Broadway opening of *Oh, Kay!* Gershwin appeared with the French-Peruvian contralto Marguerite d'Alvarez[3] in a concert she gave at New York's Hotel Roosevelt on December 4. Her overall program was uncomfortably reminiscent of the one by Eva Gauthier in 1923. It, too, emphasized selections from the traditional as well as popular repertoire.[4] However, Gershwin's salutary experience with the Gauthier recital, and of course with Whiteman's Aeolian Hall "experiment," made him favorably disposed to appear with her. Her concert, after all, was "serious" in intent, despite its inclusion of popular pieces, and offered him still another opportunity to show his weightier side as composer in a favorable light. Besides, he had been writing a number of short, "serious" piano pieces for a number of years and her recital gave him a chance to air such pieces in public.

A considerably bigger name at this point than when he had performed with Miss Gauthier, Gershwin practically hogged the d'Alvarez program as performer and composer. Though the concert was ostensibly the singer's, Gershwin was the star attraction. (Mme. d'Alvarez may have welcomed this arrangement, though possibly she had little choice, since the participation of the world-famous Gershwin obviously added luster to her concert and accrued to her credit.) In addition to performing as soloist in the premiere of his five brief preludes—a mixture of old and new piano pieces put together for the event—Gershwin used this concert to promote a two-piano version of the *Rhapsody* based on his original sketch of the piece. He played the solo part, with Isidor Gorn as second pianist. Gershwin also accompanied the diva in the popular songs on the program, nearly all of them Gershwin pieces: "The Nashville Nightingale," "Clap Yo' Hands," and "Oh, Lady, Be Good!" plus Jerome Kern's "Babes in the Woods."

In terms of press attention, the d'Alvarez concert suffered badly in comparison with its almost look-alike model, the Gauthier recital, for it received scanty, less than enthusiastic coverage; like many carbon copies, it didn't come off so well as the original. What had been inspired programming in 1923—the inclusion by Miss Gauthier of "jazz" songs in her recital—became something *déjà vu* in 1926. This, even with the *Rhapsody* and the preludes added to the d'Alvarez program and Gershwin, glamorous name, personality and all, on center stage as soloist rather than merely an accompanist for Miss Gauthier, playing in his inimitable, highly-charged manner for the filled hall. Also, though his *Rhapsody* was performed in a two-piano version rather than the original orchestral one, it was not really a novelty for the critics or the public; it had already arrived. Nor did his five preludes set the world on fire at their premiere. They were probably too small-scaled in scope to project in a strongly positive fashion at their first hearing. Nevertheless, when three of these pieces were subsequently published together in 1927 under the collective title of *Preludes for Piano* (the first and third pieces are fast and jazzy—both are marked *allegro ben ritmato e deciso*—while the middle one is bluesy and slow and marked *andante con moto e poco rubato)* they eventually went on to become world favorites, highly popular with the public and many pianists for their sensitive, attractive qualities.[5] Dedicated to Bill Daly, in expression of Gershwin's gratitude to him, these three preludes are frequently performed not only as piano pieces but in various transcriptions, including ones for orchestra and chamber ensemble.

As he had done with Eva Gauthier, Gershwin performed with Mme. d'Alvarez out of town in a repetition of their New York concert. He appeared with her in concert in Buffalo on December 15, 1926, and in Boston

Igor Stravinsky. (Courtesy Columbia Records) He refuted a commonly quoted anecdote about himself and Gershwin.

Nadia Boulanger, in a relatively early photograph and as she looked in 1962 after participating, as conductor and pianist, in a Composers' Showcase concert at the Museum of Modern Art. With her is Charles Schwartz.

Gershwin on board ship. He made five trips abroad between 1923 and 1928.

Gertrude Lawrence as Kay, in *Oh, Kay!*

on January 16, 1927. For the Boston concert, he incorporated a sixth brief piece to his collection of piano preludes, but it added little of substance to the grouping.[6] Nonetheless, these six preludes, plus the piano sketch dated "January 1925," from which the opening theme in the finale of the *Concerto* was taken, have the distinction of being among the few known solo piano pieces that Gershwin ever wrote. The only other similar piano works by Gershwin were written later in his career, and little is known of them since they have never been performed or made public. Of these latter pieces, Ira has stated: "Among the unpublished and uncopyrighted music I still possess of my brother's are a couple of short pieces which might have been intended as preludes; . . . these [were] written in the thirties."[7]

The interest Gershwin had shown in stage works about blacks, as manifested by his early opera *Blue Monday* or, tangentially, his tune for *Americana*, "That Lost Barber Shop Chord," came to the surface again in still another way in 1926. One evening in early October that year, before retiring, after a fatiguing day of rehearsals of *Oh, Kay!*, he took the time to read *Porgy*, DuBose Heyward's best-selling, widely discussed novel about the crippled beggar Porgy and life among poor Charleston blacks, published in 1925. The book had an immediate and profound effect on him. Here was a warm yet powerful, basic human story, told with feeling and compassion by a Southern white obviously familiar with the locale and the people he described. Though it concerned the poor blacks of Charleston's Catfish Row, it was applicable as well to folk all over the world. *Porgy* cried out for stage treatment, and Gershwin's instinctive theatrical sense responded immediately to its potential. Intrigued by the thought of a musical treatment of the novel, Gershwin wasted no time in writing to Heyward, expressing a desire to collaborate with him on such a project and suggesting a meeting between them. Heyward took kindly to the idea, though, unknown to Gershwin, he and his wife, Dorothy, were then writing a dramatic adaptation of the novel for the Theatre Guild that prohibited any immediate collaboration on his part.[8] Not long afterward, while Heyward was up north, he met with Gershwin to talk over the matter. At their meeting, Heyward relates,

> we discussed *Porgy*. He [Gershwin] said that it would not matter about the dramatic production [for the Theatre Guild], as it would be a number of years before he would be prepared technically to compose an opera. . . . And so we decided then that some day when we were both prepared we would do an operatic version of my simple Negro beggar of the Charleston streets.[9]

They undertook no specific plan of action at that point to realize their goal and went their separate professional ways, but the idea of writing a musical version of *Porgy* never really left George. In staking out his claim for a future collaboration with Heyward on an opera about blacks, George was only following the shrewd instincts, the professional awareness of what would come off, that made him the success he was in a tough, competitive field.[10] Such an opera not only lent itself to the popular "jazz" style for which he had become noted, since "jazz" and blacks were often equated, but it also demanded a black cast for authenticity, which practically assured an extra dimension of theatricality and uniqueness that white actors, with ór without blackface, could not possibly muster. How many stage productions were then performed by a black cast? Also, whether or not he was aware of the ramifications involved, Gershwin, by thinking "black" for his projected operatic work, was on top of the fashionable artistic trends of the time. For some of the most chic contemporary composers—Stravinsky, Ravel, and Milhaud, for instance—had already made clear in their music their indebtedness to "le jazz nègre," while many of the leading painters and sculptors, in turn, openly admitted the influence of black art on their work. The subsequent triumph of *Porgy* as a play (produced by the Theatre Guild, it opened on Broadway on September 10, 1927 and ran for 367 performances) only reinforced Gershwin's desire to write a musical vehicle based on it.

His perceptive judgment, as shown by his choice of *Porgy* as an opera, was also evidenced in the field of the visual arts. There he came to develop a taste for collecting contemporary paintings, sculpture, drawings, and prints that was remarkable for its catholicity and scope. True, this appreciation of fine modern art may have been stimulated by his exposure to quality works in the homes of many of his wealthy and elegant friends—people he eagerly emulated in such externals if he could—as well as by an awareness of the potential value of art as an investment. But Gershwin also brought to collecting a natural gift for color, line, and form that he later demonstrated in paintings and drawings of his own. He was aided in his collecting by his cousin and close friend, the artist Henry Botkin. With the assistance of Botkin, who went to Europe in 1926 to paint and study and stayed there, on and off for approximately eight years, Gershwin began to purchase paintings and other art.[11] While in Europe, Botkin scoured art dealers for Gershwin and sent photographs of art works of merit to the composer in New York for his consideration. Gershwin then notified Botkin by cable whether he wanted any or all of them bought. Botkin did the rest. Because of his connections in the art world, Botkin was able to make purchases from European dealers at a much lower price than Gershwin would have paid on his own; when in the United States, Botkin also bought art cheaply for Gershwin from American dealers. This arrangement worked out beauti-

Marguerite d'Alvarez, Gershwin's partner in a concert at New York's Hotel Roosevelt on December 4, 1926. Five of Gershwin's piano preludes received their premieres on that occasion.

Gershwin's ink drawing—one of his earliest, made in 1927—of his dog Jock, lying down. *(Courtesy Melvin Parks, Museum of the City of New York)*

Jock.

G.S.

fully for both of them. Gershwin bought a total of 144 exceptional art works at substantial savings, while Botkin received a commission from the dealers for each of the sales, a tidy sum. In later years, Botkin used his considerable skill as art connoisseur to help assemble—for a price—a number of famous collections, including those of Edward G. Robinson and Billy Rose.

Gershwin's art collecting may have been a labor of love for him, but it was hardly a financial gamble. With Botkin's help, his art choices were impeccable—he could do no wrong—and his investment heavily stacked in his favor. Just as in writing music, where he was able to earn money in abundance, in addition to fulfilling his creative impulses, Gershwin had the golden touch in collecting art. For a total money outlay estimated to be no more than about $50,000, Gershwin amassed the works of such distinguished artists as Bellows, Benton, Chagall, Derain, Eilshemius, Gauguin, Kandinsky, Léger, Masson, Modigliani, Picasso, Rouault, Rousseau, Siqueiros, Sterne, Utrillo, and Weber, among others. His collection contained, in Botkin's opinion,

> some of the greatest examples of contemporary painting that can be found in this country. . . . Besides paintings in oil by the masters, he [Gershwin] had gathered a most varied group of important examples of Negro sculpture, together with drawings, rare watercolors and lithographs. He never confined himself to the paintings of any one group or country, but was always interested in the various movements and schools of art. [12]

At his death in 1937, Gershwin's collection was worth many times over what he had paid for it. Its dollar value since then, if a price tag can be put on such a collection, must have increased at least tenfold. It is undoubtedly worth millions at the present time. The collection is now the property of the Gershwin estate, administered by Ira.[13]

The flair Gershwin demonstrated in assembling his collection[14] carried over to his own paintings and drawings. He had started dabbling in art as a boy, making simple sketches and caricatures as the mood moved him. Like Ira—whose earliest painting, a watercolor of a Bowery scene, goes back to 1911—and his sister Frances, George had apparently inherited a natural inclination toward graphic art. But it was not until he was already established as a composer that he even gave thought to the idea of becoming a painter. An important breakthrough for him occurred when he tried his hand at watercolors for the first time in 1927. Encouraged by the results, he painted and sketched whenever he had an occasional free moment and the inclination to do so. By 1929 he was motivated enough to apply himself diligently to improving his art skills. Under the tutelage of Botkin, he soon revealed a definite bent as an artist. He was particularly impressed by the paintings of Rouault. Of the many artists he admired, it was Rouault he most wanted to emulate in scope and emotional power. Every chance he could he visited galleries and museums to see his idol's work for inspiration. In his own paintings, Gershwin was partial to portraits. He had the ability to capture quickly the essence of a person in a small sketch, which was then used as the basis for a larger oil.[15] His portrait style was realistic, darkly colorful, and neo-romantic, with little or no surface modernisms; his paintings were anything but far-out. Among the portraits he painted—all insightful in one way or another—were those of himself, his father, mother, grandfather, a Negro girl, Emily Paley, DuBose Heyward, Jerome Kern, and Arnold Schoenberg. Besides portraits, he painted some still lifes and landscapes in oil and watercolors. He had more than a hundred drawings to his credit at his death, though not all of them were completed.

His dedication to painting and drawing was no less intense than his dedication to music. He threw himself into his art with the enthusiasm usually reserved for composing. At the easel, caught up in his work, he thought of little else for hours on end. It was a welcome change of pace for him, a refreshing interlude away from his musical activities. Such was his attachment to art, that he would often put a canvas on which he was working at the foot of his bed before going to sleep so that he could see it in fresh perspective immediately on arising. In his wishful moments, he even considered concentrating on art instead of music, but such flights of fancy were never realized. However, he had planned to go on a painting trip with Botkin to Palestine and the Orient and devote himself entirely to painting during his stay.[16]

Any evaluation of Gershwin as a painter must be tinged with speculation. His death before his full painting potential could be realized must be taken into account in any assessment of his true worth. Suffice it to say, his oils, watercolors, and drawings show imagination and aptitude, but they are not comparable in quality to his music. They do not have the strong individuality, the richness of personality that stamp the finest of his tunes and scores as his own. Nor do they come close to the high standards set and maintained in his collection of art works of others. Nevertheless, his paintings and drawings have some relevance to the total corpus of his creative works and, indirectly, may even be thought of as being a part —a very small part, to be sure—of music history. But unquestionably they are more valuable as mementos of a famous musician than as art, simply because Gershwin the composer overshadowed by a wide margin Gershwin the painter.[17] Posthumous exhibitions of his art work at the Marie Harriman Gallery in New York in December 1937, at Lincoln Center's Philharmonic Hall in 1963 (given in connection with a Gershwin commemora-

Gershwin watching Henry Botkin,
his cousin and art instructor, paint.
Botkin helped Gershwin to amass
an exceptional art collection.

Gershwin's ink drawing of Botkin,
made in 1931. *(Courtesy Henry Botkin)*

tive sixty-fifth birthday musical program), and at the Museum of the City of New York in 1968 (where other Gershwin memorabilia, as well as his music, were also displayed) have been important less from an artistic standpoint than as a reflection of an interesting facet of his personal life. Clearly Gershwin lives on through his music—and also through his paintings and drawings.

George, Ira, and Ira's wife Leonore on shipboard during their 1928 European holiday.

EUROPEAN HOLIDAY

$\mathbb{G}$ERSHWIN'S INITIAL WATERCOLOR attempts in 1927 were undertaken at a country estate in Ossining, New York, Chumleigh Farm by name, that he and Ira had rented for the spring and summer of that year to get a taste of the leisurely life away from the mad pace of Broadway show business. There in the quiet of this lonely rural retreat he painted his first watercolor, a still life he dated "4/25/27." Besides painting and sketching, horseback riding, and other amenities of country living at Chumleigh, he worked with Ira on the score for his next show, *Strike Up the Band*. Rehearsals for this musical went into full swing during July. Rather than endure the "hardships" and the intrusion on their time of regular commuting between Broadway and Ossining while rehearsals were in progress, the brothers quit the rustic life and their elevated status of country gentlemen—a far cry, and a substantial social upgrade, from their boyhood days on the lower East Side—to move back to their home on One Hundred Third Street. Also that summer, on July 26, Gershwin made his first appearance at City College's Lewisohn Stadium, a huge outdoor ball-park-like mecca for music lovers in uptown Manhattan. The stadium was famous for its low-priced summer concerts, though these were often marred by poor amplification and an assortment of noises, street and other. Performing as soloist with members of the Philharmonic under

Willem van Hoogstraten in both the *Rhapsody* and the *Concerto,* Gershwin drew a capacity crowd that cheered him with unabashed partisanship.[1] George, for them, was not only the man of the hour, he was *their* composer; a man of the people who had risen from their ranks. They loved him and let him know it. The hurrahs were loud and long.

The public was less enthusiastic for *Strike Up the Band,* which began its out-of-town tryouts on August 29, 1927, with a half-week's stay at the Broadway Theater in Long Branch, New Jersey. Moving on to Philadelphia's Shubert Theater on September 5, the show closed after two weeks of progressively dwindling business without ever reaching Broadway. By the end of the second week the house was nearly empty for each performance. In spite of its brief run, this musical had much going for it. It had a fine score, numbering among its tunes "The Man I Love," a strong cast featuring Vivian Hart, Jimmie Savo, Roger Pryor, Edna May Oliver, Morton Downey, and other talents, an imaginative, gifted producer in Edgar Selwyn, and a book by the rapier-witted, acidulous George S. Kaufman. All things considered, it was probably Kaufman's book that was mainly to blame for the show's early collapse. It was a humorously cynical look at how war is instigated by man against his fellowman; in this instance, tiny, perennially neutral Switzerland, no less, is made the war target of American cheese interests. For protesting a tariff of fifty percent on Swiss cheese entering the United States, Switzerland and everything it represents becomes *non grata,* first to American business interests and then to patriotic fanatics. Chauvinistic zealots soon cause all things Swiss, in addition to cheese, to be banned in America: highly moralistic tales such as *William Tell* and *Swiss Family Robinson* become unacceptable library fare and are removed from the shelves; even Swiss watches are beyond the pale, as "un-American." As patriotic fervor mounts in intensity, a war between the nations is ultimately maneuvered by American would-be cheese profiteers eager to capitalize on an explosive situation for their own selfish interests, aided by the martial strains of the title tune that galvanizes the populace into action. The imbroglio is fought on Swiss soil, but in comic-opera fashion. As the battle rages, American soldiers can be found knitting for the folks back home and singing of the delights of war, while their Swiss counterparts yodel away in similarly nonmilitary manner. Finally the war is resolved, peace is restored, and the soldiers return home, neither side really benefiting. But at the final curtain the title tune is heard again, auguring another ridiculous war, this time between America and Russia over caviar.

War profiteering, man's inhumanity to man, obtuse diplomacy, absurd militarism, misguided patriotism were all unattractive topics, but fair game

148

for Kaufman in *Strike Up the Band*. No matter how comically treated, they added up to a bleak, oppressive outlook, one too much to take for the 1927 theatergoing public: affluent, comfortable, filled with optimistic hopes that World War I had ended wars for all time and that the rising national economy would continue its upward spiral indefinitely. Nothing could have seemed more unreal than the 1929 crash or the international politics of the 1930s and 1940s. Though George's lilting music and Ira's deft lyrics, a contrasting counterpoint to Kaufman's book, helped to lighten the burden of the playwright's somber message cloaked in barbed humor, they were not enough to save the show. Probably nothing could have. This production was not "right" for its period. It was too far ahead of its time. Lost in the shuffle with the demise of *Strike Up the Band*, besides "The Man I Love," was Gershwin's gentle love duet, "Seventeen and Twenty-One." Almost as retribution for this 1927 failure, a revised, less cynical, toned-down version of *Strike Up the Band* in 1930 had a substantial run on Broadway.

Another 1927 catastrophe loomed in prospect for Gershwin when *Funny Face*, starring the Astaires, began its six-week shakedown stint out of town in preparation for its November 22 Broadway opening. Nearly everything imaginable—including the book, the score, the casting, the singing and dancing—went awry at the start of its trial run. The entire production was all thumbs and left feet. Nothing meshed. There was even a further complication. The musical was set to open in New York at a spanking new theater on West Fifty-second Street built by its producers, Aarons and Freedley. The new house, the Alvin—its title derived from the producers' first names: *Al,* from Alex, and *Vin,* from Vinton—was something very close to their hearts since it was clearly a monument to themselves. Through good luck and judicious, financially profitable producing, mainly of Gershwin musicals, they were in the enviable position after three short years or so of partnership to pamper their egos with this theatrical edifice, which practically guaranteed them the satisfaction of seeing a union of their names glowing brightly over the theater's marquee. Understandably, Aarons and Freedley were anxious to mark the gala opening of their new theater with a hit, particularly one by the Gershwins, in view of their well publicized, highly successful association with them. As November 22 drew near, however, it appeared that their planned musical would not be ready for the auspicious occasion or be a worthy successor to their other Gershwin productions: *Lady, Be Good, Tip-Toes,* and *Oh, Kay!* The prognosis for the success of *Funny Face* on Broadway looked most unpromising as it played out of town.

Initially called *Smarty,* with a book contrived by Fred Thompson and Robert Benchley, this musical could not seem to get off the ground at the start of its road tryouts.[2] It was misshapen, lumpy, swollen. The book obviously needed work. To help doctor the script, a new writer, Paul Gerald Smith, was brought in to collaborate with Thompson, as Benchley fearing the worst left what looked like a sinking ship. Nor were the producers satisfied with the score at that point. They made no bones about their dissatisfaction with the way the musical was going and blamed Gershwin's score for much of the difficulty. Aarons and Freedley could be tough and hard and obsessively demanding; they didn't become successful producers in a cruelly rapacious profession by being "nice" guys. They insisted that the score be revised.[3]

George and Ira obliged. While out of town with the show, they dropped about half of their original tunes and came up with new ones to keep pace with the new script and other revisions as they occurred. And there were many such changes. The show was in a constant state of flux as all hands pitched in to get it into shape for Broadway. For as Ira has noted, "everyone concerned with the show worked day and night, recasting, rewriting, rehearsing, recriminating—of rejoicing there was none."[4] Among the songs eliminated from the score on the road was the now-famous "How Long Has This Been Going On?" (A few months later Gershwin would find a spot for it in Ziegfeld's *Rosalie*.) In its place went the equally fine "He Loves and She Loves." One of the last-minute additions to the score was "The Babbitt and the Bromide," the delectable patter song written for the Astaires. The lyrics for the chorus of this tune were initially devised as unison chatter for them. This was then changed to have Fred and Adele alternate each phrase to heighten the zaniness of the lyrics. The following excerpt shows how it worked:

> Hello! [*Fred*] How are you? [*Adele*]
> Howza folks? [*Fred*] What's new? [*Adele*]
> I'm great! [*Fred*] That's good! [*Adele*]
> Ha! Ha! [*Fred*] Knock wood! [*Adele*]

The song was tried out in Wilmington for two hundred or less of the local citizenry—mainly pregnant housewives, according to one description —shortly before *Funny Face* reached New York. From their jubilant response that made up in volume for their lack of number, it was clear that the tune worked, Ira's deliberate non sequiturs and all. "The Babbitt and the Bromide" stayed in the show when *Funny Face* opened on Broadway the following week.

By the time the company left Wilmington for the big city, all in the show, from the producers on down, had reasonable hope that *Funny Face* had a chance of surviving the scrutiny of the tough-as-nails Broadway critics on opening night. The show was now an entirely different product from the one that had started playing on the road some six weeks earlier. What had been an almost sure-fire candidate for oblivion at the beginning of the tryouts had been turned around by hard work, constant revisions, and tightening, to the point where it now had the look of a potential winner. What followed reaffirmed the most optimistic of expectations. The critics loved *Funny Face,* and audiences taking their cue from them descended on the Alvin. Ticket sales took an immediate upward spurt. In the first week alone, box-office receipts at the Alvin were $44,000 in contrast to the piddling $6,000 that *Funny Face* grossed in Wilmington. Nor did business let up. *Funny Face* was a smash hit, a veritable gold mine at the box office during its Broadway run of 244 performances.[5]

The book for *Funny Face* was only incidental to the singing and dancing of the Astaires and the other members of the company. At best, the story line was merely a skeletal framework to show off the Gershwin score and the talented cast. The plot revolved around some jewels held by Jimmy, played by Fred Astaire, who has hidden them away for safe-keeping for his charge, Frankie, played by Adele Astaire. Frankie and her boyfriend, Peter, played by Allen Kearns, want to gain possession of the jewelry as quickly as possible. So do two bumbling crooks. Thereby hangs the tale.

Cast as Herbert, one of the thugs, was Victor Moore, in a role as offbeat as the one he had in *Oh, Kay!* He practically stole the show with his blundering attempts at jewel robbing. As unlikely a thief as one might meet, he had them rolling in the aisles, doubling over with laughter. Add to this the charm and versatility of the Astaires and the fine Gershwin tunes and lyrics and you have the ingredients for instant success. Of George's songs, "'S Wonderful" stood out. The catchy, repetitive melody of its chorus and the slurred-over, sibilant sound of its lyrics—with its "'s wonderful," "'s marvelous," "'s paradise"—were a combination not easy to ignore or to forget. Other song favorites included "My One and Only,"[6] "Let's Kiss and Make Up," and, as mentioned, "He Loves and She Loves" and "The Babbitt and the Bromide."

Aside from its qualities as a musical, *Funny Face* was also the source of a widely quoted incident, one that has been used to point up Gershwin's supreme confidence in his ability to write songs quickly and easily. According to the story, Gershwin, on his way back to New York after his stay in Wilmington during the tryout of the show, found that he had left behind two notebooks with sketches for forty or more tunes. After calling his Wilmington hotel to report the loss, he was told that his sketches could not be found. It is alleged that, in true storybook fashion, he took the news calmly, hardly ruffled by the loss of his material. He would simply write some new tunes. There were plenty more where the lost ones came from.[7]

Gershwin, however, did not have to write many new tunes for his next show, the Ziegfeld production of *Rosalie*, which opened at the New Amsterdam Theater on January 10, 1928. Merely by digging into his bag of discards from other musicals or by having Ira change the lyrics of songs already written—almost the musical equivalent of a paste-up job— he came up with a sizable number of tunes for Ziegfeld. Heading the list was the perennial discard "The Man I Love." From *Funny Face* came "How Long Has This Been Going On?" as well as "Ev'rybody Knows I Love You" (originally known as "Dance Alone with You," Ira changed its lyrics and title for *Rosalie*). Salvaged from the scuttled *Strike Up the Band* was "Yankee Doodle Rhythm." *Oh, Kay!* was the source for "Show Me the Town," while "Beautiful Gypsy" (before its change of lyrics and title, it was called "Wait a Bit, Susie") was exhumed from *Primrose*. To these Gershwin added some new tunes such as "Say So!," "New York Serenade," and "Oh Gee! Oh Joy!," none of them very well known today. From the motley assortment of new and old songs that he put together, seven were selected for the show, the most popular by far being "How Long Has This Been Going On?" Gershwin songs constituted about half of the *Rosalie* score. The rest of the tunes came from the pen of Sigmund Romberg.

At first Romberg had been designated as the sole composer for *Rosalie*. When it developed that he could not complete the music on time because of another commitment, Ziegfeld asked Gershwin to help finish the score. Though he was then out of town with *Funny Face* and up to his neck in revisions trying desperately to get that show ready for New York, he agreed to take on the job after finishing his immediate assignment. *Rosalie* was to be his first Broadway association with the famed producer, and he welcomed the experience. As a parallel to the George Gershwin—Sigmund Romberg musical collaboration, Ira agreed to share the writing of the lyrics for *Rosalie* with P. G. Wodehouse. With their tasks cut out for them, George and Ira turned their full attention to *Rosalie,* then already in rehearsal, just as soon as *Funny Face* opened in New York. Without a break between shows, they plunged right into the preparations for the Boston tryout of *Rosalie*. Since this show was built around Marilyn Miller, one of their main concerns was shaping their material to suit her.

Miss Miller was lissome, shapely, and beautiful. As a standout *Follies* alumna—she first appeared in Ziegfeld's 1918 *Follies*—at the pinnacle of her fame, and a major box-office draw, she was treated by all in the show with the deference reserved for royalty. And it was as a member of royalty that she was cast in *Rosalie*. In the script tailored for her by Guy

Bolton and William Anthony McGuire, she played the role of a princess of the mythical kingdom of Romanza who visits the United States.[8] In the course of her visit, Rosalie finds love in the arms of an army lieutenant from West Point. The drama heightens when she must return to Romanza. The lieutenant, convinced of their enduring love and undaunted by their different worlds, follows her across the ocean. Not by boat, however. Using Lindberg's 1927 flight across the Atlantic as his model, he too flies across the ocean. His persistence and bravery pay off. He finally wins Rosalie for his own.

Rosalie may have had more than its share of credibility gaps, but it gave Miss Miller the chance to sing and dance, to show off her legs and figure, and to be displayed in a cornucopic array of dress, from royal garb to street clothes. The fine supporting cast—it included Gladys Glad, Frank Morgan, Bobbe Arnst, and Jack Donahue as the lieutenant—and the talented ensemble of singers, dancers, and specialty performers in the show were really just a backdrop for Miss Miller, but one that emphasized the spit-and-polish aspects of the production, the trademark of a Ziegfeld musical. The basic material of which *Rosalie* was fabricated may have been innocuous and less than inspired, but it didn't matter. Miss Miller's radiance blinded the public to the tinsel in the rest of the show. They loved her and *Rosalie*. They kept the show running on Broadway for 335 performances, a major success from any standpoint. Thanks in large part to Marilyn Miller, Gershwin chalked up still another hit in *Rosalie*. He may not have extended himself so much as he might have for this show and possibly dredged his swamp of cast-off tunes more deeply than usual, but evidently few were aware of it. For the record, and this is what mattered for the public and professionals in terms of his career, Gershwin's batting average as a composer of successful Broadway shows remained as high as ever with *Rosalie*.

Almost concurrent with the January 10 opening of *Rosalie* on Broadway, Gershwin began working on his third orchestral composition, *An American in Paris*. For some time prior to actually committing notes to paper for this piece, he had been itching to get back into the symphonic fold. Approximately two years had gone by since the premiere of the *Concerto*. Most of his energies during that period had been expended on musical comedy. True, while so involved, he had had the satisfaction of writing the scores for several smash hits and of increasing his already high income level in the bargain. But he was now anxious to express himself once again in orchestral terms, particularly if he was to maintain his highly touted position as a double musical threat: a leading composer for Broadway as well as a promising new voice in the symphonic field; heady brew, indeed. With his *Rosalie* assignment taken care of, he could turn his attention to an extended orchestral piece to balance his career "scale," so heavily tipped in favor of musical comedy for many months. Another consideration was his promise to Damrosch, made at the latter's initiative after the well-publicized premiere of the *Concerto,* that his next symphonic opus would be written with the conductor in mind. (This promise, when fulfilled, assured a performance of the piece by the New York Philharmonic, because Damrosch had become affiliated with this ensemble during the 1928–1929 season.[9]) And so, presumably for these reasons he began his *An American in Paris* in January 1928, the date inscribed on the opening of his preorchestration sketch of the piece.

The initial stimulus for *An American in Paris* may very well have been derived from Gershwin's trip to Paris in April 1923, shortly after *The Rainbow Revue* had opened in London and flopped. As a guest of Glaenzer, Gershwin had been filled with wide-eyed wonder during his brief stay in Paris from his tour of the city's exciting cabarets and restaurants to his visit to a luxurious bordello. Some of the enchantment of his adventures then as a tyro *boulevardier,* taken in tow and shown the sights by the dapper Glaenzer, must have remained with him. For at the time he started *An American in Paris* in early 1928 he had not returned to Paris, though he had been back to England three times since 1923 in connection with various London productions of his shows. Thus any remembrances he had of Paris, implicit in the very title of the work, came from his experiences there five years earlier.

But if *An American in Paris* was triggered by his 1923 springtime adventures in France, it was further stimulated by a visit he made to Paris later, in 1928. For he had not progressed very far with *An American in Paris* when he decided that a trip abroad, including an extended stay in Paris, was in order. *Funny Face* and *Rosalie* had settled down for long runs on Broadway, and his career was running smoothly in high gear. Why not combine a vacation with a renewing and broadening of his contacts— musical, theatrical, and social—abroad? He could also work on *An American in Paris* in an appropriate French setting as well as possibly "study" with some famous musicians. In an "exclusive" interview in *Musical America* of February 18, 1928, he stated as much. He would sail for Europe in early March, he announced, to visit London and Paris. He wanted to work on an "orchestral ballet," *An American in Paris,* while abroad, and to study.[10] On March 9, 1928, the *New York Times* noted Gershwin's imminent departure for Europe to study and compose.[11] Two days later, on March 11, George along with his sister, Frances, and Ira and his wife, Leonore, left New York for London and the Continent.

On arriving in London, Gershwin took up where he had left off when he had been there last; it was almost as though he had never been away. He renewed old acquaintances and acquired new ones. He resumed his rounds of partygoing, performed at the drop of a hat, hobnobbed with royalty, ate at fine restaurants, disregarding his dietary restrictions, bought new clothes to add to his already bulging wardrobe, enjoyed the sights, and had a busy, sparkling good time. Among the many pleasures of his stay in London was his seeing Gertrude Lawrence in the closing performance of the English production of *Oh, Kay!* on March 24.

His next stop, Paris, was no less frenetic. Practically from the moment he arrived at his hotel, the Majestic, on March 25, he was besieged with invitations to this party or that, to concerts and to the ballet, along with numerous requests to talk with the press or to see a steady stream of visitors who came to pay their respects to him. Like a royal potentate, Gershwin could sit back and wait to be sought out. In Paris, as elsewhere, he was in great demand.

Most important for Gershwin during his stay in Paris were the many contacts he had with leading musicians, both at the Majestic Hotel and elsewhere.[12] At every opportunity he would play his music for them, including his unfinished *An American in Paris* (as all musicians do, he also exchanged professional gossip, usually "juicy" tidbits about one colleague or another). Among those he met were Serge Prokofiev, Darius Milhaud, William Walton, Francis Poulenc, Leopold Stokowski, Alexander Tansman, Georges Auric, Jacques Ibert, Vittorio Rieti, as well as Maurice Ravel and Mlle. Boulanger.[13] With few exceptions—Prokofiev was one of the exceptions; he had reservations about Gershwin's potential as a "serious" composer—they all responded favorably to his music and encouraged him in his work. Stokowski even gladly volunteered to conduct the premiere of *An American in Paris* if the piece were available to him; to his chagrin he learned that Damrosch had already put in his bid for the composition.

Between his meetings with musicians and the press, and his social and business obligations, Gershwin still found time to work on *An American in Paris*. Its famous blues section was written at the Majestic. He also found time to attend several performances of his music.[14] One performance hardly did him justice. This occurred on March 31, when he heard the *Rhapsody* played by the Pasdeloup Orchestra[15] under the direction of Rhené Baton at the Théâtre Mogador, usually a theater rather than a concert hall (in the close quarters of the Mogador, with its strong smell of beer from its adjacent bar, *Rose Marie* was then playing its second year). Underrehearsed, poorly interpreted, and with a two-piano team, Wiener and Doucet, dividing the solo part between them, the *Rhapsody* in the Pasdeloup's collective

155

hands was anything but the work Gershwin had originally intended it to be. Among other faults, the tempos were too slow and the jazz rhythms sloppily executed. The audience, though, hardly knew the difference. They knew *of* the piece and the Gershwin name, and that evidently was enough for them. They cheered spontaneously and loudly at the conclusion of the composition. Gershwin, however, fearing the worst, had left for the bar before the ovation started. But he quickly responded to the applause when he was called to the stage. Whereupon Wiener and Doucet, obviously prepared for this moment, burst into a well-rehearsed two-piano arrangement of "Do, Do, Do" as their encore. If Gershwin had any reservation about the *Rhapsody* à la Pasdeloup, he was won over by the reception he and his work received.

On April 16 at the Théâtre des Champs-Élysées, Gershwin attended still another performance of the *Rhapsody*, but this time in a dance version choreographed for the Ballet Russe by Anton Dolin. Drawn to the *Rhapsody* by its inherent theatricality as other choreographers have been, Dolin's ballet dramatically featured two solo dancers. One represented classical music, the other, jazz, in a "battle" for supremacy. The eventual victor, jazz, was danced by Dolin himself.

Whether heard in conjunction with the dance or in its more usual way as a purely instrumental piece, the *Rhapsody* was played practically everywhere Gershwin went. It had caught on like wildfire and had become his "motto" piece, his "trademark." Then, as now, the *Rhapsody* and "Gershwin" had become practically synonymous in the public's eye. If he needed affirmation of this point, it must have been brought home to him when he went on to Vienna from Paris. There, he and his party visited the Café Sacher as the guest of Emmerich Kálmán, the highly regarded Hungarian-born composer of Viennese operettas, who had settled in that city. To Gershwin's delight, as soon as he entered the café its little band of resident musicians immediately went into the strains of the *Rhapsody* in acknowledgment of his presence. Almost like the playing of the Austrian national anthem at a Viennese ball, the *Rhapsody* had the broadest type of recognizability for those in the café, as it clearly announced that George Gershwin was in their midst. In honor of him, too, the café's chef reputedly even tried to concoct some blue ice cream for all at Gershwin's table as a symbol of the *Rhapsody*. When that could not be arranged, homage was paid to him in another, rather significant way. Ice cream was served, but with little American flags with it.

While in Vienna, Gershwin continued to work on *An American in Paris*[16] when he wasn't socializing, performing at parties, musician "collecting,"[17] or engaged in the other activities that had become a part of his way of life and career. He was also present at the Vienna Opera for a performance of Ernst Křenek's jazz opera *Jonny spielt auf,* then sweeping Europe, and ostensibly found it commendable: if he had any reservations about the "jazz" efforts of a European rival, they were not expressed publicly. The high point of Gershwin's stay in Vienna, however, was his meeting with Alban Berg, Arnold Schoenberg's brilliant disciple, then still relatively unknown outside of avant-garde musical circles despite the big splash made by his opera *Wozzeck* when it was produced at the Berlin State Opera in December 1925. The two met at a party and took to each other immediately, though they were almost opposites, musically and personally. Berg was elegant, aristocratic, sensitively handsome, reserved, illness-prone, a Viennese intellectual whose music consciously derived from the chromatic complexities of Schoenberg, Wagner, and a long historical tradition. In contrast, Gershwin, the nonintellectual, the exuberantly outgoing human dynamo, had little or no musical tradition to fall back on other than what he could trace to his limited training and his life experiences, be they on the lower East Side or in Tin Pan Alley and Broadway musical comedy. An odd combination, Gershwin and Berg, but they responded positively to each other's music. Berg found Gershwin's work, particularly as Gershwin played and sang it at the piano, utterly fascinating, youthful, and vitally American. Gershwin, in turn, was awed by the technical mastery, the seriousness and long-lined emotionalism in the music of Berg, then forty-three years old. When he left Vienna to return to Paris, Gershwin brought with him a score of Berg's *Lyric Suite* for string quartet, inscribed to him by the Viennese composer, which he treasured. In later speaking of Berg and this piece, Gershwin exulted: "One of the high spots of my visit was my meeting with Alban Berg. . . . Although this quartet is dissonant . . . it seems to me that the work has genuine merit. Its conception and treatment are thoroughly modern in the best sense of the word."[18]

Back in Paris when Vladimir Golschmann and Dimitri Tiomkin, as previously mentioned, performed the European premiere of the *Concerto* on May 29 at the Opéra, Gershwin received still another ovation from the friendly Parisians. To add to his pleasure, he was highly satisfied with the rendition by Tiomkin and Golschmann. So were many French critics. Reviewing the work for the *Christian Science Monitor,* Émile Vuillermoz, one of the critics, proclaimed:

> Gershwin's concerto will greatly help to dissipate the last prejudices attaching to the new technique that has emerged from the novelties of jazz. . . . This very characteristic work made even the most distrustful musician realize that jazz, after having renewed the technique of dancing, might perfectly well exert a deep and beneficent in-

157

fluence in the most exalted spheres. There is, in this mixture of balance and suppleness, a whole series of indications from which the most serious music might reap advantage.[19]

With the acclaim received by the *Concerto* one of the memorable moments of his Paris stay, Gershwin began to make ready to return to New York, but not without certain misgivings. His holiday abroad had had a fairyland quality about it. Like a child in a forest of multicolored candy bars, ice-cream cones and fanciful toys to taste and to play with, he had been surrounded nearly continually by myriad pleasures.[20] He had had time to enjoy himself without worrying about any deadlines; his future looked rosier than ever; his stay had been productive; he had been fêted wherever he went and had had his wishes looked after; his career contacts had been broadened and enriched; he had had more than his share of the limelight; there had hardly been a dull moment. Indeed, Gershwin could clearly say that his time in Europe had been well spent.

So could Ira, Leonore, and Frances. They had been his almost constant companions and had been privy to many of the felicities lavished on him. Especially Ira. As George's closest associate, highly respected for his own achievements in the. theater, he was generally accepted as his brother's alter ego, thoroughly familiar with his plans and aspirations. And he was treated accordingly. Though Ira was usually content to sit back and bask in reflected glory, he inevitably shared part of the perennial spotlight thrust on George because of their professional and familial relationship. The shower of attention that followed George thus also included him and other members of the family as well. Even the youngest Gershwin, Frances, enjoyed the limelight while in Paris. She appeared as a chanteuse for a week at Les Ambassadeurs, a nightspot, singing George's songs. This was no mere capitalization on the Gershwin name. Frances had been singing and dancing from childhood on. She was *au courant* with the best torch-singing styles of the period and had learned how to use her small husky voice with considerable effectiveness. Nevertheless, irrespective of any native talent Frances may have had as a cabaret singer, her Parisian engagement received more attention and significance because she was George's sister than it would have otherwise.[21]

With his stay in Paris coming to an end, Gershwin's thoughts focused on the projects that were of most immediate concern to him. High on the list of priorities was the next Aarons-Freedley production, a Gertrude Lawrence musical due on Broadway in the fall of 1928. Gershwin had also promised to deliver *An American in Paris* to Damrosch by the fall. If he needed any prodding to get back home to put the finishing touches on that piece, he undoubtedly got it when the *New York Times* of June 6, 1928, announced that the Philharmonic would premiere it during the coming season. Before the month was out,[22] Gershwin was back in New York hard at work, the European holiday over.

Back in his regular groove, it was almost as if he had never been away, except for his memories of the trip. Among his mementos were four French taxi horns, whose unique honking sound he incorporated into *An American in Paris,* eight handsome leather-bound volumes of Debussy's complete works, and a French Mustel reed organ, which he had installed in his studio and on which he occasionally played. This little bit of Paris in New York was the closest he got to France again, for his 1928 European holiday was his last one abroad.

Otto Kahn, financier and art patron extraordinary. *(Courtesy Metropolitan Opera Company)* He paid tribute to Gershwin after the premiere of *An American in Paris*.

THE AMERICAN
"FRENCHMAN"

AS IF COMPLETING *An American in Paris*
and writing the score for the Gertrude Lawrence musical *Treasure Girl*
were not enough, Gershwin also started work on the music for Ziegfeld's
East Is West during the summer of 1928.[1] But unlike the relatively easy
success he had had with the producer's *Rosalie,* Gershwin had a most unfortunate experience with *East Is West,* for the show never got on the
boards. Actually, before his involvement with *East Is West,* he had received
a cable from Ziegfeld while he was still in Paris in the spring of 1928 inquir-
ing whether he would write the music for another show: a new Eddie Cantor
musical that was due to start rehearsals the following September. In the
event that Gershwin were not available for the Cantor musical Ziegfeld
went on to ask in his cable, "Can I depend on you to write the music for
one show?" Since Gershwin had already agreed to write the score for the
Aarons-Freedley fall production of *Treasure Girl,* he could not accept the
Cantor assignment. But on returning to New York, he did succumb to
Ziegfeld's persuasive request that he write the score for a musical adaptation
of *East Is West,* a hit play of the 1918 season. According to Ziegfeld, the
projected musical would not only star Marilyn Miller, but would also
feature the hyperthyroid buffoonery of comedians Bobby Clark and Paul
McCullough, three practically foolproof guarantees of a hit show. Ziegfeld,

moreover, assured Gershwin that he would have virtually a free hand in developing his musical material. As Ziegfeld described it, *East Is West* would not be just another musical comedy. There would be greater integration between plot and score than was customary for Broadway, and this broadened the possibilities for novel and varied musical approaches. Another attractive consideration for Gershwin was that much of the plot had Oriental overtones. It lent itself to more exotic musical treatment than anything he had tried before.

Such was the magnetism of Ziegfeld's "pitch" that George and Ira were stimulated to begin work on *East Is West* without waiting for contractual arrangements to be completed. After they had finished about half the score, still without a contract, sometime in the early part of 1929, they learned from Ziegfeld that he had "temporarily" shelved plans for *East Is West*. This postponement, however, turned out to be permanent. Ziegfeld eventually lost interest in *East Is West* and never produced it. (It would have been a very expensive production and Ziegfeld did not want to undertake the financial risk involved.) Gershwin's music for *East Is West* was not, of course, an entire loss for him; where his self-interests were involved, in hoarding material for future use he had all the miserly instincts of a Silas Marner. The famous "Embraceable You," sung in the 1930 Broadway musical *Girl Crazy*, was one of those tunes, as was "Blah, Blah, Blah" (for *East Is West* it had been titled "Lady of the Moon"), used in the 1931 movie *Delicious*. Even the incongruously "Chinese"-sounding vocal patter to "Love is Sweeping the Country" from *Of Thee I Sing*, that stunning satire on American politics, had its origins in *East Is West* before it was grafted onto the song it now supports. Gershwin's only "art" song, the little-known and seldom-performed "In the Mandarin's Orchid Garden," also came from that aborted Ziegfeld show.

Any effort Gershwin put into *East Is West* in its early stages was secondary to his main concern at that point: getting the scores for *Treasure Girl* and *An American in Paris* ready on time. He succeeded admirably in both cases. The *Treasure Girl* score was completed first to meet the show's opening deadline. After a tryout at the Shubert Theater in Philadelphia starting October 15, *Treasure Girl* opened on November 8 at the Alvin to an overwhelming chorus of nays from the battery of opening-night critics. Notwithstanding some concessive praise of the Gershwin score, the talents of Gertrude Lawrence and her supporting cast, numbering among them Clifton Webb,[2] Walter Catlett, Paul Frawley, and Mary Hay, the dancing and singing of the ensemble, and the lavish sets by Joseph Urban that realistically duplicated such diverse scenes as a spacious ballroom, a magnificent terrace, and a deserted island, the reviewers had much to complain

162

about. The book by Fred Thompson and Vincent Lawrence bore the brunt of most of the criticism. As Burns Mantle noted in the *Daily News,* the script was "pretty dreary stuff in the matter of dialogue." Brooks Atkinson, in the *Times,* was equally abrasive. He characterized the book as "humorless" and "an evil thing." Atkinson was particularly put off by the snippety role that Gertrude Lawrence, who was normally charm incarnate, was asked to play. In the person of the poor but wealth-oriented heroine, Ann Wainwright, she was a "malicious liar and spoiled child," in Atkinson's estimation, for much of the show. Nor was the grouchy realtor hero, Neil Forrester, played by Paul Frawley, any more attractive. Ann and Neil bicker constantly. But their love-hate relationship mellows in the end after Ann finds buried treasure, making her wealthy, and Neil saves her from a band of thieves. In their closing embrace, all is sweetness and light, a happy future intimated for the two, as Ann announces their engagement.

With the negative reviews of the drama critics an albatross around their aggregate necks, the *Treasure Girl* company was forced to call it quits after only sixty-eight performances. Suffering the consequences of the hasty shutdown of the show was the fine Gershwin score, which had hardly been around long enough to catch on. Some of the engaging tunes that fell by the wayside were "Feeling I'm Falling," "I Don't Think I'll Fall in Love Today," "Got a Rainbow," "Oh, So Nice," "Where's the Boy? Here's the Girl!," and "I've Got a Crush on You." The last song, in particular, has since become extremely popular, but its ultimate success can be attributed as much to a change in interpretation as anything else. In *Treasure Girl* the tune was considered a "hot" duet number. Accordingly it was sung and danced at a fast tempo by Clifton Webb and Mary Hay. George and Ira later incorporated it into the revised 1930 version of *Strike Up the Band,* where it was performed at an even faster tempo by Gordon Smith and Doris Carson. Again, the song did not get very far. Many years later, after Gershwin's death, the sensuously throaty Lee Wiley recorded the tune as a solo in a slow rendition that verged on the sentimental. Her version soon caught on and paved the way for other recordings of "I've Got a Crush on You" done the same way, slowly and with feeling.

On November 18, 1928, ten days after *Treasure Girl* opened on Broadway, the orchestration for *An American in Paris* was completed. The preorchestration sketch itself, written mostly on three and four staves as one would for a two-piano version of the piece, had been finished several months earlier, on August 1.[3] Presumably the fully orchestrated score was not ready sooner because of the demands made on Gershwin to help get *Treasure Girl* ready for Broadway. Nevertheless, during the summer of 1928, even before he had gotten very far with the orchestration, he helped beat the drums for *An American in Paris* in anticipation of its premiere in late fall, by discussing the piece in an interview that appeared in the August 18, 1928 issue of *Musical America*.[4] Discussing the one-movement work, Gershwin said for publication:

> This new piece, really a rhapsodic ballet, is written very freely and is the most modern music I've yet attempted. The opening part will be developed in typical French style, in the manner of Debussy and the Six, though the tunes are all original. My purpose here is to portray the impressions of an American visitor in Paris as he strolls about the city, listens to the various street noises, and absorbs the French atmosphere. As in my other orchestral compositions, I've not endeavored to present any definite scenes in this music. The rhapsody is programmatic only in a general impressionistic way, so that the individual listener can read into the music such episodes as his imagination pictures for him.[5]

Gershwin may not have had a specific story in mind when he wrote *An American in Paris,* but by the time of its premiere at Carnegie Hall on December 13, 1928, by the New York Philharmonic under Damrosch, a detailed narrative for the piece revolving around an American's walking tour of Paris (to appropriate "walking" themes) had been prepared by Deems Taylor in conjunction with the composer.[6] Moreover, the work was now described as "a tone poem for orchestra," with all that that implies in the way of a story.

In the orchestral realization of *An American in Paris,* Gershwin dispensed completely with the piano—his first large-scale work to do so—and concentrated instead on other instrumental resources. Evidently satisfied with the instrumental forces used for the *Concerto,* he employed an essentially similar ensemble for the tone poem, to which he added three saxophones and four taxi horns. The actual orchestra called for in *An American in Paris* consists of three flutes (the third flute doubles on piccolo), two oboes, English horn, two B-flat clarinets, bass clarinet, two bassoons, three saxophones (E-flat alto, B-flat tenor, and E-flat baritone saxophones),[7] four French horns, three B-flat trumpets, three trombones, tuba, timpani, percussion, four taxi horns (played by the percussionists), celesta, and strings. The score itself is written even more clearly and with greater care than that of the *Concerto,* and more attention is paid to accents, slurs, bowings, tempo indications, and other symbols of expression than ever before. [8] As for the actual orchestration, it is colorful, jazzy, and wholly professional. But just as some doubt was raised as to whether Gershwin had orchestrated the *Concerto* himself, so, too, a controversy erupted over the orchestration of *An American in Paris.* It did so in 1932, and Allan Lincoln Langley lighted the fuse that kindled the controversy. As violist for a performance of *An*

George S. Kaufman. His caustic, cynical book for *Strike Up the Band*, 1927 version, did not endear the show to the public.

Marilyn Miller, the star of *Rosalie*. (*Museum of the City of New York*)

Alban Berg, the brilliant Viennese composer of *Wozzeck*. He and Gershwin took to each other, though their backgrounds and personalities were highly dissimilar.

American in Paris conducted by the composer at the Metropolitan Opera House on November 1, 1932, Langley had had a chance to observe both Gershwin and Bill Daly at close range during rehearsals. He found Gershwin so strongly dependent on Daly during rehearsals that he vented his feelings in the following December's edition of *The American Spectator*. "The genial Daly," wrote Langley in the *Spectator,* "was constantly in rehearsal attendance [for *An American in Paris*], both as *répétiteur* and adviser, and any member of the orchestra could testify that he knew far more about the score than Gershwin."[9] In Langley's judgment, Gershwin had been assisted in orchestration by Daly, and this presumably explained the latter's intimate familiarity with Gershwin's music. Concluding his article with a blast at Gershwin, Langley snorted, "No previous claimant of honors in symphonic composition has ever presented so much argument and controversy as to whether his work was his own or not."[10]

Not to be outvoiced by Langley, Daly quickly jumped into the fray, coming to Gershwin's defense (Gershwin himself remained remarkably silent, letting Daly do the talking for him). Daly vehemently denied Langley's charges in a letter published in the *Times* on January 15, 1933. In his letter Daly said:

> I neither wrote nor orchestrated the "American." My only contribution consisted of a few suggestions about reinforcing the scoring here and there, and I'm not sure that Gershwin, probably with good reason, accepted them. But, then, Gershwin receives many such suggestions from his many friends to whom he always plays his various compositions, light or symphonic, while they are in the process of being written. . . . It is true that I orchestrate many Gershwin numbers for the theatre; but so does [Robert] Russell Bennett. . . . And it is true that we are close friends—to my great profit—and that I use that relationship to criticize. But that is far from the role that Mr. Langley suggests. . . . The fact is that I have never written one note of any of his compositions, or so much as orchestrated one whole bar of any of his symphonic works.[11]

The charges and countercharges aired by Langley and Daly made interesting reading, representing as they did emotionally charged viewpoints, but they hardly resolved once and for all unanswered questions relating to the orchestration of *An American in Paris*. Also unresolved through the years is the matter of revisions made in *An American in Paris* after it was finished. For as was true with the *Concerto,* changes were made in the score of the tone poem between the time it was completed and first performed.[12] Unlike the *Concerto,* however, *An American in Paris* did not have a trial reading before its premiere to help Gershwin evaluate the work. Who, then, suggested the changes? Probably Damrosch. It was he, after all, who received the score shortly after it was completed and then rehearsed and conducted the work from Gershwin's original orchestrated manuscript.[13] Presumably only a man of Damrosch's position and stature could have suggested two extensive cuts of thirty-seven measures each, plus deletions of twenty-seven and seven measures respectively, as well as some other changes—mainly minor ones, dealing with tempo and dynamics —and gotten Gershwin to go along with them.[14] The score itself, at least on the basis of deletion marks and other visual signs, does not give an unequivocal answer as to who initiated these revisions. But no matter who suggested the changes, the end result was an improved score, primarily because of the elimination of redundant material.

Shining through all the cloudy areas connected with *An American in Paris* are the unmistakable signs of Gershwin's technical progress as a composer. There is clear evidence in the tone poem of a greater diversity of musical texture than in the earlier works, mainly achieved by contrapuntally combining important thematic elements with figurations of one kind or another and with a commensurate emphasis on detail; as in a painting where added shadings of line and color increase perspective, there are generally more things "happening" at any one given point in the score than was true for the orchestral pieces that preceded it. There is also more metric fluidity in *An American in Paris* than was usual for Gershwin (possibly to show his familiarity with "progressive" metric trends), adding a "modernistic" boost to the tone poem. Almost like a poor man's Stravinsky, but without the latter's extraordinary rhythmic sensibility, Gershwin in one instance in *An American in Paris* changed the meter five times within five consecutive measures.[15]

But alongside such indications of technical advancement, there is again the all too literal repetition of material as well as the poorly articulated, haphazard, and unconvincing directional goals; one is not always sure where Gershwin is heading, though he ultimately arrives at his "destination" in spite of himself. Also, Gershwin musical mannerisms, such as blues-inflected melodies, syncopations, Charleston-like rhythms, and other conscious Americanisms derived from jazz and popular music, frequently seem to be ends in themselves, rather than means toward more lofty artistic purposes. As Olin Downes has observed, *An American in Paris* "gets no farther than the earlier works; it reveals no new artistic or emotional ground." For Downes, as a matter of fact, "Gershwin sang one song [in all his works]. It is of the city, the music hall."[16]

Considering the essentially programmatic concept of *An American in Paris,* it is perhaps understandable that the form of the piece in an absolute sense is less important than the story that the work purports to tell.

Nevertheless, in discussing the overall construction of the tone poem in the preface to his program narrative for the work, Deems Taylor remarked that "its structure is determined by considerations musical rather than literary or dramatic. The piece, while not in strict sonata form, resembles an extended symphonic movement in that it announces, develops, combines and recapitulates definite themes." Notwithstanding Taylor's musical assessment of *An American in Paris*, the work in many respects can be considered a series of themes (essentially six: three "walking" themes, a "taxicab" theme, a blues, and a Charleston theme), attractive ones to be sure, but almost as casually strung together as homemade beads. As Leonard Bernstein has commented:

> When you hear the piece, you rejoice in the first theme, then sit and wait through the "filler" until the next one comes along. In this way you sit out about two thirds of the composition. The remaining third is marvelous because it consists of the themes themselves; but where's the composition?[17]

Laying aside these reservations about *An American in Paris*, Bernstein has pointed out: "What's good in it is so good that it's irresistible. If you have to go along with some chaff in order to have the wheat, it's worth it."[18] It is the very accessibility and personal charm of Gershwin's themes, not their structural organization, that has helped entrench *An American in Paris* in the orchestral literature.

At its premiere, *An American in Paris* was done to a turn by Damrosch and the men of the Philharmonic. The carefree whimsy and broad humor of the piece had apparently struck home with them, for they played it with enormous élan, gusto, and obvious relish. The audience, nearly always on Gershwin's side to begin with, responded in kind to the sympathetic treatment the work received, particularly since there were no disconcerting musical surprises to contend with. They had come to hear Gershwin of the *Rhapsody* and the *Concerto* and were not disappointed. The tone poem was easy to listen to; it abounded in tunefulness, sprightly playfulness, jazzy instrumental effects, and feet-tapping rhythms, and it was consistent in style and content with everything they had come to expect from the composer. They were more than pleased with the results. No sooner had Damrosch put down his baton after the closing chord than they let forth a thunderous barrage of approbation directed at Gershwin, sitting grandly in a front box surrounded by family and friends. Visible to all in the hall and beaming broadly, he bowed again and again from his box to the delight of the audience. If he had had any prior apprehensions about the reception his work would get from the audience, their cordial response soon laid such fears to rest.[19]

The Philharmonic-Symphony Society of New York

FOUNDED 1842

1928 · EIGHTY-SEVENTH SEASON · 1929

CARNEGIE HALL

Thursday Evening, December 13, 1928

AT EIGHT-THIRTY

Friday Afternoon, December 14, 1928

AT TWO-THIRTY

2338TH AND 2339TH CONCERTS

Under the Direction of

WALTER DAMROSCH

PROGRAM

1. FRANCK...Symphony in D minor
   I. Lento; allegro non troppo
   II. Allegretto
   III. Allegro non troppo

INTERMISSION

2. LEKEU..Adagio for Strings

3. GERSHWIN.."An American in Paris"
   (First performance anywhere)

4. WAGNER..............................Magic Fire Scene, from "Die Walküre"

ARTHUR JUDSON, Manager
EDWARD ERVIN, Associate Manager

THE STEINWAY is the Official Piano of The Philharmonic-Symphony Society

Owing to the great demand for Philharmonic-Symphony seats, which the management is unable to supply, it is requested that subscribers return tickets which cannot be used, to Philharmonic-Symphony Offices in Steinway Hall, or to the Box Office, Carnegie Hall, to be sold for the benefit of Orchestra Pension Fund

Those who wish to obtain the scores of any of the works on this program for home study should apply at the 58th Street Branch of the New York Public Library, 121 East 58th Street, which has a large collection of music available for circulation

The program by the New York Philharmonic, under Walter Damrosch, which included the premiere of *An American in Paris*. *(Courtesy New York Philharmonic)*

In contrast to the audience, the cognoscenti of the press were less than unanimous in their reactions to the piece. Like gamblers hedging their bets as a precautionary measure, the members of the fourth estate dispersed their opinions of the work in all directions. They were as divided on the merits of *An American in Paris* as they had been for the *Rhapsody* and the *Concerto*. "Long-winded and inane" was Herbert Francis Peyser's uncomplimentary description of the tone poem in the *Telegram,* while the *World*'s Samuel Chotzinoff, extolling its virtues, found it "easily the best piece of modern music since . . . *Concerto in F.*" Oscar Thompson of the *Post* abhorred what he heard. For him the piece was "very pedestrian, indeed." On the other hand, Leonard Liebling of the *American* considered it "merry, rollicking music." Mainly noncommittal in his assessment of the piece in the *Herald Tribune,* Lawrence Gilman did comment fleetingly on "its gusto and naïveté." W. J. Henderson had mixed feelings about the work, and his *Sun* revue echoed that ambivalence. Conceding "much cleverness in the score," Henderson also found in the work "some rudeness of manner." To his way of thinking, "The American in Paris is a Broadway swaggerer, well acquainted with the music halls, the vaudeville shows and its comic opera stars." Olin Downes's report in the *Times,* too, juxtaposed the good with the bad. While paying tribute to the "material gain in workmanship and structure" in the tone poem over Gershwin's earlier orchestral pieces, Downes at the same time felt that it was easier for the composer "to invent ideas than to develop them." He went on to say that, "if the work suggests a potpourri of popular airs rather than a symphonic fragment, its lack of formality excuses its manners, and if its hilarity is noisy it is also contagious." Despite some reservations about the work, Downes labeled the Philharmonic concert "Mr. Gershwin's evening."

And so it was "Mr. Gershwin's evening," and in more ways than one. His preeminence that Thursday night of December 13, 1928, was not limited solely to Carnegie Hall. For after the concert, he was again the center of attention at a party in his honor at the Lexington Avenue home of Jules Glaenzer. Amid a houseful of gaily laughing and chattering celebrants, mainly famous and wealthy, sharing the joyful occasion with Gershwin, Otto Kahn suddenly took the floor. To the now-hushed and attentive assemblage, the financier paid tribute to Gershwin as he presented him with a handsome humidor inscribed with the signatures of many of the composer's friends.[20] In his presentation speech, Kahn touched on a number of points. Among them, he compared Gershwin with Charles Lindbergh. Stated Kahn: "Gershwin is a leader of young America in music, in the same sense in which Lindbergh is a leader of young America in aviation." He also made reference to the tragedy of the Civil War, out of which emerged

170

"the noblest, most moving and most beautiful figure among the public men of all history, Abraham Lincoln." Kahn hastened to explain that he was not wishing tragedy on the composer. But he did wish for Gershwin "an experience—not too prolonged—of that driving storm and stress of the emotions, of that solitary wrestling with your own soul, of that aloofness, for a while, from the actions and distractions of the everyday world, which are the most effective ingredients for the deepening and mellowing and the complete development, energizing and revealment, of an artistic inner being and spiritual powers."[21]

Were Kahn's exhortations to Gershwin to "suffer" as an artist an oblique invitation for him to write a "deep" work for the Metropolitan Opera, with which the financier was affiliated? Certainly the Metropolitan had shown interest in a Gershwin opera by their contract with the composer for *The Dybbuk*. Gershwin, however, dropped the idea of doing *The Dybbuk* when he could not get the stage rights to it. But if the possibility of his writing a "grand" opera was still in the realm of speculation at the premiere of *An American in Paris,* his position as an orchestral composer was a decided reality. With a third orchestral work to his credit, he unquestionably helped to solidify, if only by weight of numbers, his reputation as a composer for the symphony orchestra. He could no longer be considered a mere tunesmith with aspirations for writing orchestral works; Gershwin now was a composer of such pieces, and an experienced one at that. In terms of his potential, moreover, the technical advances in *An American in Paris* over the *Rhapsody in Blue* and the *Concerto in F* augured well for his development as a composer. For all these reasons and more, *An American in Paris* was indeed a landmark piece among Gershwin's orchestral works.

Performances of the tone poem, however, have not been limited to the orchestra alone. The piece has lent itself beautifully to the dance, in keeping with its original description as a "rhapsodic ballet." Among the many ballets adapted from the score are those for the 1929 Ziegfeld musical *Show Girl* and the 1951 Academy-Award-winning movie, *An American in Paris*. It is this very adaptability, plus its charm and tunefulness, that have helped the work to transcend any national boundaries implicit in its title. For whether or not Gershwin was the actual transposed American of the title, or whether or not the mangled musical Gallicisms in the piece were authentically Parisian, it mattered little in the long run. Somehow the piece has been able to communicate in a way that goes beyond geographical confines. Gershwin may have been the New Yorker incarnate, but ultimately he and *An American in Paris* have become highly respectable internationalists. Both now belong to the world.

Gershwin conducting.

ON THE PODIUM

ADDED TO THE hoopla surrounding the Philharmonic's playing of *An American in Paris* was the radio premiere of the piece on January 9, 1929. It was performed on the air by a New York radio orchestra conducted by Nathaniel Shilkret, an old boyhood friend of Gershwin who had made a name for himself in commercial broadcasting. Shilkret followed up the radio presentation by recording the piece for RCA Victor shortly afterward, in February. During the preparations for the recording, Gershwin proved to be more of a handicap than an asset. He kept interrupting Shilkret during rehearsal with so many performance suggestions and generally making a nuisance of himself that Shilkret finally asked him to leave the studio so that he could get his job done without impediment. It was not until he was ready to record that Shilkret allowed Gershwin back in the studio.[1]

Gershwin's behavior with Shilkret was not an isolated incident. In many respects he was quite inconstant in his dealings with people, especially as his fame increased. He could waver between being likable and considerate and, as the mood struck him, being difficult and insufferably vain and boorish. He often felt himself to be above the normal rules of the game and, therefore, entitled to the preferential treatment and privileges consistent with his position in life. At his self-centered worst, especially

173

when he had every reason to believe he could get away with it, he would not let anyone forget *he* was Gershwin. For instance, as noted earlier, he was practically never punctual for appointments, though he would often temper his lateness with some self-deprecatory remark to lighten the air. But casual asides or not, as *Gershwin,* he considered himself above reproach for this failing, as his persistent tardiness would bear out. Nor did he carry his fame lightly in other matters. When he felt the urge to carry on in some unseemly manner, such as by playing the piano loudly in a hotel lobby in the early morning hours to impress his female companion of the moment, that also was his right (at least until stopped by the hotel manager or his equivalent). As another privilege of his primacy, Gershwin would remind drivers when in their cars: "You've got *Gershwin* with you, so drive carefully." He wasn't especially reticent either about describing his own music in the most favorable terms. "Great, isn't it?" was a typical phrase he would use in discussing his work with friends and colleagues.[2] He was equally immodest when speaking of other composers. With what he considered a generous evaluation, Gershwin referred to Manuel de Falla, whose music he liked, as the "Spanish Gershwin." Even when tinged with Gershwin's own brand of artless whimsy, remarks such as these hardly covered up the colossal ego underneath.

The widely quoted story about Oscar Levant's being assigned an upper berth by Gershwin during an overnight train trip, while the composer took the lower berth, humorously points up Gershwin's assumption of rights due him because of his eminence. "Upper berth-lower berth," quipped Gershwin to Levant on preempting the more desirable lower berth for himself. "That's the difference between talent and genius."[3] Nor did Gershwin limit his proprietary privileges to dealings with close friends. He thought nothing of monopolizing conversations with all and sundry by telling stories about his past experiences and exciting future plans, or his imposing musical itinerary. He also took great delight in showing off mementos of his brilliant career at every opportunity. Bennett Cerf tells of the time at a dinner when "apropos of nothing, George suddenly said, 'Has anybody here seen my new cigarette case?' It was solid gold, and inscribed thereon were facsimile signatures of a score of famous men. It had been presented to him after a performance of his *Concerto in F.* The case was passed clear around the table."[4] Like a youngster proudly exhibiting a treasure trove of shiny trinkets to impress his peers, Gershwin *had* to show off his cigarette case to the dinner guests. On the slightest pretext, moreover, he would gratuitously offer a running commentary to complement the sizable amount of his memorabilia on display in his home. He never tired of commenting about them, for the *ohs* and *ahs* of delight and surprise wafted his way by his essen-

174

tially captive audience was an obvious source of delectation to him. Among these prized possessions in his home was his original manuscript of the *Rhapsody in Blue*. He had had it placed on an elaborate stand in a focal area, a conversation piece exhibited with the reverence shown a precious jewel in a museum showcase, so that it stood out with all the distinction it merited as his most famous work; clearly a document of historical import for the world.

Gershwin's need for ego gratification appeared to go hand in hand with his rise to the top. Once, for example, he bet a friend he would get a mutual acquaintance to purr like a contented cat and went all out to win that wager. He spent hours one day in obsequious flattery, catering to his acquaintance's every whim. Sure enough, the man finally began to emit what sounded like purrs of self-satisfaction which his friend was obliged to acknowledge. That he had proved his point was as important and as pleasurable to Gershwin as collecting his bet.

Nor was he particularly sensitive to others. On one occasion, Gershwin invited a presumably attractive woman to his apartment, sight unseen. He had spoken with her by chance on the telephone as a result of dialing a wrong number. Not only did she have a beautiful speaking voice, but he found they had many friends in common. She was thrilled with the prospect of meeting him and quickly accepted his suggestion that she come to his apartment so they could get to know each other better. For the assignation, Gershwin had readied champagne on ice, had turned the lights down to a soft romantic glow, and wore a velvet lounging robe. When she finally arrived, Gershwin was dismayed to find her grossly unattractive. He didn't even bother opening the champagne as he ended their "tryst" with great dispatch.

These boorish actions were not atypical. Another time, after keeping a close friend waiting two hours in an anteroom of his apartment without explanation, he grandly walked out to say as if to atone for his lack of hospitality, "Come, you can watch me eat." Such *chutzpah,* even if rooted in Gershwin's nature, was kept sufficiently in check in his early days so that it didn't readily show. Success changed that. For along with the glowing confidence and charismatic effervescence that were key externalizations of Gershwin's personality at his prime, went other equally noticeable, but less attractive aspects of his character.

Another consequence of Gershwin's success was his move in 1928 from the family home on One Hundred Third Street to his own luxurious penthouse apartment at 33 Riverside Drive at Seventy-fifth Street. Seventeen floors above the city, with a large terrace and a commanding view of the Hudson and the Palisades, the imposing bachelor apartment was

Some interior photographs
of Gershwin's penthouse on
Riverside Drive. *(Museum
of the City of New York)*

decorated and furnished in the latest 1920s "modern," with severely rectangular lines immersed in blacks, whites and chromes, indirect lighting, and even included a small gymnasium complete with barbells, punching bag, and rowing machine. There was a gargantuan bed covered in fur that monopolized the bedroom, and a man in white jacket who glided softly over the acres of deep-pile carpeting to greet you at the door and then magically disappear, to reappear, genie-like, when needed. Drawings, paintings, and other art objects, seemingly everywhere, were discreetly placed, a decorator's touch amply evident. There was no stinting; money was clearly no object in making the new apartment a glittering showcase of Gershwin's advanced estate.

With more room at his disposal and a fancier setting in which to disport himself, Gershwin entertained more extensively and lavishly than ever in his penthouse, almost as if to repay in kind the many parties he had attended over the years at the homes of Jules Glaenzer, Condé Nast, Carl Van Vechten, Alfred Knopf, Mary Hoyt Wiborg, Mrs. Sidney Fish, Richard Simon and other stalwarts of the New York social scene. Ira and his wife also moved to the same building as George's, to an adjoining penthouse and terrace. Close by his side, they shared in his work and play as before. Nor were George's ties with his parents and younger brother and sister radically changed by his move. He saw them almost as frequently as he always had (they were often present at his parties) and continued to be a bastion of financial support for them, as their ever-comfortable life-style would attest. Gershwin may have had his uppity moments and his share of tiffs with his family—he was often quick to anger—but there were never any deep-seated frictions. Among the most constant traits in his inconstant life were his stanch devotion and loyalty and his unstinting generosity to his family.[5] Nevertheless, in outbursts of anger, he would rail at them, particularly at Ira, who had assumed besides his lyricist's duties the responsibility for overseeing George's business affairs and financial records, the paying of his bills, and other essential managerial functions, in order to free George from these onerous chores so he could devote more time to his music. "Why don't you take better care of things for me?" would be typical of George's flash-anger tirades at his brother. Despite such plaints, Ira invariably handled George's affairs with dispatch, in a level-headed, practical, para-legalistic way and often served as a buffer between his brother and the outside world. As a matter of fact, consistent with Ira's managerial role, one finds his name listed as a litigant in hordes of civil cases in New York's courts over the years.[6] On the other hand, court records show a surprising absence of George's name in similar litigation, notwithstanding

177

hundreds of contractual involvements on his part, with all the susceptibilities for legal entanglements that these would inply.

One of the few instances in which Gershwin had recourse to legal action occurred in connection with Ziegfeld's *Show Girl*. After abandoning production plans for *East Is West,* the producer turned his energies to mounting a musical version of J. P. McEvoy's crisply crackling book *Show Girl,* adapted by William Anthony McGuire. The heroine of this musical, a Ziegfeld girl herself, is Dixie Dugan, a perky, crafty, coolly ambitious and driving dancer, who maneuvers her way from theatrical obscurity to stardom in the *Follies*. Ziegfeld recruited George and Ira in the spring of 1929 for the rush assignment of writing the *Show Girl* score in time for its Boston tryout on June 25 (even after the *East Is West* fiasco, the producer had no difficulty charming the Gershwins into working for him again). To help speed matters along, Ira, at Ziegfeld's suggestion, willingly shared the writing of the lyrics for the show with Gus Kahn.[7] The resulting score, up to the usually fine Gershwin standards, included the now-famous "Liza," one of George's own favorites, as well as "Home Blues" (devised from the blues section of *An American in Paris*), "Do What You Do!," "So Are You!," "Harlem Serenade," and "I Must Be Home by Twelve O'Clock."[8] To complement the zestful tunes and as calculated insurance for a long run, Ziegfeld packed the *Show Girl* company with a coruscating crew of show-stoppers, among them Ruby Keeler; Jimmy Durante and his manic cohorts, partners Lou Clayton and Eddie Jackson (the illustrious comic triumvirate of Clayton, Jackson, and Durante); Eddie Foy, Jr.; Harriet Hoctor; Frank McHugh; and Duke Ellington and his band. A balletic treatment of *An American in Paris* by Albertina Rasch was also incorporated into the musical to help sell tickets. Nor did Ziegfeld spare expenses on eye-catching costumes and scenery. To all this, Al Jolson added an extra boost to the show's Broadway opening on July 2 at the Ziegfeld Theater by lending the glamour of his name to the production. Not only had he married Ruby Keeler shortly before *Show Girl* opened—she was billed as Ruby Keeler Jolson in the musical—but he also contributed his talents. On opening night, Jolson, with his customary effusive vitality, jumped from his seat to run down the aisle in full-blown song, joining his wife in a rendition of "Liza." The Jolsons in duet galvanized the chic first-nighters into paroxysms of shrieking delight.

Yet despite the lavishness of the production and the glitter and tinsel surrounding it, *Show Girl* did not attract customers to the box office, finally expiring afer only 111 performances. For this poor showing, Ziegfeld must bear much of the blame. With all his theatrical expertise and calculated forethought, he missed the boat badly with this show, because in manipulating the swiftly paced satirical humor of McEvoy's script into a Broadway spectacular worthy of the Ziegfeld name, the producer obliterated much of the rapier wit of the original plot. Instead of focusing on the simple, taut outlines of Dixie Dugan's rags-to-riches rise, Ziegfeld opted for elephantine staging that emphasized fancy costumes and sets and multiple scenery changes. The production was ultimately bogged down in the mire of its own heavy-handed pretension.

Long before the Gershwins started working for Ziegfeld, he had had a reputation among the insiders of the profession for hard-nosed dealings with his cast and other hired hands, not exempting his musical staff. True to form he took the Gershwins to task for his show's lack of business. From his office chambers, Ziegfeld bombarded George and Ira with telegrams, complaining of the score and its effect on *Show Girl*. Since the Gershwins, to Ziegfeld's way of thinking, had contributed to the musical's failure, he righteously claimed he would not pay them royalties for their songs.[9] Under the circumstances, George and Ira had no alternative but to take legal action to collect payment. As a direct result of the ill will caused by this tiff, Gershwin ended his association with Ziegfeld with *Show Girl*. He never so much as wrote a tune for him again.[10]

The dispute with Ziegfeld of course touched Gershwin, but only peripherally. At worst it left only a minuscule and temporary scar. He had too many irons in the fire to dwell deeply on an essentially minor altercation, even if it involved a producer of Ziegfeld's prominence. After all, there were *other* producers standing in line for his services, among them Edgar Selwyn, who had not given up on *Strike Up the Band*. Selwyn wanted another go at producing this antiwar musical, but in a version more palatable to the public. Gershwin was only too happy to fulfill his request to refurbish the score.

By the time the reworked *Strike Up the Band* opened out of town at Boston's Shubert Theater on Christmas Eve of 1929, Gershwin had added still another dimension to his musical career—that of conductor. He had made his conducting debut the previous summer on August 26, 1929, at Lewisohn Stadium, as a dramatic followup to his earlier appearance there in 1927. Before another predictably enthusiastic crowd that jammed the stadium and overflowed the aisles,[11] Gershwin directed members of the Philharmonic in *An American in Paris* and was also soloist in the *Rhapsody in Blue,* led by Willem van Hoogstraten, the regular conductor. With all the show-biz instincts at his command, Gershwin carried off his first conducting attempt with aplomb. Certainly it was histrionically sound. He appeared poised and assured before the orchestra and wielded the baton with enough grace to carry conviction, particularly since he was the composer

179

Ira Gershwin, with pipe.
(Courtesy ASCAP) Besides
his duties as lyricist,
he handled many of
George's business and
financial affairs.

of the piece he was directing. He also enjoyed himself in his new role, as his relaxed, jaunty, loose-limbed athletics on the podium indicated. The audience, following his every move with obvious relish, roared their approval of his performance and brought him back for numerous bows. Backstage, after it was over, Gershwin was beside himself with delight, as he hugged everyone in sight. He had found still another means of displaying his talents in public. And best of all, it was so easy for him and so emotionally satisfying. What more exhilarating sense of power than to have an orchestra respond with all nuances to the mere waving of a baton? He joyfully promised his retinue of delirious well-wishers he would conduct at every opportunity henceforth.

In preparing for his conducting engagement at the stadium, Gershwin practiced baton technique by listening to records while waving his hands before a mirror. Bill Daly, always ready to assist him, was by his side to help with comments and guidance. He also got some conducting pointers from Edward Kilenyi, who claims that

> before conducting the New York Philharmonic Orchestra in playing his own music at the Lewisohn Stadium one summer—his first experience at conducting a large symphony orchestra—George was worried and asked me what I thought he might do to gain composure. "Let us go over your music together," I proposed. He played the records of the music he was about to conduct [An American in Paris] and which were recorded under his own personal supervision—that is, played the way he wanted them to be played. We spent hours in practice-conducting. I tried to give him all the practical and helpful hints I could give him as a result of my experience in conducting theatre orchestras. His concert was a triumph.[12]

With Gershwin's appetite for conducting whetted by his triumphant stadium performance, he gladly accepted an invitation to lead An American in Paris again the following November, this time at Mecca Temple,[13] with the newly formed Manhattan Symphony Orchestra, directed by conductor-composer Henry Hadley.[14] Sharing the podium with Hadley, Gershwin gave another good account of himself. As the Times noted in reporting the event, he "was recalled many times" in response to the clamorous outburst his conducting evoked.

Gaining in confidence with each conducting appearance, Gershwin next tackled the job of leading the pit orchestra for Strike Up the Band, in the show's Boston premiere as well as in its Broadway opening at the Times Square Theater on January 14, 1930.[15] This report of Gershwin at rehearsals gives some idea of how he comported himself on the podium:

To watch him at rehearsals is to see with what ease he gets the most out of the men under his baton. Baton, did I say? George conducts with a baton, with his cigar, with his shoulders, with his hips, with his eyes, with what not. . . . He sings with the principals and the chorus; he whistles; he imitates the various instruments of the orchestra; nothing but a sense of propriety, indeed, keeps him from leaping over the footlights and getting right into the show himself.[16]

Apropos of this description, Gershwin almost *did* leap on stage at the New York opening of *Strike Up the Band;* he was literally a show by himself in the pit. If wearing an enormous white tie with his tails for the occasion and a large gardenia to match were not enough to draw attention to himself in the pit, he remedied that by humming, whistling, and singing so loudly with the goings-on on stage that one reviewer pointedly suggested that it was he, not any of the principals, who was really the star of the show. There was no mistaking who was in charge of the orchestra and evidently everything and everyone else in the show that evening.

Fortified with his *Strike Up the Band* baton experiences, Gershwin conducted opening nights every chance he could for his other shows as well, often with an introductory blare of the trumpets and a glittering spotlight following him down the aisle to the pit to focus attention on him. He loved the excitement and applause that went with such appearances and always put on a fine performance—energetic and boisterous—on the podium. He subsequently also directed symphony and radio orchestras with increasing frequency, with such conducting assignments coming to be in great demand. Obviously, this demand for his services resulted not so much from his exceptional conducting gifts as from his fame as a composer. For though he eventually learned to wield a baton with a certain amount of finesse, his conducting technique remained mainly a rote-derived one, rather than one based on solid musicianship. Even as late as 1932, after leading orchestras for several years in his own music (Gershwin *never* conducted anything but Gershwin and limited sampling at that), his conducting and musical skills were questioned, as we have seen, by Langley after he had played *An American in Paris* under his direction. As one estimate of his conducting aptitude put it, Gershwin "possessed none of the traditional conductor's accomplishments. He had almost no capacity to read a score, and in addition he had a bad musical memory, except of his own works."[17] Nevertheless, for the general public Gershwin's questionable musicianship and limited conducting talent were of little or no concern; that was something for the professionals to quibble about. For them, Gershwin on the podium conducting his music with seeming authority was exciting to behold and a cause for cheering. They flocked to see him in action not only because they loved him and his music, but also because he was the embodiment of current popular musical fashion. That was more than enough for them.

Paulette Goddard with Charles Chaplin.

"LADIES' MAN"

$\mathcal{T}$HE BRUTAL CYNICISM of George S. Kaufman's original plot for *Strike Up the Band* was very much played down in the revised version of the musical. Morrie Ryskind, brought in by Edgar Selwyn to help adapt Kaufman's book for the new production, was responsible for the change.[1] No less a pacifist at heart than Kaufman, Ryskind nonetheless made the story more easily acceptable to theatergoers and thus commercially more viable by relegating America's war with Switzerland to that of a dream fantasy that never took place outside the mind of industrialist and arch militarist Horace J. Fletcher. As another "sweetening" element in the plot, chocolate rather than cheese became the bone of contention between the warring countries in the Ryskind adaptation.

With a change in script, the addition of the famous Red Nichols band, and a new cast built around the capers of comedy-team Clark (Bobby) and McCullough (Paul), went a change in score. About half of the old Gershwin tunes were dropped. Replacing them with such tidbits as "Soon,"[2] a tender duet for Margaret Schilling and Jerry Goff; the humorous patter song, "If I Became the President," incisively done in the show by Bobby Clark and Blanche Ring; "I Want to Be a War Bride"; "I Mean to Say"; "Hangin' Around with You"; and, from *Treasure Girl*, "I've got a Crush

185

on You." Retained from the 1927 edition of *Strike Up the Band* were the martial strains of the key title tune. During the writing of this song, Gershwin showed how finicky he could be before he was finally satisfied with his material: as Ira has related, George, over a period of weeks,

> had written four different marches and on each occasion I had responded with "That's fine. Just right. O.K., I'll write it up." And each time I received the same answer: "Not bad, but not yet. Don't worry. I'll remember it; but it's for an important spot, and maybe I'll get something better. [The] fifth try turned out to be it."[3]

Good as the old score was, the new one was even better, mainly because there was greater integration between plot and music than previously. The songs were not simply "set" pieces, used merely to show off the singers, dancers, and other members of the company, but were integral to the stage action. So artfully conceived was the transplant between the Gershwin music and lyrics with their sparkling colloquialisms and the sly Ryskind-Kaufman book that they seemed to merge into a unified whole. Theatrical artificiality was thus kept down to a minimum. The end result was a highly praised, yet reasonably satanic and biting musical, one that played for 191 performances after its opening in January of 1930, a very respectable run for a show that came in on the heels of the stock market crash of October 29, 1929. As one of the rewards of this musical's fine reception, its vocal score was published complete, the second Gershwin show to merit this distinction.[4] Furthermore, with this version of *Strike Up the Band*, George and Ira began a sustained association with Ryskind and Kaufman that led to the creation of *Of Thee I Sing* (1931) and *Let 'Em Eat Cake* (1933).

The close correlation between the score and the book for *Strike Up the Band* was aided by cogent orchestral commentary from the pit. Though no one was singled out as orchestrator in the printed program for *Strike Up the Band*, Isaac Goldberg, Gershwin's faithful Boswell, has attributed much of the effectiveness of the show's scoring to Gershwin and his fine ear for orchestral sounds and effects.[5] Goldberg's attribution, however, runs counter to facts.[6]

But if Gershwin's ear for orchestral sonorities is open to question, there would seem to be almost complete agreement that the composer had an uncommonly fine harmonic sense.[7] One indication of this faculty was his ability to duplicate immediately at the piano practically any chordal combination he heard. Another was his frequent habit of striking a series of chords at random at the piano before writing a song; the struck harmony obviously stimulated his creative processes. But even more conclusive evidence of his harmonic gift can be found in his piano improvisations of his

186

own music. While improvising, he would invariably introduce novel, wonderfully imaginative harmonic progressions with each variation of a tune. Seldom did he harmonize a piece twice the same way. The ever-fresh yet logical harmony that evolved as he played, so convincing and sounding so inevitable, was always a source of amazement to his listeners.

Gershwin's exceptional rhythmic flair, too, stood out in his piano improvisations as he executed, among other things, complicated runs and arpeggios in a highly poised and assured fashion. These came off so well, they seemed to have been prepared in advance and memorized. Vernon Duke, a gifted improvisor himself, has freely conceded that Gershwin's "extraordinary left hand performed miracles in counterrhythms, shrewd canonic devices, and unexpected harmonic shifts." He was also impressed by Gershwin's "faculty for abrupt yet felicitous modulations, the economy and logic of the voice-leading, and the overall sureness of touch [that] were masterly in their inevitability."[8] Rouben Mamoulian, equally generous in his assessment of Gershwin's improvisations, relates that

> George at the piano was George happy. He would draw a lovely melody out of the keyboard like a golden thread, then he would play with it and juggle it, twist it and toss it around mischievously, weave it into unexpected intricate patterns, tie it in knots and untie it and hurl it into a cascade of ever-changing rhythms and counterpoints. George at the piano was like a gay sorcerer celebrating his Sabbath.[9]

Another Gershwinophile, S. N. Behrman, tells of seeing "Kreisler, Zimbalist, Auer, and Heifetz caught up in the heady surf that inundates a room the moment he [Gershwin] strikes a chord. It is a feat not only of technique but of sheer virtuosity of personality."[10] Similar glowing tributes to his piano improvisations have come from Henry Cowell, Serge Koussevitsky, Bennett Cerf, Robert Russell Bennett, and many others.

Word of his brilliant improvisations ultimately filtered down to the general public and created a demand for them in printed form. To fulfill this demand, Simon and Schuster published a book of piano transcriptions of supposed Gershwin improvisations, illustrated by Alajálov, in September 1932.[11] Titled *George Gershwin's Song-Book,* it contained eighteen of his best-known songs, ranging from "Swanee" of 1919 to "Who Cares?," from *Of Thee I Sing,* with "improvised" variations on them by the composer. Among the other tunes in the *Song-Book* were "I'll Build a Stairway to Paradise," "Fascinating Rhythm," "Oh, Lady, Be Good!," "Somebody Loves Me," "The Man I Love," "Clap Yo' Hands," "Do, Do, Do," " 'S Wonderful," "Strike Up the Band," "Liza," and "I Got Rhythm."

The difficulty of capturing on paper the elusiveness of piano improvisations, especially of Gershwin's dynamic and very personal kind, was not very adroitly negotiated in the *Song-Book*. The published "improvisations" are rather cloddish affairs that do a disservice to his reputation as an improvisor. Question has even been raised whether the actual transcribing of the "improvisations" was done by Gershwin. For as Olin Downes speaking of the *Song-Book* pointed out in the *New York Times* in 1937, Gershwin's

> way of playing the piano was maddeningly his own. He could never write down his accompaniments as he played them, although the edition of selected songs which appeared some six years ago had affixed to them a series of laughably appropriate embroideries on the melody for the keyed instrument.[12]

But if, as Downes implies, the printed "variations" of the famous tunes in the *Song-Book* were not wholly a Gershwin product, the volume still has historical interest, albeit of a limited kind, as the only published sampling of his "improvisations." The book also has some value for Gershwin's comments—pedestrian as they are—on pianistic style in performing the transcriptions. He warned against the overuse of the sustaining pedal on the piano, understandably insisting on a "staccato" rather than a "legato" approach in performing for the proper "ragtime or jazz" quality.[13] As he put it, "The rhythms of American popular music are more or less brittle; they should be made to snap, and at times to crackle."[14] Unfortunately for posterity, Gershwin never recorded the transcriptions in the *Song-Book* for the public. The world will thus never know how he would have played the published "improvisations" himself.[15]

Just as he had dedicated his three *Preludes for Piano*, published in 1927, to Bill Daly, so, too, Gershwin dedicated his *Song-Book* to someone especially close to him: Kay Swift. When he first knew her, Kay, born Katherine Faulkner Swift, was the wife of wealthy James P. Warburg, a 1917 Phi Beta Kappa Harvard graduate who could trace his roots to three great German-Jewish banking families, the Loebs, the Schiffs, and the Warburgs.[16] Kay and James had married young, both barely out of their teens when they tied the marital knot in June 1918. Sixteen years later, in 1934, and the parents of three girls, they were divorced.

Gershwin met Kay in the spring of 1925 when he attended a party for Jascha Heifetz and other musicians at the Warburgs' New York home as the guest of Marie Rosanoff, then of the Musical Art Quartet. Not long after his arrival at the Warburgs', Gershwin was at the piano, playing and singing as usual. Suddenly he jumped up to announce, "I have to go to Europe," and rushed out of the house. He just about missed the boat that took him to England for work on *Tell Me More*, which opened in London on May 26. It was under these dramatic circumstances that he left his initial imprint on Kay Swift.

| STAGE | BROADWAY | SCREEN |

VARIETY

PRICE 25¢.

Published Weekly at 154 West 46th St., New York, N. Y., by Variety, Inc. Annual subscription, $10. Single copies, 25 cents.
Entered as second-class matter December '5, 1905, at the Post Office at New York, N. Y., under the act of March 3, 1879.

VOL. XCVII. No. 3   NEW YORK, WEDNESDAY, OCTOBER 30, 1929   88 PAGES

WALL ST. LAYS AN EGG

Going Dumb Is Deadly to Hostess In Her Serious Dance Hall Profesh

A hostess at Roseland has her problems. The paid steppers consider their work a definite profession calling for specialized technique and high-power salesmanship.

"You see, you gotta sell your personality," said one. "Each one of us girls has our own clientele to cater to. It's just like selling dresses 'in a store—you have to know what to sell each particular customer.

"Some want to dance, some want to kid, some want to get soupy, and others are just 'misunderstood husbands'."

Girls applying for hostess jobs at

Hunk on Winchell

When the Walter Winchells moved into 204 West 55th street, late last week, June, that's Mrs. Winchell, selected a special room as Walter's exclusive sleep den for his late hour nights. She shushed the Winchell kidlets when her husband dove in at his usual eight o'clock the first morning.

At noon, Walter's midnight, his sound proof room was penetra d by so many high

DROP IN STOCKS ROPES SHOWMEN

Many Weep and Call Off Christmas Orders — Legit Shows Hit

MERGERS HALTED

The most dramatic event in the financial history of America is the collapse of the New York Stock Market. The stage was Wall Street, but the onlookers severed

Talker Crashes Olympus

Paris, Oct. 29.

Fox "Follies" and the Fox Movietone newsreel are running this week in Athens, Greece, the first sound pictures heard in the birthplace of world culture, and in all Greece, for that matter.

Several weeks ago, Variety's Cairo correspondent cabled that a cinema had been wired in Alexandria, Cleopatra's

Kidding Kissers in Talkers Burns Up Fans of Screen's Best Lovers

Boys who used to whistle and girls who used to giggle when love scenes were flashed on the screen are in action again. A couple of years ago they began to take the love stuff seriously and desisted, but the talkers are reviving the ha ha for film osculators.

Heavy loving lovers of silent picture days accustomed to charming audiences into spasms of silent ecstasy when kissing the leading lady are getting the bird instead of the heartbeat. The sound accompaniment is making it tough.

Such a picture romancer as John Gilbert is getting laughs in place

Variety reports the Wall Street crash of October 29, 1929. *Strike Up The Band* of 1930 was Gershwin's first musical after the crash.

Robert Russell Bennett, who orchestrated many of Gershwin's musicals for Broadway and Hollywood.

She and Gershwin met again some months later at another party, at Walter Damrosch's apartment after the premiere of the *Concerto* in December 1925. As the hero of the evening, Gershwin naturally was surrounded by a coterie of admirers. But he did not miss Kay amid the tumult and celebrating. She was dressed in an elegant costume, sufficiently outlandish to stand out. Gershwin, ever the ladies' man, gravitated to her. They were soon chatting merrily away like old acquaintances.

They saw each other more frequently after that, for they had many common interests and mutual friends. Before long, they were warmly attached to each other and could be found together at art galleries, concerts, the theater, parties, and so on. Fortunately, James did not appear to mind his wife's friendship with Gershwin; the Warburgs were an enlightened couple who often went their separate ways without overt frictions or jealousies. Whether seeing Kay in their customary Manhattan haunts or horseback riding with her at the Warburg farm in Connecticut, Gershwin did not have to contend with a righteously indignant or jealous husband.

Besides her social position and slim attractiveness, Kay brought to her relationship with Gershwin a native wit, practical intelligence, worldly sophistication, sensitivity, as well as a musically retentive mind, a keen ear, and a background of study at the Institute of Musical Art and with Charles Martin Loeffler, a highly respected composer and pedagogue. She was also a songwriter of more than average skills. Still active today, Kay has written for Broadway, radio, the movies, and, over the years, numerous industrial shows.[17] She is probably best known for her score for the fine 1930 musical *Fine and Dandy,* which starred Joe Cook, and as the composer of the hit song "Can't We Be Friends."[18]

Convinced from the very beginning that Gershwin was a major musical talent, and with a high personal regard for him as well, Kay was only too happy to be of service to him and his career in any way possible. For her, it was a privilege to place her own musical gifts at his disposal. He had but to ask her, and Kay would be ready to help him notate his music as he played it at the piano, or proofread his scores and copy parts for them, or offer criticism of his work, or join him in piano duets for relaxation. She could always be counted on whenever he needed her.[19] Just as it was Kay who would send Gershwin a boutonniere and flowers for his concert appearances and lovingly greet him after he had performed as conductor and soloist, so it was she who often helped cheer him up when he was low in spirits. If one measures by the dedication of his *Song-Book* to her, his generous gifts of paintings, manuscripts, and other keepsakes that betokened affection, plus the many hours he spent with her, Gershwin obviously had a special place in his heart for Kay Swift.[20]

With Kay, Gershwin probably came as close to settling down with one woman as he ever did. He even queried some of his friends—though offhandedly enough, so that one couldn't really tell whether he was serious or not—about their reactions to the idea of his marrying her. For that matter, there are those who claim that Kay's divorce from Warburg in 1934 was precipitated by her hope that she and Gershwin would marry. But nothing came of it.[21] Clearly, he was too much involved with himself and his work and too fickle and unpredictable to pay more than lip service to the idea of marriage, whether to Kay or anyone else.

Nor were his numerous sexual affairs and dalliances throughout his life helpful in cementing a stable, lasting relationship with any woman, particularly in marriage. Gershwin himself frequently gave this pat and confident answer, or words to the effect, when asked why he didn't settle down to the "bliss" of married life: "Why should I limit myself to only one woman when I can have as many women as I want?" Paradoxically enough, despite this outward expression of braggadocio, there were many women who found Gershwin anything but secure and sure of himself in their presence. To them, he often seemed uncomfortable, relatively withdrawn and unable to handle even casual conversations very well. His paradoxical behavior with women was demonstrated in other ways, too. For instance, notwithstanding his own sexual adventures, he could be an insufferable prude. Thus, when he saw his sister, Frances, sitting with her dress above her knees, he insisted that she pull it down. He once even slapped her for using an expletive in public.[22]

The inconsistency of the roué and the prig existing cheek by jowl in Gershwin's psyche was but another example of the many contradictions in his personality. By the same token, his cockiness and boastfulness in talking about the countless women at his beck and call were matched on occasion by expressions of self-pity and unhappiness about his relationship with them. During fits of depression, he complained to intimate friends that he had not been able to form a lasting bond with any woman. He bemoaned in his melancholic moments that his life "was all mixed up," that, despite his material and artistic successes, he could not find a suitable mate.

Many of his friends have attributed his inability to settle down with one woman to some major quirk, some psychological insecurity, on his part. While Gershwin, they have suggested, appeared on one level to be the ultimate womanizer who coveted attractive, amenable women wherever and whenever he found them and had an immense sexual appetite to boot, on another level he set up totally unrealistic standards for them that no woman could fulfill. In their opinion, Gershwin craved and continually searched for the "ideal" mate, someone who in fact could not possibly exist except in fantasy: an extraordinarily beautiful and intelligent woman of many graces who would devote herself entirely to him, to accede to his every wish, and essentially agree with him on all important matters. Often, his friends note, the women who approached his ideal were already safely married to other men. Paulette Goddard, for example, could undoubtedly qualify as one of them. She was still married to Charles Chaplin' when Gershwin, while in Hollywood, became madly infatuated with her in the last months of his life.[23] She had the looks, the elegance, the intelligence, and the wit that he sought in a woman.[24] So did Kay Swift, who was Warburg's wife when Gershwin was first attracted to her. But whether as exceptional as Miss Goddard and Miss Swift or not, he was drawn to many women: Hollywood starlets, Broadway showgirls, socialites, and others of all physical and mental dimensions and social and educational backgrounds, especially if they presented no immediate threat to his bachelor state and imposed no long-range or permanent commitment to them on his part.

With all of Gershwin's casual sexual adventures, it is perhaps understandable that there have been rumors bandied about concerning threats of lawsuits against him—especially because of his fame and wealth—from "aggrieved" women. But even if these rumors have any validity, they have not been brought out in the open. As a matter of fact, the only scandalous public allegation related to Gershwin's numerous liaisons was made not by a woman but by a man representing himself as his son. In an article entitled, "I Am George Gershwin's Illegitimate Son," in the February 1959 issue of *Confidential*—a tabloid magazine with a masthead proclaiming that it "tells the facts and names the names"—an "Alan Gershwin," bearing a resemblance to the composer, claimed him as his father. Both in the article and in subsequent personal interviews with this writer, Alan Gershwin stated that his mother, a dancer known professionally as Margaret Manners, had "had an affair" with Gershwin.[25] He alleges he was born "between May 15 and May 18, 1928," in a private house in Altadena, California, but that his birth had never been recorded by the doctor attending his mother. According to Alan Gershwin, his mother left California shortly after his birth to return to New York, but she "disappeared from Broadway in 1930. . . . Few people knew where she had gone. She died of leukemia. She was no more than 24."[26] He claims he was raised in California and, later, in New York by his mother's sister and her husband, Fanny and Ben Schneider, both of whom died "during the 1940s," and originally used their last name as his own.[27] As a youngster, he asserts, he saw Gershwin "perhaps over a dozen times . . . [though] he would never come to the house. Always he sent for me, usually sending a new person to fetch me each time. . . . On these occasions, I never spent a night in his apartment. Always he would send me for the night to friends—who lived nearby [the friends are not identified]."[28]

Despite his published allegations, Alan Gershwin has not made public any evidence or produced any witnesses to prove that George Gershwin was his father, that the composer acknowledged him as a son, or that he had personal contact with him. Thus, irrespective of his dramatic statements in *Confidential*, Alan Gershwin, in effect, has not substantiated his relationship to the composer. Actually, at the end of his article in *Confidential*, Alan Gershwin requested assistance from the public in proving his claim by making this plea: "I hope that someone, somewhere, will read it [the article] and will remember something and will come forward to help me."[29] In essence it appears that the only basis for his case, as he has presented it, is simply his allegation that he is Gershwin's son and his resemblance to the composer.

In an effort to either corroborate or disprove the Alan Gershwin story, this writer spoke with the Gershwin family lawyer, Leonard Saxe. Saxe stated he had proof that Alan Gershwin was nothing but an imposter. But he refused to allow such "proof" to be examined, notwithstanding this writer's expressed willingness to respect completely the wishes of the Gershwin family regarding confidential material in this case placed at his disposal.

Hence, as things now stand, an Alan Gershwin, resembling the composer, has claimed consanguinity with him, without tangible facts to back up his claim. The Gershwin family, in turn, has neither publicly refuted Alan Gershwin's allegations nor legally challenged them in court,[30] though their lawyer has denied the *Confidential* allegations to this writer, without divulging any supportive evidence.

As a corollary to the *Confidential* article by Alan Gershwin and the Gershwin family's response to it, as voiced by their lawyer, one might reasonably wonder what Gershwin would have thought of this wrangle touching on his *amours* if he were alive today. Considering his courting of the reputation of "ladies' man," he might not have been displeased by the ruckus.

In Universal's *The King of Jazz* (1930), Paul Whiteman and his band played atop an enormous piano, typical of the super-colossal approach of Hollywood musicals at that time. The movie featured Gershwin's *Rhapsody in Blue*.

HOLLYWOOD MUSE

$\mathbb{H}$AVING SAVORED THE thrill of directing the orchestra and the cast, and generally being the focal point in the pit on opening night for *Strike Up the Band,* Gershwin eagerly took on again the role of conductor for his next musical, *Girl Crazy,* an Aarons-Freedley production that opened at the Alvin on October 14, 1930. He had a dream orchestra under his command in the pit for *Girl Crazy.* Among the instrumentalists hired by Red Nichols,[1] whose ensemble was featured in the show, were these now-famous jazzmen-band leaders: Benny Goodman, Gene Krupa, Glen Miller, Jimmy Dorsey, and Jack Teagarden. Gershwin found conducting as exciting as ever, though he made this complaint: "The theater was so warm that I must have lost three pounds, perspiring." But he added brightly, "The opening was so well received that five pounds would not have been too much. With the exception of some dead head friends of mine, who sat in the front row, everybody seemed to enjoy the show tremendously, especially the critics. I think the notices, especially of the music, were the best I have ever received."[2]

Girl Crazy was a fun show, with a cheerfully sassy book by Guy Bolton and John McGowan, and a young, vital cast whose exuberance spilled over the footlights. Among the principals were Ethel Merman, making her Broadway debut; Ginger Rogers, fresh from roles in *Top Speed,* a Broadway production, and *Young Man of Manhattan,* a movie; the delightfully brash comedian Willie Howard, manufactured Yiddish accent and all; and Allen Kearns, a Gershwin "regular" from such shows as *Tip-Toes* and *Funny Face*. As Danny Churchill, Allen Kearns portrayed a wealthy New York playboy, wild about girls, who has been banished to remote Custerville, a dusty, one-hotel town in Arizona, by his irate father, anxious to keep his wayward son away from the temptations of the flesh. Danny, the ever-impractical, soft-living rake, comes to Custerville in, of all things, a taxi driven by one Gieber Goldfarb, broadly played by Willie Howard, who remains there to become sheriff of the town; the incongruous sight of New Yorker Goldfarb in a Western hat, cowboy clothes, gun belt, and spurs, with a sheriff's badge pinned to his vest, was one of the funniest moments in the show. In Custerville, Danny resumes his philandering habits by opening a dude ranch replete with chorus girls and high living. But, to no one's surprise, he finally mends his ways for the love of chaste cowgirl and town postmistress Mollie Gray, the role taken by Ginger Rogers.

The show was an updated, rib-tickling satire on the Old West, when gambling and brawling were rampant and bad men flashed their guns at the slightest provocation. The tone of the show was set in the number, "Bidin' My Time,"[3] drawlingly sung by a group called The Foursome, as four lazy, tired cowboys who accompanied themselves as the spirit moved them on such simple "Western" instruments as the tin flute, jew's harp, ocarina, and harmonica. But, lethargic or not, they doffed their hats with reverence whenever "West," the word sacred to all self-respecting cowboys' hearts, was spoken. Ethel Merman, as Frisco Kate, the tough barroom gal with a heart of melted butter, also contributed to the merriment with her renditions of "Boy! What Love Has Done to Me!," an enumeration of the trials of marriage to a small-time gambler; the bluesy, comical "Sam and Delilah,"[4] and the rip-roaring "I Got Rhythm,"[5] whose ungrammatical text, as typified by its opening lines, only added to its punch:

> I got rhythm, I got music,
> I got my man—
> Who could ask for anything more?[6]

More than anything else, it was her raucous, full-voiced singing of "I Got Rhythm," which carried to every corner of the theater and the outside lobby as well, that made her a star overnight. When she belted out the tune and held a high C while the orchestra played around her, she always brought the house down.

Ginger Rogers, Allen Kearns, and Willie Howard were also well served by the Gershwin score, dividing among themselves such delights as "Embraceable You" (taken from *East Is West*), "But Not for Me," "Could You Use Me?" the satirical "When It's Cactus Time in Arizona," and the funny "Goldfarb! That's I'm," done, of course, by the inimitable Willie Howard. The infectious tunes, the talented cast, and the overall excellence of the well-knit production caught the fancy of the public. Despite the low-ebb economy of the early 1930s, *Girl Crazy* played to many well-filled houses for thirty-four weeks on Broadway (272 performances), a good run for the time.[7] Prompted by the Broadway success of *Girl Crazy*, Hollywood's RKO Studios made a film of it in 1932. It starred comedians Bert Wheeler and Robert Woolsey and contained a refreshing though limited sampling of the Gershwin score. Eleven years later, MGM, too, made a movie of *Girl Crazy* with Judy Garland and Mickey Rooney as the leads plus Tommy Dorsey and his band. To his credit, the 1943 film version included many of the original Gershwin tunes in its soundtrack.[8]

George and Ira became directly involved with Hollywood themselves when they signed a contract with Fox Studios in April 1930 to write the score the following fall—after *Girl Crazy* had opened—for *Delicious,* a film that was to star Janet Gaynor and Charles Farrell, then moviedom's beloved screen couple, who had captured the world's collective hearts with their tender, wistful portrayals as the love interests in *Seventh Heaven.* Their contract with Fox guaranteed George and Ira the combined salary of $100,000—$70,000 for George and $30,000 for Ira—a monumental sum for those post-crash days. The *Delicious* assignment was not, of course, their first experience with movies. For, as stated previously, they had written a "score" that accompanied the 1923 silent film *Sunshine Trail.* George was also paid $50,000 for allowing the *Rhapsody in Blue* to be used in *The King of Jazz,* a movie about Paul Whiteman. When *The King of Jazz* opened at the Roxy in New York in May 1930, George earned an additional $10,000 for appearing for two weeks on stage there with Whiteman as soloist in the *Rhapsody.*

It was perhaps inevitable that Hollywood would beckon the Gershwins to write a film score, inasmuch as sound-film production—a relatively new phase of filmmaking, only begun in 1926—laid great stress on musicals. To the powers that were in Hollywood of the time, movies were primarily meant to entertain. What better way to entertain the vast public than through singing and dancing on the new sound screen? In the minds of the then-ruling moguls of Cinema City, "musicals" were usually equated with Broadway's Great White Way, Tin Pan Alley, and the New York "jazz" of the Paul Whiteman variety. Because of these associations, Hollywood not only imported much of its musical talent from the east for the writing of movie scores, but many of its films also reflected

197

Kay Swift, when Gershwin knew her.
(Courtesy Radio City Music Hall)

Kay Swift today. *(Courtesy ASCAP)*

Alan Gershwin, who claims to be the son
of the composer, shown with a friend
pointing to a photograph of Gershwin.

Paulette Goddard, as she appeared with
Charles Chaplin in *The Great Dictator*.
Gershwin was greatly drawn to her.

the New York scene, especially after two of the earliest talkies, *The Broadway Melody* and Jolson's *The Jazz Singer,* both with New York locales, became smash hits. It was in a climate that can only be described as friendly that the "Broadway" Gershwins were welcomed to Hollywood with sunny smiles and open arms, and were compensated handsomely for what amounted to little more than several weeks' work on the *Delicious* score.[9]

Before his trip west, Gershwin, as was to be expected, was busily immersed in getting *Girl Crazy* ready for the boards.[10] Shortly after it opened at the Alvin, however, Gershwin was in the fortunate position of being able to say of that musical: "[It] looks so good that I can leave in a few weeks for Hollywood with the warm feeling that I have a hit under the belt."[11] And leave he did, by train, for Hollywood on November 5, 1930, three days after attending the marriage of his sister, Frances, to Leopold Godowsky, Jr. (in tribute to them, he played a condensed version of the *Rhapsody in Blue* at the piano as a wedding march), and after seeing his parents off to a Florida vacation. Going cross-country with him was a small army of friends and professional associates, including, of course, Ira. They all traveled in the style befitting Hollywood-bound luminaries, with a car completely to themselves. All had a merry time en route, as the train resounded with the noise of an almost continual round of parties.

Speaking for publication about his new Hollywood assignment, Gershwin had a few well-chosen words to say. "I go to work for the talkies like any other amateur, for I know very little about them," he stated modestly. "Because I am inexperienced with films, I am approaching them in a humble state of mind."[12] But if these remarkably demure press comments were models of understated humility, his life-style in Hollywood hardly reflected these sentiments. For example, for his stay in the movie capital, George and Ira with his wife lived in a luxurious Spanish-type home in Beverly Hills that had served as a residence for Greta Garbo. He even slept in Garbo's bed, though, as he jokingly admitted to friends, it had little effect on his sleep.

In Hollywood, Gershwin, as usual, combined work with pleasure. As he later indicated in an interview on his return to New York, "I worked hard in Hollywood, but did manage to bring my golf score down a few points."[13] And he often found time not only for golf, but tennis, swimming, hiking, and other diversions, not only in Hollywood and its environs, but as far south as Agua Caliente, Mexico, then noted for its race track, gambling, hot springs, and other attractions.[14] He also found time to attend a performance on January 15, 1931, of *An American in Paris* by the Los Angeles Philharmonic under Artur Rodzinski, and to take his share of bows on stage for the local gentry, thrilled with the piece and their good luck at seeing the celebrated Gershwin in the flesh.

Enjoying life while fully involved in the rigors of an active and demanding career had always been his policy, but in young Hollywood of that period the ratio between work and leisurely pursuits was not always so conscientiously balanced as it might have been, either for Gershwin or for others.[15] Consequently, many of the talents who were brought to Hollywood on the basis of past career achievements considered their stay in balmy Southern California as simply a high-paying reward for previous effort. Sound films, to them, had not yet collectively proved themselves as a medium. So why not take all the "gold" that Hollywood offered, they reasoned, while doing as little as possible in return, even if it meant going through the motions of work. Gershwin himself freely admitted his awareness of this practice of lying down on the job, going so far as to tell—without naming him—of a famous author he knew who had been brought out from the east at a high salary, and who then enjoyed a six-month vacation with full pay at the studio's expense without his employer's knowledge.[16] So, if under such lax Hollywood conditions, Gershwin did not extend himself so much as he might have for *Delicious,* it was perhaps understandable.

Most of the tunes he came up with for *Delicious* were taken from his grab bag of previously written material or were discards from other musicals merely fitted with appropriate lyrics by Ira to match the screenplay by Guy Bolton and Sonya Levien. The story told of a poor but pretty Scottish lass, emigrating to the United States, who meets a handsome, wealthy American polo player on board the ship taking them both to New York. The details of the Bolton-Levien script were less important for plot content than for showing off Janet Gaynor as the sweet-as-pie lass and Charles Farrell as the dashing American, who fall in love and eventually marry, but not without their share of travail, including Miss Gaynor's search through Gotham's streets for her hero. Gershwin's score was competent and to the point, but not much more inspired than the plot it supported. It included "Delishious," completed months before he went out to Hollywood, and "Blah, Blah, Blah," a spoof on the rhyming of popular ballads (much of the text for the tune's refrain consists of nothing more than "blah, blah, blah," interspersed with such rhymed clichés as "moon" and "croon," and "love" and "above"), reworked from a song originally written for *East Is West.* Gershwin even went back to his early "Mischa, Jascha, Toscha, Sascha," the witty takeoff on the names of four famous Russian violinists that he and Ira had written around 1921, but it was not used in the film. Specifically composed for *Delicious,* however, was an orchestral rhapsody that was meant to depict the noises, vitality, and tempo of bustling Manhattan, and music for a dream sequence in which reporters intoned this bit of New Yorkese: "We're from the *Journal,* the *Warheit,* the *Telegram,* and the *Times;* we specialize in interviews and crimes."

Of the various items Gershwin contributed to *Delicious,* his most ambitious musical undertaking was unquestionably his rhapsody, which drew on the technical and instrumental resources he had absorbed from writing his three earlier orchestral works. Though only a small portion of the piece was actually employed in the film, he completed a sketch of a full-blown orchestral rhapsody while under the stimulus of his Hollywood muse.[17] It featured a driving, repetitive melody that evoked the sound of riveting, for he had hit on the idea of a "rivet" theme to convey a musical image of Manhattan and its skyscrapers in the rhapsody. As he expressed it—and somewhat inelegantly at that—in speaking about this theme and its relation to the New York scene: "As the part of the picture where it is to be played takes place in many streets of New York, I used as a starting-point what I called 'a rivet theme' but, after that, I just wrote a piece of music without a program."[18] Consistent with the prominence of the theme in the rhapsody, he vacillated between calling his sketch *Rhapsody in Rivets, Manhattan Rhapsody,* and *New York Rhapsody,* before finally settling on the title of *Second Rhapsody.*[19]

Some months after his Hollywood stint on *Delicious,* he gave these reasons for writing the rhapsody:

> I wrote it mainly because I wanted to write a serious composition and found the opportunity in California. Nearly everybody comes back from California with a western tan and a pocketful of motion picture money. I decided to come back with both these things and a serious composition—if the climate would let me. I was under no obligation to the Fox Company to write this. But, you know, the old artistic soul must be appeased every so often.[20]

Thanks, then, to his movie assignment and the income that went with it Gershwin was able to bring back the sketch of his new rhapsody with him when he left Hollywood for New York on February 22, 1931. He could also take back with him some music he had written in California for his next musical, *Of Thee I Sing.* For prior to going to Hollywood, George and Ira had had a series of conferences with George S. Kaufman and Morrie Ryskind, who were then preparing the book for the show. Kaufman and Ryskind had gotten far enough along with their script to be able to give the Gershwins a fourteen-page outline to take with them to California. Between their movie chores for *Delicious* and their other business and social activities in Hollywood, the brothers still found time to

201

finish "The Illegitimate Daughter," one of the songs for their upcoming show, as well as to draft a tentative version of the title tune for this musical.

Once comfortably settled in New York, Gershwin began orchestrating the rhapsody on March 14, 1931, completing the task some two months later on May 23.[21] As was true for the symphonic works that preceded it, the orchestrated manuscript paid distinct attention to such details as phrasing, accents, bowings, and tempo indications. It had that tidy, spick-and-span, concerned-with-its-appearance look of something clearly meant to impress. The score called for these instruments: three flutes (with the third flute doubling on piccolo), two oboes, English horn, two B-flat clarinets, bass clarinet, two bassoons, four French horns, three B-flat trumpets, three trombones, tuba, timpani, percussion, harp, and strings, plus piano. The full title of the piece, printed on the title page of his score, was now *Second Rhapsody for Orchestra with Piano*. The reason for the use of "with piano" rather than "and piano" in the title may be inferred from Gershwin's comment in speaking of the work: "Although the piano has quite a few solo parts, I may make it one of the orchestral instruments, instead of solo."[22] As this statement suggests, the piano had more of a quasi-obbligato role in the work than a solo one. But extended solo part or not, Gershwin himself was the pianist when a trial performance of the rhapsody took place several weeks after he had finished the orchestration. As he had done for the *Concerto in F,* he hired an orchestra of more than fifty musicians to play through the piece so he could judge how it "sounded." The run-through took place on June 26, 1931, in one of the studios of the National Broadcasting Company. As a favor to Gershwin, moreover, Victor made a recording of the session for his own private use, the better for him to hear the piece at his leisure. That he was obviously gratified with the results may be judged from the remark he made about the work even before receiving the recording: "In many respects, such as orchestration and form, it is the best thing I've written."[23] He also had good reason to be pleased with himself on another count: relatively few revisions had to be made in the score, even after the run-through. The most noticeable changes in the score were these: the solo piano introduction was increased from four to six measures, and two measures were deleted from the orchestra (from between what are now m. 28 and m. 29 of the published score).[24] In its final state, the work was dedicated by Gershwin to Max Dreyfus in appreciation for all the publisher had done for him.[25]

The premiere of the *Second Rhapsody* did not take place until January 29, 1932, more than eight months after its completion, when it was performed in Boston by Serge Koussevitzky and the Boston Symphony. This rather long delay resulted mainly from Gershwin's belief that Arturo

Ethel Merman
as Frisco Kate in *Girl Crazy*.

Postmistress **Ginger Rogers**
in *Girl Crazy*.

Toscanini might consider conducting the first performance of the piece with the New York Philharmonic, which Toscanini then headed. He first met Toscanini at the home of critic Samuel Chotzinoff in the spring of 1931, after returning to New York from Hollywood. At the Chotzinoffs', Gershwin played piano versions of his *Rhapsody in Blue* and *Second Rhapsody* for Toscanini, who, surprisingly, was not familiar with his music. From the conductor's response, he seemed genuinely attracted to what he heard, although he made no definite commitment to schedule the new piece. The possibility of Toscanini's performing the *Second Rhapsody* got another boost when CBS chief William Paley, impressed with the work when he heard Gershwin play it at a party, strongly intimated he would use his good offices to get Toscanini to premiere it. When nothing ultimately materialized, Gershwin was only too happy to have Koussevitzky and the magnificent Boston orchestra play it. As for Toscanini, it was not until November 1, 1942, five years after Gershwin's death, that he finally played something by Gershwin, when he directed the NBC Symphony— the superb radio orchestra created specifically for the conductor in 1937 by David Sarnoff, head of National Broadcasting—in the *Rhapsody in Blue,* with Earl Wild as pianist and Benny Goodman as clarinet soloist. Notwithstanding the fine soloists and orchestra, Toscanini's interpretation was anything but definitive. Granted that he was incomparable in the classical and romantic repertoire, he had had little experience—and even less inclination—in conducting contemporary music and least of all the "jazzy" American music of Gershwin's kind. The result was dismal. As Virgil Thomson pointed out in his review of the performance in the *Herald Tribune,* "It all came off like a ton of bricks. . . . It was as far from George's own way of playing the piece as one could imagine."

The Boston Symphony's rendition of the *Second Rhapsody* was another matter. Koussevitzky had long been a champion of contemporary music and had been particularly active in promoting new American works from the start of his tenure as permanent conductor of the Boston Symphony in 1924—a post he was to hold for twenty-five years, longer than any other director of the orchestra. Moreover, Koussevitzky was wholly sympathetic to Gershwin's music and firmly convinced that Gershwin was touched with genius.[26] He and his orchestra went all out for Gershwin and did well by the *Second Rhapsody,*[27] both in its world premiere in Boston and in its first New York performance the following week, on February 5, 1932.

Gershwin was the piano soloist with the orchestra on both occasions. More celebrated than ever at this point, he attracted overflow crowds, warmly disposed to him and his work. As Lawrence Gilman noted in reporting the New York premiere of the *Second Rhapsody* at Carnegie Hall in the *Herald Tribune* of February 6, 1932:

> Only Mr. Paderewski, perhaps, could have drawn a gathering comparable in numbers if not in kind with that which stood patiently at the rear of the hall last evening while Mr. Koussevitzky cruelly delayed the appearance of George I by playing a couple of superfluous introductory numbers by Prokofiev [*Classical Symphony*] and Vincent d'Indy [*"Istar" Variations*].

And Gershwin did not disappoint his large following. As customary, he brought down the house with his breathtaking, glittering playing. But despite Gilman's passing reference in his review to composer-pianist Ignace Jan Paderewski, Gershwin was *not* a Paderewski as a pianist. Nor a Sergei Rachmaninoff. Nor the equal as concert pianist of any one of a number of famous composers who were also exceptional piano soloists. Unlike them, he could play *only* his own music in public. This he did with brilliant virtuosity, resulting from his sure-footed musical instincts and fine muscular coordination. For the pianistic flair and command of the keyboard that he invariably displayed in his improvisations were also evident in his solo performances with orchestra. But George *could not* and *did not* perform difficult works from the piano literature in concert, as did Rachmaninoff or Paderewski. His overall finger technique was too limited for such an undertaking because of deficiencies in training and practice discipline on his part. After all, his early teacher, Charles Hambitzer, can really be considered his last piano mentor, although he subsequently took a lesson now and then from his professional pianist friends. To Gershwin's credit, however, he did not hesitate to ask pianists he respected for advice in fingering to help his playing along. But that was not the same as having this technique almost automatically ingrained in his fingertips to be put at the service of *all* music. Also, his practice habits were limited mainly to improvising at the piano either at home or at parties, though occasionally he tried his hand at Czerny exercises or the equivalent. That is a far cry from spending hours practicing to acquire the skills needed to broaden one's repertoire. As for his ability to play difficult music at sight, it was practically nonexistent. His music-reading skills were never highly developed at any point in his life. Oscar Levant has inadvertently pointed up this failing in humorously describing his competition with Gershwin to win the affections of a curvaceous chorus girl they were both interested in. She was then employed in the company of *Strike Up the Band,* 1930 version, and ecstatically devoted to *La Bohème.* To Gershwin's advantage in the battle for her favors, as Levant tells it, was the Gershwin name and "the extra weight pull of a ducal fur-trimmed overcoat . . . giving him the appearance of a perpetual guest conductor." But to even things out in this apparently one-sided match for the lady's esteem was the fact that, in Levant's words, "George had difficulty in playing the Puccini score for her on the piano for two reasons: (A) It wasn't by Gershwin. (B) He didn't read other people's music very well (at that time)."[28] His reading skills did not advance very far even after 1930, despite Levant's implications that they did.

But if Gershwin's concert appearances as pianist were limited to his own works, his performances of them were certainly as authoritative as one might imagine. It was no surprise, then, that there was practically unanimity of opinion that his playing of the Second Rhapsody with the Boston orchestra was well-nigh perfect: idiomatic, musical, and exciting. Where reservations were raised about the Second Rhapsody, they touched almost exclusively on the piece itself. And reviewers found much to criticize in it, particularly its aping of the mannerisms of the Rhapsody in Blue. W. J. Henderson complained in the Sun that the Second Rhapsody "suggests the first rhapsody over and over." He described the piece as "jazz out of high school," and its orchestration as "generally too thick, which is a result of the attempt to fit the jazz style to a symphonic orchestra." Lawrence Gilman, never too sympathetic to Gershwin, was also less than complimentary in his review in the Herald Tribune. With ill-disguised irony, Gilman quoted Gershwin as saying that for his lyrical second theme in the work he "wanted merely to write a broad, flowing melody, the same as Bach, Brahms or Wagner would have done." But, commented Gilman sarcastically, in a broadside at the derivative qualities in the Second Rhapsody, "needless to say, he [Gershwin] gives us, also, music employing those idioms with which, long since, he caught the ear of the world." Olin Downes, in the Times, criticized this self-copying aspect of the work too. Although he found praiseworthy things to say about Koussevitzky's conducting of the Second Rhapsody, as well as about Gershwin's playing of the "modest piano part," Downes was critical of the composition itself. He found it "imitative in many ways of the Rhapsody in Blue," a work he considered "more individual and originative" than the Second Rhapsody. Downes also felt the Second Rhapsody was "too long for its material." Similar negative reactions to the work seemed to be the order of the day. Almost to a man, most first-line critics turned thumbs down on the piece.

And history has not proved them wrong. The work has never caught on through the years. The look-what-a-bright-boy-am-I shrewdness that Gershwin showed by bringing back from Hollywood, along with pocketfuls of movie money, an orchestral piece that eagerly sought to emulate the sure-fire surface mannerisms of the Rhapsody in Blue did not accomplish its ultimate artistic success. To be sure, the piece had all the jazzy, bluesy qualities that are the earmarks of a Gershwin orchestral opus, yet the opportunism that had always played an important part in his career did not pan out in this case. In attempting to capture consciously the hard-driving aspects of Manhattan life reflected on the movie screen, Gershwin came up with less than inspired material. Where the *Rhapsody in Blue* had been almost all instinct and extraordinary, the *Second Rhapsody* was more manipulatively contrived and dull. Especially the so-called rivet theme, all eight square measures of it. Not only are its melodic contours unexceptional, but its rhythmic patterns are monotonous in their insistency. Ironically enough, the technical advances found in his first three orchestral pieces are also noticeable in the *Second Rhapsody,* including increased metric fluidity, emphasis on detail, and thematic modifications that are often ingeniously treated. There are too many instances of intellectual processes at work in the *Second Rhapsody*—such as the breaking down of the rivet theme into more basic musical elements and then juxtaposing and combining these elements in a variety of inventive ways—not to be impressed with Gershwin's growing technical strength as a composer. Moreover, the overall structural design of the piece is simplicity itself. The rivet theme and its variants, plus transitional passages, make up the perimeters and form the bulk of the piece. A slow section, with a vaguely suggestive blues theme, constitutes its middle. A coda containing references to both themes brings the work to a close. This concentration on only two main themes within the framework of a concise three-part form plus coda is still another indication of his improved craftsmanship and increased discipline as an artist. But with all these positive signs, the work is a dud. What it primarily lacks are memorable tunes.

It is somewhat amazing that Gershwin miscalculated so badly in the *Second Rhapsody,* especially since his forte was always the quality of his tunes. He himself had reservations about the work of his leading European counterparts, because in his estimation they frequently lacked this special gift. As he phrased it after listening to a virtuoso orchestral piece by Arthur Honegger, "The European boys have small ideas but they sure know how to dress 'em up."[29] Yet not only were Gershwin's tunes in the *Second Rhapsody* third rate, but his technical expertise even if one takes into account his burgeoning experience in the symphonic field was hardly the equal of his highly trained, superbly equipped European colleagues. Possibly if he had had the technique of an Arthur Honegger, he might have been able sufficiently to "dress up" the *Second Rhapsody* so that it would have seemed better than it really is. But as it stands, the *Second Rhapsody,* despite his own high appraisal of it, marks a decline from the creative heights of the three orchestral pieces that preceded it.

In view of his expressions of satisfaction with it, including its orchestration, it seems incongruous that the published score for the *Second Rhapsody*,[30] put out in 1953, uses an orchestration by composer-arranger Robert McBride, rather than the original one for which Gershwin is credited.[31] The decision to redo the orchestration of the *Second Rhapsody* was made by Frank Campbell-Watson, music editor from 1932 to 1965 of New World Music, the publisher of Gershwin's symphonic scores.[32] As a matter of fact, Campbell–Watson is responsible for revisions in the published scores of all Gershwin's symphonic works written after the *Rhapsody in Blue*—that is, from the *Concerto in F* on. Neither the *Concerto* nor the symphonic works that followed it were published in their orchestral version during Gershwin's lifetime,[33] so he was not directly involved with these changes. But since the revisions in these published scores, except for those in the *Second Rhapsody,* were mainly simple editorial changes dealing with accents, slurs, bowings, tempo and dynamic indications, and some minor instrumentation modifications, one might reasonably assume that Gershwin would have approved of them. It is extremely questionable, however, whether he would have authorized a complete change of orchestration in the *Second Rhapsody,* by Robert McBride or anyone else.[34] For Gershwin was always sensitive to innuendoes that he could not orchestrate. At every opportunity, either he or a spokesman would proclaim that he could, and did, orchestrate his own music—both the large-scale works and some tunes for shows—notwithstanding published declarations to the contrary by such doubting Thomases as A. Walter Kramer or Allan Lincoln Langley. With that in mind, Campbell-Watson's statement, made years after Gershwin's death, as justification for reorchestrating the *Second Rhapsody* for publication, aside from its obvious inaccuracies, seems at the least a gross rationalization, if not just plain double-talk. According to Campbell-Watson, shortly before Gershwin died, he and the composer had "held a series of conferences having to do with the revision and reorchestrating of the major Gershwin works," including the *Second Rhapsody.* As Campbell-Watson tells it, with the implication that his opinions reflect Gershwin's as well, "The score [for the *Second Rhapsody*] was not completely finished. It was temporary; and in its existing form there were but few pianists and orchestras close enough to the work to negotiate the hurdles offered by the many structural barbed wire fences."[35] In Campbell-Watson's words, McBride's orchestration of the *Second Rhapsody* only "followed the preconceived plan."[36] But what he did not say in his pronunciamento was that he had asked McBride in 1952 to reorchestrate the work simply because, in his opinion, "Gershwin was not a good orchestrator."[37]

In rescoring the *Second Rhapsody* at Campbell-Watson's bidding,

McBride followed Gershwin's manuscript closely and used an orchestra identical to the composer's. Moreover, though McBride made changes in instrumentation as well as octave placement, chordal spacing, and part-leading to some extent—revisions not dissimilar to those Grofé made when he first orchestrated the *Rhapsody in Blue* for Whiteman's concert—he did not tamper with the overall structure of the piece and left the solo piano part intact.[38] Also, McBride's basic orchestral color conceptions followed those in Gershwin's score so that the "Gershwin" personality in the piece is not materially affected by the revisions. One might thus easily consider McBride's reorchestration more a breach of the spirit than a radical over-hauling of the piece. This point is strengthened by the fact that the revised published orchestration has helped not a whit to increase the popularity of the *Second Rhapsody*, or to compensate for the relative lack of inspiration in this product of Gershwin's Hollywood muse. Since it is clear in retrospect that it would take more than orchestration to save the piece, the decision to revise the original orchestration of the *Second Rhapsody* seems more questionable than ever.

Gershwin.

LATIN FROM
MANHATTAN

ALWAYS ONE TO make a big splash, Gershwin caused his customary stir when in quick succession *Delicious* was released to the public on December 3, 1931, and *Of Thee I Sing* opened on Broadway a few weeks later, on December 26. Cocky as ever, he could hardly contain himself as he spoke boastingly of both the show and the film in a letter to a friend on January 2, 1932. "The New Year is here," he wrote. "*Of Thee I Sing* is the town's big hit, having gotten the most sensational reviews of many a day from the New York critics." As for the film, he crowed, "The picture, *Delicious*, has just turned in the best week's receipts in three years (since *Cock Eyed World*)."[1]

Delicious may have gotten off to a good start at the box office and gladdened his heart in so doing, but it was anything but a good movie. "Civilization hasn't had such a setback since the Dark Ages," was the vitriolic report on the film in *Outlook and Independent*. Nor was this an isolated comment. For the film was claptrap, pure and simple, nothwithstanding the ticket-selling value of the names Janet Gaynor, Charles Farrell, and George and Ira Gershwin appended to it. As for Gershwin's score, about the only thing one could say of it was that it was easily forgettable. Little of the orchestral rhapsody was heard, and the few tunes used in the film seemed to fade into the artificial Hollywood studio scenery with the

211

unobtrusiveness and lack of impact common to many a vacuous product of the Hollywood assembly line. Not that Gershwin hadn't tried to have his music stand out more effectively. He had expected to return to Hollywood, after his initial stay there, to help in what he hoped would be the transformation of his musical contribution into something bigger than life on the screen. He had even recorded the tunes for the studio while in Hollywood, so that their appropriate styles and tempos could be properly absorbed into the film. (For the recording, Gershwin at the piano accompanied a then relatively little-known singer, Bing Crosby, who was paid all of fifty dollars for his efforts; unfortunately, this historic recording of Gershwin and Crosby has been lost.) But his effort was to no avail. Once he had returned to New York he was never called back to assist in the realization of the final musical product. Unlike Broadway musicals, where George and Ira invariably took an active part in shaping them into a personal reflection, anonymous Hollywood hands reduced the *Delicious* score to an amorphous musical blob that carried little of the Gershwin imprint.

The score of *Of Thee I Sing* was another matter. George and Ira had collaborated closely with George S. Kaufman and Morrie Ryskind from the early planning stages of the show. Thus, when the Gershwins left for Hollywood in November 1930, they could take with them a fourteen-page outline of its book and even work on two of the tunes for the show while in California. Back in New York, between his involvement with the *Second Rhapsody* and various other chores that always intruded on his hectic personal and professional life, Gershwin continued writing the score for *Of Thee I Sing* with Ira, in frequent consultation with Kaufman and Ryskind. By the time this musical, inimitably directed by Kaufman himself, opened in Boston on December 8, 1931, things were well in hand, as it spun off the stage of the Majestic Theater with the striking force of a Kansas cyclone gone haywire in Back Bay territory. Proper Bostonians may not have been fully prepared for the outrageously impudent, no-holds-barred views of Washington politics, presidential campaigns, and the country's manipulative electorate aired in *Of Thee I Sing,* but they flocked to see the show nevertheless, as it played to packed houses.

Word of mouth[2] and good Boston notices helped pave the way for an equally warm welcome at Broadway's Music Box Theater on December 26, 1931, when *Of Thee I Sing* opened to a glittering first-night audience that included politicians Jimmy Walker and Al Smith, social figures Otto Kahn and Jules Glaenzer, and hundreds of other celebrities. Clearly, many of the luminaries present were favorably disposed to the show, for they appeared to vie with one another in boisterously showing their appreciation for the score, the proceedings on stage, and Gershwin's baton-wielding in the pit. (Gershwin, not unexpectedly, was front and center on opening night, lending the weight of his name and public personality to the performance, while lapping up the bravos showered on him as both conductor and composer.) The reviewers, too, seemed to fall all over themselves in lauding the show. With few exceptions, they had high praise for the brainchild of Kaufman, Ryskind, and the Gershwins. As George Jean Nathan described it, the show was a "landmark in American satirical comedy," while Brooks Atkinson labeled it "a taut and lethal satire on national politics."

Of Thee I Sing gleefully tore into the behind-the-scenes machinations that go into the making of an American president by political bosses, those party-hack piranhas of smoke-filled rooms and ill repute. To fulfill their political needs, the bosses choose as a candidate one John P. (for "Peppermint") Wintergreen, forceful and outspoken, a manly symbol attractive to young and old. As a vote-getting maneuver, they come up with a platform for Wintergreen virtually impossible to fault: a "love" ticket. For Wintergreen, the electorate is told, is "the man the people choose," one who "loves the Irish and the Jews"—and everyone else.

All the loud and showy—and phony—hoopla surrounding political campaigning is incisively captured in the musical's opening torchlight parade. Amidst an air of exultant optimism, of band playing, of shouting and banner waving by the party's faithful (the banners proclaimed such less than reverent slogans as "Wintergreen—the Flavor Lasts," "Even Your Dog Loves Wintergreen," "Vote for Prosperity—and See What You Get," and "A Vote for Wintergreen Is a Vote for Wintergreen"), mass hysteria gradually takes over.[3] Adding impetus to the frenzy, by serving as a musical rallying cry, is the campaign chant, "Wintergreen for President," repeated several times by Wintergreen supporters against the noisy background. In its own way, "Wintergreen for President"—short and readily identifiable with the American presidential candidate it represents—is the ultimate in political theme songs. Yet its genesis was far removed indeed from American politics, inasmuch as it was conceived with old Middle Europe in mind. For Gershwin had originally written it in the mid-1920s as a pseudo-medieval march, titled "Trumpets of Belgravia," for *The Big Charade,* a musical that never got on the boards. Reminded of this long-forgotten tune by Ira while working on the score for *Of Thee I Sing,* George quickly adopted it as Wintergreen's own, despite its Old World musical implications. For that matter, that incongruously Oriental-sounding, sing-song vocal patter Gershwin added to "Love Is Sweeping the Country," also part of the *Of Thee I Sing* score, was taken from Ziegfeld's ill-fated *East Is West.* But no matter how far removed the original source or stimulation for his material may have been from the way it was ultimately used, as a busy professional he never hesitated to draw on anything that served his purpose, wherever he found it, even if it was not always the ultimate in musical refinement.[4]

One of the key stratagems in Wintergreen's bid for the presidency revolved around an Atlantic City beauty contest he and his advisers concoct for publicity. As an incentive for the contestants, a unique reward is promised the first-prize winner: she will marry Wintergreen and become first lady when he is elected. The plan backfires when Wintergreen falls in love with his secretary, sweet homespun Mary Turner, a whiz at making corn muffins, instead of the shapely contest winner Diana Devereux. But despite his change of heart, Wintergreen rallies the voters around him with his campaign slogan: "Lovers! Vote for John and Mary!" It acts as a clarion call for all the romantically inclined, as the "love" plank sweeps the country on election day, carrying Wintergreen and his ticket into office. Shortly afterward, in response to the mandate of the electorate, Wintergreen combines his presidential inauguration with his marriage to Mary. Before the august body of the Supreme Court, members of Congress, and numerous dignitaries and guests, the two are united in matrimony at the same time Wintergreen is sworn in as chief executive.

All does not remain calm and serene for the newlyweds for long. A major complication develops when the French government through its ambassador in Washington protests Wintergreen's ill treatment of Diana Devereux. By jilting her he has struck a heavy blow to France's pride, particularly since she can trace her heritage to the Bonapartes. Miss Devereux, we are told, is "the illegitimate daughter of an illegitimate son of an illegitimate nephew of Napoleon." International tension mounts over the incident. When Wintergreen refuses to divorce Mary to marry Miss Devereux, under pressure from Washington and France,[5] his political fate hangs in the balance as the Senate meets to consider his impeachment. Just when they are only a few votes shy of impeaching Wintergreen and things look very bleak for him, Mary saves the day by dramatically announcing from the Senate floor that she is soon to become a mother. Like rays of sunshine filtering through Stygian darkness, her news causes a turnabout of opinion. Never ones to trifle with motherhood, the Senate as one man reverses itself. Impeachment proceedings are dropped as all rush to congratulate the expectant parents. Even the Supreme Court, lending the weight of its judicial authority, enters the picture to express its preference for the sex of the awaited child.

Practically nothing in American politics was sacred to the authors as they nimbly castigated farcical conditions in the day-to-day affairs of government: the pervasive influence of insidious political bosses; the unscrupulous selection and manipulation of candidates; the gobbledygook and inane clichés of political prose; the chaotic circus atmosphere of party meetings and campaigning; the irrational, unprincipled behavior of all too many government officials; the argumentative yet dullard mentality often displayed in Congress; the cardboard facade and lack of power of the vice-presidency; the juridical absurdities of the black-robed men of the Supreme Court. These and other realities of American political life were but sitting ducks for the satirical shotguns of Kaufman and Ryskind, who were aided by the sharply honed Gershwin score. No government official, institution, or practice was inviolate to their scathing collective thrusts.

The saucy, bright-eyed cast kept the mad pace going with little letup as they spewed forth the impertinent lines with the inevitability and highly controlled casualness one expects of high comedy in the best tradition. There was a contagious, joyous lilt to their acting and a naturalness of speech and movement common to seasoned troupes who have played together for years, often lacking in companies assembled for one particular show, as was the case for *Of Thee I Sing*. Leading the zany tactics on stage as the romantic leads were William Gaxton as irrepressible John P. Wintergreen[6] and Lois Moran as faithful Mary Turner. As a comic and political foil to Gaxton's vigorous portrayal of Wintergreen was sad-faced, quavery-voiced, slow-moving Victor Moore, as the meek, much-abused Vice-President Alexander Throttlebottom, a man so little known in Washington he has to take a guided tour to gain entrance to the White House. In his quiet, frightened way, Moore was the perfect schlemiel, the butt of everyone's jokes, truly the low man on the political totem pole. Yet so cunningly did he play his role that, nightly, to the degree of sympathy he evoked, he got the loudest laughs in the house. Also contributing to the fun were such fine cast additions as Grace Brinkley, playing Diana Devereux; Florenz Ames, in the role of the French ambassador; and June O'Dea and George Murphy[7] as political associates of Wintergreen.

The Gershwin score not only held its own with the cast and the script, but it helped to unify the many disparate elements—the singing, dancing, acting, direction, and plot content—that go into the making of a first-rate musical. Actually, the score was the focal point of the production. Besides integrating the book with the purely musical and dancing elements of the show by providing an attractive, cogent underpinning for the stage action, it also stood out on its own merit. For its tunes and lyrics were just too good —as memorable and as incisive as one might hope for—to serve merely as a backdrop for the rest of the production, important though that function may be. The inanities of the story, replete with built-in comic situations and carryings-on of all kinds on stage, may have had audiences laughing uproariously while watching the show, but the Gershwin score had a greater

Charles Farrell and
Janet Gaynor, the stars
of *Delicious*, in a scene
from an earlier film,
Street Angel.

Serge Koussevitzky
and Gershwin in Boston
for the premiere of
the *Second Rhapsody*.

carryover once they left the theater, especially if one considers that some of its songs are still popular today, such as "Who Cares?," "Love Is Sweeping the Country," "Wintergreen for President," and the title tune with its outrageous mixture of staid propriety and suggestive earthiness in its opening line: "Of thee I sing," followed by the jivy "baby."[8] Rounding out the score are such lesser-known stalwarts as "The Illegitimate Daughter," "A Kiss for Cinderella" (combining a melody and countermelody), the droll waltz "I'm About to Be a Mother," as well as "Hello, Good Morning," "Because, Because," and "Jilted, Jilted!"[9]

George and Ira had good cause to be pleased with their efforts, for there was greater overall unity between score, book, and stage action in *Of Thee I Sing* than in anything they had done before for the theater, no matter how highly praised. Instead of concentrating on the usual "set" pieces with their customary choruses of thirty-two measures that were generally expected of musical comedy scores, they addressed themselves to creating music and lyrics that closely complemented the dialogue and theatrics of the production, without concerning themselves unduly with the length and shape of the resulting tunes. As Ira put it in describing the flexibility of the score for *Of Thee I Sing:* "In the show there are no verse-and-chorus songs." Because of its expanded scope of expression—greater, surely, than was customary for musical comedy of the time—the score for *Of Thee I Sing* has a certain affinity with operetta, but without many of the shopworn, stultifying elements often associated with this medium. But, then, the Gershwin team had really never been burdened with a sense of historical tradition in their work. In place of tradition, their instincts and pragmatic experience were usually their best creative guides. As is true with many originals, they generally went their own way and made up their own rules as they went along, developing in the process a definite Gershwin style. It is this very combination of personal style and newness of approach that makes the *Of Thee I Sing* score a genuine landmark in musical comedy.

In tribute to its quality, the complete vocal score of *Of Thee I Sing* was published in 1932, the third Gershwin musical-comedy score to receive this distinction.[10] Of even greater significance, the show itself received a Pulitzer prize in drama on May 2, 1932, the first musical comedy to be so honored. "The play is unusual," read the citation that went with the prize. "Its effect on the stage promises to be very considerable." In the competition for the award, *Of Thee I Sing* won out against such highly touted straight dramatic productions as *Mourning Becomes Electra* and *The Animal Kingdom.* Unfortunately for Gershwin, however, the judging committee felt they could not make an award to a composer of a show, no matter how tal-

217

ented, based on Pulitzer rules as they were then constituted. Through a technicality, therefore, his invaluable contribution to the success of *Of Thee I Sing* were completely ignored by the Pulitzer committee.[11] Instead, the prize went only to Kaufman and Ryskind as the authors of the show, and to Ira as its lyricist. Each got an impressive parchment scroll from the trustees of Columbia University enunciating the award, along with a total cash prize of $1,000, which was divided among the three. In dividing the money, Ira and Ryskind conceded the extra penny to Kaufman because he was the eldest of the three.

There were a number of other distinctions that set *Of Thee I Sing* apart from other Gershwin shows. Not the least of these was the publication by Alfred Knopf of the script and lyrics of the show, the first American musical comedy to be published in book form. Under the impetus of all the fanfare surrounding the show, seven printings were needed to keep up with the demand for the book. Moreover, with 441 performances to its credit, *Of Thee I Sing* enjoyed the longest run of all the Gershwin musicals. It was also the only Gershwin show to have two productions running simultaneously. After its initial Broadway run, *Of Thee I Sing* went on a rather lengthy road tour before returning to New York on May 15, 1933. At about the same time this show was back on Broadway, a second company after opening in Chicago was wending its way through the country for a run of nearly eight months.

As if all the kudos lavished on *Of Thee I Sing* were not enough, George and Ira had the added satisfaction of realizing a financial windfall from the show. Not content simply with salary and royalties connected with their score, both Gershwins along with Kaufman and Ryskind had invested in the show with its producer, Sam H. Harris. All reaped large profits from their investments, as the box office jumped with activity despite the Depression.

Another beneficiary of the smash-hit status of *Of Thee I Sing* was tunesmith Irving Berlin, the co-owner with Sam H. Harris of the Music Box Theater, which housed the show in New York. He and Harris, at a cost of $930,000, had built this beautiful theater on West Forty-fifth Street in 1921, both as a business investment and as a necessary addition to the thriving Broadway theatrical scene. Berlin also wrote the music for the first four shows—all hits—that played there: four editions of *Irving Berlin's Music Box Revue*. During the Depression, however, the Music Box like other Broadway theaters felt the effects of the economy as audiences dwindled. Since theaters are usually dependent on a percentage of box-office receipts as the major source of their income, Berlin freely admits, speaking of the

Music Box during those bleak days, "We almost lost it." But thanks to *Of Thee I Sing*, Berlin and Harris were bailed out. The jingle of coin ringing merrily at the box office saved the Music Box for them.

But not all of the stories dealing with *Of Thee I Sing* smacked of success. One that ended in failure concerned a legal action taken in 1932 by Walter Lowenfels, poet and author, against the Gershwins, Kaufman and Ryskind, and those connected with producing the show and publishing its score, book, and lyrics. Lowenfels, down on his luck at the time, charged there were forty pages of similarities between the Kaufman-Ryskind book for *Of Thee I Sing* and his own play *U.S.A. with Music*, written four years earlier, which told of a presidential aspirant who considers running on a platform of companionate marriage. Seeking redress because of plagiarism, Lowenfels in his suit demanded an accounting of the profits for *Of Thee I Sing*, a sum he estimated at close to a million dollars, claiming a share of this income. His bid for reparation, however, was promptly turned down by the presiding judge.[12]

All the profits Lowenfels had sought to share in have not yet stopped for the creators of *Of Thee I Sing*, nor is there an end in sight for mining this theatrical vein of gold. Like a blue-chip annuity, *Of Thee I Sing* long after its opening has continued to earn income for its collaborators. To a greater extent than any other Gershwin musical, American amateur and professional companies have mounted productions of it over the years, especially during election periods or whenever important or unusual political activities make headlines. Yet despite the show's profitability, revivals of *Of Thee I Sing* have not fared very well in New York, the site of its original success. For instance, an updated version of this musical opened at the Ziegfeld Theater on May 5, 1952, with Jack Carson as Wintergreen and Paul Hartman as Throttlebottom, to generally favorable reviews, but the show soon closed for lack of business.[13] What had appeared impudent and bitingly satirical in the 1930s now seemed as tired and lackluster to theatergoers as a thrice-repeated newscast. Another revival on March 7, 1969, off Broadway at the Anderson Theater on Second Avenue, did not even have good reviews to sustain it, despite some fine individual performances by Hal Holden as Wintergreen, Lloyd Hubbard as Throttlebottom, Joy Franz as Mary, and others. It closed quickly for lack of patronage.[14] The book by Kaufman and Ryskind bore the brunt of the criticism of this production from Clive Barnes of the *Times*. "It is not just bad, it is terrible," was Barnes's verdict of the script. Excoriating it further: "Nor is this entirely a matter of changing tastes, except in the respect that we do demand a new standard of wit and even literacy from our musical books nowadays." However, he had only praise for the score: "George and Ira Gershwin remain as fresh as a daisy." Said Barnes of their contributions:

> This is an extraordinarily advanced kind of musical comedy. The Gershwins were here actually straining toward proper, or more likely improper, operetta, and had the courage to use arias, ensembles, even, as unlikely as it sounds, recitatives, and the musical aspect of the show —although very inadequately given—is as new as tomorrow. They don't write musical scores like that anymore, but let's live in hope.[15]

Barnes's pleasure with the score nearly four decades after it was written reflected Gershwin's own opinion of it as well. He considered it, at least as voiced to a number of friends, just about the strongest score he had written for a Broadway show up to then. But satisfaction with his handiwork and the conviction that *Of Thee I Sing* would be at the Music Box for a long run were not enough to keep him from pressing forward with other projects. Shortly after *Of Thee I Sing* opened on Broadway on December 26, 1931, he was already up to his neck getting the *Second Rhapsody* ready for its world premiere in Boston on January 29, 1932, and its New York premiere the following February 5.

Nor did the rest of 1932 see a letup in his normally frenetic pace after the first performances of the *Second Rhapsody* were out of the way. He was as busy as ever working and socializing, though in looking back certain highlights stand out for him that year: the publication of his *Song-Book* with its piano "improvisations"; the start of study with Joseph Schillinger; the writing of *Rumba* for symphony orchestra; his appearance as soloist at Lewisohn Stadium on August 16 in the first all-Gershwin concert ever given; his conducting and performing at the Metropolitan Opera on November 1; and his involvement with *Pardon My English* (it opened in New York on January 20, 1933). With all that, Gershwin also found time during 1932 for a few vacation breaks. On one of these jaunts, he spent a brief period in Havana with Emil Mosbacher and some of his other cronies, basking in the sun, swimming, boating, golfing, gambling, making the rounds of nightspots, and generally leading the good life. Like a conquering hero enjoying the spoils of his victory, Gershwin luxuriated in his worldly and artistic success, from being wildly serenaded in the wee hours of the morning by a sixteen-piece rumba band outside his suite at the stately Almendares Hotel—to the chagrin of other hotel patrons within earshot—to disporting himself with his customarily high and diversified quota of attractive women. There was, nonetheless, one unpleasant moment for him during his Havana stay when a delectable Cuban miss he had just met broke a luncheon appointment with him. According to Bennett Cerf, Gershwin later "spied her on the Yacht Club terrace, and exclaimed, 'Hey,

A "love" rally at Madison Square Garden in *Of Thee I Sing.* Presidential candidate Wintergreen (William Gaxton), with his beloved Mary Turner (Lois Moran) beside him, exhorts the crowd to support him.

An announcement for *Of Thee I Sing* after it had won the Pulitzer Prize.

President Wintergreen (William Gaxton) and Vice-President Throttlebottom (Victor Moore) in *Of Thee I Sing.*

do you know you stood me up today?' 'Oh, I meant to phone and tell you I couldn't meet you,' said the contrite maiden, 'but do you know something? I simply couldn't think of your name!' George didn't recover for days."[16]

Aside from the myriad pleasures of the flesh the Cuban capital had to offer him, Gershwin also wrote his fifth piece for orchestra because of his 1932 visit there. During his rounds of revelry and dancing in Havana, he became so intrigued with various percussion instruments employed in the rumba, such as maracas, bongos, claves (Cuban hardwood sticks, hit together), and the guiro (a serrated gourd, scraped with a wooden stick), he decided to incorporate them into his next symphonic opus, which would evoke Cuban dance. He planned, too, to introduce the work at the all-Gershwin concert at Lewisohn Stadium that summer. Not long after returning to Manhattan from Cuba with some of these percussion instruments in tow as additions to his continually expanding collection of memorabilia, he began writing the piece, called *Rumba* (now better known as *Cuban Overture*). Working rapidly, he sketched the composition during July.[17] He orchestrated it even more quickly, between August 1 and 9,[18] in time for the Stadium concert on August 16.

Preceding his involvement with *Rumba*, he had started studying theory, composition, and orchestration with Schillinger some time in 1932, though it is not known exactly when the lessons were initiated. Speaking of these lessons Schillinger alleged in 1940 that Gershwin was "a very active student for four and a half years" and came to him because

he was at a dead end of creative musical experience. He felt his resources, not his abilities, were completely exhausted. . . . A mutual friend, Joseph Achron, . . . recommended me as teacher to George.

When we met, Gershwin said: "Here is my problem: I have written about seven hundred songs. I can't write anything new anymore. I am repeating myself. Can you help me?" I replied in the affirmative, and a day later Gershwin became a sort of "Alice in Wonderland."

Later on he became acquainted with some of the materials in this book [by Schillinger]. . . . "You don't have to compose music anymore —it's all here," he remarked.[19]

Even if Schillinger's self-proclaimed impact on Gershwin was not so all-embracing and crucial as he has implied and is not taken too literally, it seems clear that Gershwin became intellectually more aware of structural elements in music as a result of his study. This may be inferred from his rather stodgy analysis of *Rumba* for its premiere:

In my composition I have endeavored to combine the Cuban rhythms with my own thematic material. The result is a symphonic overture which embodies the essence of the Cuban dance. It has three main parts.

Some of the doodles
Gershwin made while studying
with Schillinger.

For Joseph Schillinger

In appreciation of his
great talent as a teacher &
with all my best wishes.

George Gershwin

feb. 1936

The signed photograph
Gershwin gave Schillinger.

The first part (moderato e molto ritmato) is preceded by a (forte) introduction featuring some of the thematic material. Then comes a three part contrapuntal episode leading to a second theme. The first part finishes with a recurrence of the first theme combined with fragments of the second.

A solo clarinet cadenza leads to a middle part, which is in a plaintive mood. It is a gradually developing canon in a polytonal manner. This part concludes with a climax based on an ostinato of the theme in the canon, after which a sudden change in tempo brings us back to the rumba dance rhythms.

The finale is a development of the preceding material in a stretto-like manner. This leads us back once again to the main theme.

The conclusion of the work is a coda featuring the Cuban instruments of percussion.

Well in advance of his analysis, while still in the preliminary stages of writing *Rumba*, Gershwin had already casually spelled out his general structural plans for the piece. He did so in pencil on a yellow work sheet, headed "Introduction" (now at the Library of Congress).

He spelled out his broad, general plan in this laconic manner:

INTRODUCTION
Start with ff excerpts of melodic content featuring most rhythmic fundamentals of rumba about 16 bars
subito into first theme
    A—(1) polyphonic episode leading to (B) contrasting theme in manner of 1st theme then polyphonic episode (2) again leading to A plus parts of (B)
        Slow theme
        B—canonic exposition
        ostinato based on B theme[20]

But apart from the light these plans, plus his actual analysis, shed on his preoccupation with structural aspects of *Rumba,* the piece itself shows continued evidence of his technical growth as a composer. Like the *Second Rhapsody,* the overall form of *Rumba* is clear and simple. Within its one-movement framework, it is essentially in three parts, plus an introduction and coda, with a concentration on a limited number of themes and motifs. Aided by the prominent use of percussion instruments, *Rumba* exhibits an increased textural diversity and a greater emphasis on musical detail—including the juxtaposing and combining of themes and motifs, a favorite Gershwin device—than the orchestral works that preceded it. Also, as a result of his efforts at polytonal canon, his harmony in *Rumba* is more freely chromatic and dissonant than usual.[21] But along with these advances, one still finds many of the "Gershwinisms" that were characteristic weaknesses in his scores, such as excessive repetition, both melodic and rhythmic, and a lack of any real development. Often, when he didn't know what to do with his material, he simply repeated it. Nor are the two main themes and subsidiary motifs in the piece particularly outstanding. Though they evoke Cuban dance by their rhythms, accents, and general lack of symmetry, their melodic contours are quite prosaic and dull. Mainly they meander up and down the scale. Certainly most audiences would not leave the concert hall humming the themes. This lack of an incisive profile probably resulted from his marked concern with technique in the piece. In attempting canons and strettos[22] and focusing on other technical matters, possibly to prove something to himself and the world, he may have become overly self-conscious in his writing, inhibiting his normal instinctive musical impulses. Whatever the reason, the *Rumba* tunes have little pizzazz.

Weak though they may be, the melodies for *Rumba* are cloaked in a layer of orchestration that does as well by the tunes as one might expect under the circumstances, for the scoring of *Rumba* is remarkably transparent for Gershwin, though his orchestra is essentially similar to those he used for his other pieces: three flutes (with the third flute doubling on piccolo), two oboes, English horn, two B-flat clarinets, bass clarinet, two bassoons, contrabassoon, four French horns, three B-flat trumpets, three trombones, tuba, timpani, percussion, and strings. The rather wide spectrum of instrumental colors in this composition, enhanced by the underlying sounds and rhythmic momentum of "Cuban" percussion instruments come through with considerable clarity and effectiveness, making *Rumba* a fine display piece for orchestra. The piece is relatively unencumbered by some of the unnecessary trappings; mainly excessive instrumental padding found in his earlier symphonic works. The instrumental transparency in *Rumba* may be traceable to Schillinger, since one of Schillinger's strongest assets, among his other talents as theoretician, composer, and teacher, was his sensitivity to sonorities of all kinds—including those electronically derived—combined with a scientific approach to sound which enabled him to improve the acoustical quality of his students' orchestral pieces through calculated adjustments in instrumentation.[23] Consistent with his expertise in matters of sonority, Schillinger has the distinction of composing the first work for Theremin—one of the earliest of electronic instruments—and orchestra, titled *First Airphonic Suite*. It was performed in Cleveland and New York in 1929 with Leon Theremin, the Russian inventor of the instrument, as soloist.[24]

Rumba received its first public hearing on August 16, 1932 at the Lewisohn Stadium. With Gershwin as soloist in the *Rhapsody in Blue* and the *Second Rhapsody*, and the first all-Gershwin program as bait, still another stadium attendance record was made that mid-August evening. Al-

225

ways concerned with attendance at his concerts—particularly at Lewisohn Stadium, a mammoth barometer of popularity, where it would almost regularly be announced when Gershwin appeared there that he had broken previous records—he could hardly contain his enthusiasm in describing this event in a letter to George Pallay on August 17:

> It was, I really believe, the most exciting night I have ever had, first, because the Philharmonic Orchestra played an entire program of my music, and second, because the all-time record for the Stadium concerts was broken. I have just gotten the figures: 17,845 people paid to get in and just about 5,000 were at the closed gates trying to fight their way in—unsuccessfully.

Albert Coates and Bill Daly shared the podium for the concert, alternating in conducting members of the Philharmonic in the various Gershwin works that included *Concerto in F* and *An American in Paris*. Oscar Levant performed, too. He spelled Gershwin as pianist by playing the solo part in the *Concerto*. But it was Gershwin the composer and performer the crowd had come for, a key point made in a *Musical Courier* review of the concert: "Musical history is replete with examples of composers who, if they did not suffer complete neglect at the hands of their contemporaries, could hope for little more than the encouragement and understanding of an enlightened few. George Gershwin, surveying the throngs who came to hear him, had much for which to be grateful." Grateful, indeed! While he was still around to savor every moment of the public's adulation and, possibly more important to him, to be able to boast about it to his many friends, he was lionized as few composers before or after him. If his contribution to music could be measured solely by the size of Lewisohn Stadium crowds, loudly shouting their approval, he was far and away the front runner in the ranks of the world's leading composers of all time.

Though the brief *Rumba,* judging from applause, was an attractive addition to the first all-Gershwin program, Gershwin himself felt the work suffered from being played outdoors, because its percussion sounds were badly dissipated in the broad expanse of the stadium. That problem did not occur at the next performance of the piece. In a benefit concert at the Metropolitan Opera House the following November 1, Gershwin conducted the new composition and *An American in Paris* as well as playing the solo in the *Concerto* under Bill Daly; Daly also led the orchestra in his own arrangement of four Gershwin songs with Gershwin at the piano.[25] The concert served as the setting for the famous painting by the Mexican artist Siqueiros of Gershwin on stage, alone at the piano, playing for a hoity-toity audience that filled the huge, glowing, many-tiered, horseshoe-shaped house.[26] The occasion also marked the change of title for

226

Rumba to *Cuban Overture*. After considering, Gershwin decided that the title *Rumba* connoted for the general public a piece for dance band, rather than a work for symphony orchestra. It is as *Cuban Overture* that the piece has come to be best known.[27] It is played with moderate frequency and appears most often in all-Gershwin programs—hardly enough to qualify as a staple in the concert repertoire. But irrespective of its standing in the orchestral literature, *Cuban Overture* is still another example of Gershwin's conscious utilization of popular musical elements in a work for symphony orchestra. As such, it is as much representative of Gershwin as his more famous orchestral pieces, but with a new wrinkle, at least for the composer: it attempts to capture the flavor of Cuban dance. The south-of-the-border Latin dance qualities in the piece are as overtly and liberally applied as the jazzy syncopations are in the *Rhapsody in Blue*, and for just as obvious reasons. That the *Cuban Overture* does not come off better than it does may be as much the result of Gershwin's birth and upbringing as anything else. After all, he was only nominally a "Latin" from Manhattan.

Gershwin in his East Side duplex. In the background is his
painting of a Negro girl. *(Courtesy ASCAP)*

IN ANALYSIS

G̲ERSHWIN'S ALMOST INFALLIBLE
golden touch in the theater seemed to have deserted him with *Pardon My
English,* one of the early Broadway casualties of 1933. What made his association with this failure even more ironic was the fact that neither he nor
Ira had wanted to write the score for it in the first place. They had both
been turned off by the personality problems of the hero of the musical, who
was a gentleman at one moment and a thief at another, but were talked into
lending their names to the show by Alex Aarons. He was practically broke
when he approached the Gershwins to do the score. For a number of years,
starting with *Lady, Be Good* in 1924, he and Vinton Freedley had been living high on the theatrical hog as money rolled into their coffers from a succession of hits they had produced. But when the Depression started decimat-
ing legitimate theaters left and right because of insufficient business, they,
like many other Broadway producers, suffered the consequences.[1] By May
1932 they had lost their theater, the Alvin, which reverted to its property
owners. In a bad financial bind at the time they dreamed up *Pardon My
English,* Aarons and Freedley told the Gershwins that if they didn't write
the score for the show its backers would withdraw their support and that
that would probably spell the finish of Aarons and Freedley as a producing
team.

Thus out of sympathy and loyalty to the producers—especially to Aarons, who in 1919 had sponsored *La La Lucille,* Gershwin's first full-scale musical—George and Ira took on the job, though their hearts were definitely not in it. To add to their uneasiness about the project, the script for the show was in bad shape and in an almost constant state of flux during rehearsals and out-of-town tryouts, necessitating numerous changes in the score as well. Starting with the writing-team nucleus of Morrie Ryskind and Herbert Fields, the producers worriedly brought in other librettists to help doctor the ailing book. But the hoped-for miracle of script resuscitation did not materialize, though Aarons and Freedley went through a covey of writers with the speed and ruthlessness of a tropical tidal wave during the show's various road stops in Philadelphia, Boston, and Brooklyn. By the time *Pardon My English* reached New York, of all the writers only Herbert Fields had survived the ordeal. Fields also had courage to match his staying power. He bravely allowed himself to be billed as the librettist on record for this not too promising addition to Broadway.

The plot, to put it mildly, was a mishmash of inconsequentiality: the handsome hero, a kleptomaniac as a result of blows on the head, marries the pretty daughter of a Dresden police commissioner; she is kidnapped by crooks; she is rescued; people continually fall in and out of love; and the hero is cured of his stealing proclivity by further blows on the head. The hodgepodge plot was more than matched by the babel of accents on stage: Lyda Roberti's goulash-flavored Hungarian; Jack Pearl's pig-knuckle German;[2] George Givot's comic Greek; and so on, The noted British comedian Jack Buchanan had originally been signed by Aarons to play the hero's role. But sensing impending disaster, he wisely left the show while it was still playing in Boston, though he had to pay heavily for the privilege of buying back his contract.[3]

As advance promotion for *Pardon My English,* it was announced in the New York press that the highest-priced seat for the show would be three dollars, a low tariff then for a Gershwin musical, and that the composer himself would conduct the orchestra for the opening-night performance at the Majestic Theater on January 20, 1933. Neither ploy had much effect on the ultimate success of the show. It was poorly received and closed quickly, after only forty-six performances. The do-or-die gamble by Aarons and Freedley to recoup some of their past losses and at the same time to remain leaders in their field did not pan out; *Pardon My English* quickly went down the theatrical drain. Because of the show's early collapse, Aarons and Freedley were forced to break up as a producing team under the pressure of mounting debts. Freedley even left the country for a while to get away from clamoring creditors. But his recuperative powers were such that

230

by 1934 he was back in harness again, but this time on his own as producer. His production that year of *Anything Goes,* with a book by Guy Bolton and P. G. Wodehouse and a score by Cole Porter, was a smash hit. He followed that up in 1936 with another Porter musical, *Red, Hot and Blue,* starring Ethel Merman, Jimmy Durante, and Bob Hope. It was also a hit, and there was no stopping him. With these two new successes to his credit, he was on the top rung of Broadway producers once more. He continued to produce actively on Broadway until 1950, when he turned his talents to various administrative and charitable pursuits for the theater.[4]

Unlike Freedley, Aarons never really recovered from the effects of their breakup as a team. *Pardon My English* turned out to be his last show on Broadway. He eventually moved out to the West Coast, where he held relatively minor jobs with Metro and RKO before signing with Warner Brothers to assist in the production of *Rhapsody in Blue,* the Hollywood style film on Gershwin. But his sudden death of a heart attack in 1943 at the age of fifty-two, before the movie could be made, denied him this additional and somewhat sentimental association with a name so closely linked with his.

Aarons and Freedley's assorted difficulties as a result of the poor showing of *Pardon My English* did not carry over to George and Ira. The flop status of this musical, with nary a hit tune among the lot written for it, caused no major financial or career problems for the Gershwins. From a financial standpoint, each was still getting a large paycheck regularly from *Of Thee I Sing,* as well as royalties from their other scores and tunes. And as professionals, the brothers were too strongly entrenched in their field and too highly respected to be seriously affected by the fate of one musical. Moreover, irrespective of the ineptitudes of the book and the production, the music for *Pardon My English* was never less than competent. Gershwin even spoke up for the score, judging from this story by Bennett Cerf: "One day, I happened to remark that the score of one of his infrequent failures, *Pardon My English,* was below par. George demurred. All of us were sun bathing in the nude; George insisted that we all go inside while he proved his point by going through the score from opening chorus to finale. I can still see him sitting at the piano, stark naked, playing the songs and singing them too at the top of his voice."[5] Ira, too, made some favorable comments about the score: "I've never known of any theatrical failure where, sooner or later, an author or the stage manager or one of the backers or some members of the cast didn't reminisce to the effect that there were some pretty good things in it. So, I must add: there were a couple of pretty good songs, like 'Isn't It a Pity?' and 'My Cousin in Milwaukee,' . . . in *Pardon My English.*"[6] To which one might also add these tunes: "So

231

What?," "Lorelei," "Where You Go I Go," "Luckiest Man in the World," and "I've Got to Be There."

The same period that witnessed the quick obliteration of *Pardon My English* and its producing team, and the continued devastating toll on the economy by the seemingly fathomless Depression, also saw Gershwin move in the late spring of 1933 to a considerably larger, more luxurious apartment than the penthouse he had had on Riverside Drive—one more appropriate for a leading Broadway tunesmith and symphonic composer with a yearly income in six figures. The new apartment, a huge fourteen-room duplex at 132 East Seventy-second Street, was impeccably furnished in conservative taste, a noticeable change from the severe "modernity" of the penthouse. His extensive art collection and his own paintings were proudly exhibited in its cavernous recesses, which included a "trophy" room for his memorabilia, a gymnasium, an English den, an art studio, a mammoth paneled living room, an ample dining room, and a reception room.[7] By any standards, it was an impressive showplace. But for all its elegance, it had many of the display aspects of the previous penthouse about it, especially since Gershwin for months after he moved in evinced great delight in taking his guests on a guided "tour" of the new apartment. With obvious pride, he pointed out its many features, among them its sleeping porch; its garden; a special writing desk made for him, complete with drop leaves, panels and other appendages; a variety of shelves and racks for his music; and a work cubicle for playing the piano in privacy, similar to those Broadway song pluggers used when he had started at Remick's. Like many another self-made man, Gershwin was anything but blasé about his luxurious apartment and his other impressive acquisitions.

Taking his lead from George, Ira also left Riverside Drive for the East Side. He and Leonore moved to a building across the street from George, at 125 East Seventy-second Street. Whereas before George and Ira shared adjoining terraces, they were now separated by asphalt pavement. But it hardly made any difference in their relationship. They were as close as ever, both at work and socially.

The first musical to come from their pens while living on Seventy-second Street was *Let 'Em Eat Cake,* a sequel to *Of Thee I Sing,* with the Gershwins again joining forces with George S. Kaufman and Morrie Ryskind. As before, Sam H. Harris was producer and Kaufman, director. There was a carryover in the casting as well. William Gaxton continued in the role of John P. Wintergreen, once more Lois Moran was his wife, Mary, and Victor Moore played the lovable stumblebum Throttlebottom as drolly as ever. The similarities between the two musicals just about ended there. For unlike *Let 'Em Eat Cake, Of Thee I Sing* under its layers of

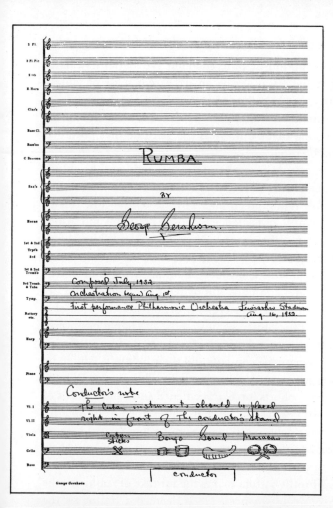

RUMBA

BY

George Gershwin.

Composed July, 1932.
Orchestration begun Aug. 1st.
First performance Philharmonic Orchestra Lewisohn Stadium
Aug. 16, 1932.

Conductor's note
The Cuban instruments should be placed
right in front of the conductor's stand.

Cuban
Sticks   Bongo   Gourd   Maracas

conductor

George Gershwin

Gershwin's title page
for *Rumba,* complete
with his comments
and drawings.

Siqueiros's painted version
of Gershwin performing
at the Metropolitan
Opera House.
(Peter A. Juley and Son)

caustic cynicism was gently optimistic in its spoofing. No matter how hard-hitting or satirical it got, there was always an irreverent sense of fantasy about *Of Thee I Sing* that was beguiling. *Let 'Em Eat Cake,* however, despite its many comical situations, was almost consistently pessimistic at its core. "Down with ev'rything that's up!"[8] was the attitude that prevailed through the scrim of laughter that surrounded it. The plot for *Let 'Em Eat Cake,* no matter how ludicrously dressed up, was not only anti-Establishment but also basically anarchistic in spirit.

In *Let 'Em Eat Cake,* Wintergreen and Throttlebottom lose out in their bid for reelection. John P. Tweedledee is chosen President and brings in his own political crew to run the country. Now out of the White House and forced to fend for themselves, the Wintergreens after borrowing money from pliable Throttlebottom start a business manufacturing blue shirts, on New York's Union Square, a famous site of political ferment and debate. They do badly at first until Wintergreen dreams up the idea of a revolution, by an army of Blue Shirts, against those in charge of government. The plan is put into action and gains momentum. Besides selling his shirts to hordes of Union Square malcontents and their followers, all led by professional agitator Kruger (aggressively played by Phil Loeb), Wintergreen and his revolutionary cohorts force Tweedledee and company out of office and set up a Blue Shirt fascist state. Once in power, the revolutionaries demand payment of past war debts owed by foreign nations. When they refuse, a baseball game is arranged between their representatives and members of the Supreme Court to settle the matter, with Throttlebottom selected as umpire. Slow-witted Throttlebottom makes the mistake of ruling for the opposition, with disastrous consequences. He is deemed a traitor by the revolutionaries and sentenced to death on the guillotine *à la* French Revolution (consistent, of course, with the title of the show). Brought to the chopping block before an angry, unruly mob eager for his blood, Throttlebottom is ready to be decapitated when Mary Wintergreen helps save his head. She and a group of friends suddenly appear to put on a sparkling fashion show for the bloodthirsty throng. The mob is diverted by the sight of pretty women attractively attired, and its mood changes. Throttlebottom is saved and eventually becomes President, as democracy is restored. John and Mary Wintergreen go back to making shirts, this time presumably for peaceful purposes.

The angry tone of *Let 'Em Eat Cake* did not endear it to reviewers when it opened at New York's Imperial Theater on October 21, 1933. "Dull and dreary" was the verdict of the production in *Newsweek,* while Brooks Atkinson in a majority opinion registered this complaint about the librettists: "Their hatreds have triumphed over their sense of humor."

Nor did the Gershwin score win many friends, though it had much to commend it. As in *Of Thee I Sing*, the music and lyrics for *Let 'Em Eat Cake* neatly matched the Kaufman-Ryskind script, from the smug pomposities in "The Union League," tiredly voiced by well-to-do octogenarians of an "exclusive" men's club, to the fire-and-brimstone denunciations of everything and everybody by agitator Kruger and his henchmen in "Union Square," to the merits of the color blue, in "Blue, Blue, Blue,"[9] expounded by the wives of Wintergreen's supporters, to Wintergreen's expressions of love and devotion for his wife, Mary, in "Mine," with its tenaciously repetitive countermelody sung by an ensemble of his followers. Gershwin himself thought very highly of the score, particularly its contrapuntal aspects. In discussing the score for the press, he stated, somewhat murkily: "I've written most of the music for this show contrapuntally, and it is this very insistence on the sharpness of a form that gives my music the acid touch it has—which points the words of the lyrics, and is in keeping with the satire of the piece. At least, I feel that it is the counterpoint which helps me do what I am trying to do." Actually, with the notable exception of the melody-countermelody format of "Mine," the amount of counterpoint in the score is considerably less extensive than Gershwin has indicated. Though several numbers in the show, such as "Union Square," alternated solo and ensemble passages, they did not really combine separate melodies, as did "Mine," and are thus not contrapuntal in the usual sense. But if his statement is not wholly accurate, it at least reflects his heightened interest at that time in technical matters.

As it had *Of Thee I Sing*, Knopf published the book and lyrics for *Let 'Em Eat Cake* in 1933, but the public largely ignored the volume. As for the show itself, with few words of praise from the press to help sustain it, it closed after only ninety performances. And an attempted road tour of *Let 'Em Eat Cake* did even worse. The failure of both *Pardon My English* and *Let 'Em Eat Cake* in succession may not have had any noticeable effect on Gershwin's standard of living, but it may very well have contributed to his decision to undergo psychoanalysis in 1934. In an attempt to relieve anxiety and depression and the chronic constipation that bothered him, he started seeing Dr. Gregory Zilboorg (1890–1959), a distinguished psychiatrist and psychoanalyst who had treated a long list of wealthy and famous patients.

Gershwin's need for psychiatric help had not developed overnight; it had been a long time brewing. Though he seemed to be the personification of exuberant confidence and self-satisfaction to many who knew him, he had had his moments of despondency and apprehension over the years, certainly from young adulthood on. Some of his friends recall that as early as 1919 he had shown signs of anxiety and despair at times, away from the public spotlight, as he nervously fretted about some real or imaginary obstacle blocking what he felt to be his predestined road to fame and fortune. However, in the more typical social situation, especially after he had established himself, he invariably appeared to be the antithesis of uncertainty and dejection. The center of attention wherever he went and doted on by his admirers, he was generally considered to be too much the star, too much the front-page demigod to be afflicted with some of the psychic ills that trouble lesser mortals. Yet surely many of the turnabout traits of his character—at one instant, charming and demure, at another, vain and boorish—that lurked under the surface of his public personality were indeed indicative of problems tormenting the inner man, as were his innumerable transitory relations with women and his inability to form a lasting union with any of them. Some insight into his troubled private self can be deduced from Rouben Mamoulian's description of his initial meeting with him in 1923 at a Rochester tavern, the Corner Club. There, in the company of pianist Artur Rubinstein, conductor-composer Eugene Goossens, and others, Mamoulian recalls that his "first impression of Gershwin during that evening was that of a rather worried and anxious young man—very ambitious and not very happy. Rather reserved and self-centered and in some curious way suspicious of the world, looking not unlike a child with more apples than he can comfortably hold in his hands and afraid that someone would take them away from him."[10]

The anxiety and insecurity Mamoulian sensed in Gershwin back in 1923 may have also helped trigger his persistent case of "composer's stomach." Gershwin himself always maintained that he first became troubled with chronic constipation in 1922 as a consequence of tensions built up during the preparations for the Broadway opening—as part of the 1922 *Scandals*—of his little jazz opera *Blue Monday*. In an attempt to alleviate his digestive infirmity, he became almost a fanatic about his diet, limiting himself mainly to the simplest and blandest of foods. He experimented, too, with a variety of fad diets to cure his condition, but nothing seemed to help. Despite his excellent overall good health and the great care expended on his diet and general well-being, his intestinal difficulty never really left him.

But possibly nothing would have helped him. According to some of his friends, he was too much the hypochondriac under the outer shell of driving energy, great physical strength, and enthusiasm not to be troubled with some aspects of his health. Where he perhaps differed in his symptoms from other hypochondriacs was his inordinate concern with his alimentary tract and his great emphasis on diet as a cure. However, irrespective of his particular hypochondriacal syndrome, it would appear in retrospect that there was an almost cause-and-effect relationship between his basic lack of inner security and his overt concern with health. For at just about the point when Gershwin scored his first major breakthrough in his career and was well on his way to conquering the world, his "composer's stomach" started acting up. And ironically enough, no matter how much his fame and wealth increased, these symptoms never disappeared or improved with any consistency.

It was while surrounded by all the accouterments of worldly success in his huge duplex on Seventy-second Street that he became a patient of Zilboorg. Just prior to seeing Zilboorg, he had complained to a number of intimate friends that he did not feel up to par: he was not sleeping or eating well and had lost some of his zest for life. One close acquaintance even remembers Gershwin's telephoning him unexpectedly to ask if he would come right over to join him for dinner at the Seventy-second Street apartment because he was low in spirits and didn't want to eat alone.[11]

In Zilboorg, Gershwin found someone who was exceptional on many levels, aside from his outstanding credentials as a psychiatrist and analyst. Zilboorg was practically a modern-day version of a Renaissance man. Before coming to the United States in 1919, he had at first been a physician in the Russian army. He subsequently served as secretary to the Minister of Labor in the cabinet of Aleksandr Feodorovich Kerenski, the moderate socialist who briefly took over as provisional Russian premier in July 1917, before being overthrown by Lenin and the Bolsheviks in the October Revolution of 1917.[12] Forced to leave Russia in 1917, Zilboorg finally settled in New York, where his numerous talents ultimately came to the fore: he was a Cordon Bleu chef of distinction; he spoke at least eight languages fluently; he was an authority on Byzantine church art; he was a highly respected photographer as well as a fine craftsman in metal and wood; and he was a member of learned societies in a host of nations. In his own field, he wrote voluminously: scientific papers, scholarly treatises, and textbooks, including *A History of Medical Psychiatry,* a major history of psychiatry written in English.[13]

During the year or so that Gershwin was Zilboorg's patient, their relationship was an exceptionally good one. Besides his respect for Zilboorg's professional skills, there were many areas of common interest because of the psychiatrist's broad background in art and related fields. As in many analyst-patient relationships, Gershwin came to lean quite heavily on Zilboorg for psychological support, as his frequent visits would suggest. Except when conflicts of schedule between them or unusual circumstances dictated otherwise, he saw Zilboorg five times a week, an hour at each session, during the period he was a patient. The fine rapport between them is also attested to by the vacation trip they made together to Mexico in 1935, along with Edward Warburg[14] (the son of Felix Warburg of the well-known banking family), then director of the American Ballet School. Warburg was also in analysis with Zilboorg at the time.

While on this trip, which lasted from late November to mid-December 1935, Gershwin spent some time with Siqueiros and Diego Rivera. One of the highlights of the trip occurred when Gershwin and his party were all invited to a dinner at which both artists were to be present. While Gershwin and young Warburg were delighted at the invitation, Zilboorg had some reservations beforehand about the dinner. He worried that the two radically oriented, outspoken Mexicans, brooking no opposition to their individual brands of social reform, would argue violently or precipitate a torrid controversy with others of differing political persuasions. Steeped in pre-Lenin revolutionary politics of Russia, Zilboorg, fearing the worst, came to dinner armed with a gun for self-protection. Fortunately for all the guests, no political tempers flared; nothing untoward happened during the meal.

As a memento of his stay in Mexico, Gershwin had hoped that Rivera would paint his portrait and suggested as much to the artist. But, for whatever the reason, Rivera did not do so. Gershwin then simply reversed the artist-sitter roles one might normally expect in these circumstances: he did a colored-pencil drawing of Rivera. On finishing the drawing, he showed it to Rivera, who smiled graciously and then wrote at the top of the portrait, "Encantado de poser para George," followed by his signature. Though Rivera said very little about the merits of the drawing, Gershwin later made a point of telling friends how highly it had been praised. For just as he had promulgated favorable stories about himself relating to his studying with various celebrated musicians, Gershwin here, too, presented himself in a more attractive light than the situation warranted.

Nor was Gershwin so circumspect as he might have been at a press conference held on his return from Mexico to New York on December 17, 1935, via the Grace liner *Santa Paula*. (Besides reporters, Gershwin, as befitted a returning composer-hero, was also met at the boat's West Twenty-first Street pier by the entire company of *Porgy and Bess*, who had just completed their seventy-fifth performance of the work.) To an attentive press, listening eagerly to his every word, he spoke out on a number of subjects. Somewhat surprising was his newfound awareness—perhaps resulting from concentrated exposure to the leftist opinions of Rivera and Siqueiros—of things political, as he suggested zealous liberal sentiments: "I am going to interest myself in politics, and it is true that in Mexico I talked a great deal with Diego Rivera and with his radical friends, who discussed at length their doctrines and their intentions."[15] About his future goals as a composer, he naïvely had this to say: "I'm going to try to develop my brains more in music to match my emotional development." Also aired was his less than generous evaluation of Mexican music. Speaking with the cumulative weight of authority of someone in his position, he stated that his most recent trip to Mexico had given him his first chance to study the country's people and music, something he had not been able to do while briefly visiting Agua Caliente during his stay in Hollywood for *Delicious*. He had left for Mexico several weeks earlier, he noted, with the hope of bringing back new ideas for use in his own music based on what he heard there; that is, possibly returning with the Mexican equivalent of *Rumba,* whose genesis dated from his Havana vacation. With this in mind, he had visited innumerable cafés and had attended many concerts of music by native composers while in Mexico City. However, he was wholly unimpressed with what he heard. Mexican music held nothing of merit for him, he announced. In his considered judgment, Mexican music was too monotonous.[16]

Shortly after the Mexican trip, Gershwin ended his sessions with Zilboorg after about a year of treatment, during which time he had complained impatiently to friends that his analysis was not benefiting him so much as he would have liked and was more drawn out than he had anticipated. Contrary to reports that Gershwin and Zilboorg parted unamiably, the two remained on friendly terms after Gershwin discontinued his analysis, but their relationship was, of course, altered by the fact that they no longer saw each other nearly daily and that Zilboorg was no longer privy to Gershwin's most intimate and revelatory confidences. There was sufficient good will between the two, however, so that after Gershwin suffered a brief blackout while appearing with the Los Angeles Philharmonic in February 1937, he felt free to call Zilboorg in New York to discuss the matter and to solicit his professional opinion. Moreover, when Gershwin became gravely ill later that year while in Hollywood, it was Zilboorg who recommended Dr. Ernest Simmel, a California psychiatrist-psychoanalyst, to look after him. Zilboorg also gave Simmel the benefit of his advice, based on his earlier treatment of Gershwin.

Another questionable report pertaining to Gershwin's psychoanalysis has attributed to Zilboorg the opinion that the composer adored his father, not his mother, and that had the reverse been true he would have been a gross neurotic.[17] Among those questioning this opinion attributed to Zilboorg is his former wife, Mrs. Ray Zilboorg. She was not only married to Zilboorg during the period he treated Gershwin,[18] but she also knew the composer and his parents. In her judgment, the conclusion attributed to Zilboorg runs counter to facts. She maintains, too, that Zilboorg was punctilious about observing the code of ethics for psychoanalysts by never discussing publicly his patients' cases in specific terms. Any assessment of Gershwin's relationship with his parents, furthermore, must take his own sentiments into account. As already stated, he felt much closer to his mother and resembled her more in overall character and personality than his father.

Where Zilboorg has publicly discussed the psychology of the creative personality—presumably including Gershwin's—he has done so in the broadest of terms. Speaking at a so-called creativity conference in 1958, sponsored by the Art Directors Club of New York, Zilboorg made such general statements as these:

> The great majority of artists, writers, musicians, creative people, when they have a neurosis, are afraid to be treated. . . . This suggests that the artist, the writer, the painter, the musician, are cherishing something, they know not what, which they are afraid to expose to the gaze of the world and, at the same time, are afraid to have touched by anyone. . . .
>
> One of the outstanding features of an artist is that if he does know what he did, he knows afterwards, not before. . . . That which is creative, which gives the spark of creativeness, is something spontaneous but not thought-out, not cerebrated. . . .
>
> You may note that artists in general, most artists, as human beings appear perhaps boastful, self-centered, constantly preoccupied only with their own petty little problems, and very sensitive. Inwardly, artists are almost always very humble. They feel that they have to get at something they are unable to get. . . .
>
> I am one of those who believe that you can help artists to develop their creative capacities. But you cannot . . . make him rich. The artist who is very rich is somehow not the artist, because adversity is in the very nature of an artist. Not that if you create adversities you will create artists—depressions will not make artists, artificial shortages of what we need will not make them. But an artist must live in adversity. The adversity is not outside himself but within him, insofar as he absorbs the spirit of his age. . . .
>
> Sometimes an artist goes above and beyond his age and turns out to be a very poor specimen of personality. Take Dostoevski, who was a gambler; take Marcel Proust, who was a frightful neurotic. . . .
>
> When the artist is able to become separated from that which he created, he might even be moved by what he created and not fully realize that it is he, himself, who made it. Emotionally, he wouldn't know. But it takes a long time before the artist can be objective, before he can objectivize his own creation. Therefore, artists are so very personal, so very sensitive, and so very, very jealous of what they have done. . . .

The best creative work is done unconsciously in the "thou shalt not touch me" sphere of man, and if you open it up artificially and expose it to the gaze of men and make it a matter of technique, you will lose the creative man.[19]

So spoke Zilboorg of the creative mentality. Were any of the characteristics of Gershwin's psyche included in these remarks? Unquestionably! For Zilboorg's comments were so very general, they could easily apply to Gershwin as well as to others of his patients. Fortunately, however, for the sanctified tradition of secrecy relating to confidences shared by analyst and patient, Gershwin's specific neuroses and their causes—no matter how dramatic and convoluted—were never spelled out by Zilboorg. Nor will they ever be. Zilboorg kept no notes or written records of his sessions with Gershwin or his other patients. Thus, when Zilboorg died, all confidential information about his many patients was lost with him. Consequently, the bases for Gershwin's many foibles and inconsistencies continue to be fair game for conjecture. And that is the way they should remain.

A caricature of Gershwin and *Porgy and Bess* by Will Cotton.

PORGY AND BESS

$\mathbb{G}$ERSHWIN'S PERSISTENT DREAM of writing a full-scale black opera finally came to pass in 1934 when he started setting to music DuBose Heyward's *Porgy*, with the author as librettist. In Heyward as collaborator, Gershwin found almost the perfect partner for realizing in musical-theatrical terms this story about the crippled beggar Porgy and the poor blacks of Charleston. Yet, except for the fact that both men were white, they had little in common. Unlike Gershwin, Heyward was widely read and a genuine intellectual. Whereas Gershwin's "black" experiences stemmed mainly from occasional forays to Harlem's famous nightspots[1] and a nodding acquaintance with a number of black musicians and entertainers, Heyward had been born in Charleston and had lived there nearly his entire life in close proximity to blacks similar to those he had written about; he had even worked for a time on Charleston's piers checking cotton bales. He was familiar with the dialects of the blacks from that locale and knew firsthand many of their customs and habits. There were other differences, too, between Gershwin and Heyward. Where Gershwin was the bumptious, quick-moving, quick-talking New Yorker, Heyward was introverted, courtly, and reserved, slowed down and physically impeded by the after-effects of a crippling attack of polio suffered in his youth. Moreover, in contrast to Gershwin's somewhat rootless Russian-

Jewish, new-immigrant background, Heyward was a Southern aristocrat of plantation-owner stock. He could trace his lineage to Thomas Heyward, one of the signers of the Declaration of Independence.

Heyward modeled his Porgy on an actual Charleston character he was familiar with, a badly crippled, coal-black beggar with bloodshot eyes and graying hair, named Samuel Smalls, who moved about the city in a little box on wheels drawn by a goat.[2] "Goat Sammy," as he was known, had the disconcerting habit on his begging rounds of staring blankly and interminably into space while awaiting the handful of coins fitfully thrown his way by the passing citizenry moved by his strange look, abject poverty, and crippled body. Belying Smalls's physical deformity was a history of antisocial behavior, mainly of beating and assaulting women, behavior that resulted in a long police record. His last known criminal act was an attempt to shoot a Maggie Barnes one Saturday evening. For this act, he was apprehended and sent to the city jail to await trial. But once in jail, "Goat Sammy" somehow disappeared. A body with his name tag on it was later found buried on one of the islands off the Charleston coast.

Though Samuel Smalls was wholly unstable—verging on lunacy—and dangerous, he had somehow left his mark on Heyward, who set about writing a novel about him after reading a brief account in the *Charleston News and Courier* about the aging beggar's arrest in connection with his assault on Maggie Barnes. Using the Charleston he knew so well as the setting for his novel, Heyward fashioned a story about a beggar, Porgy— whom Heyward initially called Porgo—in most sympathetic terms. Catfish Row of Heyward's novel had a real-life counterpart as Porgy did: Cabbage Row—dilapidated buildings for poor Charleston blacks surrounding a courtyard, formerly part of a luxurious mansion. Like "Goat Sammy," Porgy was crippled, past middle age, and dependent on a goat cart to get around, but there the primary similarities ended, for in Heyward's tale Porgy emerged as no less than a tragic hero. To be sure, he was crafty and malevolent at times, but his deeply felt love for Bess was monumental in its heartbreaking persistence against oppressive odds.

What finally emerged from Heyward's transformation of "Goat Sammy" was a best-selling novel, published in 1925. *Porgy* as a play was no less a spectacular success when it was produced two years later by the Theatre Guild. With its interspersed spirituals to evoke a black flavor and with a slightly changed text—several white characters were added to the script and the original tragic overtones of the novel somewhat softened—the play had a triumphant year's run (367 performances) after opening at the Guild Theater on September 10, 1927. Possibly not since *Uncle Tom's Cabin*, Harriet Beecher Stowe's anti-slavery novel in 1852, had a black theme captured the world's imagination and won its adulation so completely as did *Porgy*.

But along with its paeans of praise, *Porgy*, like Mrs. Stowe's *Uncle Tom* before it, had its share of detractors who criticized the stereotyped images of black life put forth by its white author. Objections were subsequently also raised to Gershwin's "white" musical treatment of Heyward's script: during the initial run of the opera such black spokesmen as musicians Duke Ellington and Hall Johnson and music critic Ralph Matthews of the *Afro-American* voiced dissatisfaction with the score. Complained Ellington: "The times are here to debunk Gershwin's lampblack Negroisms." Ellington felt that Gershwin in his opera had "borrowed from everyone from Liszt to Dickie Wells's kazoo" and that "the music does not hitch with the mood and spirit of the story." Hall Johnson, possibly more charitable than Ellington, described the work as "an opera about Negroes rather than a Negro opera" and credited much of what was good in the opera to the excellent black cast who were "able to infuse enough of their own natural racial qualities into the proceedings to invest them with a convincing semblance of plausibility. This is true even in the musical and dramatic moments most alien to the real Negro genre." Added Johnson: "If these singing actors had been as inexperienced as the composer 'Porgy and Bess' might have turned out to be as stiff and artificial in performance as it is on paper." Ralph Matthews, no less disappointed with the opera, characterized it as "a musical hybrid." As Matthews expressed it, "There are none of the deep sonorous incantations so frequently identified with racial offerings. There is none of the jubilee spirit of 'Run Little Chillun,' and none of the deep soul-stirring songs of 'The Green Pastures.' The singing, even down to the choral and ensemble numbers, has a conservatory twang."[3] Adding his voice to the chorus of black nays about Gershwin's white treatment of the opera was Virgil Thomson, himself white. In Thomson's estimation, the Gershwin work was an example of a "libretto that should never have been accepted on a subject that should never have been chosen [by] a man who should never have attempted it. . . . Folk-lore subjects recounted by an outsider are only valid as long as the folk in question is unable to speak for itself, which is certainly not true of the American Negro in 1935."[4]

If Gershwin was aware of his potential vulnerability to charges of white chauvinism and Uncle Tomism by attempting to write an opera about blacks, he gave little indication of it. Rather, from his very first reading of *Porgy*, in 1926, he had evidently shrewdly assessed the intrinsically novel and dramatic qualities the book possessed as an opera vehicle and plowed straight ahead with his plan eventually to do a musical version of the work. Thus, it was he, not Heyward, who took the initiative in expressing an interest in setting *Porgy* to music. After writing Heyward to that effect immediately on reading the novel, Gershwin met with him shortly afterward in Atlantic City, where they discussed the project. At the meeting, they both agreed in principle to collaborate on an opera of *Porgy* at some indefinite future date when they would be free to do so. With that vague commitment behind them, each then returned to his individual professional chores. However, when Gershwin later saw the Theatre Guild production of *Porgy*, he was impressed more than ever with the possibilities of the work as an opera.

Approximately six years after his first contact with Heyward, he once more took the initiative in voicing a desire to collaborate on an opera of *Porgy*. He wrote to Heyward on March 29, 1932:

> My dear Mr. Heyward:
>
> I am about to go abroad in a little over a week, and in thinking of ideas for new compositions, I came back to one that I had several years ago—namely, PORGY—and the thought of setting it to music. It is still the most outstanding play that I know, about the colored people.
>
> I should like very much to talk with you before I leave for Europe, and the only way that I imagine that would be possible would be by telephone. So if you will be good enough to either telephone me collect at TRafalgar 7-0727—or send me your telephone number by telegram, I will be glad to call you.
>
> Is there any chance of your being abroad in the next couple of months?
>
> I hope this letter finds you and your wife in the best of health, and hoping to hear from you soon, I am
>
> > Sincerely yours,
> > GEORGE GERSHWIN

Gershwin's anticipated stay abroad—actually, he never got to Europe that spring; his father's rapidly deteriorating health and ultimate death on May 14, 1932, made him cancel the trip—elicited a quick response from Heyward, who stated most affirmatively, "I would be tremendously interested in working on the book with you. I have some new material that might be introduced, and once I got your ideas as to the general form suitable for the musical version, I am pretty sure that I could do you a satisfactory story." But with Heyward now ready to proceed on the collaboration, it soon turned out that Gershwin's busy schedule precluded his working on the opera for some months. He notified Heyward on May 20, 1932, that, because of prior commitments, "there is no possibility of the operatic version's being written before January 1933." He suggested

Gregory Zilboorg,
Gershwin's psychoanalyst and friend.

Gershwin's drawing of Diego Rivera,
with Rivera's signed inscription
on it. *(Peter A. Juley and Son)*

instead that they "meet—either here or where you are—several times, before any real start is made." Gershwin also wanted more time to familiarize himself with the book. "I shall be around here most of the summer," he informed Heyward, "and will read the book several times to see what ideas I can evolve as to how it should be done. Any notions I get I shall forward to you."

The following September it was Heyward who took the initiative. He reported to Gershwin that Al Jolson was interested in *Porgy* for himself and was trying to obtain clearances. Though Heyward had reservations about Jolson's playing *Porgy,* he felt he could not turn him down without knowing more about Gershwin's plans. "I evidently have an asset in *Porgy*," Heyward wrote him, "and in these trying times this has to be considered. Therefore, before I turn this down flat, I think we should execute the customary agreement with your producer, with whom, I presume, you have already been discussing the matter. . . . It seems to me that this is very important for both of us, as certainly neither of us would wish to put our time on it without this protection." He continued: "Will you please at the earliest possible moment wire me whether your associates are prepared to enter into a definite agreement at this time, so that I may know how to handle the Jolson matter. I will then leave promptly for New York so that we may get that settled, and also have our first conference on the rewriting of the book." Almost as an afterthought, Heyward threw out this idea: "Would it be possible to use Jolson, and arrange some sort of agreement with him, or is that too preposterous?"

In his reply, Gershwin hardly appeared ruffled by the news of Jolson's bid for the *Porgy* rights. While admitting that Jolson was "a very big star, who certainly knows how to put over a song," Gershwin pointed out that "the sort of thing I had in mind for *Porgy* is a much more serious thing than Jolson could ever do. . . . It would be more a labor of love than anything else." "If you can see your way to making some ready money from Jolson's version," he counseled Heyward, "I don't know that it would hurt a later version done by an all-colored cast." Conceding that he had not yet come up with a producer for the opera, he gave Heyward this reason for the delay: "I should like to write the work first and then see who would be the best one to do it."

Several weeks later, in mid-October 1932, with Gershwin still not any further along with his plans for *Porgy*, he learned from Heyward's agent that Jerome Kern and Oscar Hammerstein II, eager to repeat the great success of their 1927 score for Edna Ferber's *Show Boat,* had aligned themselves with Jolson to write the music for his projected *Porgy.* If this information was designed to get Gershwin to act more decisively about the opera, it failed, for he continued to temporize about *Porgy*. He had no objections to Jolson's getting the rights to the book, he again told Heyward, since he felt the singer's "version would undoubtedly be the play as you wrote it with the addition of perhaps a few songs." He saw no conflict between Jolson's planned musical and his own future treatment of the work. Once more Gershwin advised Heyward: "I wouldn't want to stand in the way of your making some money with your property at the present time."

In suggesting that Heyward try to make some money from his script, Gershwin, of course, showed the best side of his nature. Yet he could afford to be generous. After all, he had no immediate need for the script himself, nor was he under any economic pressure to rush into the assignment. He was in a very sound financial position, with lucrative returns coming in regularly from that box-office bonanza *Of Thee I Sing* to augment his other income. Heyward, on the other hand, had been hard hit by the Depression. As a matter of fact, in justifying his decision finally to sell *Porgy* to Jolson, Heyward confessed to Gershwin that he was "in a fairly tight spot financially" because of economic reverses and needed money badly. Nonetheless, he also carefully assured Gershwin that "it is not my idea to work in any way upon a possible Jolson musical, but merely to sell the story. Later I shall hope to work with you." Heyward also took pains to commend Gershwin on his "attitude in this matter," which he found "simply splendid." "It makes me all the more eager to work with you some day, some time," he wrote him on October 17, 1932, "before we wake up and find ourselves in our dotage."

With the *Porgy* rights now "resolved," for the time being, in favor of Jolson, Gershwin turned his attention to matters of more immediate moment: he conducted and performed his music at the Metropolitan Opera House on November 1, 1932; he completed the score for *Pardon My English* on schedule for its out-of-town tryouts and Broadway opening on January 20, 1933; he fulfilled numerous concert engagements; he moved to his huge new duplex in the late spring of 1933; he arranged for a cross-country tour with orchestra in early 1934 to commemorate the tenth anniversary of the "birth" of the *Rhapsody in Blue*; he entered into negotiations for his own radio program; and he began work on the score for *Let 'Em Eat Cake* to ready it in time for its Broadway premiere in the fall of 1934. But with all this activity, he managed to keep abreast of *Porgy* developments. By September 1934, it became clear that disenchantment had set in for Jolson and his associates over the *Porgy* property and that they were no longer committed to mounting the work. The way was now opened up for Gershwin and Heyward to reconsider collaborating on an opera of *Porgy*. And this they did, with Gershwin finally agreeing to write the music to Heyward's libretto at his earliest convenience.

Aside from their mutual enthusiasm for the project, they still had to come up with a producer. Conceivably, Gershwin could have gotten the Metropolitan to mount the work if Otto Kahn had been alive. For this Merlin of international finance and Maecenas of the arts had long expressed an interest in having Gershwin write an opera for his beloved Metropolitan, though that of course was *not* the same thing as guaranteeing its production.[5] But with Kahn's death on March 29, 1934, at the age of sixty-seven, Gershwin lost a friend at the Metropolitan who was in an excellent position to speak up in his behalf; after all, Kahn's money—he was the Metropolitan's largest single contributor—plus his social contacts and fund-raising abilities had helped pull the opera company through many periods of economic drought. Whether Kahn's death had an effect on Gershwin's and Heyward's ultimate choice of producer is uncertain. But what is clear is that they opted for the Theatre Guild as the producer for what appear, on the surface at least, to be very practical reasons. Whereas the Metropolitan, assuming that it would have produced the work, might at best put on *Porgy* in blackface a few times a season,[6] the Guild offered them the possibility of a long Broadway run. With the novelty of an all-black—or nearly so—cast performing a musical version of a best-selling book and highly popular show, and with the magic of the Gershwin name on the score, it is easy to see why he and Heyward thought that their planned work might do well for them financially. As a matter of fact, Gershwin and Heyward—as well as Ira—even invested in the Guild production in anticipation of getting a good return on their money.[7] Heyward has explained the choice of producer this way: "We had hoped, and it was logical that the Theatre Guild would produce the opera. An excursion into that field of the theater was a new idea to the directors. But then, they had gambled once on *Porgy* and won. There was a sort of indulgent affection for the cripple and his goat on Fifty-second Street. Most certainly they did not want anybody else to do it, and so contracts were signed [on October 26, 1933]."[8] A week after the signing of the contracts, after settling various legal matters, the Guild announced to the world on November 3, 1933, its projected production of a musical version of Heyward's *Porgy*, with a score by Gershwin.

With contractual formalities out of the way and his artistic partnership with Gershwin now a reality, Heyward started preparing his libretto in earnest. From his home in Charleston, he was able to mail the first scene of his script to Gershwin in New York by November 12. In an accompanying letter, Heyward recommended that recitatives, customary in opera,

Duke Ellington. *(Courtesy ASCAP)*
He criticized *Porgy and Bess*
for its "lampblack Negroisms."

Duke Ellington today. He is with
Ambassador Mawussi of Togo and Charles
Schwartz shortly before performing in a
Composers' Showcase concert at the Whitney
Museum of American Art in 1972. During
the concert, Ambassador Mawussi presented
Mr. Ellington with an issue of stamps that
the Togo government had put out in
his honor. *(Photograph by Steve Balkin)*

Gershwin and DuBose Heyward at the time they wrote *Porgy and Bess*.

Gershwin working on the score for *Porgy and Bess* while at the home of Emil Mosbacher in Florida.

Gershwin's hectic train schedule for his 1934 tour with the Reisman orchestra.

GEORGE GERSHWIN TOUR 1934 ... Subject to Train Change without notice
Members are required to watch Bulletin Board on Stage

Sat. Jan. 13	Lv New York (Grand Central Station)	4 PM
	Ar Boston	9:30 PM
Sun. Mat. Jan. 14	Concert, Symphony Hall, Boston	
Mon. Jan. 15	Lv Boston	9:30 AM
	Ar Portland (City Hall Auditorium)	11:45 AM
Tues. Jan. 16	Lv Portland	11:30 AM
	Ar Worcester (Memorial Auditorium)	5:12 PM
Wed. Jan. 17	Lv Worcester (Boston and Alb)	9:52 AM
	Ar Springfield (City Auditorium)	11:10 AM
Thurs. Jan.18	Lv Springfield (B and A)	7:45 AM
	Ar Syracuse (Lincoln Audt. Central H.S.)	2:14 PM
Fri. Jan.19	Lv Syracuse	12:50 AM
	Ar Toronto (Massey Hall)	7:45 AM
Fri. Jan.19 Sat. Jan.20	Lv Toronto	11:30 PM
	Ar Cleveland (Music Hall, Public Audt.)	7:45 AM
Sun. Jan.21	Lv Cleveland (NYC)	8:47 AM
	Ar Detroit (Mich.Cent) (Orchestra Hall)	12:35 PM
Mon. Jan.22	Lv Detroit (Wabash)	12:30 PM
	Ar Ft. Wayne (Shrine Theater)	2:25 PM
Tues. Jan.23	Lv.Ft Wayne (Penn RR)	10:15 AM
	Ar Chicago	1:15
	(Coaches transferred to Northwestern-no change)	
	Lv Chicago	3 PM
	Ar Milwaukee (Auditorium)	4:45 PM
Wed. Jan. 24	Lv Milwaukee	10:30 AM
	Ar Madison (West H.S.Auditorium)	12:45
Thurs. Jan. 25	Lv Madison	1:10 AM
	Ar St Paul (Auditorium)	8:05 AM
Fri. Jan. 26	Lv St Paul	12:05 AM
	Ar Sioux Falls (The Coliseum)	7:35 AM
Sat. Jan. 27	Lv Sioux Falls	1 AM
	Ar Omaha (Tech. H.S.)	12:40 PM
Sun. Jan. 28	Lv Omaha (M P RR)	12 Midnight
	Ar Kansas City (Convention Hall)	8 AM
Mon. Jan. 29	Lv Kansas City (Rock Island)	8:30 AM
	Ar Des Moines (Shrine Auditorium)	2:30 PM
Tues Jan. 30	Lv. Des Moines	11:55 AM
	Ar Davenport (Masonic Auditorium)	4 PM
Wed. Jan. 31	Lv Davenport	12:48 AM
	Ar St. Louis (The Odeon)	1 PM
Thurs. Feb.1	Lv St Louis (Penn RR)	9:02 AM
	Ar Indianapolis (English Opera House)	1:45 PM
Fri. Feb.2	Lv Indianapolis	8:20 AM
	Ar Louisville (Memorial Audt)	11:20 AM

GERSHWIN TOUR 1934......Page 2

Sat. Feb 3	Lv Louisville	11:20 AM
	Ar Cincinnati (Taft Auditorium)	3:50 PM
Sat. Feb 3	Lv Cincinnati	11:45 AM
Sun. Feb 4	Ar Chicago (Auditorium Theater	7:30 AM
Mon. Feb 5	Lv Chicago	10 AM
	Ar Dayton (Memorial Hall)	5 PM
Tues.Feb 6	Lv Dayton	9:50 AM
	Ar Pittsburgh (Syria Mosque)	4:30 PM
Wed. Feb 7	Lv Pittsburgh	9:05 AM
	Ar North Philadelphia (Academy of Music) (Subways downtown)	4:46 PM
Thurs. Feb 8	Lv Philadelphia (Penn RR. 30th Station)	12:21
	Ar Washington (Constitution Hall)	3 PM
Fri. Feb 9	Lv Washington	12:01 PM
	Ar Richmond (Mosque Auditorium)	2:45
Sat. Feb 10	Lv Richmond (Broad St. Station)	8:20 AM
	Ar New York (Penn Station)	4 PM
Sat Eve Feb.10	Brooklyn (Academy of Music)	

be omitted in the score (ultimately, recitatives—which Gershwin favored —won out). "I feel more and more that all dialogue should be spoken," he wrote. "This will give the opera speed and tempo. This will give you a chance to develop a new treatment, carrying the orchestration through the performance (as you suggested) but enriching it with pantomime and action on the stage, and with such music (singing) as grows out of the action. Also, in scenes like the fight, the whole thing can be treated as a unified composition drawing on lighting, orchestra, wailing of crowd, mass sounds of horror from people, etc., instead of singing." In his reply, Gershwin had reservations about Heyward's emphasis on spoken dialogue and admitted that he had been so busy with other things that "I haven't actually started composing." "I want to do a great deal of thinking about the thing and the gathering in of thematic material before the actual writing begins," he confided.

Early in December, Gershwin had a chance to exchange ideas with Heyward once more, but this time in a face-to-face meeting, rather than by long-distance correspondence, for while traveling south with Emil Mosbacher for a Florida vacation, he stopped off briefly at Charleston to see Heyward. In advance of this stopover, he had asked Heyward if he might "see the town and hear some spirituals and perhaps go to a colored café or two if there are any." Heyward, of course, was only too happy to help him get a feel for the city.

Going on to Florida, Gershwin stayed at Mosbacher's Palm Beach home. Besides sharpening his golf game and savoring the Florida sun and surf, he worked there on *"I Got Rhythm" Variations*[9] a piece for piano and orchestra that he intended to introduce on his cross-country tour that was to start in mid-January. On his way back to New York, he visited Charleston on January 2, for another short stay, so that he could "hear some real singing," as he put it, and continue his discussions with Heyward. Apart from the inestimable value of his direct talks with Heyward so early in the planning stages of *Porgy*, these two visits to Charleston gave him his first real exposure to the setting of the opera. It also gave him a chance to patronize a local whorehouse, presumably more for self-gratification than for research in the call of duty, considering his particular need and affinity for brothels.

In a press interview on January 4 on his return to New York, he had something to say about *Porgy* and his new *Variations*. About the former, almost as justification for writing an opera about blacks, he volunteered this information: "Though of course I will try to keep my own style moving in the opera, the Negro flavor will be predominant throughout." Elaborating further on "Negro flavor," he took a professorial tone. "I'd like

253

to point out that Negro music is the prototype of jazz," he declared. "All modern jazz is built up on the rhythms and melodic turns and twists which came directly from Africa. Even the rumba."[10] He also told the press that he hoped Paul Robeson would play the lead in his opera.

In speaking of his nearly completed *"I Got Rhythm" Variations*, he showed his sensitivity to innuendos about his lack of orchestration skills by stressing the scoring of the work and his part in it. He proudly announced for publication that he had already finished fifty-three pages of its orchestration. He emphasized his singular role in the scoring by proclaiming further: "Before the night's over I've got to wash up twenty-five more [pages], so you must excuse me if I don't talk very long."[11] Right on schedule, the entire seventy-three pages of the score were finished two days later, on January 6,[12] in ample time for the January 14 opening concert of his tour.

Based on the famous tune "I Got Rhythm," from *Girl Crazy*, the *Variations* was written specifically for the Leo Reisman orchestra, Gershwin's ensemble on the tour.[13] Because of the relatively limited size of the group—approximately thirty musicians—the score for this work requires fewer instrumentalists than was customary for Gershwin's orchestral pieces. Thus, besides the solo piano, the *Variations* requires only one flute, one oboe (doubling on English horn), one bassoon, four saxophones (doubling on various instruments), three French horns, three B-flat trumpets, two trombones, tuba, percussion, and strings.[14] Undoubtedly as a result of the modest ensemble needed to perform it, the orchestration for the *Variations* is unusually transparent for Gershwin. It also incorporates, according to Vernon Duke, "a number of devices recommended by Schillinger and deftly and ingeniously applied."[15] What the work is deficient in, however, is substance. To be sure, the *Variations* was originally meant to show off Gershwin at the piano in the context of a Gershwin program geared to entertain audiences all over the country.[16] Obviously, it was not expected to be weighty. But even judged on its own terms, the *Variations* is extremely shallow. The "I Got Rhythm" tune serves as the basis for six spindly, powder-puff variations, none of which would hurt a fly.[17] Included among them are an obvious, heart-on-the-sleeve "valse triste"; a "Chinese variation," smacking more of Broadway and Hollywood than of the Orient;[18] and a variation "in jazz style," no less commonplace, with its trite bluesy syncopations and slapped-bass accompaniment.[19]

But substance aside, the *Variations* still demonstrates Gershwin's ever-improving technique as a composer. For the directional goals of the *Variations* are better controlled than ordinarily for a Gershwin orchestral composition, in large part because of the uncomplicated, squarish

Saturday Evening, February 10, 1934

Tour Celebrating 19th Anniversary "Rhapsody in Blue"
Presenting

GEORGE GERSHWIN, Composer-Pianist
James Melton, Tenor
AND THE
Reisman Symphonic Orchestra
Charles Previn, Conductor

PROGRAM OF GERSHWIN SUCCESSES
(Subject to change)

1. Concerto in F .... *Gershwin*
The "Concerto in F" is of thirty minutes duration and was published in 1925. The usual rhythmic effects are conveyed throughout the work which is unmistakably Gershwin. It has been played by Walter Damrosch, the Boston Symphony, the Philharmonic Orchestra under Mengelberg and Van Hoogstraten; the Milwaukee Orchestra, the Minneapolis Orchestra under Verbrugghen; the Cincinnati Orchestra and the Pasdeloup Orchestra of Paris.
MR. GERSHWIN

2. a. Swanee ....
   Do It Again (Sam and Delilah)
   Lady Be Good .... *Gershwin*
   b. Mine
   c. Strike Up the Band ....
ORCHESTRA

3. a. Hills of Home .... *Oscar Fox*
   b. Home on the Range .... *David Guion*
   c. Carry Me Back to the Lone Prairie ... *Carson Robinson*
JAMES MELTON

4. Rhapsody in Blue .... *Gershwin*
The famous "Rhapsody in Blue," the foundation stone of Gershwin's reputation, is the first of the composer's work in the larger forms. Jazz and nobility of thematic material stalk through the Rhapsody in alternating moods and the difficulty of the piano part is matched by its brilliance. This is a work which any audience will enjoy from beginning to end.
MR. GERSHWIN

INTERMISSION

5. An American in Paris .... *Gershwin*
Deems Taylor wrote an analysis of "An American in Paris," which follows: "By its composer's own confession, 'An American in Paris' is an attempted reconciliation between two opposing schools of musical thought. It is program-music in that it engages to tell an emotional narrative; to convey, in terms of sound the successive emotional reactions experienced by a Yankee tourist adrift in the City of Light. It is absolute music as well, in that its structure is determined by considerations musical rather than literary or dramatic. The piece, while not in strict sonata form, resembles an extended symphonic movement in that it announces, develops, combines and recapitulates definite themes. Only, whereas the ordinary symphonic movement is based upon two principal themes, 'An American in Paris' manipulates five."
ORCHESTRA

Program Continued on following page

The Mason & Hamlin is the Official Piano of the Brooklyn Academy of Music

The final program of Gershwin's tour,
on February 10, 1934, at the
Brooklyn Academy of Music.

Dr. Albert Sirmay, Gershwin's music editor
for many of his published works. (*Courtesy
Chappell Music*) He helped Gershwin get
Porgy and Bess ready on time.

overall form of the piece: six brief variations set between an introduction and presentation of the theme, and a coda. All of the variations, moreover, are distinct entities, their individuality heightened by simple basic differences of tempo, key, meter, melodic outline, instrumentation, texture, rhythm, and harmony. The orchestration for the piece, too, speaks well for Gershwin, though Schillinger apparently had a part in it. But as in Gershwin's other symphonic pieces, one cannot gauge from the actual score itself the extent of the assistance he received in orchestrating the *Variations,* since the score is entirely in his hand. On the surface, at least, everything in the score is presumably of his own making.[20]

The tour program in which the *Variations* was first heard assured audiences their money's worth. They not only got a generous sampling of Gershwin music, including *An American in Paris* and a number of famous show tunes, but they also saw Gershwin almost continuously in action on stage as the soloist in the *Variations,* the *Rhapsody in Blue,* and the *Concerto in F.* Except for briefly turning over the spotlight to tenor James Melton, who lustily sang a few non-Gershwin songs (sentimental favorites such as "Hills of Home"), Gershwin was clearly the center of attention as composer and performer throughout the long concert. The physical demands of this program on him must have been enormous, considering that he was constantly on the go on stage and then afterwards, when he traveled to his various destinations. But he thrived on it. Between the opening concert in Boston's Symphony Hall on January 14, 1934, and the final one in Brooklyn's Academy of Music on February 10, he and his group traveled approximately 12,000 miles and visited such widely dispersed cities as Toronto, Detroit, Omaha, and Richmond, yet Gershwin seemed almost as fresh and vigorous when he finished the tour as when he had started it. If he had any regrets about the tour, they touched almost wholly on finances, for he had expected the tour to make a substantial profit and had eagerly invested in it. (He was always amenable to making a killing on the basis of his talents.) Unfortunately, however, the tour lost money despite largely packed halls. As he explained it, "The tour was a fine artistic success for me and would have been splendid financially if my foolish manager hadn't booked me into seven towns that were too small to support such an expensive organization as I carried."[21] Nonetheless, he conceded that "it was a very worthwhile thing for me to have done and I have many pleasant memories of cities I had not visited before."

Shortly after the tour, when he had hardly had a chance to catch his breath, he was again running full steam. For on February 19 he began his own New York-based radio program, *Music by Gershwin,* heard twice weekly on Monday and Friday evenings from seven-thirty to seven-forty-five, over WJZ. On the air Gershwin served as the pleasant, all's-right-with-the-world host, as well as star composer and performer, for which he received a reported salary of $2,000 weekly. Ironically enough in view of his persistent plaints about constipation, the sponsor of the program was Feenamint, a chewing-gum laxative. But if the sponsor's product and Gershwin's digestive failings represented a compatibility of interests, the actual radio program did not. Gershwin found radio broadcasting, save for its high financial dividends, anything but to his liking. In an interview published in the *New York Times* on March 4, 1934, he compared broadcasting unfavorably with concert touring. Speaking of his tour, he stressed that "the activity during those twenty-eight days was more physical than mental, for while we covered 12,000 miles in less than a month, our program was unchanged in the various cities in which we played." Conversely, he pointed out, broadcasting emphasized change and was more mental than physical. "It means preparing an entirely different program for each broadcast," he complained. "At that rate it doesn't take long to exhaust even an extensive repertoire. The microphone is like a hungry lion the way it eats up material." Somewhat worriedly, yet at the same time boastfully, he added: "It's really liable to prove something of a strain even to a composer who is in the habit of turning out melodies more ·or less on schedule. And I've written close to a thousand songs."

But despite his lack of enthusiasm for broadcasting, it was the ample monetary return offered by radio—and other "commercial" ventures—that helped subsidize the operatic version of *Porgy,* in the opinion of DuBose Heyward. Heyward, an advocate of "commercial" assignments for artists as a modern-day version of the old patronage system, has advanced his argument this way:

> It is the fashion in America to lament the prostitution of art by the big magazine, the radio, the moving pictures. With this I have little patience. Properly utilized, the radio and the pictures may be to the present-day writer what his prince was to Villon, the king of Bavaria was to Wagner.
>
> At no other time has it been possible for a writer to earn by hiring himself out as a skilled technician for, say, two months, sufficient income to sustain him for a year. And yet the moving pictures have made it possible. I decided that the silver screen should be my Maecenas [Heyward wrote the screen versions of Eugene O'Neill's *The Emperor Jones* and Pearl Buck's *The Good Earth*], and George elected to serve radio. . . .
>
> Statistics record the fact that there are 25,000,000 radios in America. Their contribution to the opera was indirect but important. Out of them for half an hour each week poured the glad tidings that Feenamint could be wheedled away from virtually any drug clerk in America

for one dime—the tenth part of a dollar. And with the authentic medicine-man flair, the manufacturer distributed his information in an irresistible wrapper of Gershwin hits, with the composer at the piano.

There is, I imagine, a worse fate than that which derives from the use of a laxative gum. And, anyhow, we felt that the end justified the means.[22]

On February 26, 1934, a week to the day after starting his Feenamint program, Gershwin was able to write Heyward this good news: "I have begun composing music for the first act, and I am starting with the songs and spirituals first." And it was the now well-known lullaby, "Summertime," heard shortly after the opera opens, that he wrote first. But promising as that start was, he did not get so much work done on the opera as he would have liked until the following summer when, with the radio show off the air until the fall, he could devote himself fully to *Porgy*.[23] However, most of his composing that summer was not done on East-Seventy-second Street, but in the South, for he left New York for Charleston in mid-June so as to be near Heyward and the actual site of *Porgy* while working on the opera. Joining him on the trip was his artist-cousin Henry Botkin.[24]

Gershwin and Botkin stayed at Folly Beach, a small island ten miles from Charleston, where the Heywards had a summer home. Close by the Heywards, they rented a four-room frame cottage, since blown down. In contrast to the luxuries of Gershwin's New York duplex, the beach cottage offered only the basic necessities. His small room, where he worked and slept, consisted only of an old upright piano, a primitive iron bed and a few nondescript pieces of furniture, a washbasin, and some hooks for hanging clothes—baggage and shoes were stored under the bed. Nor was Botkin's room any fancier. For drinking-water, they depended on the bottled variety. They also shared the experience of having sand crabs crawl all over their rooms and of being interrupted in their sleep by the sounds of bugs and insects doing a mad dance against the cottage screens and by crickets shrilly proclaiming their rights of eminent domain. But of all the noise, the cricket chirping troubled Gershwin the most. After one particularly sleepless night that left him nervous and irritable because of a persistent barrage from the crickets, he decided to take the situation into his own hands. Convinced that the bombardment of his ears came from a tree near his cottage, he borrowed a ladder and went looking for the culprits in the nearby tree the following day. Fortunately for the cricket population of Folly Beach, he could not find them, the hunting expedition a decided failure.

Along with the primitive living on Folly Beach went the privacy that allowed Gershwin to work for long stretches of time on *Porgy* without inter-

Three of the stars of *Porgy and Bess*: John Bubbles (Sportin' Life),
Todd Duncan (Porgy), and Anne Brown (Bess).

The inhabitants of Catfish Alley huddling together
in the hurricane scene in *Porgy and Bess*.

ruption from the telephone—there was none on the island—or from the various pressures that constantly intruded on his life in New York. With few social responsibilities to contend with, he thought nothing of not shaving for days at a time or of wearing only a bathing suit to keep cool as he focused his energies on the opera. (As a result of his sparse dress, he became heavily tanned from the baking sun.) There may have been few of the luxuries of life on Folly Beach that he normally took for granted in his Manhattan tower, but as a workplace for *Porgy,* this sandy island was Nirvana itself. Besides the necessary solitude, Folly Beach also gave him the chance to observe at close range the blacks of the vicinity, especially the Gullahs, who inhabited adjacent James Island. In many ways, the Gullahs were the real-life counterparts of the characters in *Porgy.* Like those of the residents of Catfish Row, a good many of their habits, superstitions, ecstatic incantations, singing, dancing, foot stamping and handclapping, and even their dialect, had unmistakable African origins. The Gullahs, through isolated living on the islands off the Charleston and Georgia shores for many years, had resisted outside influences to a greater extent than did their fellow blacks on the mainland. By being physically and emotionally removed from the mainstream of American life, they had retained more of their African heritage in their customs and language than probably any black group in the United States. Heyward has conceded that it was just this carryover of African tradition in the Gullahs' way of life that made them so invaluable as a collective model for *Porgy,* for he has admitted that the "primitive" Gullahs furnished Gershwin and himself "with a laboratory in which to test our theories as well as an inexhaustible source of folk material." Gershwin, for his part, immersed himself in what he saw and heard. For him, these experiences were "more like a homecoming than an exploration," in the judgment of Heyward, who noted, too: "The quality in him which had produced the *Rhapsody in Blue* in the most sophisticated city in America, found its counterpart in the impulse behind the music and bodily rhythms of the simple Negro peasant of the South."[25]

Gershwin responded to the stimulus of his surroundings with an exuberant, creative outflow. Musical ideas poured forth quickly and steadily at the piano as if from some limitless subterranean well. Most of the ideas he incorporated into his opera immediately; others he laid aside for future use, including the incantations he devised for his Catfish Row residents praying for protection from a threatening hurricane (in the fourth scene of the second act). He had heard similar invocations when he was taken by Heyward to a prayer meeting by a small group of black Holy Rollers. While still outside the ramshackle cabin of these people, he had been stopped in his tracks by the sounds he heard coming from within. For though each of the congregants chanted his prayer in a different, highly individual fashion, the totality of the effect of all voices combined in loud, rhythmic polyphony was so dramatically intense that it made a lasting impression on him. Several months later in New York, he drew on this experience to come up with his own prayer music, as he explained to Heyward in a letter on November 5, 1934: "I start and finish the storm scene with six different prayers sung simultaneously. This has somewhat the effect we heard in Hendersonville as we stood outside the Holy Rollers' Church."

Busy as he was with *Porgy* on Folly Beach, there were occasional breaks for shopping and sightseeing on the mainland, for boating and swimming, and for partying at the homes of Charleston's most distinguished citizens. In his spare moments, Gershwin also joined Botkin in painting and drawing, both as a respite from composing and to keep his hand active as a visual artist. Thus, when he returned to Manhattan in August, he brought back samples of his art work in addition to his bulging portfolio of manuscripts for the opera.

Encouraged by continued progress on *Porgy* as loose ends gradually fell into place and confident that he had picked a winner, he often seemed even cockier than usual when discussing the opera. Shortly after arriving at Folly Beach, he had this to say to the press about *Porgy:* "If I am successful it will resemble a combination of the drama and romance of *Carmen* and the beauty of *Meistersinger,* if you can imagine that. I believe it will be something never done before."[26] (Strong words, indeed, when one considers that opera as Gershwin simplistically described it was often "just singing in costume," and that his familiarity with the medium at the time was practically nil—consisting almost solely of a few opera performances he had attended.) Nor was he reluctant to characterize his opera to Dorothy Heyward as "the greatest music composed in America." Undoubtedly contributing to his ebullience and optimism was his and Heyward's decision to have Ira join them in their collaboration. For with George and Heyward usually separated by a thousand miles of Eastern seaboard and largely dependent on the mails for communication, Ira was brought in as a kind of middleman to add his own special brand of expertise to many of the lyrics for the tunes, thereby assuring both their viability in the theater and their distinct Gershwin flavor. Heyward, of course, still remained responsible for the basic libretto, which he submitted to Gershwin in the form of scenes and lyrics. But then, as Heyward relates, "the brothers Gershwin, after their extraordinary fashion, would get at the piano, pound, wrangle, sweat, burst into weird snatches of song, and eventually emerge with a polished lyric." In this manner, Ira collaborated with Heyward on such lyrics as those for

"I Got Plenty o' Nuttin'," "Bess, You Is My Woman," and "It Takes a Long Pull to Get There." On his own, Ira is credited with the words for "There's a Boat Dat's Leavin' Soon for New York" and "It Ain't Necessarily So," among others. Heyward, in turn, contributed the texts for still other songs, including "My Man's Gone Now," "Summertime," and "A Woman Is a Sometime Thing." So efficacious was this working arrangement that even if one quibbles with the Amos-and-Andy quality of many of the lyrics devised by Heyward and Ira there is still a consistency of style among the various song texts; one cannot easily tell where Southerner Heyward leaves off and New Yorker Ira begins.

On his return to New York from South Carolina, Gershwin showed no letup in the creative pace he had set for himself on Folly Beach. Music for *Porgy* rolled from his fingertips as easily as ever, even though he now had to contend with the many distractions of life in the big city. Among the demands on his time where those connected with his radio show, which returned to the air in October—fortunately, the program seemed less onerous to him the second time around because it was presented only once a week, for half an hour. But radio show or not, he pressed forward on the opera, buoyed by the fact that the completion of *Porgy* was in sight. Planning ahead, he wrote to Heyward as early as November 5, 1934, to say he "would like to set a tentative date for rehearsals," and suggested that performers be auditioned starting "January or February so that those people we choose for the parts can be learning the music." By December, he already had a singer in mind for one of the leads and excitedly gave Heyward this news: "I heard about a man singer who teaches music in Washington and arranged to have him come and sing for me on Sunday several weeks ago. In my opinion he is the closest to a colored Lawrence Tibbett I have ever heard. He is about six feet tall and very well proportioned with a rich booming voice. He would make a superb Crown and, I think, just as good a Porgy. . . . I shall ask the Guild to take an option on his services." With the Guild acceding to his recommendation, the singer, Todd Duncan, was signed for *Porgy* and went on to play the title role. A letter from Gershwin to Duncan on January 24, 1935, discusses the progress of the opera and the singer's projected part in it: "I am leaving for Florida this weekend where I begin the task of orchestrating the opera. I just finished a trio in the last scene for Porgy, Serena, and Maria which I think will interest you very much. While I am away the Theatre Guild or Mr. Wachsman will get in touch with you to do whatever ironing out there has to be done. Before I leave I am sending two acts of the opera to my publishers and a copy will be made available to you as soon as they are printed."

As promised, the vocal score for the first two acts of *Porgy* went to his publisher before he entrained for Palm Beach. But there was a new wrinkle, for the publisher was not Harms, with whom Gershwin had had a contract for many years, but the Gershwin Publishing Company, no less, a new organization set up in the composer's name by Max Dreyfus as a subsidiary of Chappell and Company. Dreyfus left Harms to head Chappell.[27] He also brought with him Dr. Albert Sirmay, Gershwin's music editor at Harms.[28] The Gershwin Publishing Company went on to publish not only the opera[29] but subsequent Gershwin songs as well, including selections from his film scores for *Shall We Dance, A Damsel in Distress,* and *The Goldwyn Follies,* and a number of posthumous tunes.

On arriving at Palm Beach after another brief stopover on January 30, 1935, at Charleston, Gershwin stayed at Emil Mosbacher's, where he occupied himself with the orchestration of *Porgy,* between breaks for pleasure and diversion. He touched on the tediousness of scoring the opera in a letter to Ira from Palm Beach in early February: "I'm sitting in the patio of the charming house Emil has rented, writing to you after orchestrating for a few hours this morning. Expect to finish scoring Scene II, Act I this week. It goes slowly, there being millions of notes to write." Several months later the scoring for *Porgy* was still laborious going for him, judging by the letter he wrote Schillinger on May 16, 1935, to say he had finished "the orchestrations of the first act and am now working on the second act scoring, but it goes slowly." In his letter he also asked if he might see Schillinger "to take some lessons."[30] Besides Schillinger's help in scoring *Porgy* that summer, Gershwin as a further safeguard indulged himself in the luxury of having an orchestral run-through of the opera in mid-July as he had done for the *Concerto in F* and the *Second Rhapsody.*[31] For the *Porgy* tryout, he had the generous help of William Paley, head of CBS, who put at his disposal an ensemble of forty-three musicians for a two-and-a-half-hour rehearsal session.

Refreshed by his Palm Beach interlude, Gershwin pushed himself even harder than usual when he got back to New York. Setting his sights on the start of rehearsals in August, he worked against that deadline to complete all the musical elements for *Porgy* on time, including the necessary vocal and instrumental scores. (In preparing his material, he was aided by, among others, Dr. Albert Sirmay, who supervised the editing, and Kay Swift, who spent long hours copying parts and proofreading.) He also auditioned and selected performers; met frequently with the press to publicize the opera; exchanged ideas constantly with Heyward, Ira, and the executives of the Theatre Guild; and generally kept on top of the many details that required his personal attention, such as the hiring of the principal musical personnel. At his say-so, Alexander Smallens, an experienced conductor of orchestral and operatic works, was engaged as musical director and Alexander Steinert, equally versatile, as vocal coach.[32] In choosing the cast, Gershwin attended literally hundreds of auditions of black performers, many of them recruited from the vaudeville and nightclub circuits. Among the cast members finally selected besides Todd Duncan, were Anne Brown as Bess, Warren Coleman as Crown, Georgette Harvey as Maria, Ruby Elzy as Serena, Edward Matthews as Jake, and John Bubbles, of the dancing team of Buck and Bubbles, as Sportin' Life. Complementing them on stage was the Eva Jessye Choir. Rouben Mamoulian, who had staged *Porgy* as a play, directed the opera as well. He gladly took a leave of absence from Hollywood, where he had been directing films, for the chance to join Gershwin and Heyward in the new Broadway venture.

Three days before the start of rehearsals (August 26, 1935), Gershwin wrote on the last page of his long orchestral score, "finished August 23, 1935." Actually, there was still work to be done on the score, as this notation appended to the first page of the orchestrated manuscript would indicate: "finished September 2, 1935." Nor was there a letup in the demands made on him during rehearsals. Not only were there cuts and other revisions to be made in the score, but the cast had to be welded into a cohesive unit. Their backgrounds varied enormously. Some, for example, had had conservatory training, while others, such as John Bubbles, could not read a note of music and had to learn their parts by rote.[33] There was also the matter of getting the company to use "authentic" dialects, suitable for blacks living in Charleston. As one sign of the times, the job of coaching the cast in the black dialect written for them by Heyward and Ira fell to George, Heyward, and their white associates. The black performers on stage excepted, the entire production was white-created and controlled, from the composer and librettist, to the stage director, to the orchestra and conductor in the pit, to the vocal coach, to the Theatre Guild staff.

Although Gershwin and Heyward had always intended to call their opus *Porgy*, they ultimately decided on the title of *Porgy and Bess* in order to avoid any possible confusion in the public's mind between the play and the opera. And it was while speaking of the opera that Gershwin admitted to a reporter, "I'm very happy it's finally finished and yet it leaves me a little empty." Nervously chewing gum while dapperly dressed in a gray fedora and suit and brown shoes, and with a yellow, ivory-handled cane in his hands, he made this comment in the alleyway of the Guild Theater during rehearsals of *Porgy and Bess*. As he spoke, he peered intently through an open door, watching every move on stage, only to interrupt the interview and quickly vanish into the theater on hearing his name called,[34] for he was a man in motion during the rehearsals. Nor did he slow down away from the theater. As Rouben Mamoulian recalls, "Once during rehearsals he invited me to spend a weekend with him and some friends in Long Beach. 'You must come out, Rouben, to relax and forget *Porgy and Bess* and my music for a while,' he said. I couldn't go, but on Monday morning I asked Alexander Steinert, who was in the party, what did they do over the weekend at George's. Alex replied, 'We played *Porgy and Bess* Saturday and Sunday —all day and all night.' "[35]

Shortly before *Porgy and Bess* opened at Boston's Colonial Theater on September 30, 1935, for its shakedown stint, the entire company went through their paces at Carnegie Hall before a small audience of invited guests to get their reactions to the folk opera, as the work was now designated. They loved it, even without benefit of scenery, costumes, or stage action. The reception in Boston was equally cordial.[36] Not atypical were the comments of Francis D. Perkins, reviewing the work for the *New York Herald-Tribune*. He found the opera a "notable achievement in a new field. It tells of unusually effective craftsmanship; it reflects a marked advance in Mr. Gershwin's progress." Moses Smith of the *Boston Transcript*, also pleased with *Porgy and Bess*, characterized the opera as "unique" and felt that Gershwin "must now be accepted as a serious composer."

Reviewers in New York, too, found much to praise in the opera at its glittering opening on October 10, 1935, at the Alvin Theater. But the criticisms of the work far outweighed the praise, especially since they came from some of the most powerful members of the music-critic fraternity. For Olin Downes, in the *Times,* Gershwin had "not completely formed his style as an opera composer. The style is at one moment of opera and another of operetta or sheer Broadway entertainment." However, Downes readily conceded that "many of the songs in the score of 'Porgy and Bess' will reap a quick popularity." Downes's colleague, Brooks Atkinson, from the drama-critics' side of the aisle, took more kindly to the production, though he questioned the use of recitatives in the work. "Why commonplace remarks that carry no emotion have to be made in a chanting monotone is a problem of art he cannot fathom," grumbled Atkinson. "Even the hermit thrush drops into conversational tones when he is not singing. . . . Turning 'Porgy' into opera has resulted in a deluge of casual remarks that have to be thoughtfully intoned and that amazingly impede the action." Also commenting on the action was music reviewer William J. Henderson of the *Sun,* who found "the work much too long." He cited "I Got Plenty o' Nuttin" as "without question the 'song hit' of the night," but added, "It was many miles from opera." Lawrence Gilman of the *Herald-Tribune* and Samuel Chotzinoff of the *Post* were both of the opinion that the opera was essentially a succession of song hits. According to Gilman, "Perhaps it is needlessly Draconian to begrudge Mr. Gershwin the song hits which he has scattered through the score and which will doubtless enhance his fame and popularity. Yet they mar it. They are cardinal weaknesses. They are the blemishes upon its musical integrity." Nor was Chotzinoff, usually favorably disposed to Gershwin, any more sympathetic. Chotzinoff found *Porgy and Bess* "a hybrid, fluctuating constantly between music-drama, musical comedy, and operetta. It contains numerous 'song hits' which would be considered ornamental in any of the composer's musical shows. . . . Yet they are too 'set' in treatment, too isolated from the pitch of opera for us to accept them as integral parts of a tragic music-drama."

Gershwin had a chance to answer his critics and generally speak his mind about the opera in a long article in the *New York Times* on October 20, 1935. Speaking with assurance, if not always razor-sharp logic, he touched on many points in his article, propagandizing all the while for himself and his work. Equating ersatz folk music with the real thing, he began by discussing his use of the term "folk opera" to describe *Porgy and Bess:*

> *Porgy and Bess* is a folk tale. Its people naturally would sing folk music. When I first began work on the music I decided against the use of original folk material because I wanted the music to be all of one piece. Therefore I wrote my own spirituals and folk-songs. But they are still folk music—and therefore, being in operatic form, *Porgy and Bess* becomes a folk opera.

He then went on to talk about his novel use of "Negro" material, almost as if he were spokesman for black musical America.

> Because *Porgy and Bess* deals with Negro life in America it brings to the operatic form elements that have never before appeared in opera and I have adapted my method to utilize the drama, the humor, the superstition, the religious fervor, the dancing and the irrepressible high spirits of the race. If, in doing this, I have created a new form, which combines opera with theater, this new form has come quite naturally out of the material.

The Metropolitan Opera Company was next on his agenda, at least by indirection. He took a pot shot at the company, whether or not he was aware of it, by alluding to the sponsorship of *Porgy and Bess* in this manner: "The reason I did not submit this work to the usual sponsors of opera in America was that I hoped to have developed something in American music that would appeal to the many rather than to the cultured few."[37] After some passing references to the entertainment value of *Porgy and Bess* ("because the Negroes, as a race, have all these qualities inherent in them"), to the humor in the opera ("for instance, the character of Sportin' Life, instead of being a sinister dope-peddler, is a humorous dancing villain who is likable and believable and at the same time evil"), and to several other items, self-inflatingly described, he turned his attention to justifying the hit-song syndrome in his opera by claiming that very same quality in other well-known composers. As Gershwin saw it, "Nearly all of Verdi's operas contain what are known as 'song hits.' *Carmen* [by Bizet] is almost a collection of song hits." He also had some good things to say about his use of recitatives, a source of bitter complaint by many reviewers: "The recitative I have tried to make as close to the Negro inflection in speech as possible, and I believe my song-writing apprenticeship has served invaluably in this respect, *because the song writers of America have the best conception of how to set words to music so that the music gives added expression to the words* [this writer's emphasis]." Nor did he neglect the lyrics by Heyward and Ira for his songs. He praised their texts, pidgin English and all, for their "fine synchronization of diversified moods," and gave examples of the lyrics for "Oh, de Lawd Shake de Heavens," "It Ain't Necessarily So," "Summertime," and "There's a Boat Dat's Leavin' Soon for New York" to back up his commendation. He concluded his pitch with this statement: "All of these are, I believe, lines that come naturally from the Negro. They make for folk music. Thus *Porgy and Bess* becomes a folk opera—opera for the theater, with drama, humor, song and dance."[38]

Gershwin's hard sell in the *Times* article may have appeased the drummer within him, but it didn't cause a run on the box office. After only 124 performances, *Porgy and Bess* quietly folded its tent at the Alvin.[39] A tour by the company that followed was even briefer, closing in Washington, D.C., on March 21, 1936, after the opera had been on the road less than two months. The smart money that had invested in the opera for profit had little to show for it at the posting of the closing notice. All of the investment of approximately $70,000 that went into mounting the opera was eaten up by production costs. Gershwin did not even recoup enough to cover his copying expenses.

The saga of *Porgy and Bess* of course did not end at that point. Gershwin had somehow managed—through tough-nosed shrewdness, instincts, or both—to cover himself in case the opera floundered. Simply by his hit-song approach, he offset the risk of commercial failure. After all, his opera by his own admission was geared to "appeal to the many rather than the cultured few." In following that very dictum, he helped to insure his musical and financial investment in the work. Thus, even when *Porgy and Bess* went off the boards, it was not too difficult, considering his fame and the publicity attendant to the production, to get a number of outstanding tunes from the opera performed and recorded.[40] By repeated

267

hearings on the air lanes, on private turntables, as well as in nightclubs, and concert and dance halls, tunes such as "Summertime," "It Ain't Necessarily So," and "I Got Plenty o' Nuttin' " began to make inroads on the public taste and consciousness and gradually to build up a groundswell of interest not only in the tunes themselves but in the work as a whole.[41] Out of the context of the opera and judged solely on their own terms, these songs have all the tunefulness, all the broad appeal and instant recognizability that are the earmarks of the best of Gershwin's pieces, whether for the theater or the concert hall. To be sure, there are also advances of a technical nature in the opera itself—such as a more varied harmonic palette and more elaborate use of counterpoint than was customary for Gershwin—that make the work the high point of his career. But these improvements alone, welcome as they are, could not have possibly saved *Porgy and Bess*, especially when one considers that hundreds of works yearly fall by the wayside by composers with more technique at their disposal than Gershwin could ever have mustered.

Gershwin never saw another production of *Porgy and Bess* after the original closed, but not because he didn't work at it. For by March 1937, negotiations were under way for a revival of the opera on the West Coast.[42] (Unfortunately, Gershwin died before this production became a reality.) He also promoted the opera by frequently conducting and performing portions from it, including a five-movement suite for orchestra that he had fashioned.[43] Interestingly, despite the "authenticity" of the suite, since it is presumably solely by Gershwin, it has never come close to matching the popularity of Robert Russell Bennett's colorful orchestral synthesis of the opera, titled *A Symphonic Picture,* written in 1941–1942 for the Pittsburgh Symphony at the behest of its conductor, Fritz Reiner.

The first revival of *Porgy and Bess*—the one Gershwin had started negotiating for prior to his death—began its run on the West Coast on February 4, 1938, under the sponsorship of Merle Armitage. With Todd Duncan and Anne Brown again in the leading roles and other cast holdovers (Avon Long, however, replaced Bubbles as Sportin' Life), this production practically duplicated the original one. Also borrowed from the first production was Alexander Steinert, who conducted. After playing to enthusiastic audiences in Los Angeles, Pasadena, and San Francisco for over a month, prospects for a long run for the revival looked encouraging, for many cities in the West had indicated interest in booking it. But this possibility was cut short when California suddenly underwent a serious flood siege which inundated many parts of the state, putting a crimp on normal activities. Dramatically overwhelmed by the elements, *Porgy and Bess* had to end its brief run, with disastrous economic consequences. Like the original production, the revival did not earn enough to recover its investment.

There was a financial upswing for the opera, however, several years later. Under Cheryl Crawford's auspices, a production of *Porgy and Bess* finally showed a profit. Miss Crawford first put on the opera for a week in October 1941, in Maplewood, New Jersey, usually the site for summer stock, but in a version that all but eliminated recitatives and cut approximately forty-five minutes from the performing time. Encouraged by the results, Miss Crawford then began thinking seriously of invading Manhattan. After a tryout at Boston's Shubert Theater starting December 29, 1941, Miss Crawford brought her version of *Porgy and Bess* to the Majestic Theater in New York on January 22, 1942. With a smaller cast and reduced orchestra to help streamline the production while cutting overhead costs, Miss Crawford came up with a taut and fast-paced *Porgy and Bess* instead of a leisurely one as before. Aiding the flow of action was the experienced cast on stage, led by Todd Duncan and Anne Brown, and the conducting of Alexander Smallens in the pit. The revival quickly won over New York. As Burns Mantle expressed it, almost in chorus with the ecstatic huzzahs of his press confreres, the new *Porgy and Bess* was "a smoother and more melodious production than the original."[44] And the public apparently agreed, as they turned out en masse to see the revival during its eight months on Broadway. The opera then went on a prolonged tour of the country, before returning to New York again for a limited engagement—all the while enriching the till. By the time the revival had run its lengthy course, a sizable profit had accrued to it. Among the investors who shared in the pickings was Mrs. Rose Gershwin, George's mother. Almost as retribution for George's money loss in the original production, Mrs. Gershwin realized a handsome return for investing in the Crawford revival.[45]

Since the Crawford production, *Porgy and Bess* has become "big business" and has been performed with and without Gershwin's original recitatives in most major cities of Europe, including Moscow and Leningrad, as well as in Central and South America, Israel, Egypt, and Morocco, not to mention cities throughout the United States and parts of Canada. Greatly assisting in the promulgation of interest in *Porgy and Bess* abroad has been the State Department sponsorship of several tours of the opera as a representation of American culture. But that has only been part of the story. For over the past several decades, especially during the 1950s and 1960s, there appeared to be genuine curiosity throughout the world in an opera about poor American blacks by Mr. Musical America himself, George Gershwin. Certainly crowds have flocked to see the opera wherever it has been performed. Even Samuel Goldwyn's 1959 technicolor extravaganza of the

269

Ruby Elzy (Serena), arms outstretched, sings
"My Man's Gone Now" in *Porgy and Bess*.

Alexander Smallens,
the conductor of *Porgy and Bess*.

opera, replete with wide screen, dubbed singing, and stereophonic sound, has not lessened interest in it. But for a work purported to be an artistic depiction of blacks in southern America during this century, *Porgy and Bess* has never gotten much support from American blacks themselves. Taking their lead from such key black musicians as Duke Ellington and Hall Johnson, who originally disputed the validity of the opera, blacks have generally been indifferent to the work. *Porgy and Bess* has become fat-cat Establishment over the years, and audiences for it by and large have been white and middle class, *not* black. In our present age of increased black consciousness and vocalism over black issues, the opera has even become downright embarrassing to many whites as well as to blacks. They question not only the Uncle Tomisms in the opera but the underlying conceit of the work—that Gershwin could set himself up as musical spokesman for the blacks represented in *Porgy and Bess*. Whether *Porgy and Bess,* as an operatic entity, can survive such questioning, or whether it will deteriorate instead into merely a series of isolated song hits, remains to be seen. But one thing seems reasonably certain. Just as long as the name of George Gershwin remains on the tongues of men, some aspects of *Porgy and Bess* will always be remembered.

George and Ira shown working on the score for
Damsel in Distress.

THE FINAL CURTAIN

AFTER MORE THAN two decades of hard-fought professional gains on Broadway, Gershwin decided in 1936 that there were greener pastures elsewhere than on the Great White Way. Though a large portion of his income had always come from Broadway shows, theater in New York in the mid-1930s seemed to be on its last legs, suffering the effects of the intense gravitational pull of the Depression. Somehow he had managed to prosper on Broadway after the 1929 crash because of such sparkling musicals as *Strike Up the Band* (1930), *Girl Crazy* (1930), and *Of Thee I Sing* (1931). And while working on *Porgy and Bess* he had been amply supported—and by his own estimate, he needed approximately $1,000 weekly just to meet his high-flying living expenses— by his radio show, concert engagements, and royalties. But by 1936, after three flops in a row—*Pardon My English* (1933), *Let 'Em Eat Cake* (1933), and *Porgy and Bess* (1935)—Gershwin could not consider the prognosis for commercial theater on Broadway particularly promising. As a matter of fact, during the 1935–1936 season, which saw *Porgy and Bess* open at the Alvin, there were some fifty fewer productions on Broadway than the year before, and most of the shows that were mounted did not even recoup their investments, much less show a profit. Things were so bad in the theater that the Federal Theater Project was initiated in 1935, as part of President

273

Franklin D. Roosevelt's New Deal, to help subsidize employment for theatrical professionals, while bringing shows to the public at prices they could afford.[1]

But if Broadway was struggling for survival, Hollywood was prospering. At a time when millions of Americans were unemployed and on relief rolls, Hollywood's movie mills were working overtime grinding out films for a voracious public hungry for the diversion they offered from their financial and other woes. Moreover, through technological advances in making films and mass distribution, large doses of celluloid make-believe were able to be projected on the movie screens of the country at a relatively modest cost to the eager public. With little competition from the floundering theater, films quickly became the major entertainment industry of the 1930s.

Sensing the trend, Gershwin let it be known that he was interested in a movie contract. Broadway may have been his first love, but financial expediency dictated that he go West. By early February 1936, he had sent word to Hollywood that the asking price for a Gershwin movie score was $100,000 plus a percentage of the film. But in a tough horse-trader's market, there were no takers at that price, especially since Gershwin had not written a smash musical since *Of Thee I Sing,* light-years earlier, and had aggravated that sore point by composing a flop, long-hair opera—a near-fatal sin in the eyes of Hollywood producers, who now viewed him suspiciously as having gone highbrow and lost his common, man-in-the-street touch as a tunesmith. After an exchange of letters and telegrams over a period of several months with a number of film agents on the Coast in quest of the best deal, he learned from agent Arthur Lyons[2] in early June that RKO wanted Ira and him to write the score for the next Fred Astaire-Ginger Rogers movie, then titled *Watch Your Step.* Their best offer, however, was only $60,000 for twenty weeks' work, quite a salary drop from his original asking price. Since future bargaining rights were at stake, he did not accept the studio offer without haggling over terms. As a counter proposal, he suggested that he and Ira be paid $75,000 for twenty weeks' work, or $60,000 for sixteen weeks at the studio. George and Ira finally came to terms with RKO after receiving this impassioned telegram on June 24 from Pandro S. Berman,[3] the producer of the film:

DEAR GENTS VERY MUCH SURPRISED HEAR FROM ARTHUR LYONS YOU HAVE DESCENDED TO COMMERCIAL MINDEDNESS THOUGHT EVERYTHING BETWEEN US WAS IN A HIGHER REALM STOP NOT BEING A BUSINESS MAN MYSELF AND HAVING HEARD FROM THE TRADE YOU ARE ARTISTS WAS SURE WE HAD NOTHING MORE TO TALK

ABOUT ESPECIALLY IN VIEW YOUR PROTESTATION OF WILLINGNESS TO SACRIFICE ALL FOR GOOD OLD RKO A SPIRIT WHICH I HAVE ADMIRED SINCE DEWITT CLINTON DAYS AND ONE WHICH LED ME BELIEVE WE HAD MADE A DEAL STOP SERIOUSLY I THINK YOU ARE LETTING A FEW THOUSAND DOLLARS KEEP YOU FROM HAVING A LOT OF FUN AND WHEN YOU FIGURE THE GOVERNMENT GETS EIGHTY PERCENT OF IT DO YOU THINK ITS NICE TO MAKE ME SUFFER THIS WAY STOP PLEASE ADVISE LYONS CLOSE DEAL ACCORDING MY TERMS AND ALL WILL BE FORGIVEN BEST REGARDS

PAN BERMAN

On June 26, George and Ira settled contract arrangements with RKO. The terms: $55,000 for sixteen weeks' work on the movie, with an option by the studio for a follow-up film at a salary of $70,000, again for sixteen weeks.

In the months preceding his move to California in August 1936, Gershwin wrote only one new tune for the New York scene—"King of Swing," with lyrics by Albert Stillman. It was introduced by Buck and Bubbles on May 28, 1936, as part of a Radio City Music Hall stage revue called *Swing Is King*,[4] but it has hardly been heard from since. Ira was represented in somewhat better fashion in New York during this same period. He wrote the lyrics to music by Vernon Duke for the successful *Ziegfeld Follies of 1936*,[5] which opened at the Winter Garden on January 30, 1936. It was not until the end of 1936, when the Gershwins were living in Hollywood, that they both contributed to a New York production again. At that, it was only one song, "By Strauss,"[6] their witty takeoff on the Viennese waltz. This tune was included in Vincente Minnelli's revue *The Show Is On* when it opened at the Winter Garden on December 25, 1936.

Though he may not have been very active on Broadway at this time, Gershwin's name continued to appear regularly in the news. For instance, on January 5, 1936, a reception and concert in his honor was tendered at the Plaza Hotel by Mailamm, the American Palestine Music Association, with appropriate press fanfare. He also got plenty of attention when he went before the House Patents Committee in Washington, D.C., on February 25, along with Irvin Berlin, Rudy Vallee, and Gene Buck of ASCAP, to speak against the Duffy bill, an attempt to amend 1909 copyright legislation. Nor was there a letup in his concertizing. As always, he performed before the public at every opportunity, including two all-Gershwin evenings at Lewisohn Stadium on July 9 and 10, his last appearances in New York.

Obviously two nights of Gershwin at the stadium were planned in anticipation of a rush of his many fans. For the expected huge turnouts, several sure-fire Gershwin chestnuts were announced in advance: *An American in Paris, Rhapsody in Blue,* and the *Concerto in F,* with Gershwin as soloist in the *Rhapsody* and the *Concerto* and Alexander Smallens[7] conducting the New York Philharmonic. In addition, Todd Duncan, Anne Brown, Ruby Elzy, and the Eva Jessye Choir, all from the original production of *Porgy and Bess,* were booked to sing selections from the opera. But despite these goodies, the attendance was meager on both nights. As the *New York Times* reported on July 10, 1936, "It was George Gershwin night at the Lewisohn Stadium, and there were empty seats in the amphitheatre last night. That is news." The *Times* then went on to explain why only 7,000 people showed up for the first concert: "Against the hottest day in the city's records Mr. Gershwin's popularity could not prevail." Since the weather for the second concert was as warm as for the first, attendance was sparse again for the same reason. However, Gershwin was so very much wrapped up with stadium attendance records that he didn't immediately grasp why his numerous fans had deserted him. For as Oscar Levant tells it, a friend of his visited Gershwin backstage at the stadium to find him "in conversation with Mrs. Charles Guggenheimer, director of the stadium concerts. She was exuding enthusiasm for the performance, but George seemed detached and inattentive. When she paused for a moment he said, 'How's the crowd?' 'Grand,' she answered. . . . With a shake of his head, Gershwin observed, 'Last year we had seventeen thousand.' The friend interrupted, 'Don't forget, George—this was the hottest day in the history of New York.' He brightened a little at this and remarked, with that curious mixture of irrelevance and seriousness, 'That's right. I know four friends of mine who were supposed to come, but they were overcome by the heat.' "[8]

On August 10, 1936, after winding up their business in New York and putting their furniture and other belongings in storage, George and Ira flew to California to take up their movie duties there. By August 22, they had leased a magnificent creamy-white Spanish-style home at 1019 North Roxbury Drive in Beverly Hills, with swimming pool, tennis court, and Ping-Pong table, and they settled down to the civilities of Hollywood living. This meant an almost continual round of dinners and parties for George in the evening. During the day, when he wasn't visiting the movie lot or working at home, he was usually outdoors playing golf or tennis or participating in some other pleasurable athletic pastime, frequently in the company of other "expatriate" New Yorkers like himself who had come West for their share of movie gold. It was an easygoing, well-paid existence that appealed to him. In comparison with his last stay in the movie colony, in connection with *Delicious,* he now found life there more to his liking. As he noted in a letter, "Hollywood has taken on quite a new color since our last visit six years ago. There are many people in the business today who talk the language of smart showmen and it is therefore much more agreeable working out here. We have many friends here from the East, so the social life has also improved greatly." Speaking with all the conviction of a zealot, newly converted to the merits of small-time life, he also had something good to say about the camaraderie existing among Hollywood songwriters: "All the writingmen and tunesmiths get together in a way that is practically impossible in the East. I've seen a great deal of Irving Berlin and Jerome Kern at poker parties and dinners and the feeling around is very 'gemutlich.' " With old friends everywhere he looked and new ones added regularly, it wasn't long before the Gershwin household was jumping with social activity. Among his large circle of Hollywood friends were Moss Hart, Lillian Hellman, Edward G. Robinson, Rouben Mamoulian, Oscar Levant, Harold Arlen, Harry Ruby, and E. Y. "Yip" Harburg, nearly all "refugees" from the East.

Gershwin became friendly, too, with famed "twelve-tone" composer Arnold Schoenberg, who in 1936 joined the faculty of the University of California at Los Angeles.[9] Always impressed by name musicians of recognized attainments, he had publicly shown his respect for the brilliant Viennese master as early as September 1933, even before he had met him, by contributing toward some scholarships for Schoenberg's students at the newly formed Malkin Conservatory in Boston,[10] where Schoenberg taught for one season after coming to the United States in October 1933 as an émigré from Nazi Germany. In Hollywood, Gershwin and Schoenberg shared a love for tennis. They not only played together frequently, but Gershwin also extended a standing invitation to the older man to use his tennis court regularly. Any aesthetic, intellectual, and personality differences between them were glossed over in the easygoing, chitchat exchanged by two tennis enthusiasts. However, on at least one occasion the underlying dissimilarities in their makeup surfaced briefly. One day, following a concert of Schoenberg's abstruse string quartets, the two met on the tennis court, when, as Oscar Levant relates, "talk turned to the concert of the previous day. 'I'd like to write a quartet some day,' said George. 'But it will be something simple, like Mozart.' Schoenberg mistakenly interpreted Gershwin's typically irrelevant reflections as a comment on his work and answered, somewhat nettled, 'I'm not a simple man—and, anyway, Mozart was considered far from simple in his day.' "[11]

George and Ira had little difficulty keeping up with the pace of the movie they had been hired for. By the end of September 1936 they had still not gotten a completed script from the studio, even though they were on salary. But George and Ira did not sit idly by while Hollywood chieftains deliberated on an appropriate script that would best utilize the talents of their "hot" Astaire-Rogers property. Rather, they went ahead on their own and prepared a number of tunes for possible inclusion in the film. They quickly impressed producer Berman, director Mark Sandrich, and Fred Astaire with their wares. By the time the score was just about completed, in early December, the Gershwins had established themselves so favorably that RKO, exercising its option, asked them to work on still another Astaire film. Among the tunes the Gershwins wrote for their first movie—ultimately called *Shall We Dance* rather than *Watch Your Step*—which helped cinch their second RKO contract were these: "Let's Call the Whole Thing Off," "They Can't Take That Away from Me," and "They All Laughed," classics all, as well as "Slap That Bass" and the title song.[12] Two of the tunes composed for the film have only lately been published. One of them, an instrumental interlude called "Walking the Dog," was published in 1960 as a piano solo titled "Promenade," while another one, "Hi-Ho," never used in the film, came out in 1967.

Gershwin added to his Hollywood income by performing in public when it didn't interfere with his movie duties. He usually got a $2,000 fee for each engagement, besides the applause, adulation, and attention—all of which he loved—that went with concertizing. Moreover, his concerts required practically no advance preparation from him, since he generally performed over and over again the same pieces—all his own—in his limited repertoire. Thus, between movie assignments, he gladly took on some concert dates between December 15, 1936, and February 11, 1937. Starting with a concert in Seattle on December 15, Gershwin performed in such cities as San Francisco, Berkeley, Detroit, and Los Angeles over the two-month period, with time out for rest and relaxation. In almost every case the concerts drew capacity crowds who were clearly pro-Gershwin. But there were also grumblings to be heard from some critics who deplored the program content as well as the show-biz aspects of the concerts. For instance, in reviewing two all-Gershwin programs that he gave with the Los Angeles Philharmonic on February 10 and 11,[13] Richard Drake Saunders of the *Musical Courier* complained: "In more ways than one it was a show, rather than a concert. Gershwin has a certain individual flair, and an occasional work of his on a program is all very well, but an entire evening is too much. It is like a meal of chocolate eclairs." Concluding his review with some "positive" attributions to the Gershwin program, Saunders remarked sarcastically: "It fulfills a purpose in making a certain class of people conscious of such a thing as symphonic ensemble. It was obvious that a large number had never been in the auditorium before. Anyway, they saw some movie stars."[14]

It was during Gershwin's engagement with the Los Angeles Philharmonic that the first portent of his fatal illness showed itself. While playing the *Concerto in F* with the orchestra, conducted by Alexander Smallens, he suffered a mental lapse and blundered during the performance. It went practically unnoticed, but it had special significance for him since he had never stumbled like this before. He later recalled experiencing a disagreeable smell of burning rubber when his mind went blank.[15] In discussing the incident afterward with Dr. Zilboorg by phone, Gershwin was told that the cause was probably physical rather than psychical in origin. But a medical checkup in late February showed him to be a fine physical specimen.

He quickly forgot the entire matter in the press of daily living. High on the list of his priorities was the score for the new Astaire film *A Damsel in Distress*. The movie, based on a script by P. G. Wodehouse,[16] of *Jeeves* fame, featured Joan Fontaine in the feminine lead, replacing Astaire's perennial partner, Ginger Rogers.[17] Gershwin's music for this film turned out to be prime Gershwin, if only for two hardy perennials: "A Foggy Day" and "Nice Work If You Can Get It." One of the more novel aspects of the score was his inclusion in it of two pieces for chorus because of his displeasure with the way studio bigwigs had treated his music for *Shall We Dance*. As he explained it, "In our next picture *Damsel in Distress* we have protected ourselves in that we have a madrigal group of singers and have written two English type ballads for background music so the audience will get a chance to hear some singing besides the crooning of the stars." Despite his implication of substantial musical fare, both ballads for chorus are little more than trifles. Of these two "protection" pieces, the livelier one, "The Jolly Tar and the Milkmaid," with its quaint use of such phrases as "a hey and a nonny," has been heard now and then outside of its movie context. The second, "Sing of Spring," has been practically ignored, mock Old English text and all. ("Piminy mo" and "tilly-tally-tillo" are some of the phrases Ira created for it.) It was not until 1969 that "Sing of Spring" was first performed in concert.[18]

Even with the pressure of movie deadlines, Gershwin found ample time for romance. Not only that, his name was continually linked in the press with one pretty young thing or another from the movie-colony set. All of this interest in his affairs of the heart was, of course, aided and abetted by the *macho* image he had built up over the years as one of music-dom's most talked-about Don Juans.[19] Gossip columnists had a field day keeping up with his numerous amours and reporting them breathlessly to their many devoted readers. Just as one gossip item was printed and circulated it was quickly superseded by another one. Reports of his friendship with Simone Simon, the French actress, however, did not have so brief a run in the press as did most of the others, principally because there was a carryover beyond his death. When Miss Simon, who had come to Hollywood in 1935, first met him, she was often seen in his company. She was then just making a name for herself in the movies and had let it be known that Gershwin was planning a light-opera career for her as her sponsor.[20] But some of the more personal details of their relationship became public knowledge only after he had died, when Miss Simon brought charges in 1938 against her former private secretary, Sandra Martin, for having pilfered close to $11,000 from her bank account. In court, while attempting to answer the charges against her, the defendant divulged how Miss Simon had given a "friend" a gold-plated key and holder with the initials "G. G." on it to her West Los Angeles mansion. The "friend" also got from her a pair of gold-backed hairbrushes, similarly initialed, the court was told. When asked to identify the "friend," Miss Simon smilingly declined. "You will never know," she coyly replied. Shortly afterward, some newsmen got wind of the fact that Gershwin's mother had found an initialed, gold-plated key and sapphire-encrusted holder among his personal effects in her apartment. In no time at all the recipient of Miss Simon's symbols of friendship was exposed.

Keeping his fingers in as many Hollywood pies as possible, Gershwin put out some feelers in the spring of 1937 to see whether the movie industry was interested in buying his life story. He also plunged into a new movie assignment just as soon as he had finished the score for *A Damsel in Distress*. On May 12 he noted, "We started this week on the *Goldwyn Follies,* a super, super, stupendous, colossal, moving picture extravaganza which the 'Great Goldwyn' is producing. Ira and I should be taking a vacation by this time, having just finished eight songs for the second Astaire picture *Damsel in Distress,* but unfortunately Goldwyn cannot put off a half million dollars' worth of principal salaries while the Gershwins bask in the sunshine."[21] During this same period of intense activity, he became smitten, too, with the chic charm of Paulette Goddard. Strongly drawn to her, Gershwin persisted in seeing her as frequently as possible, though generally away from the public spotlight, since she was still married to Charles Chaplin. (She had been the comedian's protégée before marrying him in 1935.) In Miss Goddard, Gershwin felt he had finally found his ideal woman and went so far as to ask her to leave Chaplin and marry him. When she turned him down, it was a major blow to his ego.

On top of this rejection, he began to complain of headaches and dizzy spells in early June. He assumed at first that they resulted from overwork. When they persisted, Dr. Ernest Simmel, a Los Angeles psychoanalyst recommended by Dr. Zilboorg, examined him. Like Zilboorg, Simmel believed the symptoms were physical rather than mental in nature and referred Gershwin, in turn, to Dr. Gabriell Segall for a checkup.[22] When Gershwin saw Segall for the first time on June 9 it was found that the

> two major complaints dealt with headaches and dizzy spells, the latter occurring over a three-month period. Headaches tended to occur during the early morning hours, awakening Gershwin about 6 A.M., and consisted of neuralgic pain in the right side of the face and occasionally a dull ache at the top of the head. The headaches disappeared after eating. Dizzy spells consisted of momentary giddiness which lasted for about thirty seconds. These attacks were associated with a disagreeable, foul-smelling olfactory sensation. Dizzy spells took place at least once daily and were usually present in the early morning hours when Gershwin awoke, recurring during periods of emotional tension—for example, during the performance of a concert or even while playing tennis. Gershwin was unaware of ever having lost consciousness or having convulsions. Physical examination failed to reveal any abnormalities: an electrocardiogram showed no evidence of heart damage; the urinalysis and blood count were normal; and the blood pressure was 110/80.[23]

A neurological examination on June 20 also proved negative, except for one detail: there was an impairment of his sense of smell in his right nasal passage. Further diagnostic tests at the Cedars of Lebanon Hospital between June 23 and 26, including X rays of the skull and blood studies, showed nothing irregular.[24] While in the hospital, Gershwin categorically rejected as being too painful and time-consuming the suggestion that a spinal tap be performed to check for a possible brain tumor. He considered his malady nothing serious and was anxious to leave the hospital and get back to composing.

On returning home, he was placed on sedation with a nurse in constant attendance and examined daily by doctors. It was hoped that extended rest might help him bounce back to his normal self. For added privacy, he was even moved to a friend's house nearby, away from visitors, noise, and distractions. But to the mystification of his friends and relatives—many of whom speculated that he was unconsciously rebelling against Hollywood and the way his music had been treated in the movies—his inexplicable ailment did not go away. Despite fewer headaches in his almost perpetually drowsy state, his condition deteriorated. Whereas he had been like a brave young bull only weeks before, sure of his powers and ready to take on anything, he was now enfeebled and pitiful. As the vital forces within him ebbed away, he lived in a world of drawn shades, for lights bothered him. Nor could he walk without support or eat without having his food cut up for him. He was now a shadow of himself, his voice weak, his coloring pale, his eyes lusterless, his handshake limp, his coordination limited.

At the request of his doctor, Gershwin played the piano on the morning of July 9. He was still able to get around the keyboard. But in the late afternoon he fell into a deep coma. Rushed to the hospital, he was examined by Dr. Carl Rand, a neurosurgeon, whose notes show that Gershwin

> could not be aroused even by superorbital pressure. However, he occasionally would move an arm or a leg, but he did not make purposeful movements. . . . The eyegrounds showed recent swellings of the discs, elevation of about 2 diopters with fresh hemorrhages and overfilled vessels. He did not move the right arm nor right leg quite as much as the left, although upon stimulation they were moved. Blood pressure 105/60. The abdominal and epigastric reflexes could barely be obtained on the left, but not on the right. The deep reflexes were generally subdued throughout.[25]

By July 10, after getting the results of a spinal tap, there was no longer any doubt about the cause of his condition. He had a brain tumor, and it was crucial that surgery be performed as quickly as possible.

What transpired next was ordered frenzy. Dr. Harvey Cushing, the eminent brain specialist, was first approached to perform the delicate operation, but he declined—he had not done any recent surgery and feared his reflexes might not be so sharp as they should be. Attempts were then made, without success, to reach Dr. Walter Dandy, of Johns Hopkins, another brilliant brain surgeon. He was cruising somewhere on Chesapeake Bay with Governor Harry W. Nice of Maryland on the state yacht *Du Pont*. Not giving up easily, two of Gershwin's friends, completely independent of each other, took dramatic action: George Pallay, in California, called the White House for help, while Emil Mosbacher, in New York, appealed directly to the Coast Guard. Through their separate or combined efforts the Coast Guard intervened and located Dr. Dandy. He was taken to Cambridge, on the Eastern shore of Maryland, and then flown to Newark. There, Mosbacher had arranged to have a plane in readiness for the trip to California. But in talking by telephone from Newark with Gershwin's doctors in California, Dandy was told that it would be too dangerous to delay the operation until he could get there. After discussing his case in detail with the attending physicians, Dandy agreed with them that immediate surgery was called for. He then flew back to Maryland.

Gershwin playing on the set for *Shall We Dance*. Seated are Fred Astaire and Ginger Rogers. Standing, from the left, are Hermes Pan, ballet choreographer; Mark Sandrich, director; Ira; and Nathaniel Shilkret, musical director.

Fred Astaire and Ginger Rogers dancing to the tune of "They All Laughed" in *Shall We Dance*.

Another scene from *Shall We Dance*, with Fred Astaire surrounded by a bevy of beautiful women, each wearing a mask of Ginger Rogers.

Prior to surgery, Gershwin's doctors had diagnosed his condition as a tumor of the right temporal lobe. The operation itself was performed in the early hours of Sunday morning, July 11, 1937, and portions of a cystic tumor removed from his brain. About five hours after the operation at 10:35 A.M., he died without regaining consciousness. However, even if the tumor could have been completely removed and he had survived the operation, there was every chance he would have suffered another tumor attack in short order, for as Dr. Dandy pointed out, on receiving a report of the operation from one of the attending physicians,

> I do not see what more you could have done for Mr. Gershwin. It was just one of those fulminating tumors. There are not many tumors that are removable, and it would be my impression that although the tumor in a large part might have been extirpated and he would have recovered for a little while, it would have recurred very quickly since the whole thing fulminated so suddenly at the onset. I think the outcome is much the best for himself, for a man as brilliant as he with a recurring tumor it would have been terrible; it would have been a slow death.[26]

Word of Gershwin's death quickly spread around the world—the news met with shock and dismay. Outpourings of grief and tributes to his talent soon followed, with political figures, friends, and professional associates outdoing each other in eulogizing him. Typical of the panegyrics was this from Paul Whiteman: "Speaking as a member of the world of modern music, I would say that the death of George Gershwin is a great blow to those millions of music lovers who received his arresting compositions so enthusiastically. We feel he had only scratched the surface of the fame that would have been greater still had he lived to continue his works. It is through his writings that the symphony concert halls of the world have been opened for modern music."[27]

Equally lavish were the two simultaneous funeral services for Gershwin on July 15, one on the West Coast at Hollywood's B'nai B'rith Temple, and the other at Manhattan's Temple Emanu–El, where Gershwin's body, after being brought from California, rested in a flower-draped coffin before the ark. At the New York services, approximately 3,500 people—most of them prominent in the theater, the music world, or politics—filled huge Emanu–El, while more than a thousand waited outside in a drizzling rain. Inside the hushed temple, huge banks of flowers from many of Gershwin's friends filled the chancel and sides of the sanctuary and added to the aura and drama of the occasion. So did the list of honorary pallbearers, headed by Mayor Fiorello La Guardia, and including George M. Cohan, former Mayor Jimmy Walker, Walter Damrosch, Sam H.

Harris, Edwin Franko Goldman, and Gene Buck. After prayers, further eulogies, and some small doses of solemn, appropriate funeral music, the casket, followed by members of the Gershwin family, was taken to Mount Hope Cemetery, Hastings-on-Hudson, for burial.[28] While the New York ceremonies were going on, many of moviedom's big names crowded Hollywood's B'nai B'rith Temple for equally impressive funeral services. As a further Hollywood tribute to his memory, all movie studios halted work for a moment of silence synchronous with the start of funeral services on both coasts.

Despite the Gershwins' great loss, they handled themselves with poise and forbearance during the days preceding and following his death and funeral, as befitted one of America's best-known families. And they have maintained this good public posture ever since, with disagreements and frictions among themselves invariably kept as private family matters. Thus, when Ira and Rose Gershwin both sought to be declared administrator of George's estate almost concurrent with his death and each set legal machinery in motion toward this end, there was no public acrimony between them. If there were any hard feelings when Mrs. Gershwin was ultimately declared administrator and George's sole heir, inheriting a net estate of close to $350,000,[29] it did not show publicly. For that matter, when Ira, following Mrs. Gershwin's death in December 1948, disputed the terms of his mother's will that left his brother and sister each forty percent of her estate and himself only twenty, that family squabble, too, was handled legalistically and quietly; no one but those involved knew what took place.[30] Also kept quiet were the family grumblings when Rose Gershwin, years after her husband's death, was duped out of money and valuables by a man, considerably her junior, who had attracted her interest. Even when news touching on George or the family has gotten less than attractive treatment in the press—as was the case when Arthur Gershwin was sued for divorce and he was unflatteringly described by his wife as living in the shadow of George, or when "Alan Gershwin" claimed he was George's illegitimate son—the Gershwins have usually taken a lofty stance and tended to ignore such reports, letting them die of their own accord.

At the time of George's death, he and Ira had nearly completed five songs (mainly the verses required further work for these tunes) for *The Goldwyn Follies,* among them "I Love to Rhyme," "Love Walked In," "I Was Doing All Right," and "Love Is Here to Stay." The fifth tune, "Just Another Rhumba," was dropped from the movie, though it was eventually published in 1959. To help complete the score, Vernon Duke was brought in. Besides fleshing out some of Gershwin's verses,[31] Duke also wrote new ballet music, plus two tunes with Ira, only one of which—"Spring Again"

285

Simone's Key in Gershwin 'Chest'

The back of the golden key which Simone Simon gave to the late George Gershwin. Note the sapphire slide (arrow). (Copyright, 1938, by N. Y. Daily Mirror)

By RAY DOYLE and ARNOLD PRINCE.

(Copyright, 1938, by Daily Mirror, Inc. Reproduction in whole or in part forbidden.)

The mystery of the golden key to her West Los Angeles mansion that Simone Simon gave an unnamed friend was solved in New York yesterday with the revelation of a beautiful association between the petite French film actress and a great musical genius.

The recipient of the gold-sheathed key, which bore the initials "G. G.," was George Gershwin, noted composer, whose untimely death in Hollywood last July blighted the dainty actress dreams of a light opera career he had planned for her.

Existence of the key was disclosed in a Los Angeles court last week when the pert French star appeared as a witness against her former secretary, Sandra Martin, charged with having pilfered $11,000 from her bank account.

Asked to identify the admitted friend to whom she had given the key and a pair of $295 gold backed hair brushes bearing the same monogram, Miss Simone smilingly declined.

"You will never know," she replied.

Mother Has Key

Yesterday, Gershwin's mother, Mrs. Rose Gershwin, produced the golden key in her apartment at 25 Central Park West, and turned it over to the Daily Mirror.

She had found it in a small box where Gershwin kept his most precious relics and into which his most treasured personal effects were put after his death.

Gave Composer Friendship Symbol

SIMONE SIMON.
Gershwin called her voice "greatest in world."
(Other photos on Page 1)

Arnold Schoenberg.
He and Gershwin shared
a love for tennis.

The article in the *New York Daily Mirror* which revealed that Simone Simon gave Gershwin the key to her mansion. *(Used by permission of the Hearst Corporation)*

Jacques d'Amboise and *corps de ballet* in George Balanchine's 1970 ballet, *Who Cares?* based on seventeen of Gershwin's famous tunes. *(Courtesy the New York City Ballet)*

—was actually heard in the film. Of Gershwin's tunes for Goldwyn's *Follies,* "Love Walked In" and "Love Is Here to Stay"[32] have both become major hits, with the latter's popularity greatly boosted by its subsequent use in the movie *An American in Paris.*

Gershwin left behind him a number of notebooks and manuscripts containing about one hundred songs in various stages of completion, which Ira has drawn on from time to time.[33] For example, in 1938, Ira, with the collaboration of Kay Swift, adapted the chorus of one unpublished tune and the verse of another into "Dawn of a New Day," which became the official march of the 1939 New York World's Fair. In 1946, again with Kay Swift's assistance, Ira shaped a score for the Betty Grable–Dick Haymes film *The Shocking Miss Pilgrim,* from George's unpublished material and came up with such pleasers as "Aren't You Kind of Glad We Did?," "Changing My Tune," "The Back Bay Polka," and "For You, For Me, For Evermore." Ira had less impressive results with the score for the 1964 Billy Wilder movie *Kiss Me Stupid,* especially in view of the advance publicity the music got. On February 17, 1964, the *New York Times* gave front-page attention to the news that a batch of Gershwin's unpublished tunes in Ira's possession would be released in the future and that three of these tunes—"Sophia," "I'm a Poached Egg," and "All the Livelong Day"—would be in the forthcoming *Kiss Me Stupid.* Advance publicity or not, all three *Kiss Me Stupid* tunes, without exception, have made little headway with the public. The movie itself, starring Dean Martin and Kim Novak, was hardly up to Billy Wilder's usual standards and suffered badly in comparison with such Wilder gems as *Some Like It Hot* and *The Apartment,* which preceded it.

Ever since moving west with George in 1936, Ira has remained a resident of Beverly Hills, preferring the slower pace and warmer climate of Southern California to that of New York. He and his wife live in a palatial home at 1021 North Roxbury Drive, next door to the address they once shared with George. Shorter, stockier, less flamboyant than George, and less compulsive about work, Ira, even if he had wanted to, would hardly have been able to fill the void caused by his brother's death. He has generally preferred to lead a quiet life, away from the public spotlight, doing the things that appeal to him most: reading, going to the race track, or enjoying some other leisurely pursuits. He has also spent much time building up and maintaining archives on George and in keeping an eye on matters touching directly on his brother's reputation. He has been a zealous watchdog of the latter and of all the Gershwiniana in his possession. This caretaker function on Ira's part undoubtedly stems from his admiration and affection for George. Yet it also helps control what is said about *all* the Gershwins, including Ira himself. Not that Ira's reputation as a lyricist is in danger of being slighted. Having proved his worth while George lived, Ira is probably at the peak of his prestige and fortune as the surviving member of a famous team. Moreover, since George's death, Ira has collaborated on a number of fine scores for Broadway and Hollywood with such distinguished company as Kurt Weill, Jerome Kern, Aaron Copland, Arthur Schwartz, Harry Warren, Burton Lane, and Harold Arlen. For Broadway, he was Weill's partner for the musicals *Lady in the Dark* (1941) and *The Firebrand of Florence* (1945), and joined forces with Arthur Schwartz in writing the score for *Park Avenue* (1946). His film contributions include collaborations with Aaron Copland on *North Star* (1943), with Jerome Kern on *Cover Girl* (1944), and with Kurt Weill on *Where Do We Go from Here?* (1945), as well as with Harry Warren on *The Barkleys of Broadway* (1949), with Burton Lane on *Give a Girl a Break* (1953), and with Harold Arlen on *A Star Is Born* (1954) and *The Country Girl* (1954).

During Gershwin's last stay in Hollywood, he frequently spoke of writing a variety of "serious" pieces on completing his movie obligations. Like a musical Robin Hood taking from the wealthy to assist the less affluent, he had planned to underwrite the poor-cousin status of his projected long-hair compositions with Hollywood movie-score gold. Depending on his mood, or on to whom he spoke, he mentioned his intention to subsequently write a string quartet, another opera, a symphonic piece, a ballet, and so on.[34] If his death had not prevented it and some of these works had actually been born, they undoubtedly would have been a mixture of crudity and sophistication, as was true of the "serious" pieces that preceded them and of Gershwin himself, for he was a mass of inconsistencies as a musician and as a person. Who can claim really to have known the "true Gershwin," whose image was clouded by so many contradictions? Kind, thoughtful, and sensitive in his relations with some, he could also be vain, difficult, and unpredictable with others. Whereas many remember him as dynamic, ebullient, and sure of himself, others found him troubled, confused, and insecure. He had innumerable problems with the opposite sex and was a habitué of brothels, yet innumerable intimates considered him a "ladies' man" of the first magnitude. Seemingly comfortable in the drawing rooms of Park Avenue and eager to emulate the rich and the powerful around him, he was never able to "smooth out" his own lower East Side background. Outwardly a fine physical specimen, he nonetheless tended toward hypochondria and was plagued all his adult life by constipation and digestive problems. He had pretensions of intellectualism, but often lacked the most basic kind of apodictic reasoning. A painter who took himself seriously, he was little more than a Sunday artist. A white man who could empathize with blacks, he was also guilty of unfeeling presumptuousness in setting himself up as a musical spokesman for them. A musician touched with natural genius who coveted the respectability of the concert hall, he never developed his composing skills beyond the point of rather prosaic technical obstacles. He had few peers as an improvisor of his own music, yet he never gained enough pianistic know-how to play the standard repertoire or even to read scores fluently. He presented himself as a professional conductor, but was little more than a rote baton waver who never attempted a serious study of the conducting art. He boasted of his ability to orchestrate his own music, yet was dependent on others for scoring help. A creature of the glitter and tinsel of Tin Pan Alley, Broadway, Hollywood, and the news media, he also hobnobbed with some of the most important names in serious music and was often the object of their admiration. Gershwin was a living, breathing, striving, plotting mass of contradictions—always on the run, always out to conquer the world, always seeking the adulation of the vast, unknown public (possibly this was the love affair he was eternally seeking). He played hard; he worked hard; he died hard. He was a child of his age who never became old enough to outlive his usefulness. And he had more than enough weaknesses and strengths, talents and failings, good points and bad, to go around. He had a little of all of us in him, and it showed.

NOTES

CHAPTER 1: *Family Background*

1. Morris's family name has also been reported to have once been Gershkovitz.

2. Some of Gershwin's problems as an adult, particularly in relation to women, may very well have derived in part from the weak masculine model he had as a child.

3. The family rumor may be only a romanticization of the Gershwin past: a tendency common to many families.

4. On Morris's death certificate, the cause of his death is listed as "chronic lymphatic leukemia—cardiac failure." Morris died at fifty-nine in his apartment at the Hotel Broadmoor in Manhattan.

5. George died without leaving a will, and any strained relations that already existed between Ira and his mother were probably intensified by the legal proceedings that followed. Both Rose, a New York resident, and Ira, who had lived in California since 1936, petitioned the courts in their respective states to be judged administrator of George's estate. On the legal determination that George was a resident of New York even though he had a home in California when he died, Rose was declared administrator. She also became the sole beneficiary of George's estate. On her death in 1948, Rose bequeathed to Frances and Arthur forty percent each of the annual net income from her estate, while Ira received only twenty percent—another indication of the presumed schism between Ira and his mother. Ira immediately challenged his brother and sister over the terms of his mother's will. This dispute was resolved only when Ira waived claims for personal property he alleged his mother owed him, in return for sharing her estate equally with his brother and sister. An agreement to this effect, dated December 21, 1948, is on file in Manhattan's Surrogate Court.

6. Ira has come to be known as "Mr. Words" corresponding to George's "Mr. Music."

291

CHAPTER 2: *Boyhood Years*

1. Robert Payne (*Gershwin*, p. 33) claims that Gershwin was a pianist at a Catskill Mountains hotel during the summer of 1912. This date would seem to be too early, as Gershwin had not had enough experience as a pianist by then to have undertaken a professional assignment, even one as modest as this one obviously was. On the other hand, Edward Jablonski and Lawrence D. Stewart in *The Gershwin Years* (1958), p. 46, allege that the composer worked in the Cat-skill during the summer of either 1914 or 1915. These dates, in this writer's opinion, would have conflicted with Gershwin's employment at Remick's.

2. Isaac Goldberg (*George Gershwin*, p. 66) states that Gershwin had not yet appeared in public as a pianist before this occasion. There would appear to be general agreement, how-ever, that this was his initial appear-ance as *both* pianist and composer.

CHAPTER 3: *The Young Professional*

1. Approximately 125 piano rolls have thus far been attributed to Gershwin. The exact number he recorded, how-ever, is still not certain.

2. Among those most active in propagat-ing the claim that there are Jewish elements in Gershwin's music have been Isaac Goldberg and Robert Payne. But neither of them has de-tailed these Jewish characteristics in specific musical terms.

3. Isaac Goldberg (*George Gershwin*, pp. 39–40) claimed that he had seen sketches for *The Dybbuk* and had heard them played by the composer at the piano. But in a letter to this writer, Ira Gershwin affirmed that "no manuscript exists of, or for, *The Dybbuk*."

4. The relationship between " 'S Won-derful" and the Goldfaden number was first brought to this writer's at-tention by Sholom Secunda.

5. This contract is now at the Library of Congress.

6. Dreyfus first became associated with Harms in 1901 when he bought a twenty-five percent interest in the company.

7. Jerome Kern was Dreyfus's first im-portant "find." Kern's first hit, "How Would You Like to Spoon with Me?" was published by Dreyfus in 1905.

8. In the movie *Rhapsody in Blue*, the heavy-set, gregarious Charles Coburn played Max Dreyfus. In real life, Dreyfus was a small, reserved, soft-spoken, slightly-built man.

9. Levant had come to the performance because his uncle, Oscar Radin, con-ducted the orchestra.

10. As a high-school student at Townsend Harris Hall in 1918, Ira had been one of the editors of *The Academic Herald*. While at City College, be-tween 1914 and 1916, he wrote for *The Campus* and *Cap and Bells*—both school publications. He had also contributed humorous comments and short poems to the "Conning Tower" and Don Marquis's column "The Sun Dial," in the *Evening Sun*; in May 1917, Marquis printed in his column Ira's first song lyrics: "You May Throw All the Rice You Desire (But Please, Friends, Throw No Shoes)."

CHAPTER 4: *Onward and Upward*

1. During the first few decades of this century, with production costs a frac-tion of what they are today, Broad-way shows did not necessarily have to run for many months to be con-sidered modest successes. *La La Lucille* was such a show.

2. In an article titled "How to Write a Popular Song" in the New York *Telegraph* of June 23, 1906, Alfred

Aarons frankly admitted he had written a number of successful songs simply by borrowing melodies from such composers as Wagner, Verdi, Mascagni, and Victor Herbert.

3. Aarons and Freedley first became a producing team in 1923 when they presented *The New Poor* on Broadway for a six weeks' run.

4. Based on a farce by Pinero called *The Magistrate*, this show was first produced in England under the title *The Boy*. Opening at the Shubert Theater on February 6, 1919, *Good Morning, Judge* ran for 140 performances and contained these Gershwin songs: "I Was So Young, You Were So Beautiful," lyrics by Irving Caesar and Al Bryan; and "There's More to the Kiss Than the X-X-X," lyrics by Irving Caesar, both modest successes.

5. Gershwin's "Some Wonderful Sort of Someone," first used in *Ladies First*, and "Something About Love," lyrics by Lou Paley, were interpolated into this musical, which opened at the Lyric Theater on May 12, 1919, and ran for forty-eight performances.

6. Of the six songs that Gershwin contributed to this revue, only "Poppyland" and "Limehouse Nights"—both with lyrics by B. G. De Sylva and John Henry Mears—were published. Produced by Morris Gest, this musical opened at the Century Grove, atop the Century Theater, on December 27, 1919, and lasted for 110 performances.

7. *Lullaby* has been published by New World Music in the original version for string quartet as well as in a version for string orchestra.

8. The amount of time claimed to have been needed to complete "Swanee" has apparently decreased over the years. Some years ago it was reported that the song was written in about half an hour. That figure was reduced to fifteen minutes in a later report. In an interview with this writer more recently, Caesar claimed the song "was written in eight minutes."

9. Some idea of the popularity of "Swanee" abroad can be gotten from a letter that George wrote to Ira on visiting England in 1923: "A funny thing happened yesterday which made me very joyful and for the moment very happy I came here. The boat was in dock at Southampton and everyone was in line with their passports and landing cards. When I handed my passport to one of the men at a table he read it, looked up and said, 'George Gershwin, writer of "Swanee"?' It took me off my feet for a second. It was so unexpected, you know. Of course I agreed I was the composer. . . . I couldn't ask for a more pleasant entrance into a country."

10. Lou Paley wrote the lyrics for such Gershwin songs as "Something about Love" (heard in the 1919 musical *The Lady in Red* and in the 1926 London production of *Lady, Be Good*) and "Oo, How I Love to Be Loved by You" (sung in *Ed Wynn's Carnival* of 1920), and was the co-lyricist with Ned Wayburn for "Come to the Moon," which was used in the 1919 *Capitol Revue*. Paley, who died on July 5, 1952, was also the lyricist for a number of unpublished Gershwin songs.

11. Among those who attended these Saturday gatherings were S. N. Behrman, Groucho Marx, Irving Caesar, B. G. De Sylva, and Howard Dietz. Dietz, who then lived in an apartment below the Paleys', was introduced to these Saturday sessions when his chandelier started shaking. Going upstairs to complain to the Paleys, Dietz found a large group seated on the floor, listening intently to Gershwin's singing and playing. Dietz became so entranced with Gershwin that he soon forgot about his chandelier. He and his wife became Saturday regulars at the Paleys'.

12. Gershwin may not have been a fashion plate in the beginning, but he still spent heavily for dress—that is, relative to income. In later years, for example, he claimed that even when he earned only twenty-five dollars weekly he paid twenty-two dollars for shoes.

13. The cold-blooded side of Gershwin, in relation to women, comes through in this widely quoted tale. On being told that a girl he had been interested

in had married another, Gershwin is reputed to have said, "I'd feel terrible if I weren't so busy."

14. Bennett Cerf, "In Memory of George Gershwin," *Saturday Review of Literature* (July 17, 1943), p. 16. Cerf has included this article in his *Try and Stop Me*, a collection of anecdotes.

15. A self-made millionaire from oil and investments, down to earth and resourceful, Mosbacher is the father of Emil, Jr., the famous boatman who was Chief of Protocol for President Richard M. Nixon.

16. Isaac Goldberg, *George Gershwin*, p. 63.

17. *Ibid.*, p. 62.

18. This opinion runs counter to that generally expressed about Gershwin: that he was the epitome of industriousness in seeking to master the technical skills of his craft.

19. Oscar Levant, *A Smattering of Ignorance*, p. 160.

20. This writer learned of Gershwin's lessons with Bodanzky from Robert Russell Bennett, the orchestrator, composer, and conductor.

21. Most of Kilenyi's work has been for Broadway and Hollywood. He is the father of pianist Edward Kilenyi, Jr.

22. Some sources have stated that Gershwin studied with Kilenyi for a longer period. This writer, however, agrees with the statement made by Henry Osborne Osgood in his 1926 book *So This is Jazz*, p. 174, that Gershwin "studied harmony on and off for two years, more off than on [with Edward Kilenyi]." Osborne's statement is consistent with the fact that the extant harmony exercises of Gershwin's studies with Kilenyi cover a two-year period, 1919 to 1921. Kilenyi himself clouded this entire question—possibly deliberately—by alleging, in response to a query from this writer, that he did not remember how long Gershwin studied with him or the total number of lessons involved. Kilenyi died on August 15, 1968, at the age of eighty-four.

23. Edward Kilenyi, "George Gershwin as I Knew Him," *Etude* (October 1950), p. 12.

24. This writer learned of the ramifica-

tions of this incident from the pianist Josefa Rosanska, who was a friend of Gershwin when it occurred.

25. Isaac Goldberg's *George Gershwin*, p. 64, was the initial source of this remark. It has since been quoted, with varying degrees of modification, in numerous other works on Gershwin.

26. Little is known of Gershwin's studies with Riegger except that they lasted for several months during the second half of the 1920s, after Gershwin had started collecting paintings. It has been reported that Riegger was very much impressed with his art collection.

27. Gershwin's lessons in counterpoint with Cowell were frequently interrupted for personal as well as professional reasons.

28. The exact dates that Gershwin studied with Schillinger are not known, though the lessons began in 1932, prior to Gershwin's writing *Rumba* or *Cuban Overture* for orchestra in July of that year. Schillinger, in the preface to his book *Kaleidophone*, claimed that Gershwin was his student for four and a half years.

29. Gershwin and White had first met during rehearsals for *Miss 1917*. White had been employed as dancer for the show and Gershwin as pianist.

30. Another salary figure—seventy-five dollars weekly—has been given by Isaac Goldberg, *George Gershwin*, p. 124.

31. The opera's standing with the public was not improved by the inclusion of an excerpt from it in the movie *Rhapsody in Blue*.

32. Information contained in a letter to this writer from Dr. Garbat dated May 15, 1967. Dr. Garbat died on August 12, 1968, at the age of eighty-three.

33. Gershwin's one tune in *The Sweetheart Shop*, "Waiting for the Sun to Come Out," used lyrics by Arthur Francis. This song was the first one published by Ira under his pseudonym. In one year's time, Ira earned close to $1300 in royalties from this tune, a good start for a tyro lyricist.

34. Among the performers in the 1922 *Scandals* was W. C. Fields, who also

helped write the book for the revue.
35. Fred and his sister Adele had started dancing together as children in Omaha. Then their last name was still Austerlitz. The team broke up in 1932

when Adele married an English lord.
36. "Tra-La-La," somewhat revised, was used to good advantage in the 1951 award-winning film *An American in Paris*.

CHAPTER 5: *Jazz and the Concert Hall*

1. Miss Gauthier gave her last concert in 1937 when she appeared with the Boston Symphony in Stravinsky's *Perséphone*, with the composer conducting. She died in 1958.
2. She also claimed that she introduced Gershwin to New York society at a jazz party given after her concert. Actually, this was only one of numerous occasions on which George mingled with the social élite during this period.
3. Merle Armitage (editor), *George Gershwin*, p. 194.
4. See Miss Gauthier's article, "The Roaring Twenties," *Musical Courier* (February 1, 1955), p. 42.
5. John Wilson, "Misunderstood Pioneer," *The New York Times* (December 30, 1967), p. 24.
6. *Ibid.*
7. Whiteman's original recording of "Whispering" is included in a 1968 reissue of early record hits by his band (RCA Victor LPV-555).
8. Paul Whiteman (and Mary Margaret McBride), *Jazz*, pp. 93–94.
9. *Ibid.*, p. 94.
10. Whiteman even moved his concert date ahead to February 12, 1924—he had originally planned to give his concert later—on learning that a rival band was planning a similar event. This ensured that his concert, rather than his rival's, would get the bulk of attention.
11. Numerous sources have erred in attributing the news report of January 4, 1924, to the *New York Herald Tribune*; there was no paper by that name in New York then. There was instead a *New York Herald* and a *New York Tribune*. These two papers merged on March 19, 1924, when their title then became the *New York Herald-New York Tribune*. It was not until May 31, 1926, that

the title *New York Herald Tribune* came into existence.
12. Its original title was *A Perfect Lady*.
13. He at first had wanted to call the work *American Rhapsody*, but changed the title at Ira's suggestion.
14. Compared with his generally pedestrian writing style, this quotation is more literate than one might expect. Isaac Goldberg's *George Gershwin*, pp. 138–39, is the source for this quotation. Though the thought behind the words is evidently Gershwin's, the actual language may have been improved on by Goldberg or someone else.
15. On the basis of this date, one has additional evidence for concluding that Gershwin finished his draft of the *Rhapsody* about January 25.
16. According to Vernon Duke, Gershwin "could ill conceal his grudging admiration for the roly-poly Grofé, who was just as much at home among brasses and woodwinds as Gershwin was in the company of his beloved piano." See Duke's article, "Gershwin, Schillinger, and Dukelsky," *The Musical Quarterly* (January 1947), p. 107.
17. The manuscript of this orchestration of the *Rhapsody* by Grofé along with the holograph of his 1926 arrangement for a larger orchestra, plus Gershwin's original manuscript sketch of the piece are all at the Library of Congress in Washington, D.C.
18. Ewen, in particular, has claimed that Gershwin could have orchestrated the *Rhapsody* without Grofé. Gershwin, himself, two years after the premiere of the *Rhapsody*, claimed in a letter published in *Singing* (October 1926), pp. 17–18, that Grofé "worked from a very complete piano and orchestral sketch in which many of the orchestral colors were indicated."

19. These exercises are at the Library of Congress.
20. Grofé made that statement in 1938; see Merle Armitage (editor), *George Gershwin*, p. 28. Some thirty years later, in a telephone interview with this writer, Grofé reiterated that Gershwin could not have orchestrated the *Rhapsody* when it was written. Grofé died on April 3, 1972 at the age of eighty.
21. As further substantiation of the fact that the clarinet glissando was not part of the original *Rhapsody* score, one need only compare Grofé's 1924 orchestration of the work with his 1926 arrangement for larger ensemble (both of these manuscripts are at the Library of Congress). While the 1924 version does not have a glissando, the 1926 arrangement—*after* the glissando had become a regular feature of the work—*does*.
22. Paul Whiteman (and Mary Margaret McBride), *Jazz*, p. 96.
23. Tickets were moderately priced to help attract an audience.
24. Alden Whitman, "Paul Whiteman," *The New York Times* (December 30, 1967), p. 24.
25. *Ibid.*
26. Also of doubtful veracity are a number of widely quoted stories by Whiteman pertaining to his Aeolian Hall concert. In one of them he claimed, after Gershwin's death, that he and the composer cried during the premiere of the *Rhapsody*. According to Whiteman, "somewhere about the middle of the score I began crying. When I came to myself, I was eleven pages along, and until this day I cannot tell you how I conducted that far. Afterward, George, who was playing with us, told me he experienced the same sensation. He cried, too." This story does not jibe with the numerous accounts of Gershwin's great show of confidence and pleasure as he performed at the piano. Questionable, too, is Whiteman's report of preconcert fears of which he told in his 1926 book, *Jazz*, pp. 98–99, co-authored by Mary Margaret McBride, a public-relations expert and radio raconteuse. In a posture of inordinate humility and modesty, White-

man declared that before the concert began "black fear simply possessed me. I paced the floor, gnawed my thumbs and vowed I'd give $5,000 if we could stop right then and there." But, as Whiteman tells it, "the curtain went up and before I could dash forth, as I was tempted to do, and announce that there wouldn't be any concert, we were in the midst of it."
27. Downes's description of Whiteman, as conductor of the *Rhapsody*, also deserves mention: "And then there was Mr. Whiteman. He does not conduct. He trembles, wobbles, quivers —a piece of jazz jelly, conducting the orchestra with the back of the trouser of the right leg."
28. See Osgood's *So This is Jazz*, p. 186.
29. Many sources have given the erroneous impression that Gershwin had not had time to prepare the cadenza and thus had no alternative but to improvise it. Gershwin's cadenza is to be found in the readily available published orchestral score of the *Rhapsody* by Grofé.
30. This Whiteman recording of the *Rhapsody* for RCA Victor (record number 35822) was reissued in 1951 (RCA Victor LPT–29) and again in 1968 (RCA Victor LPV–555). Like numerous other recordings of the *Rhapsody*, this recording is a considerably shortened version of the real thing, for it lasts slightly less than nine minutes. Among the jazz musicians in Whiteman's band who participated in the 1927 recording were Jimmy and Tommy Dorsey and Bix Beiderbecke.
31. See the unsigned article "Stop the *Rhapsody*," *Downbeat* (April 8, 1949), p. 1.
32. The many key signatures that Gershwin used in the *Rhapsody* may have served as an end in itself; to demonstrate his musical know-how. It is also possible that the frequent changes of key signature resulted from an ingrained habit of his acquired from long hours spent improvising at the piano. Vernon Duke recalls that Gershwin would often "be found at his piano, playing tirelessly for hours, never practicing in the Czerny sense, just racing through

new tunes, adding new tricks, harmonies, 'first and second endings' and
changing keys after each chorus [this
writer's emphasis]." See Vernon Duke,
Passport to Paris, p. 93.

33. The relationship between the opening material and the rest of the
Rhapsody is discussed further in Appendix I.

34. Virgil Thomson, "George Gershwin,"
Modern Music (November-December 1935), p. 13.

35. *Ibid.*, p. 14. Thomson recently told
this writer that his views about the
Rhapsody have not changed since he
wrote this Gershwin article in 1935.

36. Leonard Bernstein, "A Nice Gershwin Tune," *The Atlantic Monthly*
(April 1955), pp. 40–41. This article
is also found in Bernstein's book *The
Joy of Music*.

37. The piano cuts, none of which is of
major importance, consisted of ten
measures between what is now m. 222
and m. 223 in the published score, a
total of twenty-six measures between
what is now m. 347 and m. 382, and
eight measures between what is now
m. 414 and m. 415.

38. The orchestral measures eliminated
were between what is now m. 155 and
m. 156 in the published score.

CHAPTER 6: *Success Personified*

1. Desmond Carter and/or Ira wrote
the lyrics for the entire score for
Primrose except for the song "Some
Far-Away Someone." This tune,
which contains the same melody used
for the song "At Half Past Seven,"
from the show *Nifties of 1923*, used
lyrics by Buddy De Sylva and Ira. Ira
was now confidently using his own
name, a practice he had begun a little earlier when he wrote the lyrics
for *Be Yourself*, a musical based on a
book by George S. Kaufman and
Marc Connelly which opened on
Broadway on September 3, 1924.

2. The *Primrose* score was published in
England by Chappell and in the
United States by Harms.

3. Gershwin sources have generally reported that he orchestrated three of
his songs in *Primrose*, though it has
never been made clear which ones
they were or how important a part
they played in the production. Ira,
however, has stated that George orchestrated only "a number or two"
for the show; see Armitage (editor),
Gershwin, p. 20.

4. Technically speaking, "Fascinating
Rhythm" can be considered to be
polyrhythmic, with different and distinct rhythms used in the melody and
accompaniment, as well as poly-
metric—that is, the melody and accompaniment can be thought to be
in different meters heard simultaneously.

5. It is not completely clear where or
when the party took place. Some
Gershwin sources, however, have reported that Kahn first heard "The
Man I Love" aboard the very ship
that brought Gershwin back to New
York from London after *Primrose*
had opened.

6. This house is still in use today, though
it is no longer in prime condition.
It is divided into ten apartments, two
apartments to a floor.

7. See Armitage (editor), *Gershwin*, pp.
237–39, for this account by Nanette
Kutner.

8. S. N. Behrman, "Troubadour," *The
New Yorker* (May 25, 1929), p. 27; or
Armitage (editor), *Gershwin*, pp. 212–
13.

9. Through Damrosch's initiative, the
commission resulted.

10. Save for these contracts, six copies
of which are on file at the Library
of Congress, this writer has not been
able to find any legal evidence directly concerned with the commissioning itself, such as a letter of agreement between Gershwin and the Society specifying the terms of the commission. It may be that such a document never existed or, if it did, is no
longer extant. Possibly these contracts
of April 17, 1925, served such a purpose. Though they ostensibly dealt
with Gershwin's appearances as soloist in his concerto, they may also be
considered proof both of his agree-

ment to write the work and of the Society to perform it.

11. Gershwin sources have generally given the impression that he performed the concerto seven times, as originally called for.

12. Goldberg, *Gershwin*, was one of the earliest sources for this story.

13. Even after completing the concerto, Gershwin had rather naïve notions about its form, once characterizing it, rather grandly, as being "in perfect form" because it was "in three movements."

14. Its original title was *My Fair Lady*.

15. Writer-photographer Carl Van Vechten, in his diary, noted that "on July 24, 1925, George dined with us and played some of the themes of the *Concerto in F.* He has had some of these in mind for months . . . but many of them are new. . . . George started the concerto two days ago and has already written five pages."

16. Goldberg, *Gershwin*, p. 6. (This biography, published in 1931, was an "authorized" one; written with Gershwin's approval and his full cooperation. It was the first major study of the composer and played an important part in building the Gershwin legend.)

17. *Ibid.,* p. 10.

18. Levant, *A Smattering of Ignorance*, p. 170. Levant's sardonic wit was silenced on August 14, 1972 when he died of a heart attack in his California home at the age of sixty-five.

19. Much has been written about Gershwin's great pleasure in performing his music—often entire scores—at the piano. This extraordinary zeal on his part was once humorously deprecated by George S. Kaufman, who was associated with him in a number of productions. "If you play that score one more time before we open," Kaufman chided Gershwin, "people are going to think you're doing a revival." It was Kaufman, too, who said of Gershwin: "I'd bet on George any time in a hundred yard dash to the piano." In collaboration with Moss Hart, Kaufman also modeled a character on Gershwin: Sam Frankel —a composer who played his music every chance he could—in *Merrily*

We Roll Along of 1934. The following year, Gershwin, as pianist, also figured in Cole Porter's *Jubilee*. In this musical, perennial hostess Eve Standing (really Elsa Maxwell) boasts that the great novelty of one of her most elaborate parties is that Gershwin will *not* play the piano.

20. S. N. Behrman had this to say about Gershwin's playing at parties: "He [Gershwin] told me once that his mother had cautioned him against playing too much at parties. With engaging candor Gershwin admitted that there might be some truth in this, but . . . add[ed]: 'You see the trouble is, when I don't play, I don't have a good time!' "

21. Levant, *A Smattering of Ignorance*, p. 184.

22. Armitage (editor), *Gershwin*, p. 53.

23. In his diary, Carl Van Vechten reported that in October 1925 Gershwin had "completed the concerto lacking two bars."

24. On the outside cover of this manuscript is the printed indication, "October-November." Both his sketch and his orchestration manuscript of the concerto are now at the Library of Congress along with a number of work sheets and eight pages of preliminary orchestration for the piece.

25. George outlined the "development" of his material for his so-called *New York Concerto* in this fashion:
    Charleston
    First (dotted) theme
    Percussion effect
    Effects for piano
    Effects for brass
    Double Charleston

26. Isaac Goldberg, *Tin Pan Alley*, Introduction (by Gershwin).

27. These eight pages of orchestration are written in a less careful hand than the "final" orchestration.

28. Information received by this writer from personal interviews with Vernon Duke, the composer of "April in Paris," "Autumn in New York," "Taking a Chance on Love," and many other popular song hits. Duke —also known as Vladimir Dukelsky, the name he used for many of his "serious" compositions—died on January 17, 1969, at the age of sixty-five.

29. Gershwin not only never specified what assistance he received from Schillinger in the realization of *Porgy and Bess,* but he also consistently claimed publicly that he had orchestrated the opera himself.

30. Schillinger's claim was made before his own death in 1943, at the age of forty-seven.

31. See Ira's letter in *Newsweek* (October 23, 1944), p. 14.

32. It is not clear exactly when Gershwin decided to change the title of the piece from *New York Concerto* to *Concerto in F.* The latter title appears on the outside folder of the orchestral score, completed November 10, 1925, and the former title on George's manuscript sketch, completed "September 1925."

33. Gershwin admitted that his "greatest musical thrill" occurred when he heard the *Concerto* at its trial hearing; see Hyman Sandow, "Gershwin to Write New Rhapsody," *Musical America* (February 18, 1928), p. 5.

34. In the first movement of the *Concerto* cuts were made between what is now m. 94 and m. 95 in the published score and between what is now m. 350 and m. 351; in the second movement a cut was made between what is now m. 101 and m. 102; in the finale, what is now m. 225 to m. 232 was given to the solo piano instead of being played by the ensemble, sixteen measures cut between what is now m. 256 and m. 257, a measure of silence added at what is now m. 345, and a measure in triple meter became three measures in quadruple meter, now m. 390 to m. 392.

35. These dealt mainly with the elimination or addition of instrumental doublings and the adding of choral filler in the piano part.

36. Apparently the uncertainty about the amount of assistance that Gershwin received in the realization of the *Concerto in F* prompted A. Walter Kramer, a composer and music critic, to claim that the orchestration for the *Concerto* had not been done by Gershwin but by "someone else." Kramer made his allegation in an article, "I Do Not Think Jazz 'Belongs,' " in *Singing* (September 1926),

pp. 13–14. Kramer's claim was based not on knowledge of the *Concerto* score but on Gershwin's limited background as an orchestral composer. In rebuttal, Gershwin sent a letter to *Singing* (October 1926), pp. 17–18, along with a page (p. 70) in his own hand from the *Concerto* score. In his letter Gershwin asserted that the work "was orchestrated entirely by myself" and cited the page from the score as proof of that fact. Irrespective of the merits of Gershwin's claim, one might reasonably ask how a page in his hand from the *Concerto* score actually proved he had not been helped in orchestration.

37. Osgood, *So This Is Jazz,* pp. 134–35. The symphony mentioned by Osgood was the Fifth, in B-flat, by the Russian composer. This work as well as Rabaud's *Suite Anglaise,* arranged from music written by composers at the court of Queen Elizabeth I, were heard at the concert in which the *Concerto* received its premiere.

38. This description by Gershwin was used in connection with the premiere of the *Concerto.*

39. Gershwin's analysis, printed in the *New York Herald–New York Tribune* of November 29, 1925, was not so accurate as it might have been. In describing the instruments that introduced the "Charleston motif," he included the bassoon, which does not play it.

40. There was criticism in some quarters over Damrosch's commissioning of the *Concerto.* One of the Damrosch dissidents was Allan Lincoln Langley (1892–1949), a composer (a student of George Chadwick), orchestrator, and conductor, as well as violinist and violist. In an article, "The Gershwin Myth," in *The American Spectator* (December 1932), p. 1, Langley alleged that Damrosch had commissioned the *Concerto* more for publicity for himself and his orchestra than from artistic conviction. To Damrosch's credit—or possibly his luck—the ultimate success of the *Concerto* vindicated his decision to commission the work, no matter what his true motives were in the first place.

299

41. Golschmann, in 1919, organized the Concerts Golschmann in Paris with the support of a wealthy patron. The

Concerto received its European premiere at one of these concerts.

CHAPTER 7: *Perennial Troubadour*

1. One of those impressed with Gershwin's score for *Tip-Toes* was the literary wag and critic Alexander Woollcott of the caustic and vitriolic wit. Woollcott described it as "the best score anyone has written for our town this season."
2. According to Dushkin, he and Gershwin collaborated equally in arranging *Short Story*.
3. This writer has seen manuscripts in Gershwin's hand for these two "Novelettes" in the possession of Josefa Rosanska, who received them as gifts from Gershwin in the early 1920s.
4. Schott has published *Short Story*.
5. Verna Arvey, "George Gershwin Through the Eyes of a Friend," *Opera and Concert* (April 1948), p. 11.
6. On contacting Knopf, the publisher of Borzoi books, for a copy of this advertisement, this writer was told that a copy was not on file and could not be located.
7. Igor Stravinsky, on the basis of his meeting with Gershwin in 1925, described him as being "very nervously energetic"; see the article by Igor Stravinsky and Robert Craft, "Some Composers," *Musical America* (June 1962), p. 6 (this article is also included in Stravinsky and Craft's 1963 book *Dialogues and a Diary*).
8. George stopped smoking cigars for a period in the early 1930s in an attempt to improve his "composer's stomach." He never completely quit smoking, however.
9. Igor Stravinsky and Robert Craft, "Some Composers," in *Musical America* (June 1962), p. 6 (also in their *Dialogues and a Diary*).
10. *Ibid.*, pp. 6–8.
11. Jablonski and Stewart, *The Gershwin Years* (1958), p. 118. In a similar version of the story by Eva Gauthier, Ravel is purported to have told Gershwin that study with him "would probably cause him to write bad

'Ravel' and lose his great gift of melody and spontaneity"; see Armitage (editor), *Gershwin*, p. 199.
12. See Ewen's *A Journey to Greatness* (1956), p. 161, or his 1970 edition of the book, *George Gershwin: His Journey to Greatness*, p. 132.
13. According to Glaenzer, Ravel never visited his home, contrary to Ewen's statement. As additional confirmation of this fact, one does not find Ravel's name listed in Glaenzer's guest book.
14. Ewen, *A Journey to Greatness*, pp. 161–62, or *George Gershwin: His Journey to Greatness*, p. 132. Also see Wilfred Mellers, "Gershwin's Achievement," *The Monthly Musical Record* (January 1953), p. 14, for his account of this story.
15. Nicolas Slonimsky, "Musical Oddities," *Etude* (April 1955), p. 5. Slonimsky's version of the Gershwin-Ravel anecdote is, of course, almost identical with the story usually associated with Gershwin and Stravinsky.
16. Information contained in a letter from Slonimsky to this writer.
17. Information contained in a letter from Ewen to this writer.
18. Edward Jablonski, "Gershwin After 20 years," *Hi-Fi Music at Home* (July-August 1956), p. 23.
19. Information received from students of Mlle. Boulanger.
20. Before it was called *Oh, Kay!*, it had been titled *Mayfair, Miss Mayfair*, and then *Cheerio*.
21. Ira Gershwin, *Lyrics on Several Occasions*, p. 261.
22. As was true for many of George's tunes for Broadway musicals, "Dear Little Girl" was dropped from *Oh, Kay!*, only to be later resurrected. "Dear Little Girl" had to wait longer than most Gershwin tunes to make its mark, but it was finally published in 1968 after being featured in the Julie Andrews movie *Star*, a film about Gertrude Lawrence.
23. S. N. Behrman has described Gersh-

win performing his songs at the piano in this manner: "He sings. He makes elaborate gestures. . . . Illuminated and vitalized by his own music, his own voice, his own eager sense of the rhythm of life, Gershwin instantly conveys that illumination and that vitality to others."

CHAPTER 8: *Collector and Painter*

1. Ira Gershwin, *Lyrics on Several Occasions*, p. 185.
2. Another alumnus of *Americana* was Charles Butterworth, the laconic, long-faced comedian, who later went on to Hollywood fame.
3. Mme. d'Alvarez (1892–1953) was originally known as Margarita Amelia Alvarez de Rocafuerte. She has been widely quoted as saying that she wanted Gershwin's *Concerto in F* played over her grave when she died.
4. Carl Van Vechten, a mutual friend of Gershwin and Mme. d'Alvarez, brought the two together. He also introduced Gershwin and Eva Gauthier to each other. Van Vechten strongly espoused the combining of traditional and popular music in concert programming.
5. It took a while for the *Preludes for Piano* to catch on. In 1931, Isaac Goldberg, *Gershwin*, p. 223, commented that "of all Gershwin's compositions they are the least known." The publisher of *Preludes for Piano* is New World Music.
6. Besides the three preludes that make up the *Preludes for Piano*, Gershwin performed as part of his concert venture with Mme. d'Alvarez the two "Novelettes" of *Short Story*, and a song-like piece, which Ira titled "Sleepless Nights" after the composer's death. The latter piece remains unpublished.
7. Information in a letter to this writer from Ira.
8. Dorothy Heyward first began the stage adaptation of the novel on her own, without her husband's knowledge. Ultimately, it became a joint effort of the Heywards and was so presented by the Theatre Guild.
9. Armitage (editor), *Gershwin*, p. 35.
10. Writing to a friend in April 1925, even before meeting with Heyward, Gershwin expressed his interest in doing an opera about blacks this way:

"An opera must be lyric, and to me it must be fantastic. I think it should be a Negro opera, almost a Negro *Scheherazade*. Negro, because it is not incongruous for a Negro to live jazz. It would not be absurd on the stage. The mood could change from ecstasy to lyricism plausibly, because the Negro has so much of both in his nature."

11. During his European period, Botkin returned to the United States every fourteen months or so. After three or four months at home, Botkin would resume this sojourn abroad.
12. Armitage (editor), *Gershwin*, p. 138.
13. Some art works from Gershwin's collection, notably Picasso's *Absinthe Drinker*, were sold by the Gershwin estate after his death. The collection is still an extraordinary one, however.
14. In any consideration of Gershwin's role as a collector, one should not overlook the possibility that the competitive spirit that made him want to excel as a tunesmith and a composer of "serious" works made him want to excel as a collector, too.
15. Gershwin at times also used photographs of his subjects as an aid in painting their portraits. His painting of Jerome Kern, for instance, was derived mainly from a photograph.
16. Information received from Henry Botkin.
17. Though some might consider Gershwin the painter little more than a talented amateur, he would probably have taken strong exception to such an assessment, judging by this story by Bennett Cerf: "At a memorable dinner one evening he [Gershwin] said, 'A man told me today that I need never write another note; I could make a fortune with my palette and brush!' 'Isn't it amazing,' said one awed lady, 'that one man should possess a genius for two of the arts!' 'Oh, I don't know,' said George

modestly. 'Look at Leonardo da Vinci!' " See Cerf's article, "In Memory of George Gershwin," *Saturday* *Review of Literature* (July 17, 1943), p. 16 (or see Cerf's *Try and Stop Me*).

CHAPTER 9: *European Holiday*

1. Reports of the estimated size of the audience at this concert range from 16,000 to 18,000.
2. On the road, *Funny Face* opened in Philadelphia. It also played Atlantic City, Washington, D.C., and Wilmington before reaching New York.
3. To add insult to injury, Aarons and Freedley even charged Gershwin for some of the costs incurred in orchestrating the new score.
4. Ira Gershwin, *Lyrics on Several Occasions*, p. 24.
5. Because of the success of *Funny Face*, Paramount considered doing a movie version of it and asked the Astaires in 1928 to test for roles in the projected film. On the basis of the test Paramount decided against making the film, for it was felt that Fred Astaire had limited potential as a movie personality. Astaire's ultimate triumphs as a movie star have of course strongly disproved that decision.
6. Like " 'S Wonderful," the melody for "My One and Only" bears some relationship to Jewish music. (See Appendix I for a further discussion.) But unlike the " 'S Wonderful" melody, which was purportedly taken from the Goldfaden operetta *Akeidas Izchok*, there are no specific Jewish origins known for "My One and Only" at this point.
7. Like many legends, much of the Gershwin legend was built up by stories, not necessarily completely true but repeated again and again until accepted as gospel. Though evidence certainly points to the fact that Gershwin generally composed quickly and easily, all the details in this particular story may not have been accurately or completely given. For as the story stands, Gershwin emerges as a hero figure too good to be believed, rather than as an earthy Broadway tunesmith who *never* discarded any promising material. If it didn't fit in one show, he would use it in another, since it

presumably meant money in his pocket. Probably, if nothing else, he must have railed at the reputed loss of his music, if only briefly.
8. The role was somewhat topical. It was based on the visit to America by Marie, Queen of Rumania, not long before *Rosalie* was written.
9. The New York Symphony, which Damrosch had headed, and the Philharmonic were merged into one organization, the present New York Philharmonic, at the beginning of the 1928–1929 season, with Arturo Toscanini as principal conductor. Damrosch, his power base weakened by the consolidation of the orchestras, was reduced to guest conductor of the merged ensemble. He also conducted children's concerts for the orchestra. Consistent with these concerts, Damrosch helped to foster music-appreciation lessons for students in the public schools, with excellent results.
10. Hyman Sandow, "Gershwin to Write New Rhapsody," *Musical America* (February 18, 1928), p. 5. Shortly after this interview was published, Gershwin met Maurice Ravel at Eva Gauthier's, on March 7, 1928. This meeting presumably stimulated Gershwin's interest in "studying" with Ravel.
11. Practically anything that Gershwin, the major celebrity, did at that point was newsworthy. Any information supplied the press by any of a variety of people or organizations in his behalf—such as his publisher, his producers, Ira, or even himself—was almost automatically guaranteed to be printed. This obviously worked to great advantage for him, particularly since his public image was such a good one. While fulfilling the press's need for continual items of interest to feed an all-consuming public, Gershwin nourished his own career at the same time.

12. Paris was then the leading music center of the world, as it had been for a number of years, and a beehive of musical activity. Musicians from all over the world thronged there to visit, to live, and to work.

13. It was during this stay in Paris that Gershwin spoke with Mlle. Boulanger and Ravel about studying with them.

14. Gershwin's presence in Paris, with its attendant publicity, undoubtedly stimulated the playing of his work.

15. Vernon Duke has described the Pasdeloup Orchestra as "a worse than mediocre Paris orchestra whose idea of jazz was the Folies Bergère."

16. It has been reported that the occupant of the apartment next to Gershwin's in Vienna complained about the repetitive "noises" coming from his place as he went over passages of *An American in Paris* again and again at the piano. The complaints stopped,

of course, when the identity of the "noisemaker" became known.

17. Franz Lehár, the composer of *The Merry Widow*, was among the musicians Gershwin met with in Vienna.

18. Hyman Sandow, "Gershwin Presents a New Work," *Musical America* (August 18, 1928), p. 12.

19. Vuillermoz's review of the *Concerto* was printed in the July 7, 1928 edition of the *Christian Science Monitor*.

20. Among the pleasures of his stay in Europe must be counted Gershwin's friendship with the beautiful Countess de Ganny, whom he met in Paris. Elsa Maxwell has even claimed that he gave thought to marrying her.

21. To help ensure that Frances's singing stint would get off to a good start, George served as her accompanist on opening night.

22. The *New York Times* of June 20, 1928, reported the return of the Gershwins to New York from Europe.

CHAPTER 10: *The American "Frenchman"*

1. There have been reports that Gershwin did not start on *East Is West* until 1929. However, Ira, in his *Lyrics on Several Occasions*, p. 30, has stated unequivocally that "in the summer of 1928 my brother and I were busy on ... *East Is West* for Ziegfeld."

2. Though on Broadway he was known as a song-and-dance man, Webb later became famous in Hollywood mainly in non-musical roles.

3. "August 1, 1928" and "November 18, 1928" are the completion dates Gershwin inscribed on his preliminary sketch and orchestrated score respectively of *An American in Paris*.

4. As a professional in a tough "racket," Gershwin was fully aware of the value of publicity and was hardly diffident about helping to shape stories about himself and his work, or of seeing his name in print.

5. Hyman Sandow, "Gershwin Presents a New Work," *Musical America* (August 18, 1928), p. 5. Contrary to Gershwin's claim, there are no overt stylistic resemblances between *An American in Paris* and the music of either Debussy or "Les Six." The

"opening part" of *An American in Paris*, to which Gershwin refers, has more of an affinity with the humorous musical Americanisms found in such works as John Alden Carpenter's *Krazy Kat* and Zez Confrey's "Kitten on the Keys" than anything "in typical French style." Moreover, by lumping together "Les Six" and Debussy in his statement, Gershwin showed a certain lack of savvy. The members of "Les Six" (a group of six young "French" composers— Georges Auric, Louis Durey, Arthur Honegger, Darius Milhaud, Francis Poulenc, and Germaine Tailleferre; they were arbitrarily labeled "Les Six" in 1920 by Henri Collet, a French music critic), like their musical and aesthetic godfather Erik Satie (1866–1925), were essentially anti-Debussy, anti-Wagner, and "anti" anything else that represented "tradition."

6. Taylor's narrative for *An American in Paris* was included in the New York Philharmonic program notes for the work.

7. In Gershwin's orchestrated manu-

script for *An American in Paris*, the three saxophones all double on B-flat soprano saxophones, and the tenor and baritone saxophones also play E-flat alto saxophones. In the published version of *An American in Paris*, however, the three saxophones do not double on any other saxophones.

8. Undoubtedly the greater care lavished on the score of *An American in Paris* in comparison with that of the *Concerto* resulted simply from time factors. The tone poem was orchestrated in over four months, between August and November 18, 1928, while the orchestration for the *Concerto* was done in less than two months, between early October and November 10, 1925.

9. Allan Lincoln Langley, "The Gershwin Myth," *The American Spectator* (December 1932), p. 2.

10. *Ibid.*

11. Daly's reply to Langley can be found in Armitage (editor), *Gershwin*, pp. 33–34, as well as in the New York *Times*.

12. For whatever the reason, this aspect of the work seems to have been overlooked in Gershwin sources.

13. Both Gershwin's preliminary sketch and his orchestrated manuscript of *An American in Paris*, along with a number of work sheets for the piece, are now at the Library of Congress.

14. Of the cuts mentioned, thirty-seven measures were deleted from between what is now m. 571 and m. 572 in the published score, as were thirty-seven measures between what is now m. 591 and m. 592, twenty-seven measures between what is now m. 611 and m. 612, and seven measures between what is now m. 628 and m. 629.

15. These metric changes are not technically necessary to the score. By means

of phrasing the measures in question could have been written with a primarily fixed, rather than variable metric pattern. At any rate, between m. 207–12 in the published score, the meter is changed in consecutive measures from 2/4, to 3/4, 5/4, 4/4, 3/4, and 2/4.

16. These comments by Downes were originally printed in the *New York Times* of July 18, 1937. They are also found in Armitage (editor), *Gershwin*, p. 221.

17. Leonard Bernstein, "A Nice Gershwin Tune," *The Atlantic Monthly* (April 1955), p. 41 (also in Bernstein's *The Joy of Music*).

18. *Ibid.*

19. Gershwin's exceptional confidence in himself always stood him in good stead on such occasions as premieres. But in the case of *An American in Paris* he had the extra assurance of an ingenuously cheerful story told him by his father in advance of the work's first performance. Mr. Gershwin claimed he had dreamed that, after the piece was played, Damrosch turned around to the Philharmonic audience to ask them if they wanted to hear it again. "Yes!" they yelled out as one. And so, according to Mr. Gershwin, Damrosch gladly repeated the work for the Carnegie Hall throng.

20. Through his association with Cartier's, Glaenzer had arranged for the signatures to be etched on the humidor. Many of the signatures were taken from Glaenzer's guest book.

21. Otto Kahn's remarks with some deletions were first printed in the January 3, 1929, edition of the *Musical Courier*, p. 31. They are found in their entirety in Armitage (editor), *Gershwin*, pp. 126–28.

CHAPTER 11: *On the Podium*

1. Shilkret also drafted Gershwin to play the celesta for the recording. Though Gershwin straggled through the unfamiliar celesta part, the re-

cording itself (RCA Victor 35963/4) is an excellent one, with an appropriately "jazzy" 1920s quality about it. This recording was subsequently reissued in 1951 (RCA Victor LPT–29).

2. Consistent with Gershwin's lack of modesty is this description of him by the sculptor Isamu Noguchi, who made a bust of him in 1929. For Noguchi, Gershwin had "an exterior of self assurance verging on conceit."

3. Oscar Levant, *A Smattering of Ignorance*, p. 170.

4. Bennett Cerf, "In Memory of George Gershwin," *Saturday Review of Literature* (July 17, 1943), p. 16 (also in Cerf's *Try and Stop Me*).

5. There are many evidences of Gershwin's allegiance to his family. Among these must be counted the fact that Ira's entrée into lyric writing was aided immeasurably by George's efforts in his behalf. George also did what he could to help Frances succeed in the musical field and the theater. For example, besides accompanying her opening night in her engagement at the Parisian cabaret Les Ambassadeurs, he also sought to interest George White in the talents of his sister by writing him: "You gave the first Gershwin his chance, why not another?" In addition to his family, there are numerous instances of Gershwin's loyalty and generosity to his friends, especially professional colleagues like Bill Daly, Vernon Duke, and Oscar Levant.

6. As part of Ira's active court record, one must not overlook his litigation with his mother and then his sister and brother after George's death.

7. The producer actually had owed Kahn, the lyricist for Ziegfeld's production of Eddie Cantor's *Whoopee*, a musical-comedy assignment prior to his affiliation with *Show Girl*. By employing Kahn for *Show Girl*, Ziegfeld not only fulfilled his obligation to him, but also expedited the writing of the lyrics for the show.

8. Among the fine tunes cut from *Show Girl* were "Feeling Sentimental" and "I Just Looked at You," which was a reworking of "Lady of the Moon" from *East Is West*. It subsequently became "Blah, Blah, Blah" in the 1931 movie *Delicious*.

9. Besides the heavy financial losses of *Show Girl* and Ziegfeld's normal rambunctiousness, another reason given for the producer's shabby treatment of the Gershwins was his stock-market reverses at about that time.

10. Ira, however, wrote the lyrics to Vernon Duke's music for another Ziegfeld show after *Show Girl*, the *Ziegfeld Follies of 1936*. But this was after Ziegfeld's death in 1932. Moreover, the show was produced by the Shuberts.

11. Practically every time Gershwin appeared at Lewisohn Stadium, it was announced that the stadium's attendance record had been broken. However, it was not always possible to determine exactly how many attended these events. The attendance for the August 26, 1929, concert, for example, has been estimated at anywhere from 15,000 to 20,000. One can only question the validity of these records and wonder whether they were not actually the result of press agentry.

12. Edward Kilenyi, "George Gershwin as I Knew Him," *Etude* (October 1950), p. 64. From Kilenyi's remarks, it is clear that the Shilkret recording of *An American in Paris*, the only complete recording of the piece at that time, proved helpful to Gershwin in learning to conduct. But it is also clear that Gershwin's "personal supervision" of the recording was considerably less pervasive than Kilenyi gives him credit for, inasmuch as he had been banished from the studio for getting in Shilkret's hair during the prerecording rehearsal of the tone poem.

13. Mecca Temple is now City Center, on Manhattan's West Fifty-fifth Street.

14. Hadley (1871–1937) led the Manhattan Symphony between 1929 and 1932.

15. Hilding Anderson was the regular conductor for the show.

16. Goldberg, *Gershwin*, p. 247.

17. Robert Payne, *Gershwin*, p. 114.

1. Ryskind and Kaufman worked well together. In addition to their association with *Strike Up the Band,* the two of them wrote the scripts for *Cocoanuts* and *Animal Crackers,* two vintage Marx Brothers' films, in 1929.
2. "Soon" was derived from a four-bar melodic fragment from the first-act finale of *Strike Up the Band* of 1927 that Gershwin expanded into a full-blown tune.
3. Ira Gershwin, *Lyrics on Several Occasions,* p. 225.
4. Along with the vocal score of *Strike Up the Band*—published by New World Music in 1930—some of the tunes from the show, like "Soon," "I've Got a Crush on You," "I Mean to Say," and the title tune, were published individually as well.
5. Goldberg's *Gershwin,* particularly pp. 255–56, contains a number of favorable remarks about Gershwin as orchestrator for *Strike Up the Band.* Somewhat parenthetically, Vernon Duke has ascribed the orchestration of Gershwin musicals, in part, to the composer. Duke has stated that Gershwin *told* him he orchestrated "at least two numbers" in *all* his shows (see Duke's *Listen Here!,* p. 58).
6. According to Robert Russell Bennett, who orchestrated many Gershwin musicals for Broadway and Hollywood, Gershwin, essentially late in his career, orchestrated "a number now and then" for a few shows, such as *Girl Crazy* and *Of Thee I Sing,* but that, largely, was the extent of it. Bennett is free to admit that Gershwin's music lends itself to orchestration by Gershwin or anyone else because of its rhythmic variety and natural vibrancy. Nevertheless, according to Bennett, Gershwin, possibly because of a defect in his inner or outer ear, could not always hear subtle distinctions in orchestral sonorities and thus would often be relatively easily satisfied with orchestrated versions of his music. Bennett tells, for instance, of scoring problems that plagued *Of Thee I Sing,* with which he was associated as orches-

trator. Because of. these difficulties, changes in orchestration had to be made on almost a daily basis during rehearsals. On one occasion, Bennett remembers the orchestration as being particularly inept, but Gershwin, not hearing the orchestral sonorities accurately, expressed his approval. It was undoubtedly this inability to accurately conceptualize and to distinguish fine gradations in orchestral sounds that prompted Gershwin to have trial readings of his *Concerto* and, at a later date, his *Second Rhapsody* and *Porgy and Bess.*
7. This was the consensus among musician-friends of Gershwin interviewed by this writer.
8. Vernon Duke, "Gershwin, Schillinger, and Dukelsky," *The Musical Quarterly* (January 1947), p. 105. Of course, Gershwin was not always intellectually or consciously aware of the technical features in his improvisations described by Duke, since they were primarily instinctive manifestations. Moreover, speaking further of Gershwin's piano improvisations in his *Passport to Paris,* p. 93, Duke has noted that the composer "never changed tempo, nor played rubato, the relentless 4/4 beat carrying him along—it was physically difficult for him to stop." This propulsive aspect of Gershwin's playing superficially resembled the stride style of such jazz pianists as James P. Johnson, Willie "The Lion" Smith, and Fats Waller, but without the special "swinging" qualities found in the work of these major jazzmen.
9. Armitage (editor), *Gershwin,* p. 54.
10. S. N. Behrman, "Troubadour," *The New Yorker* (May 25, 1929), p. 28; or Armitage (editor), *Gershwin,* p. 216.
11. In May 1932, several months before the release of the Simon and Schuster book, Random House published a limited edition of three hundred copies of these transcriptions. Each volume was signed by the composer and Alajálov and contained, as an extra bonus, a cover-insert of "Mischa,

Yascha, Toscha, Sascha," a humorous takeoff on the names of four famous Russian violinists: Mischa Elman, Jascha Heifetz, Toscha Seidel, and Sascha Jacobsen. George and Ira (Arthur Francis) had originally written this tune around 1921. Gershwin frequently sang and played it at parties, particularly when any of the violinists who inspired the title were present.

12. Downes's statement first appeared in the *New York Times* on July 18, 1937. It can also be found in Armitage (editor), *Gershwin*, p. 220.

13. *George Gershwin's Song-Book,* Introduction (by Gershwin).

14. *Ibid.*

15. There are, of course, other recorded examples of ·Gershwin at the piano, if not of the "improvisations." The latter, however, have been recorded by Leonid Hambro for Walden and by William Bolcom for Nonesuch.

16. At his death in 1969 at the age of seventy-two, Warburg's career had successfully encompassed many areas, including that of lieutenant in the Navy Flying Corps during World War I, financier, government official, prolific author of more than thirty books, and lyricist (under the name of Paul James) for numerous popular songs.

17. Kay has also worked as staff composer for Radio City Music Hall and as assistant director of entertainment for New York's 1939 World's Fair.

18. James P. Warburg, alias Paul James, was the lyricist for "Can't We Be Friends."

19. Kay, in her 1943 "autobiography," *Who Could Ask for Anything More?,* has discussed some aspects of her life, starting with her 1939 marriage—her second—to a rodeo rider, Chris Heyward. Though she does not touch on her friendship with Gershwin in her book, the "giving" side of Kay's personality comes through in this description of herself, as she was shortly before her marriage to Heyward. In her words (pp. 3–4): "I was a city slicker, a Gal About Town (whatever that means), a confirmed New Yorker. . . . I had friends, a charming apartment, beaux and delicious clothes. In

short, a fast-moving life that held about everything I wanted, save one. Only that corny old wish common to most women, of being vitally necessary to someone you love." Notwithstanding the important role Chris Heyward had in her "autobiography," Kay Swift subsequently divorced him and married Hunter Galloway.

20. It is posterity's loss that Gershwin's letters to Kay Swift, which might have given further insights into their relationship, have been destroyed by her.

21. Among the reasons proffered by Gershwin's friends for his not marrying Kay are these: She had three children from her marriage to Warburg; she was a divorcée; she was not Jewish; his interest in Kay had lessened; he would never marry anyone, including Kay.

22. These incidents occurred before Frances's marriage.

23. In view of Miss Goddard's marital status at the time, Gershwin often used various ruses when seeing her in public, to avoid causing too much talk about their relationship. For instance, he might go to a nightclub in the company of friends, knowing in advance she would be there. Once in the nightclub, he would leave his friends to join her table. She and Chaplin, of course, were ultimately divorced in 1941. She later married the famous German novelist Erich Maria Remarque, who has since died.

24. Among other aspects of her personality that attracted him were her offbeat remarks to him, such as: "George, why don't you compose music people will hiss to?"

25. Alan Gershwin, "I Am George Gershwin's Illegitimate Son," *Confidential* (February 1959), p. 13. In the article, Alan Gershwin alleges that his mother's real name was Margaret Charlestein, but that she generally used the name "Charleston" in private life. As a dancer, he notes, she was usually known as "Margaret Manners"; occasionally, as "Margaret Erickson."

26. *Ibid.,* p. 45.

27. *Ibid.,* p. 46.

28. *Ibid.,* p. 45.

29. *Ibid.*, p. 46.
30. The Gershwins evidently decided to let the Alan Gershwin claim "die" quietly by ignoring it rather than draw attention to it by legal or other action on their part. This writer has brought the case up solely because it touches on an important, though little known, aspect of George's life. It deserves further clarification.

CHAPTER 13: *Hollywood Muse*

1. Besides his eminence as a jazz cornetist and leader of the famous Five Pennies, Nichols also conducted pit and radio orchestras, particularly during the 1930s.
2. Gershwin made these comments in a letter to Isaac Goldberg, written on October 16, 1930, two days after the opening of *Girl Crazy.*
3. The title of this tune was taken by Ira from the last line of a four-line poem he had submitted to City College's monthly *Cap and Bells*, when he was a student there briefly. The poem appeared in the June 1916 issue of the monthly under the name of "Gersh." The last line of the poem read "I'm going to Bide My Time."
4. Miss Merman demonstrated her flair for handling lyrics when she sang "Sam and Delilah." In this tune, she had to sustain "hooch" (slang for whiskey) and "kootch" (derived from "hootchy-kootchy," a belly dance) so that they each sounded like only a single phonetic unit, rather than "hoo-ch" or "koo-tch." She did it with ease.
5. As originally conceived (some time before *Girl Crazy*), the tune had less impact, for it was in a much slower tempo.
6. Ira deliberately chose "I Got Rhythm" instead of "I've Got Rhythm" as the title of the tune because of its colloquial flavor. For a while, he had considered "Who Could Ask for Anything More?" as a possible title, since that line is so prominent in the lyrics, but rejected it as not being snappy enough. That phrase, however, was used as the title of autobiographies by Ethel Merman and Kay Swift.
7. As already noted, Broadway productions of the 1920s, 1930s, and earlier, generally cost a fraction of what they do today. They therefore didn't usually have to run so long as present-day shows to recoup their investments or to be considered hits. *Girl Crazy* was unquestionably a hit for its period.
8. Another movie based on *Girl Crazy* was made by MGM in 1965. Titled *When the Boys Meet the Girls*, its plot bore little resemblance to the original. However, sprinkled through the movie were these, by then, Gershwin classics: "Embraceable You," "I Got Rhythm," "Bidin' My Time," and "But Not for Me."
9. Though the Gershwins' talents were eagerly solicited for *Delicious* by movie-industry entrepreneurs, the fact remains that, generally speaking, Hollywood's interest in musicals had waned somewhat by 1930 for the simple reason that they were no longer the novelty they had been when sound films first appeared. Nevertheless, Gershwin was quoted in the *Herald Tribune* of March 3, 1931, as stating optimistically: "The future of talking pictures with music is very promising, despite the recent decline in their popularity."
10. Gershwin also found time to appear at Lewisohn Stadium on August 28, 1930, his third stint there. He conducted *An American in Paris* and was the soloist in the *Rhapsody in Blue* and *Concerto in F* under Willem van Hoogstraten. A somewhat smaller crowd than usual for a Gershwin appearance, about 13,000 people, attended the event. But as was customary for Gershwin, he got the lion's share of applause from the audience.
11. These sentiments were expressed in Gershwin's letter to Isaac Goldberg of October 16, 1930, mentioned previously.
12. Goldberg reported Gershwin's re-

marks in both the *Boston Evening Transcript* of November 29, 1930, and his book *Gershwin*, p. 270.

13. He was so quoted in the *Herald Tribune* of March 3, 1931.

14. While in Agua Caliente, at a party given by producer Joseph Schenck, Gershwin reportedly saw a performance by a Spanish dancing team, the Cansinos. One of the dancing Cansinos was the now-famous Rita Hayworth.

15. Some idea of the good life that went with being a Hollywood tunesmith in the early days of movies can be gotten from this description by Bob Crawford, head of First National Pictures, of the work demands made on the song writers in his employ: "Our boys at First National have it pretty nice. We give them about everything they want. They have big, beautiful rooms to work in. There's a nice quiet atmosphere; some of the boys have windows with a view of the mountains—just the atmosphere for the composition of melodies. Why, we even let the boys do their work at home if they want to. We don't expect too much from them, either. When they've done two or three songs I make them go off on a vacation and do some fishing. I usually give them about six weeks in which to do an assignment. They don't have to turn anything in until three or four of those six weeks have elapsed."

16. The *Herald Tribune* of March 3, 1931, reported this information.

17. The date "January 1931," inscribed on the cover of Gershwin's sketch of the piece, gives only a general indication of when it was written. This pre-orchestration draft, like those of his earlier orchestral pieces, is written mainly on three and four staves, almost as if it were a two-piano work.

18. Information in a letter from Gershwin to Isaac Goldberg, dated June 30, 1931.

19. The title *Second Rhapsody* is on the cover of the sketch of the piece. Both this sketch and Gershwin's orchestrated score of it are at the Library of Congress.

20. From his letter of June 30, 1931 to Isaac Goldberg.

21. Both dates are clearly indicated in his orchestrated manuscript.

22. From his letter of June 30, 1931, to Isaac Goldberg.

23. *Ibid.;* as he expressed it in the letter, George didn't expect to get the recording until July 1, 1931.

24. These relatively minor revisions could easily have been planned or anticipated in advance and then confirmed at the trial performance.

25. Dreyfus learned of the dedication while in London. He immediately cabled Gershwin to say he was "touched beyond words" at the act. Dreyfus stated gratefully: "It is about the nicest thing that has happened to me." Interestingly, neither Gershwin's sketch nor his orchestrated manuscript of the *Second Rhapsody* contains a dedication inscription to Dreyfus. For that matter, only the published two-piano version of the piece, which came out during Gershwin's lifetime contains the inscription, "Dedicated to my friend Max Dreyfus." The published orchestral score does not.

26. In reminiscing about Gershwin in 1938, Koussevitzky spoke of him as an "extraordinary being too great to be real."

27. After the first rehearsal with the Boston orchestra, Gershwin said of Koussevitzky: "The man is marvelous. He knows the score inside out." And of the orchestra itself, he exclaimed: "What sight readers his players are! It's great to feel that you're in such wonderful hands." These comments were reported by Isaac Goldberg in the *Boston Evening Transcript* of January 30, 1932.

28. Oscar Levant, *A Smattering of Ignorance*, pp. 154–55.

29. Vernon Duke, "Gershwin, Schillinger, and Dukelsky," *The Musical Quarterly* (January 1947), p. 108.

30. The title of this work for publication became *Second Rhapsody for Piano and Orchestra*, rather than the title on Gershwin's orchestrated manuscript, discussed earlier.

31. The amount of assistance that *Gershwin* may have received in orchestrating the *Second Rhapsody*—as was

true for his symphonic compositions that preceded it—is conjectural.

32. New World Music was an offshoot of T. B. Harms Music, the publisher of most of Gershwin's songs. Gershwin, as already mentioned, was first signed to Harms by Max Dreyfus.

33. Prior to their publication, his symphonic scores from the *Concerto* on were available on a rental basis.

34. Gershwin usually had no objections to one or another kind of special-purpose arrangement of his orchestral works made by Bill Daly and others for radio broadcasts, concerts, or the like. But such arrangements cannot be considered to be on the same level as that of a published, and presum-ably definitive, version of a piece by Gershwin.

35. See the "Preamble" to the orchestral score of Gershwin's *"I Got Rhythm" Variations,* published in 1953, for Campbell-Watson's comments.

36. *Ibid.*

37. Information contained in a letter to this writer from Robert McBride.

38. The solo piano part is identical with the one found in the published two-piano version of the *Second Rhapsody,* which came out during Gershwin's lifetime and presumably reflected his approval. This solo part contains six additional measures, m. 101–06, not found in the original manuscript.

CHAPTER 14: Latin from Manhattan

1. Thus he wrote exuberantly in a letter to George Pallay.

2. In his own way, Gershwin helped to stimulate interest in *Of Thee I Sing* by inviting numerous friends to rehearsals of the show. This practice bothered Kaufman, who hated to be watched while directing. Kaufman, in his inimitably caustic manner got back at Gershwin by warning him one day after rehearsal: "This show is going to be a terrible flop. The balcony was only half filled today."

3. The slogans, approximately twenty in number, were all written by Kaufman and Ryskind.

4. Though the "Wintergreen for President" chant has a minor-key, quasi-European sound to it—possibly the antithesis of an American campaign song—it served its purpose effectively in *Of Thee I Sing,* especially since quotations from such American musical chestnuts as "Hail, Hail the Gang's All Here," and "Stars and Stripes Forever," were juxtaposed along with it. Oscar Hammerstein, for example, cited "Wintergreen for President" as an excellent example of a tune whose lyrics matched its melody, and vice versa. Moreover, the "Chinese" flavor of the vocal patter added to "Love Is Sweeping the Country," despite the stylistic mismatch, did not detract from the song's effectiveness in the show or adversely affect its overall popularity.

5. As a real-life corollary to the shenanigans on stage and just about as far-fetched, representatives of the Franco-American Society protested flippant remarks in the show about France's unpaid war debts to America and the way the French ambassador was made to appear ridiculous. In reply, Kaufman stated he was amenable to making changes in the script if the society could come up with lines and situations as humorous as any of those deleted. That apparently ended the matter.

6. Along with Gaxton's enormous vitality in playing the role went a propensity for altering the Kaufman-Ryskind script and improvising during performances. Angered at Gaxton's liberties, Kaufman, in his typically dry fashion, sent the actor this often-quoted telegram: "I am watching your performance from the rear of the house. Wish you were here."

7. As is well known, George Murphy in real life went on to become a Hollywood star and then a major political figure in California.

8. Kaufman never liked "baby" in the lyrics for the title tune. Before *Of Thee I Sing* opened he strongly pushed for the excision of the word from the lyrics. Kaufman also wanted

310

the tune to be a straight love song, rather than one with a "martial strain," as he put it. History, of course, has proved Kaufman wrong on both counts.

9. In the interest of expediency, Ira, like George, settled at times for less than the ideal in his work. For example, in "Jilted, Jilted!," for no apparent reason other than rhyming expediency, he rhymed "she" with the Scottish "dee," for "die," not the best of choices.

10. Besides the complete vocal score, New World Music published individually some of the more popular songs from *Of Thee I Sing*, such as "Who Cares," "Love Is Sweeping the Country," "Wintergreen for President," and the title tune.

11. Subsequently, the Pulitzer prize has been awarded to a composer of a score for a musical. When *South Pacific*, for example, received the Pulitzer prize in drama in 1950, Richard Rodgers shared the award with Oscar Hammerstein III and Joshua Logan. In 1944 Rodgers and Hammerstein also received a special citation from the Pulitzer committee (no Pulitzer prize in drama was awarded in 1944) for their *Oklahoma*.

12. Though the litigants may have had some disquieting moments in connection with the suit, the presiding judge, John M. Woolsey of the United States District Court, evidently enjoyed himself during the legal proceedings, irrespective of his decision. For the press, he described the plagiarism action presented before him as his "favorite kind of case."

13. References to bank closings, Prohibition, the League of Nations, and the Hoover Moratorium, found in the original production, had little relevance for 1952 audiences. So, to make this revival more palatable for them, such dated references were eliminated and more topical ones substituted. Yet these changes had little effect on the box office. Perhaps the generally acknowledged political apathy of the 1950s had something to do with the lack of interest in this production.

14. One might speculate that the tumultuous political and social events of 1968 (such as the Robert Kennedy and Martin Luther King assassinations, the campus unrest, the difficulties at the Democratic Convention at Chicago, and so forth) may have contributed to the bitter mood that made this revival of *Of Thee I Sing* unacceptable to the public.

15. Barnes's review appeared in the *New York Times* of March 8, 1969. In a more recent production of *Of Thee I Sing*, a ninety-minute special shown on American television screens on October 25, 1972, the score was again praised in the *Times* as being "remarkably fresh and delightful," but the musical itself drew criticism from television reviewer John J. O'Connor. "Back in 1931, 'Of Thee I Sing' hit the Broadway musical stage and thousands cheered," he wrote and then added, "Millions may wonder what the cheering was all about."

16. Bennett Cerf, "In Memory of George Gershwin," *Saturday Review of Literature* (July 17, 1943), p. 16 (also in Cerf's *Try and Stop Me*).

17. Gershwin's sketch for *Rumba* shows some of the effects of the speed at which it was written, for the bar lines appear quickly drawn and the actual notation seems less clear than usual for Gershwin. The date "July 1932" is written on the front page of the sketch to indicate when it was written. Like the sketches of his earlier orchestral pieces, the preorchestration draft of *Rumba* is written mainly on three and four staves.

18. On the title page of his orchestrated score, he noted that *Rumba* was "composed July, 1932" and the "orchestration begun Aug. 1st." On the final page of his orchestration, he wrote, "finished Aug. 9, 1932." Besides the sketch and the orchestrated score of *Rumba*, there are numerous work sheets for the piece, in no particular order, at the Library of Congress. Included in this material are three pages, titled "coda," which serve as the conclusion of the piece and feature percussion instruments, as well as other pages, titled "stretto

I" and "stretto II," which have also been incorporated into the work.

19. See the "Preface" to Schillinger's *Kaleidophone*. As stated earlier, these lessons with Schillinger lasted on and off for about four years and were generally subordinate to Gershwin's many assignments for Broadway and Hollywood.

20. Though Gershwin had indicated in this outline that the introduction would be "about 16 bars," it is actually twenty-six measures long. The introduction is found only in his orchestrated score, not in his sketch of the piece. Apparently he wrote the introduction *after* completing the sketch.

21. By and large, Gershwin showed a natural flair for imitative counterpoint and canon in his piano improvisations. For instance, Vernon Duke, as mentioned, reported that Gershwin's "extraordinary left hand performed . . . shrewd canonic devices" while improvising. Obviously, then, what had been essentially instinctive while playing became conscious in *Rumba*. As for Gershwin's claim that the canonic section of the piece is treated "in a polytonal manner" (that is, two or more tonalities or keys heard simultaneously), there are some moderate dissonances in this section which support his allegation.

22. In the usual sense, stretto (taken from the Italian *stringere*, "to tighten") refers to a technique used in writing fugues where a theme or subject is imitated in close succession: that is, the imitation of the subject comes in even before the latter has been fully stated. The resulting dovetailing of the theme and its imitation increases intensity and is a common device for bringing a fugue to a climactic conclusion. In *Rumba*, Gershwin's "stretto-like" treatment consists of a number of melodic fragments heard in quick succession against a rhythmic background similar to one played throughout much of the work. Presumably it is the close proximity of these fragments that constitutes the "stretto-like manner" to which he refers. However, his handling of this

dovetailing technique might be considered more a watered-down Gershwinian adaptation than the real thing.

23. Any part Schillinger played in the orchestration of *Rumba* does not show in the score for the piece, which is written clearly and neatly in Gershwins own hand. The score exudes a polished professional look, starting with the title page containing Gershwin's drawings of the percussion instruments featured in the work and his specification that they "be placed right in front of the conductor's stand," obviously to make them stand out both visibly and audibly. About the only telltale signs of haste occur close to the end of the work, at m. 329–54 of Gershwin's manuscript. Here to save time Gershwin used only a skeletal version of the actual orchestration, inasmuch as these measures repeat verbatim an earlier portion of the piece (m. 154–79).

24. Theremin's family name was originally Termen, before he changed it to the one he is now known by. His namesake, the Theremin, still in use today, generates pitches or tones from two electrical oscillators geared to different radio frequencies; the interaction between these frequencies produces recognizable tones. The unusual, "ethereal" sound of the Theremin probably became most familiar to the general public by its use in Miklos Rozsa's score for *Spellbound*, a popular movie of the 1940s, starring Gregory Peck and Ingrid Bergman.

25. The concert was for the benefit of the Musicians' Symphony, an orchestra made up of two hundred unemployed musicians. Sandor Harmati, the director of the orchestra, conducted music by Franck in the first half of the program. As already noted, Allan Lincoln Langley, as a result of playing in the orchestra for this concert, raised questions about Gershwin's musicianship and his ability to orchestrate.

26. Siqueiros, a close friend of Gershwin (he was his house guest for a period of time in the 1930s), painted this picture in 1936, in New York. He

simulated a Metropolitan Opera House background in his painting, reminiscent of the one for the concert on November 1, 1932. He also painted himself and friends and family of Gershwin into the picture, seated in the front rows of the parquet, watching the composer perform.

27. The work was published under that title some years after Gershwin's death. The published version of *Cuban Overture* follows his orchestrated manuscript quite closely. About the most extensive change in the published version is the elimination of seven measures for percussion instruments alone—found in Gershwin's original score, as part of the "coda"—between what are now m. 354 and m. 355 in the printed score.

CHAPTER 15: *In Analysis*

1. It has been estimated that two-thirds of the legitimate theaters in New York were forced to close by 1931 for lack of patronage. Subsequently, under President Franklin D. Roosevelt's administration, the Federal Theater Project was organized in 1935, as part of the New Deal, to help support the theater and to give employment to actors, singers, musicians, and other entertainers. The Federal Theater Project continued until 1939, by which time it employed over 12,000 persons, and was then discontinued by Congress on the ground that it was socially radical and extravagant.

2. Pearl's accent in *Pardon My English* was a carryover from his famous radio portrayal of Baron Munchhausen, whose usual retort, "Vas you dere, Sharlie?" had become a household phrase.

3. Ira, in his *Lyrics on Several Occasions*, p. 325, reports he heard "it cost him [Buchanan] twenty thousand dollars" to get out of the show, although he concedes that "this is probably an exaggeration."

4. Among Freedley's later activities were serving as president of the American National Theater and Academy (ANTA) as well as of the Actors Fund of America and of the Episcopal Actors Guild of America. Freedley died in 1969 at the age of seventy-seven.

5. Bennett Cerf, "In Memory of George Gershwin," *Saturday Review of Literature* (July 17, 1943), p. 16 (also in Cerf's *Try and Stop Me*).

6. Ira Gershwin, *Lyrics on Several Occasions*, pp. 325–26.

7. For all its impressive size and layout, the apartment apparently had one major drawback for Oscar Levant. In his *A Smattering of Ignorance*, p. 181, Levant complains that in his "bachelor apartment of fourteen rooms, George had managed to devise a layout that omitted even a single guest room. I once confronted him with this insistence of exclusiveness, accusing him of foreseeing the occasion when I might want to stay over some night."

8. One of the lines from the tune "Union Square" in the show.

9. The unusual way the twenty-four-measure chorus of this tune is put together is indicative of the overall flexibility of the score: an eight-measure phrase is followed by a different four-measure phrase in contrasting rhythm; the melody of the first eight measures is then repeated, with a new four-measure phrase brought in to conclude the chorus.

10. Armitage (editor), *Gershwin*, p. 48.

11. Besides Gershwin's depressed mental state, the high regard in which Zilboorg was held undoubtedly contributed to his decision to start psychoanalytic treatment. Also, psychoanalysis was one of the "in" things among many of Gershwin's friends. By undertaking psychoanalysis, Gershwin was following one of the more commonly accepted practices of the élite with whom he mingled.

12. By general calendar designation, the revolution took place between No-

vember 5 and November 7, 1917. But in the Julian calendar, then in use in Russia, the dates were October 23 and October 25, 1917. This explains the expression "October Revolution."

13. In addition to his many talents and broad interests, Zilboorg was notable for his close personal involvement with religion. Born into an orthodox Jewish family (his father was a scholarly Kiev grocer), Zilboorg became a Quaker when he came to America. In 1945 he embraced Catholicism.

14. Contrary to a report that Marshall Field went on the trip as well, Field was *not* on the trip according to Warburg.

15. Though his intentions may have been good, Gershwin, contrary to the implications of this pronouncement, did not show much derring-do in political matters. Save possibly for his token support of Fiorella La Guardia's candidacy as Fusion Mayor of New York City in 1934 preceding the press conference, he did not become very much involved in politics. During the Joseph McCarthy era, however, the senator from Wisconsin did include Gershwin among the names of composers and other artists whose "Americanism" he questioned.

16. His opinions of Mexican music were published in the *Herald-Tribune* of December 18, 1935, with this bold-face heading: "Gershwin Disappointed in the Music of Mexico; Reports Quest for Fresh Ideas Hits Snag of Monotony."

17. Ewen has made this wholly questionable attribution to Zilboorg in his *A Journey to Greatness* (1956), p. 34, and repeated it in his *George Gershwin: His Journey to Greatness* (1970), p. 6. According to Ewen, Zilboorg "has said that in his opinion, had the situation been otherwise, had Gershwin adored his mother and only respected his father, he would have become a hopeless psychoneurotic. Gershwin's adjustment to his work and to his life, says Dr. Zilboorg, was made possible only because his relations to his mother and father were exactly what they were." As noted earlier, since Gershwin's death, attempts have been made to denigrate his relationship with his mother.

18. Zilboorg remarried in 1946, after Gershwin's death.

19. For Zilboorg's remarks, titled "The Psychology of the Creative Personality," see Paul Smith (editor), *Creativity*, pp. 21–32.

CHAPTER 16: *Porgy and Bess*

1. The Cotton Club, Connie's Inn, Small's Paradise, and the Saratoga Club were some of the many Harlem cabarets that flourished in the 1920s and 1930s, mainly because they catered to whites who ventured uptown for the "exotic" atmosphere there.

2. Because of his own bout with polio, Heyward could easily identify with the cripple Smalls.

3. These comments by Duke Ellington, Hall Johnson, and Ralph Matthews were included in an article by Robert Garland, "Negroes Are Critical of 'Porgy and Bess.'" in the *New York World-Telegram* of January 16, 1936, p. 14.

4. Virgil Thomson, "George Gershwin,"

Modern Music (November-December 1935), pp. 16–17.

5. In statements to the press, Gershwin claimed on a number of occasions that the Metropolitan had offered to premiere *Porgy*, but that he had declined the offer. On checking with the Metropolitan, this writer has not been able to find substantiation for this claim. Although Gershwin, with the help of Kahn, had signed a contract with the Metropolitan in 1929 for *The Dybbuk*, there is no evidence that the opera company *ever* entered into serious negotiations with him for undertaking the original production of *Porgy*. Knowing of Gershwin's history of stretching the truth in other circumstances and spreading

stories to put himself in the most favorable light, one might reasonably assume he did the same thing here.

6. Shortly after the Guild production of the opera had opened on Broadway, Gershwin was reported in the press as saying that he hoped the Metropolitan would mount the work with Lawrence Tibbett in the role of Porgy. Such a production, of course, would require that Tibbett and other members of the cast perform in blackface. However, for whatever reasons, the Metropolitan has never presented the opera.

7. While in Florida in February 1935 at the Palm Beach home of Emil Mosbacher, Gershwin wrote Ira that he hoped he would join him in investing a total of $10,000 in the opera. According to Gershwin, "That 10 thousand represents 25% based on a 40 thousand dollar production," though he conceded "the cost may go higher." In his opinion, the investment "would not be risking too much and yet we'd have a good interest in the undertaking."

8. The original source for Heyward's statement was his article "Porgy and Bess Return on Wings of Song," in the October 1935 edition of *Stage Magazine*. Heyward's comments can also be found in Armitage (editor), *Gershwin*, p. 40.

9. Some reports have alleged that while in Florida he wrote most of the *Variations* away from the piano. Since by his own admission he composed at the piano, this claim is indeed questionable. Moreover, according to Mosbacher, he had a piano in his Palm Beach home, which Gershwin used when he was there.

10. Gershwin was so quoted in the *Herald-Tribune* of January 5, 1934, where he was characterized as "an eager student of Negro music."

11. *Ibid.*

12. This date appears on the last page of Gershwin's orchestrated score for the *Variations*. There is no other date indicated, in either the sketch or the orchestrated score for the work, so it is not completely clear when he began writing the piece or when he started orchestrating it.

13. For the tour, Charles Previn, who had long been associated with Gershwin (Previn had directed the orchestra for *La La Lucille,* back in 1919; he also later conducted *Of Thee I Sing*), led the Reisman ensemble. This touring orchestra was not a permanent one, but a pickup unit with the Reisman name added to it. Since most of the men in this group had not played regularly together, they did not have one common playing uniform. Instead, they all wore tuxedos or the equivalent (dark suits with black bow ties), while Gershwin often wore tails.

14. In Gershwin's original orchestrated score for the *Variations,* the four saxophones—two E-flat alto, one B-flat tenor, and one E-flat baritone—also double between them on B-flat clarinets, bass clarinet, and B-flat soprano saxophones. But the published version of the work put out in 1953 after Gershwin's death does not require saxophones. The published score, which is geared for a full symphonic complement, has cross-cued the original saxophone parts to other wind instruments. However, except for the increased number of instruments and some minor editorial and orchestrational revisions, the published orchestral score closely follows Gershwin's manuscript.

15. Vernon Duke, "Gershwin, Schillinger, and Dukelsky," *The Musical Quarterly* (January 1947), p. 110. The orchestration devices to which Duke refers may have been such sophisticated coloristic effects in the score as back-of-the-bridge playing and pizzicato glissandos in the violins (in the published score, the pizzicato glissandos have been changed to bowed glissandos).

16. The *Variations* was also supposedly written in dedication to Ira, though there is no dedicatory statement in either Gershwin's sketch or in his orchestrated manuscript for the piece. There is no dedication, either, in the published orchestral score. Only the published two-piano version of the *Variations* (a close replica of the original sketch of the piece), which came out while Gershwin

lived, contains this statement: "To my brother Ira." Like the *Variations,* only the published two-piano version of the *Second Rhapsody,* not the orchestral score itself, has a dedication to Max Dreyfus.

17. The *Variations* is so blatantly lightweight in conception, it might easily qualify now as high camp. Incidentally, before writing the *Variations,* Gershwin prepared a succinct descriptive outline of the work, just as he had done for some of his other orchestral pieces. This outline, now at the Library of Congress reads:

1—Simple
2—Orch melody—piano chromatic variation
3—Orch rich melody in 3/4 piano variation P
4—Chinese variation interlude
5—Modal variation
6—Hot variation finale

18. Gershwin got a "Chinese" musical flavor—the kind often associated with the background music of some bad Hollywood movies—in this variation simply by using many parallel intervals (fourths, fifths, and seconds) in conjunction with elements of a five-note pentatonic scale, the basis of the "I Got Rhythm" melody itself.

19. To get a "slapped" effect on the bass, its strings are almost simultaneously hit or "slapped" with the hand and *then* plucked.

20. Both his sketch and orchestrated score for the *"I Got Rhythm" Variations* are now at the Library of Congress. Like his other symphonic scores, his orchestration manuscript for the *Variations* has a glossy, professional look and pays considerable attention to performance details, such as tempo indications, accents, and phrasing.

21. The "foolish manager" referred to was none other than Harry Askins, who had helped to interest Max Dreyfus in Gershwin years earlier.

22. Armitage (editor), *Gershwin,* pp. 37–38.

23. On March 8, 1934, he had written Heyward that composing for *Porgy* "doesn't go too fast." By May 23, 1934, he had finally finished the first scene of the opera.

24. Botkin came along on the trip as a companion and fellow painter for Gershwin. Botkin, incidentally, was then very much interested in painting blacks.

25. Heyward has told a number of stories which clearly demonstrate Gershwin's empathy with the music of the Gullahs. In one of them, Heyward relates that, on attending "a Negro meeting on a remote sea island, George started 'shouting' with them. And eventually to their huge delight stole the show from their champion 'shouter.' I think that he is probably the only white man in America who could have done it."

26. His remarks were reported in the *New York Herald-Tribune* of July 8, 1934.

27. Dreyfus had sold his interest in Harms in 1929 for a price reputed to be between $8 and $10 million, but continued to be associated with Harms until his switch in 1935 to the American branch of Chappell. His brother Louis headed the venerable London branch.

28. Sirmay was a close friend of Gershwin and edited many of his publications, both at Harms and at Chappell. In an interview with this writer prior to his death on January 15, 1967, at the age of eighty-five, Sirmay said that he had made "pianistic adjustments" where necessary in Gershwin's works to make them more playable and changed or added minor details such as dynamic and metronomic markings where they were called for.

29. Before publication by the Gershwin Publishing Company, the vocal score for *Porgy and Bess* was put out by Random House in October 1935 in a special limited edition of 250 copies, each signed by George, Ira, Heyward, and Rouben Mamoulian.

30. This letter was discussed earlier.

31. For whatever reason, the July run-through of *Porgy* has met with a conspiracy of silence in key Gershwin sources. One can only wonder why this tryout has been ignored.

32. Steinert, a pianist, composer, and conductor himself, had served as vocal coach for the Russian Opera Company before his association with

Porgy. He got his *Porgy* job by a chance meeting with Gershwin at a Town Hall concert of Stravinsky's music during the winter of 1935. Gershwin, who was familiar with Steinert's reputation, simply tapped him on the shoulder and asked him if he would be interested in the coaching job. Steinert quickly accepted.

33. Getting Bubbles to learn his part proved to be a problem because he had difficulty with rhythm, pitch, tempo, and the memorization of his lines. Oscar Levant tells of the time Bubbles kept making so many mistakes in one scene during rehearsals that Alexander Smallens angrily stopped what was going on to ask if his conducting was at fault. Bubbles contritely replied, "If I had the money of the way you conduct I'd be a millionaire." Ultimately, Bubbles redeemed himself, at least in Gershwin's eyes, by his fine portrayal of Sportin' Life as well as by this magnificent telegram he and his dancing partner, Buck, sent Gershwin on opening night: "MAY THE CURTAIN FALL WITH THE BANG OF SUCCESS FOR YOU AS THE SUN RISES IN THE SUNSHINE OF YOUR SMILE."

34. This interview, complete with a description of his dress and gum chewing, appeared in the *New York Herald-Tribune.*

35. Mamoulian tells another revealing story about Gershwin that evolved from the rehearsals of the opera. After Mamoulian's first rehearsal session—a difficult one that left him feeling exhausted and depressed—the phone rang in his hotel suite and Gershwin was announced at the other end. In need of some encouragement and praise, Mamoulian, in his words, "picked up the receiver and said 'Hello' with eager anticipation. George's voice came glowing with enthusiasm: 'Rouben, I couldn't help calling you. . . . I just *had* to call you and tell you how I feel. I am so thrilled and delighted over the rehearsal today.' (My heart started warming up and I already began to feel better!) 'Of course,' he went on, 'I always knew that *Porgy and Bess*

was wonderful, but I never thought I'd feel the way I feel now. I tell you, after listening to that rehearsal today, I think the music is so marvelous—I really don't believe I wrote it!' "

36. The opening-night audience in Boston was filled with socialites and celebrities, including Irving Berlin and Cole Porter.

37. Gershwin apparently spoke through both sides of his mouth as far as the Metropolitan was concerned. On one hand, he stated that the Metropolitan had originally offered to produce *Porgy,* but that he had turned them down in favor of the Theatre Guild—though, as mentioned, this writer has found no evidence to substantiate this claim about the Metropolitan. On the other hand, he publicly expressed the hope shortly after *Porgy and Bess* had opened that the Metropolitan would produce the work with Lawrence Tibbett in the role of Porgy.

38. Although many of Gershwin's remarks in his article have a definite racist ring to them by today's standards, they must be viewed in the context of the period in which they were made. Also, he was so ego-involved with the opera, his perspective was undoubtedly affected.

39. By normal opera standards, such a run would be considered extraordinarily good. But *Porgy and Bess* had been brought to Broadway with the hope of making money for its sponsors and creators. George, Ira, and Heyward had even invested in the production with the idea of increasing their take from the work. Viewed in this light, *Porgy and Bess* was a definite Broadway failure.

40. Gershwin may have written his opera score with Catfish Row residents in mind, but individual tunes from *Porgy and Bess* have been performed mainly by whites rather than blacks, presumably because there are more of the former than the latter. The phenomenon of whites singing tunes from the opera in the "black" dialect of Ira and Heyward is one of the more incongruous aspects of such renditions.

41. Even at this late date, *Porgy and Bess*

is unquestionably better known because of the wide popularity of some of its tunes rather than for the merits of the opera as a total entity.

42. Earlier, in 1936, Gershwin had asked Max Dreyfus to try to arrange a tour abroad of *Porgy and Bess,* but nothing came of it despite Gershwin's belief that the opera "might prove to be a sensation all through Europe." Also, in connection with two all-Gershwin programs with the Los Angeles Philharmonic on February 10 and 11, 1937, in which excerpts from *Porgy and Bess* were performed, Gershwin had written Heyward that he hoped the excerpts "might whip up some enthusiasm for picture possibilities on the part of the studios who, as you know, are keen about it [the opera], but slightly afraid on

account of the color question." Here, too, nothing panned out for the opera.

43. The Philadelphia Orchestra premiered the suite on January 21, 1936, Alexander Smallens conducting. The five movements of the suite are titled "Catfish Row," "Porgy Sings," "Fugue," "Hurricane," and "Good Morning, Brother."

44. Heyward died in 1940, before the Crawford revival, so he did not live to see his artistic judgment vindicated. For as he had argued, Gershwin's recitatives impeded the pacing of the original production.

45. Inasmuch as Gershwin dedicated *Porgy and Bess* "to my parents," Mrs. Gershwin's benefits from the opera were not solely financial.

CHAPTER 17: *The Final Curtain*

1. By the time the Federal Theater Project was discontinued by Congress in 1939 it had become a $7-million enterprise. Over 15 million people attended shows that it sponsored.

2. Arthur Lyons and his brother, Sam, comprised the firm of A. and S. Lyons, theatrical agents, with Arthur handling film matters and Sam, Broadway shows. The latter represented Gershwin for a number of Broadway musicals.

3. At the time RKO, through Berman, indicated an interest in having the Gershwins write the score for *Watch Your Step,* the Astaire-Rogers team was at the peak of its popularity as a result of such movie successes as *Top Hat* and *Follow the Fleet,* both with music by Irving Berlin, and *Swing Time,* with a Jerome Kern score. One of the motivating factors that induced Berman to sign the Gershwins was that he wanted to add their names to the list of tunesmiths—which included Berlin, Kern, and Cole Porter —who had worked for him.

4. All the music for the *Swing Is King* revue was by Gershwin.

5. The 1936 *Follies* starred, among others, Fanny Brice, Josephine Baker, and Bob Hope. The famous

tune, "I Can't Get Started," came from that show.

6. "By Strauss" was subsequently used in the 1951 movie *An American in Paris* with great effect.

7. Smallens died on November 24, 1972 at the age of eighty-three.

8. Oscar Levant, *A Smattering of Ignorance,* pp. 167–68.

9. Gershwin's "association" with U.C.L.A. did not result solely from his friendship with Schoenberg. For in 1936, he and Ira presented a revised version of the tune "Strike Up the Band" to U.C.L.A. for use by its band at sports events. In adapting the tune for U.C.L.A., Ira completely rewrote its lyrics. For Ira's part in the adaptation, he has been rewarded with two season passes annually for U.C.L.A. home football games in lieu of royalties.

10. As was true for almost everything he did, Gershwin's scholarship contribution was duly reported in the press. (A number of papers printed the story on September 26, 1933.)

11. Oscar Levant, *A Smattering of Ignorance,* pp. 188–89.

12. "Shall We Dance" was not written until the spring of 1937, after the movie had gotten its new label.

13. The two programs with the Los Angeles Philharmonic featured these Gershwin staples: *An American in Paris, Rhapsody in Blue, Concerto in F, Cuban Overture,* and selections from *Porgy and Bess.*

14. Saunders's review of the concert appeared in the *Musical Courier* of February 27, 1937.

15. There have been a number of variations of this episode reported, nearly all of which have some basis in fact. There would seem to be complete agreement in all versions of the story, however, that the first ominous sign of his fatal brain tumor occurred during his engagement with the Los Angeles Philharmonic in February 1937.

16. Wodehouse has offered some incisive commentary on how Hollywood can bungle badly. According to him, the studio took the original script for *Damsel in Distress* and "gave it to one of the RKO writers to adapt, and he turned out a script all about crooks—no resemblance to the novel. Then it struck them that it might be a good thing to stick to the story, so they chucked away the other script and called me in."

17. Fred Astaire and Ginger Rogers, following their long string of hit musicals together, finally decided to go their separate ways after *Shall We Dance.* However, after a separation of fifteen months the two were reunited in *Carefree* (1938). They subsequently made *The Story of Vernon and Irene Castle* (1939) and *The Barkleys of Broadway* (1949).

18. "Sing of Spring" received its concert premiere on April 15, 1969 in the Composers' Showcase concert series directed by this writer in New York. It was performed at the Whitney Museum of American Art by the Collegiate Chorale, led by Abraham Kaplan.

19. With all the care that he had always lavished on himself, his physique and looks had weathered the years very well. Save for thinning hair (which he tried to alleviate by electric suction treatments to the scalp, without any noticeable benefits), his appearance in 1936 and 1937 had changed little from the mid-1920s, when he

had first attracted world attention with the *Rhapsody in Blue.* Hollywood women thus found him as attractive as did nearly all other women. If anything, more so. For Gershwin, after all, was a visiting VIP from the East to the women of the movie-colony set.

20. It is not clear what he actually thought of her voice. Miss Simon attempted a singing role in a legitimate musical, *Three After Three* in the 1940s, but the show never reached Broadway.

21. Gershwin did not especially enjoy his tenure with Goldwyn. The producer not only threw his weight around, but he also frequently exhorted him to write hits "like Irving Berlin."

22. Among his other qualifications, Dr. Segall had the distinction of having been Greta Garbo's doctor.

23. Noah D. Fabricant, M.D., "George Gershwin's Fatal Headache," *The Eye, Ear, Nose and Throat Monthly* (May 1958), p. 333.

24. One press report, issued shortly after his death, claimed that he had been taken to the hospital after collapsing on the Goldwyn lot and that it had been thought that he had suffered a nervous breakdown.

25. Fabricant, M.D., *The Eye, Ear, Nose and Throat Monthly* (May 1958), p. 334.

26. *Ibid.*

27. Arnold Schoenberg added his praises to the many good things said about Gershwin at his death. Reminiscing, Schoenberg stated: "Many musicians do not consider George Gershwin a serious composer. But they should understand that, serious or not, he is a composer—that is, a man who lives in music and expresses everything, serious or not, sound or superficial, by means of music, because it is his native language. . . . It seems to me beyond doubt that Gershwin was an innovator. What he has done with rhythm, harmony, and melody is not merely style. It is fundamentally different from the mannerism of many a serious composer. . . . His melodies are not products of a combination, nor of a mechanical union, but they are units and could

therefore not be taken to pieces. Melody, harmony, and rhythm are not welded together, but cast."

28. Gershwin is buried in a mausoleum there.

29. Exclusive of his fabulous collection of paintings as well as personal belongings, Gershwin left a gross estate appraised at only $430,841. Of this amount, the residuary value of his total musical works was appraised at the surprisingly low figure of $50,125 —a most modest appraisal, possibly kept down for inheritance-tax purposes. For instance, *Rhapsody in Blue* was valued at only $20,000; *An American in' Paris*, at $5,000; the score for *Of Thee I Sing*, at $4,000; the *Concerto in F*, at $1,750; and the score for *Porgy and Bess*, at only "nominal" value of $250. His main liquid assets included $228,811 in cash and insurance, and $141,615 in securities. After deducting funeral and administration expenses of $50,941 and debts of $38,810 from the appraised gross estate, Mrs. Gershwin was left a net estate appraised at $341,089.

30. This dispute, as stated earlier, was quietly resolved when Ira waived claims for personal property he alleged his mother owed him in return for sharing her estate equally with his sister and brother.

31. According to Duke, he completed the verses for "three Gershwin songs, anonymously of course" for *The Goldwyn Follies*.

32. "Love Is Here to Stay" has the distinction of being the last tune Gershwin wrote. This is one of the songs that Duke worked on for Goldwyn's *Follies*.

33. Ira has stated publicly that, of the approximately one hundred unpublished songs George left behind, at least fifty of them were "completed" tunes.

34. There was no guarantee, of course, that he would have followed through in writing all the works he talked about if he had lived. For instance, in 1929 or so, he spoke enthusiastically of writing a choral setting for Lincoln's Gettysburg Address, with a singer of Lawrence Tibbett's stature in the role of Lincoln, but he never got around to writing the piece. A Gershwin ballet, however, *did* come out after his death. It stemmed indirectly from *The Goldwyn Follies*. Both Gershwin and George Balanchine had hoped to collaborate on a ballet for this movie, before Gershwin's illness made this impossible. In 1964, Ira followed through on the originally planned Gershwin-Balanchine collaboration by sending the choreographer fourteen posthumous songs by Gershwin for consideration as a ballet. Though Balanchine did not do anything with the posthumous songs (he was quoted in the press on February 18, 1964, as saying that they were "much better for a Broadway show than for a ballet"), he did fashion a ballet in 1970 for the New York City Ballet from seventeen of Gershwin's most famous tunes. (The seventeen tunes are "Strike Up the Band," "Sweet and Low-Down," "Somebody Loves Me," "Bidin' My Time," "'S Wonderful," "That Certain Feeling," "Do, Do, Do," "Oh, Lady, Be Good!" "The Man I Love," "I'll Build a Stairway to Paradise," "Embraceable You," "Fascinating Rhythm," "Who Cares?," "My One and Only," "Liza," "Clap Yo' Hands," and "I Got Rhythm.") The resulting ballet, *Who Cares?*, conscientiously tried to recapture memories of the 1920s and the 1930s. It turned out to be a huge success. On reviewing the ballet in the *New York Times* of February 6, 1970, Clive Barnes noted "how potent such cheap music is" and how "happily nostalgic."

APPENDIX I
SOME FURTHER REMARKS ABOUT GERSHWIN'S MUSIC

WRITING GOOD POPULAR songs requires its own special talents. Gershwin had those talents in abundance. It was almost child's play for him to concoct his ditties. He enjoyed doing it, and it came easily and naturally to him at the piano. Many of his tunes mirror that spontaneity, just as they often reflect their piano evolution by their "oom-pah" accompaniments, "walking" bass lines, and the finger-doodling, stepwise movement of their harmony. Like any other tunesmith worth his salt, Gershwin made no bones about trying to cater to public taste. He also made it a point to speak simply and directly in his songs, in the best tradition of Broadway and Tin Pan Alley. As he well knew, if his tunes were to succeed, they had to be likable, singable, and easily remembered. To help the memory of the public along, most of his songs make use of the typically repetitive refrain formulas of Tin Pan Alley in which the opening melodic phrase—usually eight measures long—makes up the bulk of the tune. The *A-A-B-A* format was the one he used more than any other. In this pattern the starting phrase, or *A,* is repeated almost exactly. After some new *B* material— again, usually eight measures long— is introduced, a near facsimile of the opening phrase is heard once more, ending the refrain. " 'S Wonderful," "Liza," "Oh, Lady Be Good!," and "The Man I Love" are just a few of his well-known tunes that are struc-

321

tured the *A-A-B-A* way. But Gershwin, of course, did not limit himself merely to this format. He employed other, equally uncomplicated patterns as well. For instance, "Embraceable You," "Of Thee I Sing," "Who Cares?," and "That Certain Feeling" fall into an *A-B-A-C* mold; "Do It Again" and "But Not for Me" make use of an *A-B-A-B* structure; and so on. Within the limits of such prescribed patterns, he drew from his bag of tunesmith's wiles tunes catchy enough to withstand so much reiteration. Where the melodic line was persistently repetitive, as in " 'S Wonderful" or "The Man I Love," he invariably changed the underlying harmony each measure or so, to offset any inherent monotony. In all this he was usually aided by complementary lyrics—mainly those by Ira—which helped to dress up the tunes further, making them even more palatable to the public.[1]

As any sharp young New York tunesmith weaned on Tin Pan Alley fare would be, he was admittedly influenced by ragtime and jazz. His tunes are full of such conscious Americanisms as jazzy syncopations and "blue" notes.[2] This is what the public wanted, and he gave it to them. Equally appealing in his music are some characteristics whose derivations are less obvious and possibly unconsciously derived for the most part. Their origins probably go back to his early roots. These are the so-called Jewish elements in his music. A number of writers have touched on these Jewishisms in his compositions without spelling them out in concrete musical terms, presumably because of the difficulties involved, for any attempt to isolate Jewish musical elements presupposes a music that is specifically and uniquely Jewish, a problematic area to define. However, at least one acknowledged expert in this field, A. Z. Idelsohn (1882–1938), in his numerous writings and in his monumental ten-volume *Thesaurus of Hebrew–Oriental Melodies,* has helped to establish some musico-scientific principles for evaluating Jewish music. One of the points Idelsohn has made is that Jewish music from its very beginnings has been conceived on a melodic basis. According to Idelsohn,

> The Jewish folk has never attempted to add harmonic combinations to its music. The song remains for single voice. In all likelihood because of his Oriental origin, the Jew prefers melody. To him, music means melody, means a *succession* rather than a *combination* of tones. . . . Song, to him, is a means by which to sanctify his life, by which to flood with warmth and light the sanctuaries of his family home and of the home of his faith—his Synagogue.[3]

Idelsohn found, too, that one of the distinguishing aspects of Jewish music is its emphasis on a "minor" sound. In a study, for instance, of East

European Jewish folk song—an important musical influence among Jews in the United States, particularly in the big cities of the northeastern seaboard states—Idelsohn discovered that about eighty-eight percent of this music either makes use of elements of "the minor scale or at least has minor character."[4] Moreover, Idelsohn has been able to isolate typical Jewish song motifs and melodies. In Idelsohn's examples, the interval of a minor third plays an important part in giving them a Jewish profile.[5]

Many of Gershwin's tunes, judged on a purely melodic basis, bear some relationship to Idelsohn's examples and have a "minor" tinge to them, one readily associated with Jewish sources because of their prominent use of the minor third.[6] For instance, his melody for " 'S Wonderful," the one he purportedly borrowed from Abraham Goldfaden, emphasizes this interval. By itself, the " 'S Wonderful" melody clearly passes for Jewish, though when combined with Gershwin's major harmony for it, its character is changed. This also occurs with the simple melody for "Funny Face." Heard alone, this melody appears Jewish by reason of its focus on the minor third. But this identity is quickly obfuscated by his harmonization for the tune, with its up-to-date chromatically altered, Broadwayish chords. (The intervals of the minor third are indicated by brackets in the melody for "Funny Face" and in other cited examples of Jewishisms in Gershwin's melodies.)

"Funny Face"*

Even the melody for his famous second "Prelude," the slow, middle one from his three *Preludes for Piano,* seems Jewish on account of its stress on the minor third. This stress is especially noticeable when the melody for this "Prelude" is separated from its jazz context, inherent in the "walking," repetitive bass.

*FUNNY FACE (George & Ira Gershwin), © 1927 New World Music Corporation. Copyright renewed All rights reserved.

"Second Prelude"*

"Wintergreen for President," from *Of Thee I Sing*, "Soon," from *Strike Up the Band*, "I Love You," from *George White's Scandals of 1921*, and such tunes from *Porgy and Bess* as "My Man's Gone Now," "A Woman Is a Sometime Thing," and "It Ain't Necessarily So" are but a few of his numerous works whose melodies emphasize the minor third, with a resultant Jewish sound. The significance of this interval in giving Jewish character to many of his melodies is made more meaningful in the light of this conclusion by Idelsohn, based on his studies: "When closely analyzed, all the motifs of a nation, be they ever so numerous, can be reduced to a few motifs, and these to a few intervals."[7]

The Jewishisms in Gershwin's music are not limited solely to his use of the minor third in his melodies. For his tunes also exhibit the declamatory and expressive traits found in Biblical prayer chant, as well as characteristics associated with Jewish secular pieces. For instance, the melody for "My One and Only," from *Funny Face*, closely resembles Jewish cantillation, with its *parlando* and melismatic passages, and seems to have emerged almost intact from the Old Testament and the synagogal tradition. (In the prayer-like Gershwin examples shown, circles are used to indicate the equivalent of chanting tones in Jewish cantillation. In addition, brackets outline the interval of the minor third in the more expressive parts of the melody.)

"My One and Only"**

The melody for "In the Mandarin's Orchid Garden," his only "art" song, is also similar to Jewish cantillation. The Jewishisms inherent in its prayer-like melody are made even more noticeable by the use of the minor-third interval at cadential points.

"In the Mandarin's Orchid Garden"*

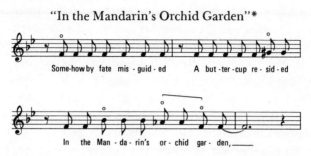

A resemblance between Gershwin's music and snappy Jewish folk-dance tunes called *frailachs* can also be noted. *Frailachs* are often performed at Jewish festive functions such as weddings by a small, variable number of musicians who are familiar with Jewish performance practices.[8] One of his tunes that resembles *frailachs* is "Seventeen and Twenty-One," from *Strike Up the Band* (1927 version). One need only compare "Der Patch Tanz" ("Hand-Clapping Dance") and the "Schuster and Schneider Tanz" ("Shoemaker and Tailor Dance"), two traditional *frailachs,* with "Seventeen and Twenty-One" to see the broad melodic resemblance among them. All three seem to have been cut from the same melodic cloth, with their reiterated, stepwise mannerisms.

"Der Pach Tanz" ("Hand Clapping Dance")

"Schuster and Schneider Tanz" ("Shoemaker and Tailor Dance")

"Seventeen and Twenty-One"**

Though many of the melodies for both Gershwin's popular tunes and large-scale works on close examination seem to spring from Jewish roots, his work as a whole was geared primarily for American audiences and was expected to be performed according to American—not Jewish—performance practice standards. After all, he emphasized the American aspects of his music by using only English texts and by pushing for performances of his work by singers and instrumentalists familiar with the musical language of Tin Pan Alley, Broadway, and jazz. As a result, audiences invariably hear his works as American, rather than focusing on any Jewish melodic traits in it.[9] Nor did he make any public statements that would alter this picture, especially pronouncements on whether Jewish characteristics were consciously or unconsciously expressed in his work.[10] Moreover, his wide acclaim as a uniquely American composer has helped to obscure further for the public any Jewish traits in his music. And that is the way matters stand today.

Besides the motley mixture of Jewish melodic characteristics and overt musical Americanisms, Gershwin's work has other idiosyncratic features. For instance, he had a natural flair for imitative counterpoint, and his music—especially his orchestral pieces—is full of it. His work teems with many literal repetitions of melodies and motifs, rhythmic ostinatos, and sequences. Disjunctive pauses also stand out. For, again and again, when he had difficulty getting from one section to another in his orchestral works, he would simply pause abruptly to mark the end of one section and the beginning of a new. Such awkward touches as these are so commonplace in his large-scale pieces that they have come to be accepted as part of the Gershwin musical personality.

His harmony is unmistakably his own, too. It generally avoids extreme dissonances. Since his musical style is pretty much the same for his popular and serious works, his harmony in turn is quite consistent for all his compositions. Mainly, it is piano-influenced and diatonic. It features unresolved seventh chords and quick, unprepared for parallel-motion shifts from the tonic to neighboring tonalities, usually a half step or a whole step away (such as these chord progressions: G-F-G-B flat-B natural-C). Where his harmony is chromatic, it also shows the influences of the piano in the stepwise and parallel movement of the inner voices. Moreover, quick shifts in harmony are most always used where there is a sustained note in the melody. Despite frequent chordal changes, he customarily limited himself to one key signature in his popular tunes to keep them as simple as possible. However, in his orchestral pieces, with a broader canvas to work on, he often changed key signatures, not only to add an element of variety, but presumably also to show the world his musical "sophistication."[11]

Like his harmony, his rhythms for his popular tunes do not differ in kind from those for his serious compositions. In either medium, he had a gift for creating concise rhythmic patterns that are distinct and memorable. With his flair for rhythms, he often based his songs or smaller pieces on one prime rhythmic-melodic motif. "The Man I Love," for example, revolves around one recurring rhythmic pattern (♩. ♫♪♫♩ | ♩. ♫♪♩); "I Got Rhythm" around another (♩ ♪♫. | ♩.♩♩). The slow "Prelude," from his three *Preludes for Piano,* grows out of this germinal rhythm (♫♩ | ♪♩.),[12] while the first "Prelude" highlights this rhythm (♫♩ ♫.) and the third "Prelude," this ($\overline{3}$ ♫♫♫ ♫♩♩ | ♩.). Of course, he used syncopation liberally. Hundreds of examples of syncopation in his work can be cited, including this pattern in the *Rhapsody in Blue* (♫♫♩♫♫♩), or this one from the *Concerto in F* (♪♩ ♩ ♩ ♪♪♪ ♩ ♩ ♪). Because of the distinctive quality of many of his rhythms, they often stand out clearly even when combined with other rhythms. For instance, his simulation of a black prayer meeting in *Porgy and Bess* (Act II, scene IV) combines six rhythmically different prayer settings sung simultaneously with great effect. His adroit handling of rhythms piled on one another is especially discernible in *An American in Paris* and the orchestral works written after it. In these compositions, he had gained enough experience to be able to combine convincingly an assortment of melodies, motifs, and figurations; despite the numerous musical details heard simultaneously, the individual rhythms come through. Another illustration of his rhythmic bent can be seen in the slow *(andantino moderato)* section of the *Rhapsody in Blue.* Here he juxtaposes this simple, recurring rhythm (♫♩ ♩ ♩) against the famous theme of this section, but in a way that gets maximum variety from the limited pitches (D-sharp, D-natural, C-sharp, in the example shown on page 328) used in the persistent rhythmic pattern.

Growing up with the music of Tin Pan Alley and Broadway in his ears, Gershwin felt completely at home in the popular-song field. He composed hundreds of songs on order to meet the needs of Broadway producers or other show-business entrepreneurs. More important, he had a knack for coming up with winning combinations of music and lyrics (greatly aided, to be sure, by Ira in the lyrics department) and could write a hit tune with the best of them. As a composer of serious works, however, he was no longer on

327

*Rhapsody in Blue** (beginning of the slow section)

home territory. He had loads of *chutzpah,* but practically no grounding in the technique of large-scale composition for undertaking the conquest of the concert hall and opera house. But mainly by following his instincts, he somehow put together pieces that managed to fall into the serious music category. Aided by reams of press releases and other publicity, they have even taken their place in the standard repertoire. For the most part, his serious works are merely extensions of his popular songs. But while the latter are models of their kind because of their brevity, the serious compositions are filled with structural defects, resulting from his limited experience in developing his materials. Often, his serious pieces consist of little more than attractive tunes separated by filler material, with the tunes quite commonly repeated literally—save perhaps for negligible differences in key, harmonization, and instrumentation—over and over. Fortunately, many of the tunes are so good they serve almost as a ballast for technical deficiencies. Moreover, alongside the ineptitudes in his serious pieces there are also some evidences of motif and thematic transformation that is surprisingly sophisticated. Since intellectuality whether from a musical or any other standpoint was not his forte, it would appear that these sophisticated elements came about through instinct rather than from design. In all likelihood, he didn't even know they existed.

Even in his first orchestral piece, the *Rhapsody in Blue,* signs of relatively sophisticated motif transformation can be detected. As a matter of fact, the opening fourteen measures serve as the basis for much of the piece. Within these measures three important motifs, melodically and rhyth-

* *Op. cit.*

mically distinct from one another, are heard (m. 2–5; m 6–11; m 11–14). Each of the three motifs, in turn, bears a relationship to other material found in the work. Some idea of this derivative relationship can be seen by examining the first of these motifs. The initial motif is presented by the clarinet after the glissando passage of the first measure.

*Rhapsody in Blue,** m. 2–5, initial motif

At least two important themes seem to be related to the initial motif. One of these well-known themes is heard at m. 138.

Rhapsody in Blue, m. 138–41, a variant of the initial motif

When this variant is broken down into its component parts, a resemblance can be seen between m. 138 and an inverted version of m. 3 (to facilitate comparison with m. 138, m. 3 will be shown in its original state, and then, in successive steps, transposed and lowered, and finally inverted).

Rhapsody in Blue, m. 3 (of the initial motif), in its original state

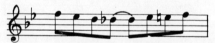

Rhapsody in Blue, m. 3, transposed and lowered to the bass clef

Rhapsody in Blue, m. 3, transposed, lowered, and inverted (for comparison with m. 138)

Rhapsody in Blue, m. 138 (of the initial-motif variant)

* *Op. cit.*

For its part, m. 139 of the variant (), with its scalewise melody and syncopation, bears a tangential resemblance to m. 3 of the initial motif (). A relationship between m. 140–41 of the variant and m. 2 of the initial motif can also be seen by augmenting the eighth-note triplets at the last beat of m. 2 to quarter-note triplets, lengthening the half note at the beginning of the measure (m. 2), and then retrograding—or playing backwards—this material.

*Rhapsody in Blue,** m. 2 (of the initial motif), in its original state

Rhapsody in Blue, m. 2, transposed and lowered to the bass clef

Rhapsody in Blue, m. 2, transposed, lowered, augmented, and retrograded (for comparison with m. 140–41)

Rhapsody in Blue, m. 140–41 (of the initial motif variant)

The renowned theme of the slow section of the *Rhapsody in Blue* is another example of sophisticated motif transformation. The beginning of this theme, m. 303, appears to be related to the initial-motif variant cited (m. 138–41).

Rhapsody in Blue, m. 303–06, the start of the theme of the slow *(andantino moderato)* section

* *Op. cit.*

A resemblance between the beginning of the slow-section theme and m. 138 can be seen if the eighth notes of the latter measure are augmented to quarter notes and a drop of an octave, rather than a reiteration of the same pitch, takes place at the fourth beat. To illustrate this point, m. 138, in its original state, then in a transposed, augmented version with the fourth note lowered an octave, is compared with m. 303 of the slow section.

*Rhapsody in Blue,** m. 138 (of the initial motif variant), in its original state

Rhapsody in Blue, m. 138, transposed and raised to the treble clef

Rhapsody in Blue, m. 138, transposed, raised, and augmented, with the fourth note dropped an octave (for comparison with m. 303)

Rhapsody in Blue, m. 303 (of the slow-section theme)

Too much, of course, should not be made of *ex post facto* evidences of sophisticated handling of material in Gershwin's serious works. Such evidences are far outweighed by examples of musical crudities. But then, the usual criteria for judging serious compositions do not really apply in his case. For first and foremost he was a celebrated writer of popular songs. If he had limited himself solely to his tunesmith's trade, he would have still been a figure to reckon with. But by his successful "dabbling" in concert-hall and operatic music he became a unique institution, one set apart from even such famous fellow tunesmiths as Jerome Kern, Cole Porter, Richard Rodgers, and Irving Berlin. Gershwin may never have come close to reaching Parnassus in his serious pieces, but that has never mattered to his vast, international public, who after all mold what is acceptable and fashionable by the cumulative strength of their collective dollars. They are the ones who buy the records, purchase the music, attend the concerts. True, their tastes have been shaped considerably by the inordinate amounts of publicity attendant on nearly everything connected with the Gershwin name. But, at the same time, one cannot overlook his special flair for

* *Op. cit.*

speaking a musical language they readily understand and savor. In return, they have ensconced in the standard repertoire his *Rhapsody in Blue, Concerto in F, An American in Paris,* and *Porgy and Bess.* What consequence, then, if technical evaluations show that his music is often put together poorly or that "enlightened" aesthetic assessments—always a thorny and highly subjective matter to define and discuss—complain of intrinsic vulgarity in his approach to serious art. The end result is little more than nitpicking. Gershwin is too strongly entrenched in the minds and hearts of his followers everywhere. Professionals and critics may always find fault with his serious work, but not so the Average Joes of the world. Their rallying cry for Gershwin and his music will probably always be *"Viva Gershwin."* And such loyalty counts the most in the long run in keeping his name and his music alive.

NOTES

1. In creating his popular songs, Gershwin wrote the music first in the vast majority of cases—some ninety-odd percent of the time. The lyrics were then fitted to the music, with some adjustments made where necessary in both the music and the lyrics to assure that they went well together.

2. "Blue" notes are closely associated with jazz. They are notes—usually the third, fifth, or seventh degrees of the scale—whose pitch has been altered slightly to evoke a jazz or blues feeling. The pitch deviations are usually indicated by flatted half steps, though in performance they may be of the microtonal variety.

3. A. Z. Idelsohn. "The Distinctive Elements of Jewish Folk-Song," *M. T. N. A., Proceedings* (1924), unnumbered pages.

4. A. Z. Idelsohn, "Musical Characteristics of East-European Jewish Folk-Song," *The Musical Quarterly* (October 1932), p. 636.

5. The characteristic Jewish song motifs and melodies which Idelsohn has isolated, and to which this writer refers, can be found in Idelsohn's article "The Distinctive Elements of Jewish Folk-Song," in the 1924 *M.T.N.A., Proceedings,* as well as in his *Thesaurus of Hebrew-Oriental Melodies,* Volume II, p. 29.

6. The interval of a minor third, in certain contexts, can of course be regarded as a jazz "blue" note. However, in evaluating so-called Jewishisms in Gershwin's music, this writer has considered his use of the minor third in its broadest sense and not limited it to its jazz context.

7. Idelsohn, "The Distinctive Elements of Jewish Folk-Song," *op. cit.*

8. Jewish performance practices have evolved through the years as a matter of tradition. They have been passed on from generation to generation of musicians mainly aurally, rather than through written or notated means. Jewish performance practices touch on such aural factors as timbre, intonation, ornamentation, speech inflection (derived from Yiddish and Hebrew), rhythm, tempo, intensity, and various types of glissandos. Of course, other national and ethnic groups have their own characteristic performance practices as well.

9. The Jewishisms in his music would, of course, be relatively easy to detect if his pieces were performed in a manner consistent with Jewish performance practices.

10. While he lived, numerous claims of Jewishisms in his music were made by Isaac Goldberg and others. Obviously, Gershwin was familiar with these claims, though he did not discuss them publicly. But even if he had

332

spoken out, there is no guarantee that he would have shed much light on the question of Jewishisms in his work. For distinctions between "Jewishisms" and "Americanisms" in his music—as well as in the work of many other tunesmiths of his generation and background—are not always clear-cut or absolute.

11. His numerous changes of key signature in his serious pieces, as noted earlier, may have been an offshoot of his piano improvisations. While improvising on his tunes, he often changed keys after each chorus.

12. He used a three eighth-note upbeat figure in a number of his works, including the second movement of his *Concerto in F*—all three themes of this movement start this way.

APPENDIX II
COMPOSITIONS BY
GEORGE GERSHWIN

1913

Since I Found You (lyrics, Leonard Praskins)
Ragging the Traumerei (lyrics, Leonard Praskins)

1916

When You Want 'Em, You Can't Get 'Em, When You Got 'Em, You Don't Want 'Em (lyrics, Murray Roth)
When the Armies Disband (lyrics, Irving Caesar)
THE PASSING SHOW OF 1916. Book and lyrics mainly by Harold Atteridge. Music mainly by Sigmund Romberg and Otto Motzan. Produced by the Shuberts at the Winter Garden, June 22, 1916, with Ed Wynn, the Ford Sisters, Stella Horban, Frances Demarest, Florence Moore, Herman Timberg, and Fred Walton; 140 performances.

*Making of a Girl (music, Sigmund Romberg and George Gershwin; lyrics, Harold Atteridge)
Not Used: *My Runaway Girl* (lyrics, Murray Roth)

1917

*Rialto Ripples (piano rag; music, Will Donaldson and George Gershwin)

1918

HITCHY-KOO OF 1918. Book and lyrics mainly by Glen MacDonough. Music mainly by Raymond Hubbell. Produced by Raymond Hitchcock at the Globe Theater, June 6, 1918, with Irene Bordoni, Leon Errol, and Raymond Hitchcock; 68 performances.
*You-oo Just You (lyrics, Irving Caesar)

(* denotes publication of individual works as well as complete musical scores)

LADIES FIRST. Book and lyrics by Harry B. Smith; Music mainly by A. Baldwin Sloane. Produced by H. H. Frazee at the Broadhurst Theater, October 24, 1918, with Nora Bayes, William Kent, Lew Cooper, Florence Morrison, and William Norris; 164 performances.

*Some Wonderful Sort of Someone (lyrics, Schuyler Greene)
*The Real American Folk Song (lyrics, Arthur Francis, Ira Gershwin's pseudonym; first published in 1959)

HALF PAST EIGHT. Opened at the Empire Theater, Syracuse, New York, December 9, 1918 and never reached Broadway. Cast included Joe Cook and Sybil Vane.

Cupid
Hong Kong
Ten Commandments of Love
There's Magic in the Air (lyrics, Arthur Francis)

1919

GOOD MORNING, JUDGE. Book by Fred Thompson, based on The Magistrate by Sir Authur Wing Pinero. Music mainly by Lionel Monckton and Howard Talbot. Produced by the Shuberts at the Shubert Theater, February 6, 1919, with Charles and Mollie King, George Massell, and Margaret Dale; 140 performances.

*I Was So Young, You Were So Beautiful (lyrics, Irving Caesar and Al Bryan)
*There's More to the Kiss than the X-X-X (lyrics, Irving Caesar)
*O Land of Mine, America (lyrics, Michael E. O'Rourke)

THE LADY IN RED. Book and lyrics mainly by Anne Caldwell. Music mainly by Robert Winterberg. Produced by John Slocum at the Lyric Theater, May 12, 1919, with Adele Rowland, Donald MacDonald, and Franklyn Ardell; 48 performances.

*Something about Love (lyrics, Lou Paley)
*Some Wonderful Sort of Someone (lyrics, Schuyler Greene; revised version)

LA, LA, LUCILLE. Book by Fred Jackson. Lyrics by Arthur J. Jackson and B. G. De Sylva. Produced by Alex A. Aarons at the Henry Miller Theater, May 26, 1919, with Janet Velie, John E. Hazzard, Eleanor Daniels, J. Clarence Harvey, Helen Clark, and Alfred Hall; 104 performances.

*From Now On
*Nobody But You
*Somehow It Seldom Comes True
*Tee-Oodle-Um-Bum-Bo
*The Best of Everything
*There's More to the Kiss than the X-X-X (lyrics, Irving Caesar)
It's Great to Be in Love
It's Hard to Tell
The Ten Commandments of Love
When You Live in a Furnished Flat

Not Used: Kisses
Money, Money, Money!
Our Little Kitchenette
The Love of a Wife

CAPITOL REVUE. Produced by Ned Wayburn for the opening of the Capitol Theater, October 24, 1919.

*Come to the Moon (lyrics, Lou Paley and Ned Wayburn)
*Swanee (lyrics, Irving Caesar)

MORRIS GEST MIDNIGHT WHIRL. Book and lyrics by B. G. De Sylva and John Henry Mears. Produced by Morris Gest at the Century Grove (atop the Century Theater), December 27, 1919, with Bessie McCoy Davis, Helen Shipman, the Rath Brothers, and Bernard Granville; 110 performances.

*Limehouse Nights
*Poppyland
Baby Dolls
Doughnuts
Let Cutie Cut Your Cuticle
The League of Nations
*Lullaby (for string quartet; first published in 1968)

1920

DERE MABLE. Opened at the Academy of Music in Baltimore on February 2, 1920. Closed out of town.

336

We're Pals (lyrics, Irving Caesar)
Yan-Kee (lyrics, Irving Caesar)
Swanee (published as the *Sinbad* version, "successfully introduced by Al Jolson")
ED WYNN'S CARNIVAL. Book, lyrics and songs mainly by Ed Wynn. Produced by J. C. Whitney at the New Amsterdam Theater, April 5, 1920, with Ed Wynn and Marion Davies; 64 performances.
 Oo, How I Love to Be Loved by You (lyrics, Lou Paley)
GEORGE WHITE'S SCANDALS OF 1920. Book by Andy Rice and George White. Lyrics by Arthur Jackson. Produced by George White at the Globe Theater, June 7, 1920, with Ann Pennington, Lou Holtz, George White, George "Doc" Rockwell, Ethel Delmar, the Yerkes Happy Six, and Lester Allen; 318 performances.
 Idle Dreams
 My Lady
 On My Mind the Whole Night Long
 Scandal Walk
 The Songs of Long Ago
 Tum On and Tiss Me Everybody Swat the Profiteer
 Not Used: *My Old Love Is My New Love*
THE SWEETHEART SHOP. Book and lyrics mainly by Anne Caldwell. Music mainly by Hugo Felix. Produced by Edgar J. MacGregor and William Moore Patch at the Knickerbocker Theater, August 31, 1920, with Helen Ford, Zella Russell and Harry K. Morton; 55 performances.
 Waiting for the Sun to Come Out (lyrics, Arthur Francis, Ira Gershwin's first published song under this pseudonym)
BROADWAY BREVITIES OF 1920. Book by Blair Traynor and Archie Gottlier. Lyrics by Arthur Jackson. Produced by George LeMaire at the Winter Garden, September 29, 1920, with Eddie Cantor, George LeMaire, and Bert Williams; 105 performances.
 Lu Lu
 Snow Flakes
 Spanish Love (lyrics, Irving Caesar)

1921

Dixie Rose (lyrics, Irving Caesar and B. G. De Sylva)
Swanee Rose (the same tune as "Dixie Rose," but with "Swanee" substituted for "Dixie" in the lyrics and in the title)
Tomale (I'm Hot for You) (lyrics, B. G. De Sylva)
A DANGEROUS MAID. Book by Charles W. Bell. Lyrics by Arthur Francis. Produced by Edgar MacGregor, with this cast: Vivienne Segal, Vinton Freedley, Johnnie Arthur, Amelia Bingham, Creighton Hale, and Juanita Fletcher. Opened in Atlantic City, March 21, 1921, and closed in Pittsburgh the following May without ever reaching Broadway.
 Boy Wanted
 Dancing Shoes
 Just to Know You Are Mine
 Some Rain Must Fall
 The Simple Life
 Not Used: *Anything for You*
   The Sirens
GEORGE WHITE'S SCANDALS OF 1921. Book by Arthur "Bugs" Baer and George White. Lyrics by Arthur Jackson. Produced by George White at the Liberty Theater, July 11, 1921, with Ann Pennington, George White, Lester Allen, Olive Vaughn, Bert Gordon, and Theresa "Aunt Jemima" Gardella; 97 performances.
 Drifting Along with the Tide
 I Love You
 She's Just a Baby
 South Sea Isles
 Where East Meets West
 Mother Eve (Opening)
Figured Chorale (for clarinet, two bassoons, two horns, cello, and bass; a manuscript at the Library of Congress)
THE PERFECT FOOL. Book, lyrics, and songs mainly by Ed Wynn. Produced by A. L. Erlanger at the George M. Cohan Theater, November 7, 1921, with Ed Wynn, Janet Velie, and Greg Robertson; 256 performances.
 My Log-Cabin Home (lyrics, Irving Caesar and B. G. De Sylva)
 No One Else but That Girl of Mine (lyrics, Irving Caesar)

1922

THE FRENCH DOLL. Book and lyrics by A. E. Thomas. Produced by E. Ray Goetz at the Lyceum Theater, February 20, 1922, with Irene Bordoni, Edna Hibbard, and Thurston Hall; 120 performances.
 *Do It Again (lyrics, B. G. De Sylva; this tune in a slightly revised version was prominently featured some forty years later in the movie Thoroughly Modern Millie, which starred Julie Andrews)
FOR GOODNESS SAKE. Book by Fred Jackson. Lyrics mainly by Arthur Jackson. Music mainly by William Daly and Paul Lannin. Produced by Alex A. Aarons at the Lyric Theater, February 20, 1922, with Fred and Adele Astaire, Helen Ford, Vinton Freedley, and Marjorie Gateson; 103 performances.
 *Someone (lyrics, Arthur Francis)
 *Tra-La-La (lyrics, Arthur Francis; this tune, somewhat revised, was effectively used in the 1951 film An American in Paris)
SPICE OF 1922. Book and lyrics by Jack Lait. Produced by Arman Kaliz at the Winter Garden, July 6, 1922, with George Price, Arman Kaliz, Valeska Suratt; 73 performances.
 *Yankee Doodle Blues (lyrics, Irving Caesar and B. G. De Sylva)
The Flapper (lyrics, B. G. De Sylva)
GEORGE WHITE'S SCANDALS OF 1922. Book by George White, Andy Rice, and W. C. Fields. Lyrics by B. G. De Sylva and E. Ray Goetz. Produced by George White at the Globe Theater, August 28, 1922, with Jack McGowan, W. C. Fields, George White, Winnie Lightner, Lester Allen, and Paul Whiteman's Orchestra; 88 performances.
 *Across the Sea
 *Argentina (lyrics, B. G. De Sylva)
 *Cinderelatives (lyrics, B. G. De Sylva)
 *I Found a Four Leaf Clover (lyrics, B. G. De Sylva)
 *I'll Build a Stairway to Paradise (lyrics, B. G. De Sylva and Arthur Francis)

 *Oh, What She Hangs Out (lyrics B. G. De Sylva)
 *Where Is the Man of My Dreams?
 I Can't Tell Where They're From When They Dance
 Just a Tiny Cup of Tea
Blue Monday Blues (a one-act opera). Libretto by B. G. De Sylva. Orchestrated by Will H. Vodery. Withdrawn after the opening night performance, August 28, 1922, as part of George White's Scandals of 1922. (Retitled 135th Street and reorchestrated by Ferde Grofé, the opera received its concert-hall premiere on December 29, 1925, at Carnegie Hall, by Paul Whiteman's Orchestra and this cast: Blossom Seeley, Benny Fields, Jack McGowan, Charles Hart, Austin Young, and Francis Howard.)
OUR NELL. Book by A. E. Thomas and Brian Hooker. Lyrics by Brian Hooker, with music by George Gershwin and William Daly. Produced by Ed Davidow and Rufus Le Maire (Hayseed Productions) at the Nora Bayes Theater, December 4, 1922, with Emma Haig, Mr. and Mrs. Jimmie Barry, John Merkyl, and Olin Howland; 40 performances.
 *By and By (music, George Gershwin)
 *Innocent Ingenue Baby
 *My Old New England Home (music, George Gershwin)
 *Walking Home with Angeline (music, George Gershwin)
 Gol-Durn!
 Little Villages
 Madrigal
 Names I Love to Hear
 Oh, You Lady!
 The Cooney County Fair (music, George Gershwin)
 We Go to Church on Sunday (music, George Gershwin)
Not Used: The Custody of the Child

1923

THE DANCING GIRL. Book and lyrics by Harold Atteridge and Irving Caesar.

Music mainly by Sigmund Romberg. Produced by the Shuberts at the Winter Garden, January 24, 1923, with Marie Dressler, Jack Pearl, Arthur Margetson, Tom Burke, and Trini; 126 performances.
  *That American Boy of Mine (lyrics, Irving Caesar)
THE RAINBOW. Book by Albert de Courville, Noel Scott, and Edgar Wallace. Lyrics mainly by Clifford Grey. Produced by Albert de Courville at London's Empire Theatre, April 3, 1923, with Grace Hayes, Earl Rickard, Stephanie Stephens, Jack Edge, and Ernest Thesiger.
  *Beneath the Eastern Moon
  *Good-Night, My Dear
  *In the Rain
  *Innocent Lonesome Blue Baby (lyrics, Brian Hooker and Clifford Grey; music, George Gershwin and William Daly)
  *Moonlight in Versailles
  *Oh! Nina
  *Strut Lady With Me
  *Sunday in London Town
  *Sweetheart (I'm So Glad That I Met You)
  Any Little Tune
GEORGE WHITE'S SCANDALS OF 1923. Book by George White and William K. Wells. Lyrics by B. G. De Sylva, E. Ray Goetz, and Ballard MacDonald. Produced by George White at the Globe Theater, June 18, 1923, with Winnie Lightner, Beulah Berson, Lester Allen, Tom Patricola, Johnny Dooley, and Richard Bold; 168 performances.
  *Let's Be Lonesome Together (lyrics, B. G. De Sylva and E. Ray Goetz; published in two editions)
  *Lo-La-Lo (lyrics, B. G. De Sylva)
  *(On the Beach `at) How've-You-Been? (lyrics, B. G. De Sylva)
  *The Life of a Rose (lyrics, B. G. De Sylva)
  *There Is Nothing Too Good for You (lyrics, B. G. De Sylva and E. Ray Goetz)
  *Throw Her in High! (lyrics, B. G. De Sylva and E. Ray Goetz)
  *Where Is She? (lyrics, B. G. De Sylva)
  *You and I

Katinka
Laugh Your Cares Away
Little Scandal Dolls
Look in the Looking Glass
THE SUNSHINE TRAIL (a silent film). Produced by Thomas H. Ince. Directed by James W. Horne. Released by First National Films. Cast included Edith Roberts, Douglas MacLean, and Rex Cherryman.
  *The Sunshine Trail (lyrics, Arthur Francis)
LITTLE MISS BLUEBEARD. Book and lyrics by Avery Hopwood. Music by Gershwin and others. Produced by E. Ray Goetz and Charles Frohman at the Lyceum Theater, August 28, 1923, with Irene Bordoni, Eric Blore, and Bruce McRae; 175 performances.
  *I Won't Say I Will But I Won't Say I Won't (lyrics, B. G. De Sylva and Arthur Francis; published in two editions)
NIFTIES OF 1923. Book and lyrics by William Collier and Sam Bernard. Music by Gershwin and others. Produced by Charles Dillingham at the Fulton Theater, September 25, 1923, with Van Schenck, Ray Dooley, Bernard Collier, Helen Broderick, and Frank Crumit; 47 performances.
  *At Half Past Seven (lyrics, B. G. De Sylva)
  *Nashville Nightingale (lyrics, Irving Caesar)

1924

SWEET LITTLE DEVIL. Book by Frank Mandel and Laurence Schwab. Lyrics by B. G. De Sylva. Produced by Laurence Schwab at the Astor Theater, January 21, 1924, with Constance Binney, Ruth Warren, Marjorie Gateson, Irving Beebe, William Wayne, and Franklin Ardell; 120 performances.
  *Hey! Hey! Let 'Er Go!
  *Mah-Jongg
  *Pepita
  *Someone Believes in You
  *The Jijibo
  *Under a One-Man Top
  *Virginia Don't Go Too Far
  Hooray for the U.S.A.

Just Supposing
Strike, Strike, Strike
The Matrimonial
Handicap
Quite a Party (Opening)
Not Used: Be the Life of the Crowd
My Little Ducky
Sweet Little Devil
You're Mighty Lucky
*Rhapsody in Blue (for jazz band and piano). Orchestrated by Ferde Grofé. First performed by Paul Whiteman and his Palais Royal Orchestra, with George Gershwin as piano soloist, at Aeolian Hall, February 12, 1924, in "An Experiment in Modern Music."
GEORGE WHITE'S SCANDALS OF 1924. Book by George White and William K. Wells. Lyrics by B. G. De Sylva. Produced by George White at the Apollo Theater, June 30, 1924, with Winnie Lightner, Lester Allen, Tom Patricola, Will Mahoney, Helen Hudson, Richard Bold, the Elm City Four, and the William Sisters; 192 performances.
*I Need a Garden
*Kongo Kate
*Mah-Jongg
*Night Time in Araby
*Rose ofMadrid
*Somebody Loves Me (lyrics, B. G. De Sylva and Ballard MacDonald; published in two editions)
*Tune In (to Station J.O.Y.)
*Year after Year
*PRIMROSE. Book by Guy Bolton and George Grossmith. Lyrics by Desmond Carter and Ira Gershwin. Produced by George Grossmith and J. A. E. Malone at the Winter Garden Theatre, London, September 11, 1924, with Heather Thatcher, Leslie Henson, Margery Hicklin, Percy Heming, Vera Lennox, and Ernest Graham.
*Boy Wanted
*Isn't It Wonderful
*Naughty Baby
*Some Far-Away Someone (lyrics, Ira Gershwin and B. G. De Sylva; the melody for this tune is the same as that for "At Half Past Seven" in Nifties of 1923)
*That New-Fangled Mother of Mine (lyrics, Desmond Carter)

*This Is the Life for a Man (lyrics, Desmond Carter)
*Wait a Bit, Susie (Ballet)
Beau Brummel (lyrics, Desmond Carter)
Berkeley Square and Kew (lyrics, Desmond Carter)
Can We Do Anything? (Finale)
Four Little Sirens (lyrics, Ira Gershwin)
I Make Hay When the Moon Shines (lyrics, Desmond Carter)
Isn't It Terrible What They Did to Mary Queen of Scots (lyrics, Desmond Carter)
It Is the Fourteenth of July (Finale; lyrics, Desmond Carter)
Roses of France (Opening; lyrics, Desmond Carter)
The Mophams (lyrics, Desmond Carter)
Till I Meet Someone Like You (lyrics, Desmond Carter)
When Toby Is Out of Town (lyrics, Desmond Carter)
LADY, BE GOOD. Book by Guy Bolton and Fred Thompson. Lyrics by Ira Gershwin. Produced by Alex A. Aarons and Vinton Freedley at the Liberty Theater, December 1, 1924, with Fred and Adele Astaire, Cliff Edwards, Walter Catlett, Patricia Clarke, Alan Edwards, Gerald Oliver Smith, and duo-pianists Phil Ohman and Victor Arden; 184 performances.
*Fascinating Rhythm (published in two editions)
*Hang on to Me (published in two editions)
*Little Jazz Bird (published in two editions)
*Oh, Lady, Be Good! (published in two editions)
*So Am I
*The Half of It, Dearie, Blues (published in two editions)
A Wonderful Party
Juanita
Seeing Dickie Home (Opening)
Swiss Miss (lyrics, Ira Gershwin and Arthur Jackson)

340

The End of a String
The Robinson Hotel
(Opening)
We're Here Because
Not Used: *The Man I Love
Evening Star
Rainy Afternoon Girls
(Opening)
Singin' Pete
The Bad, Bad Men
Weather Man (Opening)
Will You Remember Me?
Used in the 1926 London production:
*I'd Rather Charleston
(lyrics, Desmond Carter)
*Something about Love
(lyrics, Lou Paley)
Buy a Little Button from
Us (Opening; lyrics,
Desmond Carter)

1925

*Short Story. "Arranged by Samuel
Dushkin" for violin and piano from
two "Novelettes" for piano. First
performed by Samuel Dushkin,
February 8, 1925, at the University
Club in New York.
TELL ME MORE. Book by Fred
Thompson and William K. Wells.
Lyrics by B. G. De Sylva and Ira
Gershwin. Produced by Alex A.
Aarons at the Gaiety Theater, April 13,
1925, with Phyllis Cleveland,
Alexander Gray, Emma Haig, and Lou
Holtz; 32 performances.
*Baby!
*Kickin' the Clouds Away
*My Fair Lady
*Why Do I Love You?
*Tell Me More!
*Three Times a Day
How Can I Win You Now?
In Sardinia
Love Is in the Air
Mr. and Mrs. Sipkin
The Poetry of Motion
Ukulele Lorelei
When the Debbies Go By
Not Used: I'm Somethin' on
Avenue A
Once
Shop Girls and Mannikins
The He-Man

Used in the 1925 London production:
*Murderous Monty (and
Light-Fingered Jane)
(lyrics, Desmond Carter)
Love, I Never Knew
(lyrics, Desmond Carter)
*Concerto in F (for piano and
orchestra). First performed by the New
York Symphony Orchestra conducted
by Walter Damrosch, with George
Gershwin as piano soloist, at Carnegie
Hall, December 3, 1925.
TIP-TOES. Book by Guy Bolton and
Fred Thompson. Lyrics by Ira
Gershwin. Produced by Alex A.
Aarons and Vinton Freedley at the
Liberty Theater, December 28, 1925,
with Queenie Smith, Allen Kearns,
Andrew Tombes, Robert Halliday,
Harry Watson, Lovey Lee, Jeanette
MacDonald, Amy Revere, and
duo-pianists Phil Ohman and Victor
Arden; 194 performances.
*Looking for a Boy
*Nice Baby! (Come to
Papa!)
*Nightie-Night
*Sweet and Low-Down
*That Certain Feeling
*These Charming People
*When Do We Dance?
Harbor of Dreams
Lady Luck
Our Little Captain
Tip-Toes
Waiting for the Train
Not Used: *It's a Great Little World!
Dancing Hour
Gather Ye Rosebuds
Harlem River Chanty
Life's Too Short to be Blue
We
SONG OF THE FLAME. Book and
lyrics by Oscar Hammerstein II and
Otto Harbach. Music by George
Gershwin and Herbert Stothart.
Produced by Arthur Hammerstein at
the Fourty-fourth Street Theater,
December 30, 1925, with Tessa Kosta,
Guy Robertson, Greek Evans, Hugh
Cameron, Dorothy Mackaye, and the
Russian Art Choir; 219 performances.
*Cossack Love Song (Don't Forget
Me)
*Midnight Bells (music, George
Gershwin)
*Song of the Flame

The Signal (music, George
  Gershwin)
You Are You
Vodka
  Far Away
  Tar-Tar
  Women's Work Is Never Done

1926

AMERICANA. Book and lyrics by J. P.
McEvoy. Music by Gershwin and others.
Produced by Richard Herndon at the
Belmont Theater, July 26, 1926, with
Helen Morgan, Lew Brice, Charles
Butterworth, and Roy Atwell; 224
performances.
  That Lost Barber Shop Chord
    (lyrics, Ira Gershwin)
OH, KAY!. Book by Guy Bolton and
P. G. Wodehouse. Lyrics by Ira
Gershwin. Produced by Alex A. Aarons
and Vinton Freedley at the Imperial
Theater, November 8, 1926, with
Gertrude Lawrence, Oscar Shaw, Victor
Moore, the Fairbanks Twins, Harland
Dixon, and duo-pianists Phil Ohman
and Victor Arden; 256 performances.
  Clap Yo' Hands
  Dear Little Girl (dropped
    after one performance;
    first published in 1968)
  Do, Do, Do
  Fidgety Feet
  Heaven on Earth (lyrics,
    Ira Gershwin and
    Howard Dietz)
  Maybe
  Oh, Kay (lyrics, Ira
    Gershwin and Howard
    Dietz)
  Someone to Watch over Me
    Bride and Groom
    (Opening)
    Don't Ask!
    The Woman's Touch
Not Used: *Show Me the Town*
    Ain't It Romantic?
    Bring on the Ding Dong
      Dell
    Guess Who (the melody
      for this tune is the same
      as that for "Don't Ask!")
    Stepping with Baby
    The Moon Is on the Sea
    The Sun Is on the Sea
    What's the Use?

When Our Ship Comes
  Sailing In
Preludes for Piano. Gershwin performed
five preludes for piano for the first
time on December 4, 1926, at the Hotel
Roosevelt, in a recital he gave with
Mme. Marguerite d'Alvarez, contralto.
Three of these preludes became the
Preludes for Piano and were published
in 1927.

1927

STRIKE UP THE BAND. Book by
George S. Kaufman. Lyrics by Ira
Gershwin. Produced by Edgar Selwyn.
Opened at the Shubert Theater in
Philadelphia, September 5, 1927, with
Vivian Hart, Herbert Corthell, Jimmie
Savo, Morton Downey, Lew Hearn,
Roger Pryor, and Edna May Oliver;
closed out of town.
  Military Dancing Drill
  Seventeen and Twenty-One
  Strike Up the Band!
  The Man I Love
  Yankee Doodle Rhythm
    Fletcher's American Cheese Choral
      Society
    Homeward Bound
    Hoping That Someday You'll Care
    How About a Man Like Me
    Meadow Serenade
    O, This Is Such a Lovely War
    Patriotic Rally
    The Girl I Love
    The Unofficial Spokesman
    The War That Ended War
    Typical Self-Made American
FUNNY FACE. Book by Paul Gerard
Smith and Fred Thompson. Lyrics by
Ira Gershwin. Produced by Alex A.
Aarons and Vinton Freedley at the
Alvin Theater, November 22, 1927,
with Fred and Adele Astaire, Victor
Moore, Allen Kearns, Betty Compton,
William Kent, and duo-pianists Phil
Ohman and Victor Arden; 244
performances.
  Dance Alone with You
  Funny Face
  He Loves and She Loves
  High Hat
  Let's Kiss and Make Up
  *My One and Only (What
    Am I Gonna Do)*
  'S Wonderful

342

*The Babbitt and the
Bromide
*The World Is Mine
Birthday Party
Come Along, Let's Gamble
(Finale)
If You Will Take Our Tip
(Opening)
Tell the Doc
The Finest of the Finest
Those Eyes
We're All A-Worry, All
Agog (Opening)
When You're Single
Not Used: *How Long Has This Been
Going On?
Acrobats
In the Swim
Once
Sing a Little Song

1928

ROSALIE. Book by Guy Bolton and
William Anthony McGuire. Lyrics by
Ira Gershwin and P. G. Wodehouse.
Supplementary music by Sigmund
Romberg. Produced by Florenz
Ziegfeld at the New Amsterdam
Theater, January 10, 1928, with
Marilyn Miller, Jack Donahue, Frank
Morgan, Gladys Glad, and Bobbe
Arnst; 335 performances.
    *Ev'rybody Knows I Love
    Somebody (lyrics, Ira
    Gershwin; the melody
    for this tune is the same
    as that for "Dance Alone
    with You" in Funny
    Face)
    *How Long Has This Been
    Going On? (lyrics, Ira
    Gershwin)
    *Oh Gee! Oh Joy!
    *Say So!
    Let Me Be a Friend to You
    (lyrics, Ira Gershwin)
    New York Serenade (lyrics,
    Ira Gershwin)
    Show Me the Town (lyrics,
    Ira Gershwin)
Not Used: *Beautiful Gypsy (lyrics,
    Ira Gershwin; the melody
    for this tune is the same
    as that for "Wait a Bit,
    Susie," in Primrose)

*Rosalie (lyrics, Ira
Gershwin)
*Yankee Doodle Rhythm
(lyrics, Ira Gershwin)
Follow the Drum (lyrics,
Ira Gershwin)
I Forgot What I Started to
Say (lyrics, Ira Gershwin)
The Man I Love (lyrics, Ira
Gershwin)
You Know How It Is
When Cadets Parade
(lyrics, Ira Gershwin)
TREASURE GIRL. Book by Fred
Thompson and Vincent Lawrence.
Lyrics by Ira Gershwin. Produced by
Alex A. Aarons and Vinton Freedley at
the Alvin Theater, November 8, 1928,
with Gertrude Lawrence, Paul Frawley,
Walter Catlett, Clifton Webb, Mary
Hay, Ferris Hartman, and duo-pianists
Paul Ohman and Victor Arden; 68
performances.
    *Feeling I'm Falling
    *Got a Rainbow
    *I Don't Think I'll Fall in
    Love Today
    *I've Got a Crush on You
    *K-ra-zy for You
    *Oh, So Nice
    *What Are We Here For?
    *Where's the Boy? Here's
    the Girl!
    According to Mr. Grimes
    Place in the Country
    Skull and Bones
Not Used: A-Hunting We Will Go
    Dead Men Tell No Tales
    Good-bye to the Old Love,
    Hello to the New
    I Want to Marry a
    Marionette
    This Particular Party
    Treasure Island
    What Causes That?
*An American in Paris (a tone poem for
orchestra). First performed by the New
York Philharmonic conducted by
Walter Damrosch, December 13, 1928,
at Carnegie Hall.

1929

SHOW GIRL. Book by William Anthony
McGuire and J. P. McEvoy. Lyrics by
Ira Gershwin and Gus Kahn. Produced

by Florenz Ziegfeld at the Ziegfeld
Theater, July 2, 1929, with Ruby Keeler
Jolson, Clayton, Jackson, and Durante,
Harriet Hoctor, Eddie Foy, Jr., Barbara
Newberry, and Frank McHugh; 111
performances.

*Do What You Do!
*Harlem Serenade
*I Must Be Home by Twelve
O'Clock
*Liza (All the Clouds'll Roll
Away)
*So Are You!
"An American in Paris"
(Ballet)
Black and White
Follow the Minstrel Band
Happy Birthday
Home Blues
How Could I Forget
(Finaletto)
Lolita
My Sunday Fella
One Man
Not Used: *Feeling Sentimental
Adored One
At Mrs. Simpkin's
Finishing School
Home Lovin' Gal
Home Lovin' Man
I Just Looked at You
I'm Just a Bundle of
Sunshine
I'm Out for No Good
Reason To-night
Minstrel Show
Somebody Stole My Heart
Away
Someone's Always Calling a
Rehearsal
Tonight's the Night!
*In the Mandarin's Orchid
Garden (lyrics, Ira
Gershwin)

1930

*STRIKE UP THE BAND. Book by
Morrie Ryskind, based on a book by
George S. Kaufman. Lyrics by Ira
Gershwin. Produced by Edgar Selwyn
at the Times Square Theater, January
14, 1930, with Clark (Bobby) and
McCullough (Paul), Jerry Goff, Dudley
Clements, Blanche Ring, Kathryn
Hamill, Gordon Smith, Doris Carson,

Margaret Schilling and Red Nichols
and his band; 191 performances.

*Hangin' Around with You
*I Mean to Say
*I Want to Be a War Bride
*I've Got a Crush on You
*Mademoiselle in New Rochelle
*Soon
*Strike Up the Band
A Man of High Degree
A Typical Self-Made American
Fletcher's American Chocolate
Choral Society Workers
First There was Fletcher
He Knows Milk (Finaletto)
How About a Boy Like Me?
If I Became the President
In the Rattle of the Battle
(Opening)
Military Dancing Drill
Ring a Ding a Ding Dong Bell
The Unofficial Spokesman
This Could Go On for Years
Three Cheers for the Union!
Unofficial March of General
Holmes

*GIRL CRAZY. (Vocal score published
in 1954 by New World Music.) Book by
Guy Bolton and John McGowan.
Lyrics by Ira Gershwin. Produced by
Alex A. Aarons and Vinton Freedley at
the Alvin Theater, October 14, 1930,
with Ethel Merman, Ginger Rogers,
Allen Kearns, Willie Howard, William
Kent, the Foursome, and Red Nichols
and his band; 272 performances.

*Bidin' My Time
*Boy! What Love Has Done
to Me!
*But Not for Me
*Could You Use Me?
*Embraceable You
*I Got Rhythm
*Sam and Delilah
*Treat Me Rough (first
published in connection
with the 1943 film
version of Girl Crazy)
Barbary Coast
Broncho Busters
Goldfarb! That's I'm!
(Finaletto)
Land of the Gay Caballero
(Opening)
The Lonesome Cowboy
When It's Cactus Time
in Arizona

344

Not Used: *And I Have You*
Something Peculiar
The Gambler of the West
You Can't Unscramble
Scrambled Eggs

1931

DELICIOUS. Screenplay by Guy Bolton and Sonya Levien. Lyrics by Ira Gershwin. Produced by Winfield ("Winnie") Sheehan for Fox Film Studios (film released December 3, 1931). Cast included Janet Gaynor, Charles Farrell, El Brendel, and Mischa Auer.

Blah-Blah-Blah
Delishious
Katinkitschka
Somebody from Somewhere
(Dream sequence: "We're from the *Journal*, the *Warheit*, the *Telegram*, the *Times*. We specialize in interviews and crimes.")
(Rhapsody excerpt; the basis for *Second Rhapsody*)
You Started It
Not Used: *Mischa, Yascha, Toscha, Sascha* (first published in 1932)
Thanks to You

OF THEE I SING. Book by George S. Kaufman and Morrie Ryskind, Lyrics by Ira Gershwin. Produced by Sam H. Harris at the Music Box Theater, December 26, 1931, with William Gaxton, Victor Moore, Lois Moran, Grace Brinkley, June O'Dea, Florenz Ames, George Murphy, Dudley Clements, Edward H. Robins, and Ralph Riggs; 441 performances.

Because, Because
Love Is Sweeping the Country
Of Thee I Sing
The Illegitimate Daughter
Who Cares?
Wintergreen for President
A Kiss for Cinderella
Garçon, S'il Vous Plait
Hello, Good Morning (Opening)

I Was the Most Beautiful Blossom
I'm About to Be a Mother (Who Could Ask for Anything More?)
Jilted, Jilted!
Never Was There a Girl So Fair (Finaletto)
On That Matter No One Budges (Finale Ultimo)
Posterity Is Just Around the Corner
Some Girls Can Bake a Pie
The Dimple on My Knee
The Senatorial Roll Call
Trumpeter, Blow Your Golden Horn
Who Is the Lucky Girl to Be?
Not Used: *Call Me Whate'er You Will*

1932

Second Rhapsody (for orchestra with piano). First performed by the Boston Symphony Orchestra under Serge Koussevitzky, January 29, 1932, at Boston's Symphony Hall, with George Gershwin as pianist. (Gershwin completed the *Second Rhapsody* on May 23, 1931.)

You've Got What Gets Me (lyrics, Ira Gershwin; written for the 1932 film version of *Girl Crazy*)

Cuban Overture (Rumba) (for orchestra). First performed by Albert Coates conducting the New York Philharmonic, August 16, 1932, at the Lewisohn Stadium.

George Gershwin's Song-Book (piano transcriptions of eighteen songs). Published in September 1932 by Simon and Schuster, with illustrations by Alajálov (a limited edition of 300 copies, with each book signed by George Gershwin and Alajálov and containing an inserted copy of "Mischa, Yascha, Toscha, Sascha," was published earlier, in May 1932, by Random House). The eighteen songs in the volume are: "Swanee," "Nobody But You," "I'll Build a Stairway to Paradise," "Do It Again," "Fascinating Rhythm," "Oh, Lady, Be Good!," "Somebody Loves Me," "Sweet and Low-Down," "That Certain Feeling,"

"The Man I Love," "Clap Yo' Hands,"
"Do, Do, Do," "My One and Only,"
" 'S Wonderful," "Strike Up the
Band," "Liza," "I Got Rhythm," and
"Who Cares?"

1933

PARDON MY ENGLISH. Book by
Herbert Fields. Lyrics by Ira Gershwin.
Produced by Alex A. Aarons and
Vinton Freedley at the Majestic
Theater, January 20, 1933, with Jack
Pearl, Lyda Roberti, George Givot,
Barbara Newberry, Josephine Huston,
Carl Randall, and Cliff Hall; 46
performances.
  *Isn't It a Pity
  *I've Got to Be There
  *Lorelei
  *Luckiest Man in the World
  *My Cousin in Milwaukee
  *So What?
  *Where You Go I Go
  Dancing in the Streets
  Hail the Happy Couple
  He's Not Himself (Finale)
  In Three-Quarter Time
    (lyrics published in Ira
    Gershwin's Lyrics on
    Several Occasions, 1959)
  Pardon My English
  The Dresden Northwest
    Mounted
  Tonight
  What Sort of Wedding Is
    This? (Finale)
Not Used: Bauer's House
  Fatherland
  Freud and Jung and Adler
  Mother of the Band
  Poor Michael! Poor Golo!
  Together at Last
LET 'EM EAT CAKE. Book by George
S. Kaufman and Morrie Ryskind.
Lyrics by Ira Gershwin. Produced by
Sam H. Harris at the Imperial Theater,
October 21, 1933, with William
Gaxton, Victor Moore, Lois Moran,
Philip Loeb, Dudley Clements, Florenz
Ames, Edward H. Robins, and Ralph
Riggs; 90 performances.
  *Blue, Blue, Blue
  *Let 'Em Eat Cake
  *Mine
  *On and On and On

  *Union Square
  A Hell of a Hole
  Climb Up the Social
    Ladder
  Cloistered from the Noisy
    City
  Comes the Revolution
  Double Dummy Drill
  Down with Everything
    That's Up (also included
    in "Union Square" as
    an "Interlude")
  Hanging Throttlebottom
    in the Morning
  I Knew a Foul Ball
  Let 'Em Eat Caviar
  Oyez, Oyez, Oyez
  No Better Way to Start a
    Case
  No Comprenez, No Capish,
    No Versteh!
  Shirts by the Millions
  That's What He Did
  The Union League (lyrics
    published in Ira
    Gershwin's Lyrics on
    Several Occasions, 1959)
  Throttle Throttlebottom
  Tweedledee for President
  Up and at 'Em! On to
    Vict'ry
  What More Can a General
    Do?
  Why Speak of Money?
  Wintergreen for President
  Who's the Greatest———?
Not Used: First Lady and First Gent
  *Till Then (lyrics, Ira
    Gershwin)

1934

*"I GOT RHYTHM" VARIATIONS
(for piano and orchestra). First
performed by the Leo Reisman
Orchestra conducted by Charles
Previn, with George Gershwin as
soloist, on January 14, 1934, at Boston's
Symphony Hall.

1935

*PORGY AND BESS. Libretto by
DuBose Heyward. Lyrics by DuBose
Heyward and Ira Gershwin. Produced
by the Theatre Guild at the Alvin

Theater, October 10, 1935, with Todd Duncan, Anne Wiggins Brown, John W. Bubbles, Warren Coleman, Edward Matthews, Ruby Elzy, Abbie Mitchell, Georgette Harvey, Helen Dowdy, J. Rosamond Johnson, Ford L. Buck, Ray Yeates, and the Eva Jessye Choir; 124 performances.

    (in order of performance)
      Overture

ACT I
  Scene 1: *Summertime
      *A Woman Is a Sometime
        Thing
      Here Comes de Honey
        Man (Street Cry)
      They Pass By Singin'
      Oh Little Stars (Crap
        Game)
      Crown and Robbins' Fight
  Scene 2: Gone, Gone, Gone
      Overflow
      *My Man's Gone Now
      Leavin' fo' the Promis'
        Lan' (Train Song)

ACT II
  Scene 1: It Takes a Long Pull to
        Get There
      *I Got Plenty o' Nuttin'
      Woman to Lady
      *Bess, You Is My Woman
      Oh, I Can't Sit Down
  Scene 2: *It Ain't Necessarily So
      What You Want wid Bess?
  Scene 3: Time and Time Again
      Strawberry Woman
        (Street Cry)
      Crab Man (Street Cry)
      *I Loves You, Porgy
      Storm Music
  Scene 4: Oh, de Lawd Shake de
        Heavens
      A Red Headed Woman
      Oh, Doctor Jesus

ACT III
  Scene 1: Clara, Clara (Don't You
      Be Downhearted)
  Scene 2: *There's a Boat Dat's
      Leavin' Soon for New
      York
  Scene 3: *Oh, Bess, Oh Where's My
      Bess?
      Oh Lawd, I'm On My Way

Not Used:
ACT I
  Scene 1: Jasbo Brown Blues
      (Piano Music)

ACT II
  Scene 1: Buzzard Song
      I Hates Yo' Struttin' Style
  Scene 2: I Ain' Got No Shame
  Scene 4: Oh, Hev'nly Father (Six
      Prayers)
ACT III
  Scene 3: Good Mornin', Sistuh!
      Good Mornin', Brudder!
      Sure to Go to Heaven

1936

Catfish Row (a five-movement suite for orchestra adapted from *Porgy and Bess*). First performed by the Philadelphia Orchestra conducted by Alexander Smallens, January 21, 1936, at Philadelphia's Academy of Music.
  I.   *Catfish Row*
  II. *Porgy Sings*
  III. *Fugue*
  IV. *Hurricane*
  V. *Good Morning, Brother*

*King of Swing (lyrics, Albert Stillman)
*Strike Up the Band for U.C.L.A. (lyrics, Ira Gershwin)

THE SHOW IS ON. Book by David Freedman and Moss Hart. Lyrics by Ira Gershwin and others. Music by George Gershwin and others. Produced by the Shuberts at the Winter Garden, December 25, 1936, with Beatrice Lillie, Bert Lahr, Reginald Gardiner, Mitzi Mayfair, Paul Haakon, Gracie Barrie, Charles Walters, and Vera Allen; 237 performances.
    *By Strauss (lyrics, Ira Gershwin)

1937

SHALL WE DANCE. Screenplay by Allan Scott and Ernest Pagano. Lyrics by Ira Gershwin. Produced by Pandro S. Berman for RKO Radio Pictures. Film released May 7, 1937. Cast: Fred Astaire, Ginger Rogers, Edward Everett Horton, Eric Blore, Jerome Cowan, Ketti Gallian, William Brisbane, Frank Moran, Ann Shoemaker, and Harriet Hoctor.
    *(I've Got) Beginner's Luck
    *Let's Call the Whole
      Thing Off
    *Shall We Dance

*Slap That Bass
*They All Laughed
*They Can't Take That
   Away from Me
   Walking the Dog (an
   instrumental interlude;
   published in 1960 as a
   piano solo, titled
   "Promenade")
Not Used: *Hi-Ho (first published in
   1967 in connection with
   the Gershwin Exhibition
   at the Museum of the
   City of New York in
   1968; a limited edition
   of 250 autographed
   copies, signed by Ira
   Gershwin, was released
   as a benefit for the
   museum)
   Wake Up, Brother, and
   Dance (this tune was the
   basis for "Sophia," used
   in the 1964 film Kiss
   Me, Stupid)
A DAMSEL IN DISTRESS. Screenplay
by S. K. Lauren, Ernest Pagano, and
P. G. Wodehouse. Produced by Pandro
S. Berman for RKO Radio Pictures.
Film released November 19, 1937. Cast:
Fred Astaire, Joan Fontaine, Reginald
Gardiner, George Burns, Gracie Allen,
and Ray Noble.
   *A Foggy Day
   *I Can't Be Bothered Now
   *Nice Work If You Can
      Get It
   *Stiff Upper Lip
   *The Jolly Tar and the
      Milk Maid
   *Things Are Looking Up
   Put Me to the Test
   Sing of Spring
Not Used: Pay Some Attention to Me

1938

THE GOLDWYN FOLLIES. Screenplay
by Ben Hecht. Lyrics by Ira Gershwin.
Produced by Samuel Goldwyn. Film
released by Goldwyn-United Artists on
February 23, 1938. Cast: Vera Zorina,
Adolphe Menjou, Andrea Leeds, the
Ritz Brothers, Ella Logan, Bobby
Clark, Edgar Bergen and Charlie
McCarthy, Phil Baker, Helen Jepson,

Kenny Baker, and Jerome Cowan.
   *I Love to Rhyme
   *I Was Doing All Right
   *Love Is Here to Stay
   *Love Walked In
Not Used: *Just Another Rhumba
      (first published in 1959)
   *Dawn of a New Day (lyrics, Ira
   Gershwin; the tune, a posthumous one,
   was completed with the help of Kay
   Swift and became the official march
   of the 1939 New York World's Fair)

1943

*Treat Me Rough (lyrics, Ira Gershwin;
this tune, originally used in Girl Crazy
of 1930, was published in connection
with the 1943 film version of that
musical)

1946

THE SHOCKING MISS PILGRIM.
Screenplay by George Seaton. Lyrics by
Ira Gershwin. Posthumous score by
George Gershwin, as adapted by Kay
Swift in cooperation with Ira Gershwin.
Produced by William Perlberg for
20th Century-Fox. Cast: Betty Grable,
Dick Haymes, Allyn Joslyn, Gene
Lockhart, and Anne Revere.
   *Aren't You Kind of Glad
      We Did?
   *Changing My Tune
   *For You, For Me, For
      Evermore
   *One, Two, Three
   *The Back Bay Polka
   Demon Rum
   Stand Up and Fight
   Sweet Packard
   Waltzing Is Better Sitting
      Down
   Welcome Song
Not Used: Tour of the Town

1959

*The Real American Folk Song (lyrics
Ira Gershwin; this tune was first used
in Ladies First of 1918 when Ira used
the alias Arthur Francis)
*Just Another Rhumba (lyrics, Ira

Gershwin; this tune was first used in *The Goldwyn Follies* of 1938)

1960

*Promenade (piano solo; this piece was originally an instrumental interlude in *Shall We Dance* of 1937)

1964

KISS ME, STUPID. A Billy Wilder production for the Mirisch Corporation. Lyrics by Ira Gershwin. Posthumous score by George Gershwin, as adapted by Ira Gershwin. Cast featured Dean Martin and Kim Novak.
*All the Livelong Day (And the Long, Long Night)
*I'm a Poached Egg
*Sophia (this tune is based on "Wake Up, Brother, and Dance," which

was written for, but not used in, the 1937 film *Shall We Dance*)

1967

*Hi-Ho (this tune was originally written for, but not used in, *Shall We Dance*)

1968

*Lullaby (for string quartet; first written in 1919)
*Dear Little Girl (originally written for *Oh, Kay!* of 1926 but not published until it was used in connection with *Star*, a 1968 Julie Andrews film)

1971

*Two Waltzes in C (piano solo; based on a musical sequence written for, but not used in, *Pardon My English* of 1933, as edited by Ira Gershwin and adapted by Saul Chaplin)

APPENDIX III
FILMS BASED ON GERSHWIN WORKS

1932

GIRL CRAZY. An RKO Radio Picture production, directed by William A. Seiter. Released March 27, 1932. Cast: Bert Wheeler, Robert Woolsey, Arline Judge, Eddie Quillian, and Dixie Lee. Songs: "But Not for Me," "Could You Use Me?," "Embraceable You," "I Got Rhythm," "Sam and Delilah," and "You've Got What Gets Me."

1940

STRIKE UP THE BAND. An MGM production, directed by Busby Berkeley. Released September 17, 1940. Cast: Judy Garland, Mickey Rooney, June Preisser, William Tracy, and Paul Whiteman and his orchestra. Featured Gershwin song: "Strike Up the Band."

1941

LADY, BE GOOD. An MGM production. Cast included Eleanor Powell, Ann Sothern, and Robert Young. Featured Gershwin songs: "Fascinating Rhythm," "Hang on to Me," and "Oh, Lady, Be Good!"

1943

GIRL CRAZY (second film version). An MGM production, directed by Norman Taurog. Released August 3, 1943. Cast: Judy Garland, Mickey Rooney, June Allyson, Guy Kibbee, Nancy Walker, Rags Ragland, Gil Stratton, and the Tommy Dorsey Orchestra. Songs: "Barbary Coast," "Bidin' My Time," "But Not for Me," "Could You Use Me?," "Embraceable You," "Fascinating Rhythm," "I Got Rhythm," "Sam and Delilah," "Treat Me Rough," and "When It's Cactus Time in Arizona."

1945

RHAPSODY IN BLUE. Produced by Jesse Lasky for Warner Brothers. Cast: Robert Alda, Alexis Smith, Joan

Leslie, Charles Coburn, and Oscar Levant. Gershwin compositions included excerpts from *135th Street* (originally titled *Blue Monday Blues*), *Rhapsody in Blue*, *Concerto in F*, and *An American in Paris*, and the songs: "Bidin' My Time," "Clap Yo' Hands," "Delishious," "Do It Again," "Embraceable You," "Fascinating Rhythm," "I Got Plenty o' Nuttin'," "I Got Rhythm," "I'll Build a Stairway to Paradise," "It Ain't Necessarily So," "Liza," "Love Walked In," "Oh, Lady, Be Good!," "Somebody Loves Me," "Someone to Watch Over Me," "Swanee," " 'S Wonderful," "Summertime," "The Man I Love," and "Yankee Doodle Blues."

1951

AN AMERICAN IN PARIS. Produced by Arthur Freed for MGM. Directed by Vincente Minnelli. Cast: Gene Kelly, Leslie Caron, Oscar Levant, Georges Guetary, and Nina Foch. Gershwin compositions included excerpts from *Concerto in F* and *An American in Paris* and the songs: "By Strauss," "Embraceable You," " I Don't Think I'll Fall in Love Today," "Liza," "I Got Rhythm," "I'll Build a Stairway to Paradise," "Love Is Here to Stay," "Nice Work If You Can Get It," "Strike Up the Band," " 'S Wonderful," and "Tra-La-La."

1957

FUNNY FACE. Produced by Roger Edens for Paramount Pictures. Directed by Stanley Donen. Cast: Fred Astaire, Audrey Hepburn, Kay Thompson, Michel Auclair, and Robert Flemyng. Songs: "Clap Yo' Hands," "Funny Face," "He Loves and She Loves," "How Long Has This Been Going On?," "Let's Kiss and Make Up," and " S Wonderful."

1959

PORGY AND BESS. Produced by Samuel Goldwyn for Columbia Pictures. Directed by Otto Preminger. Cast: Sidney Poitier (Porgy), Dorothy Dandridge (Bess), Sammy Davis, Jr. (Sportin' Life), Brock Peters (Crown), Pearl Bailey (Maria), and Diahann Carroll (Clara). Much of the original opera score was included in the film.

1965

WHEN THE BOYS MEET THE GIRLS (third film version of *Girl Crazy*). An MGM production, directed by Alvin Ganzer. Released December 6, 1965. Cast: Harve Presnell, Connie Francis, Liberace, Louis Armstrong, and Herman's Hermits. Songs: "Bidin' My Time," "But Not for Me," "Embraceable You," and "I Got Rhythm."

APPENDIX IV

A SELECTED
GEORGE GERSHWIN
DISCOGRAPHY

GEORGE GERSHWIN has not been ne-
glected on records. Thousands of recordings of his music have been made
and released over the years. In such a climate of abundance, the quality of
the recordings has often been variable. There has also been a large turnover
of recorded Gershwiniana, for record companies, always sensitive to supply
and demand factors, have often dropped recordings of waning popularity
from their catalogues in favor of new ones, presumably of more-promising
commerciality. The field of recorded Gershwiniana is replete with records
of one kind or another that have been taken out of circulation and are no
longer readily available. For reasons of quality and inordinate quantity in
connection with Gershwin recordings, a culled discography serves a wholly
practical function, notwithstanding the subjectivity of choice inherent in
the culling. The following Gershwin discography in the interest of his-
toricity lists some key 78 rpm recordings that are now virtually impossible
to obtain, along with more current LP selections, including those of doubtful availability. In this listing, recordings that have been long out of print
and considered collectors' items are listed with one asterisk (*), while
recordings of more recent vintage, but of doubtful availability, are marked
by two asterisks (**). Recent recordings, more readily available, are

listed without any asterisks. Records marked "†" are especially recommended.

CONCERT AND OPERATIC WORKS

Rhapsody in Blue (1924)

†*Paul Whiteman's Orchestra, with George Gershwin as soloist (recorded June 10, 1924) Victor 55225-A.

†*Paul Whiteman's Orchestra, with George Gershwin as soloist (recorded April 21, 1927); RCA Victor 35822.

†**Paul Whiteman's Orchestra, with George Gershwin as soloist (a 1951 reissue of the April 21, 1927 recording); RCA Victor LPT-29.

†Paul Whiteman's Orchestra, with George Gershwin as soloist (a 1968 reissue of the April 21, 1927 recording); RCA Victor LPV-555.

†George Gershwin as soloist (piano version); Archive of Piano Music X-914 (Everest Records).

†**George Gershwin as soloist (piano version); RCA Victor LSP-2058, LPM-2058.

†**George Gershwin as soloist (piano version); Distinguished Recordings 107.

†Columbia Symphony Orchestra, with Leonard Bernstein as pianist and conductor; Columbia MS-6091, MS-7518.

Philadelphia Orchestra, Eugene Ormandy, conductor, with Philippe Entremont as soloist; Columbia MG-30073.

**Philadelphia Orchestra, Eugene Ormandy, conductor, with Oscar Levant as soloist; Columbia CL-700, CS-8641.

Boston Pops Orchestra, Arthur Fiedler, conductor, with Earl Wild as soloist; RCA Victor LSC-2367, LSC-2746.

†ape   **Morton Gould's Orchestra, with Morton Gould as soloist; RCA Victor LM-6033.

Berlin Symphony Orchestra, Samuel Adler, conductor, with Eugene List as soloist (in a version based on the original one for piano and "jazz" ensemble); Turnabout TV-S 34457.

Monte Carlo Opera Orchestra, Edo de Waart, conductor, with Werner Hass as soloist; Philips 6500118.

**Eastman-Rochester Orchestra, Howard Hanson, conductor, with Eugene List as soloist; Mercury 90002.

Boston Pops Orchestra, Arthur Fiedler, conductor, with Peter Nero as pianist; RCA Victor LSC-2821.

London Symphony Orchestra, with André Previn as pianist and conductor; Angel S-36810.

André Kostelanetz's Orchestra, with André Previn as soloist; Columbia CS-8286.

Hollywood Bowl Symphony Orchestra, Felix Slatkin, conductor, with Leonard Pennario as soloist; Seraphim S-60174.

Pittsburgh Symphony Orchestra, William Steinberg, conductor, with Jesús Sanroma as soloist; Everest 3067.

Concerto in F (1925)

†**New York Philharmonic, André Kostelanetz, conductor, with Oscar Levant as soloist; Columbia CL-700, CS-8641.

André Kostelanetz's Orchestra, with André Previn as soloist; Columbia CS-8286.

London Symphony Orchestra, with André Previn as pianist and conductor; Angel S-36810.

Boston Pops Orchestra, Arthur Fiedler, conductor, with Earl Wild as pianist; RCA Victor LSC-2586.

Boston Pops Orchestra, Arthur Fiedler, conductor, with Peter Nero as pianist; RCA Victor LSC-3025.

Philadelphia Orchestra, Eugene Ormandy, conductor, with Philippe Entremont as soloist; Columbia MG-30073.

**Eastman-Rochester Orchestra, Howard Hanson, conductor, with Eugene List as soloist; Mercury 90002.

Monte Carlo Opera Orchestra, Edo de Waart, conductor, with Werner Hass as soloist; Philips 6500118.

**Morton Gould's Orchestra, with Morton Gould as soloist; RCA Victor LM-6033.

Preludes for Piano (1926)

Frank Glazer (soloist); Concert Disc 217.

tapeOscar Levant (soloist); Columbia MS-7518.

Grant Johannesen (soloist); Golden Crest S-4065.

Leonard Pennario (soloist); RCA Victor LSC-2731, LSC-5001.

Eugene List (soloist); Turnabout TV-S 34457.

tape**Morton Gould (soloist); RCA Victor LM-6033.

An American in Paris (1928)

†*RCA Victor Symphony Orchestra, Nathaniel Shilkret, conductor (recorded February 4, 1929); RCA Victor 35963/4.

†**RCA Victor Symphony Orchestra, Nathaniel Shilkret, conductor (a 1951 reissue of the February 4, 1929 recording); RCA Victor LPT-29.

†New York Philharmonic, Leonard Bernstein, conductor; Columbia MS-6091, MG-31155.

Boston Pops Orchestra, Arthur Fiedler, conductor; RCA Victor LSC-2367, VICS-1423.

Philadelphia Orchestra, Eugene Ormandy, conductor; Columbia MG-30073, MS-7258, MS-7518.

London Symphony Orchestra, André Previn, conductor; Angel S-36810.

**Minneapolis Symphony Orchestra, Antal Dorati, conductor; Mercury 90290.

Utah Symphony Orchestra, Maurice Abravanel, conductor; Vanguard C-10017, Westminster 8122.

tape **Morton Gould's Orchestra; RCA Victor LM-6033.

Hollywood Bowl Symphony Orchestra, Felix Slatkin, conductor; Seraphim S-60174.

Second Rhapsody (1931)

tape **Hollywood Bowl Symphony Orchestra, Alfred Newman, conductor, with Leonard Pennario as soloist; Capitol SP-8581.

**Morton Gould's Orchestra, with Oscar Levant as soloist; Columbia ML-2073.

**Paul Whiteman's Orchestra, with Roy Bargy as soloist; Decca 8024.

**Pro Musica Orchestra of Hamburg, Hans Jurgen Walther, conductor, with Sondra Bianca as soloist; MGM E-3307.

Cuban Overture (1932)

Boston Pops Orchestra, Arthur Fiedler, conductor; RCA Victor LSC-2586.

**Cleveland Pops Orchestra, Louis Lane, conductor; Epic BC-1047, LC-3626.

**Eastman-Rochester Orchestra, Howard Hanson, conductor; Mercury 90290.

**André Kostelanetz's Orchestra; Columbia ML-4481.

"I Got Rhythm" Variations (1934)

Monte Carlo Opera Orchestra, Edo de Waart, conductor, with Werner Hass as soloist; Philips 6500118.

Boston Pops Orchestra, Arthur Fiedler, conductor; RCA Victor LSC-2586.

tape **Hollywood Bowl Symphony Orchestra, Alfred Newman, conductor, with Leonard Pennario as soloist; Capitol SP-8581.

**Morton Gould's Orchestra, with Oscar Levant as soloist; Columbia ML-2073.

**Pro Musica Orchestra of Hamburg, Hans Jurgen Walther, conductor, with Sondra Bianca as soloist; MGM E-3307.

**Paul Whiteman's Orchestra, with Buddy Weed as soloist; Coral 57021.

Porgy and Bess (1935)

Complete Opera (with minor cuts):

†**Lawrence Winters, Camilla Williams, Inez Mathews, Avon Long, Warren Coleman, Edward Mathews, J. Rosamund Johnson Chorus, with Lehman Engel conducting the chorus and orchestra; Columbia OSL-162.

Excerpts from the Opera (includes renditions freely derived from score):

†Todd Duncan, Anne Brown, the Eva Jessye Choir, and members of the original cast, with Alexander Smallens conducting the Decca Symphony Orchestra; Decca DL-79024. (A simulated stereo version of the original monaural recording).

**Leontyne Price, William Warfield, McHenry Boatwright, and John W. Bubbles, with Skitch Henderson, conductor; RCA Victor LSC-2679.

Douglas Singers, and orchestra; World Wide 20010.

**Rise Stevens, Robert Merrill, and the Robert Shaw Chorale; RCA Victor LM-1124.

**Cab Calloway, Helen Thigpen, and others; RCA Victor LPM-3158.

tape **Louis Armstrong, Ella Fitzgerald, and orchestra; Verve 64068.

Miles Davis featured; orchestra conducted by Gil Evans; Columbia CS-8085.

**Sammy Davis, Jr., Carmen McRae, and orchestra; Decca DL-78854.

Orchestral Syntheses of the Opera:

Catfish Row (a five-movement suite from *Porgy and Bess*, by George Gershwin):

**Utah Symphony Orchestra, Maurice Abravanel, conductor; Westminister 14063, 18850.

A Symphonic Picture (by Robert Russell Bennett):

†RCA Symphony Orchestra, Robert Russell Bennett, conductor; RCA Victor VICS-1491.

Philadelphia Orchestra, Eugene Ormandy, conductor; Columbia MS-7258, MG-30073, MS-7518.

Boston Pops Orchestra, Arthur Fiedler, conductor; RCA Victor LSC-3130.

**Minneapolis Symphony Orchestra, Antal Dorati, conductor; Mercury 90394.

Pittsburgh Symphony Orchestra, William Steinberg, conductor; Command S-11307.

Porgy and Bess Suite (by Morton Gould):
**Morton Gould's Orchestra; RCA Victor LM-6033.

COLLECTIONS OF SONGS

"Bing Crosby Sings Songs by George Gershwin":
**Bing Crosby sings "Embraceable You," "I Got Plenty o' Nuttin'," "It Ain't Necessarily So," "Love Walked In," "Maybe," "Somebody Loves Me," "Summertime," and "They Can't Take That Away from Me"; Decca DL-5081.

"Columbia Album of George Gershwin":
**Percy Faith and his orchestra perform instrumental versions of over twenty Gershwin works: "Fascinating Rhythm," "A Foggy Day," "Soon," "Clap Yo' Hands," "Embraceable You," "Mine," "Somebody Loves Me," "I Got Plenty o' Nuttin'," "Summertime," "Bess, You Is My Woman," "My Man's Gone Now," "Nice Work If You Can Get It," "For You, For Me, For Evermore," "Liza," "'S Wonderful," "Love Is Here to Stay," "They Can't Take That Away from Me," "The Man I Love," "Preludes (Nos. 2 and 3)," "Maybe," "Someone to Watch over Me," "They All Laughed," "Bidin' My Time," and "I Got Rhythm"; Columbia C2L-1.

"Dorothy Kirsten Sings Songs of George Gershwin":
**Dorothy Kirsten, with Percy Faith conducting the orchestra and chorus, sings "Do, Do, Do," "Embraceable You," "I've Got a Crush on You," "Love Is Here to Stay," "Love Walked In," "Mine," "Someone to Watch over Me," and "Soon"; Columbia ML-2129.

"Eddie Condon and Co., Vol. 1; Gershwin Program":
†A simulated stereo version of an earlier release ("George Gershwin Jazz Concert"; Decca DL-5137) by Eddie Condon and his orchestra, with Lee

358

Wiley, Bobby Hackett, Jack Teagarden, Pee Wee Russell, Edmond Hall, and others. They perform "But Not for Me," "Embraceable You," "Fascinating Rhythm," "I'll Build a Stairway to Paradise," "My One and Only," "Oh, Lady, Be Good!," "Somebody Loves Me," "Someone to Watch over Me," "Summertime," "Swanee," " 'S Wonderful," and "The Man I Love"; Decca DL-79324.

"Ella Fitzgerald Sings the George and Ira Gershwin Song-Book":
**Ella Fitzgerald, with Nelson Riddle conducting the orchestra, sings over fifty songs (five discs), many of them Gershwin classics; Verve 629–5.

"Ella Sings Gershwin":
**Ella Fitzgerald sings "But Not for Me," "How Long Has This Been Going On?," "I've Got a Crush on You," "Looking for a Boy," "Maybe," "My One and Only," "Nice Work If You Can Get It," "Oh, Lady, Be Good!," "Someone to Watch over Me," and "Soon," plus two non-Gershwin tunes; Decca 8378.

"Embraceable You: A Tribute to George Gershwin":
**Wally Stotts and his orchestra perform "Embraceable You," "Liza," "Love Is Here to Stay," "Somebody Loves Me," "Someone to Watch over Me," "Strike Up the Band," "Summertime," and "The Man I Love"; Epic LG-1009.

"George Gershwin Plays *Rhapsody in Blue* and Other Favorites" (recorded from piano rolls):
†Gershwin plays a piano version of the *Rhapsody in Blue* and four selections by other composers: "Make Believe" (Shilkret), "Grieving for You" (Gold), "Land Where the Good Songs Go" (Kern), and "Some Sunday Morning" (Whiting); Archive of Piano Music X-914 (Everest Records).

"George Gershwin Revisited":
†Barbara Cook, Bobby Short, Elaine Stritch, and Anthony Perkins, along with an orchestra directed by Norman Paris, perform thirteen Gershwin tunes, many of them relatively unknown: "Changing My Tune" (posthumous; *The Shocking Miss Pilgrim*), "Drifting Along with the Tide" (*Scandals of 1921*), "Feeling Sentimental" (*Show Girl*), "Oh Gee! Oh Joy!" (*Rosalie*), "Nashville Nightingale" (*Nifties of 1923*), "Rose of Madrid" (*Scandals of 1924*), "Scandal Walk" (*Scandals of 1920*), "The Back Bay Polka" (posthumous; *The Shocking Miss Pilgrim*), "There's More to the Kiss than the X-X-X" (*Good Morning, Judge* and *La, La, Lucille* of 1919), "Three Times a Day" (*Tell Me More*), "Tra-La-La" (*For Goodness Sake*), "Under a One-Man Top" (*Sweet Little Devil*), and "Virginia Don't Go Too Far" (*Sweet Little Devil*); Painted Smile PS-1357.

"Gems from Gershwin":

**Jane Froman, Sunny Skylar, and Felix Knight, with Nathaniel Shilkret conducting the orchestra, sing excerpts from *Lady, Be Good*, *Tip-Toes*, *Girl Crazy*, *Of Thee I Sing*, and *Porgy and Bess*; RCA Victor LPT-3055.

"Gershwin Plays Gershwin":

†**Gershwin as pianist, with Fred Astaire. Songs: "Clap Yo' Hands," "Do, Do, Do," "Fascinating Rhythm," "Hang on to Me," "I'd Rather Charleston," "Someone to Watch over Me," "Sweet and Low-Down," "That Certain Feeling," and "The Half of It, Dearie, Blues"; Heritage 0073.

"Gershwin Plays *Rhapsody in Blue*" (recorded from piano rolls):

†**Gershwin as pianist plays *Rhapsody in Blue*, "Kickin' the Clouds Away," "Sweet and Low-Down," and "That Certain Feeling," as well as Jerome Kern's "Left All Alone Again Blues" and "Whose Baby Are You?," Richard Whiting's "Ain't You Coming Back to Dixie?," and Sam Coslow's "Grieving for You"; Distinguished Recordings 107.

"Gershwin Rarities" (Volume 1):

**Kaye Ballard, David Craig, and Betty Gillet, accompanied by pianists David Baker and John Morris, perform ten Gershwin tunes: "Aren't You Kind of Glad We Did?," "Funny Face," "Isn't It a Pity," "Kickin' the Clouds Away," "Seventeen and Twenty-One," "Shall We Dance," "Soon," "Stiff Upper Lip," "They All Laughed," and "Things Are Looking Up"; Walden 302.

"Gershwin Rarities" (Volume 2):

**Louise Carlyle and Warren Galjour, accompanied by the John Morris Trio, perform ten additional Gershwin songs: "A Foggy Day," "How Long Has This Been Going On?," "I Want to Be a War Bride," "Let's Kiss and Make Up," "Oh, So Nice," "Nice Work If You Can Get it," "Nightie-Night," "Sweet and Low-Down," "That Certain Feeling," and "Where's the Boy? Here's the Girl!"; Walden 303.

"Heifetz Plays Gershwin and Music of France":

Jascha Heifetz, with Brooks Smith at the piano, plays his transcriptions for violin and piano of "A Woman Is a Sometime Thing," "Bess, You Is My Woman," "It Ain't Necessarily So," "My Man's Gone Now," "Summertime," and "Tempo di Blues" (based on "There's a Boat Dat's Leavin' Soon for New York"), all from *Porgy and Bess*, plus Gershwin's three "Preludes"; RCA Victor LSC-2856.

"Heifetz Encores" (Volume 2):

Heifetz, with Brooks Smith at the piano, includes among his "encores" his transcriptions for violin and piano of "Bess, You Is My Woman," "It Ain't Necessarily So," and "Summertime" from *Porgy and Bess*; RCA Victor LSC-3256.

"Music of George Gershwin":

**Gershwin, Fred Astaire, Larry Adler, Hildegarde, and others, perform "Bess, You Is My Woman," "Do, Do, Do," "Fascinating Rhythm," "I Got Plenty o' Nuttin'," "It Ain't Necessarily So," "My One and Only," "Summertime," "Sweet and Low-Down," " 'S Wonderful," "The Half of It, Dearie, Blues," "The Man I Love," and "There's a Boat Dat's Leavin' Soon for New York"; Columbia AAL-39.

"Music of George Gershwin":

**André Kostelanetz and his orchestra perform instrumental versions of "Embraceable You," "Fascinating Rhythm," "Maybe," "Oh, Lady, Be Good!," "Someone to Watch over Me," "Soon," " 'S Wonderful," and "The Man I Love"; Columbia ML-2026.

"Oscar Peterson and Buddy de Franco Play Gershwin":

**Oscar Peterson, piano, and Buddy de Franco, clarinet, with an orchestra conducted by Russ Garcia, perform "Bess, You Is My Woman," "I Got Rhythm," "It Ain't Necessarily So," "I Was Doing All Right," "Someone to Watch over Me," "Strike Up the Band," " 'S Wonderful," "The Man I Love," and "They Can't Take That Away from Me"; Norgren MGM-1016.

"Piano Transcriptions of Eighteen Songs" (from *George Gershwin's Song-Book* of 1932):

**Leonid Hambro performs Gershwin's "improvisations" for piano of "Swanee," "Nobody But You," "I'll Build a Stairway to Paradise," "Do It Again," "Fascinating Rhythm," "Oh, Lady, Be Good!," "Somebody Loves Me," "Sweet and Low-Down," "That Certain Feeling," "The Man I Love," "Clap Yo' Hands," "Do, Do, Do," "My One and Only," " 'S Wonderful," "Strike Up the Band," "Liza," "I Got Rhythm," and "Who Cares?"; Walden 200.

"Sarah Vaughan Sings George Gershwin":

**Sarah Vaughan includes many of the verses for the tunes in this album. Songs: "Isn't It a Pity," "Of Thee I Sing," "I'll Build a Stairway to Paradise," "Someone to Watch over Me," "Bidin' My Time," "The Man

I Love," "How Long Has This Been Going On?," "My One and Only," "The Lorelei," "I've Got a Crush on You," "Summertime," "Aren't You Kind of Glad We Did?," "They All Laughed," "Looking for a Boy," "He Loves and She Loves," "My Man's Gone Now," "I Won't Say I Will But I Won't Say I Won't," "A Foggy Day," "Let's Call the Whole Thing Off," "Things Are Looking Up," "Do It Again," and "Love Walked In"; Mercury MGP-2-101.

"Songs of George Gershwin":
**Eddy Duchin's piano renditions of "Embraceable You," "Love Walked In," "Somebody Loves Me," "Someone to Watch over Me," "Summertime," "'S Wonderful," "The Man I Love," and "They Can't Take That Away from Me"; Columbia CL-6103.

"'S Wonderful, 'S Marvelous, 'S Gershwin":
A recorded version of a television special by that title, presented on NBC on January 17, 1972 by Bell Telephone, with Jack Lemmon, Fred Astaire, Leslie Uggams, Peter Nero, Larry Kert, Robert Guillaume, and Linda Bennett performing a potpourri of Gershwin hits, including excerpts from *An American in Paris, Concerto in F, Porgy and Bess, Rhapsody in Blue,* and these tunes: "A Foggy Day," "But Not for Me," "Embraceable You," "Fascinating Rhythm," "I'll Build a Stairway to Paradise," "I've Got a Crush on You," "Let's Call the Whole Thing Off," "Looking for a Boy," "Love Is Here to Stay," "My One and Only," "Oh, Lady, Be Good!," "Someone to Watch over Me," "'S Wonderful," "The Man I Love," "They All Laughed," and "They Can't Take That Away from Me"; Daybreak DR-2009.

"The Best of Astaire":
**Fred Astaire sings these tunes from the movies *Shall We Dance* and *A Damsel in Distress*: "A Foggy Day," "I Can't Be Bothered Now," "Let's Call the Whole Thing Off," "Nice Work If You Can Get It," "Slap That Bass," "They All Laughed," "They Can't Take That Away from Me," and "Things Are Looking Up"; Epic LN-3137.

"The Gershwin Years":
**Paula Stewart, Lynn Roberts, and Richard Hayes, with George Bassman conducting the orchestra and chorus, sing over fifty Gershwin tunes (three discs), ranging from "When You Want 'Em, You Can't Get 'Em, When You Got 'Em, You Don't Want 'Em," of 1916 to "Love Is Here to Stay," written in 1937 for *The Goldwyn Follies;* Decca DXS-7160.

"The Popular Gershwin":

**Eddie Fisher, Frankie Carle, Eartha Kitt, Lou Monte, Jaye P. Morgan, Dinah Shore, June Valli, and others, perform "A Foggy Day," "Bidin' My Time," "But Not for Me," "Do It Again," "Embraceable You," "Fascinating Rhythm," "How Long Has This Been Going On?," "I Got Rhythm," "I'll Build a Stairway to Paradise," "I've Got a Crush on You," "Let's Call the Whole Thing Off," "Liza," "Looking for a Boy," "Love Is Sweeping the Country," "Love Walked In," "Mine," "Nice Work If You Can Get It," "Of Thee I Sing," "Oh, Lady, Be Good!," "Somebody Loves Me," "Someone to Watch over Me," "Song of the Flame," "Strike Up the Band," "Swanee," "'S Wonderful," "They All Laughed," "They Can't Take That Away from Me," "Who Cares?," and Wintergreen for President"; RCA Victor LPM-6000.

MUSICALS

Oh, Kay! (1926)

**Barbara Ruick, Jack Cassidy, Allen Case, Roger White, and pianists Cy Walter and Bernard Leighton, with Lehman Engel conducting the chorus and orchestra, perform the "Overture," "The Woman's Touch," "Don't Ask!," "Dear Little Girl," "Maybe," "Clap Yo' Hands," "Bride and Groom," "Do, Do, Do," "Someone to Watch over Me," "Fidgety Feet," "Heaven on Earth," "Oh, Kay," and the "Finale"; Columbia OS-2550, OL-7050.

Girl Crazy (1930)

Mary Martin, Louise Carlyle, and Eddie Chappell, with Lehman Engel conducting the chorus and orchestra, perform the "Overture," "The Lonesome Cowboy," "Bidin' My Time," "Could You Use Me?," "Broncho Busters," "Barbary Coast," "Embraceable You," "Sam and Delilah," "I Got Rhythm," "But Not for Me," "Treat Me Rough," "Boy! What Love Has Done to Me!," "When It's Cactus Time in Arizona," and the "Finale"; Columbia COS-2560.

Of Thee I Sing (1931)

A recorded version of a television special, presented on CBS on October 24, 1972, with Carroll O'Connor, Cloris Leachman, Jack Gilford, Michele Lee, Jesse White, Jim Backus, Herb Edelman, Paul Hartman, and others, performing a shortened adaptation of the score. Included in this version is an "Overture," "Wintergreen for President," "Who Is the Lucky

Girl to Be?," "The Dimple on My Knee," "Because, Because," "Mine" (from *Let 'Em Eat Cake*), "Love Is Sweeping the Country," "Of Thee I Sing," "I Was the Most Beautiful Blossom," "Who Cares?," "The Senatorial Roll Call," "Jilted, Jilted!," "I'm About to Be a Mother (Who Could Ask for Anything More?)," and a "Finale"; Columbia S-31763.

**An earlier version of the musical, based on the 1952 Broadway revival of the show, was recorded by Jack Carson, Paul Hartman, Jack Whiting, and others, with Maurice Levine conducting the orchestra and chorus; Capitol S-350.

MOVIES

Girl Crazy (1943)
    **Judy Garland, Mickey Rooney, and others, sing tunes from this ,1943 MGM film of the musical, including "Bidin' My Time," "But Not for Me," "Could You Use Me?," "Embraceable You," "Fascinating Rhythm," and "I Got Rhythm"; Decca 5412.

An American in Paris (1951)
    **Gene Kelly, Georges Guetary, Johnny Green and the MGM Orchestra are represented in this recording taken from the soundtrack of the film by MGM. They perform *An American in Paris* (the ballet sequence from the film), "I Got Rhythm," "I'll Build a Stairway to Paradise," "Love Is Here to Stay," and " 'S Wonderful"; MGM S-552 (a 1966 stereo-enhanced reissue of a 1951 release—MGM E-93).

Funny Face (1957)
    **Audrey Hepburn, Fred Astaire, and Kay Thompson are featured in this recording taken from the soundtrack of Paramount's movie version of this musical. Heard in the recording are "Clap Yo' Hands," "Funny Face," "He Loves and She Loves," "How Long Has This Been Going On?," "Let's Kiss and Make Up," and " 'S Wonderful"; Verve MGV-15001.

Porgy and Bess (1959)
    Robert McFerrin and Adele Addison are the voices of Porgy and Bess —not Sidney Poitier and Dorothy Dandridge, as the record jacket would imply—in this recording taken from the soundtrack of Samuel Goldwyn's movie production of the opera. André Previn conducts the orchestra and chorus. These selections are heard: "Overture," "Summertime," "A Woman Is a Sometime Thing," "Gone, Gone, Gone," "My Man's Gone

Now," "I Got Plenty o' Nuttin'," "Bess, You Is My Woman," "Oh, I Can't Sit Down," "It Ain't Necessarily So," "I Ain' Got No Shame," "What You Want wid Bess," "Strawberry Woman," "Crab Man," "I Loves You, Porgy," "A Red Headed Woman," "Clara, Clara (Don't You Be Downhearted)," "There's a Boat Dat's Leavin' Soon for New York," "Oh, Bess, Oh Where's My Bess?," and "Oh Lawd, I'm On My Way"; Columbia OS-2016.

BIBLIOGRAPHY

There seems to be almost no limit to the amount of bibliographic material on George Gershwin. What with press reports and reviews, program notes, articles of all kinds, and biographies and monographs of assorted lengths and quality, the subject of George Gershwin appears to be amply covered in a variety of languages. If to these sources one adds repositories of memorabilia, music, and other Gershwiniana—such as is found in the Music and Theater Divisions of the New York Public Library, the Gershwin Collection at the Library of Congress, the George and Ira Gershwin Collection at the Museum of the City of New York, and the George Gershwin Memorial Collection at Fisk University—the Gershwin bibliographic cup truly runneth over. Because of such amplitude, a complete Gershwin bibliography is probably not realizable. For practical purposes, a selected bibliography, based on one by this author that has been published by the College of Music Society in its *Bibliographies in American Music* series, is compiled here. This bibliography contains annotations for a number of references, with some information about their contents. References that are considered of particular interest to the Gershwin reader are marked with an asterisk (*).

"American Classic Sings Anew," *Life* (June 15, 1959), 70–7. Discusses the motion picture *Porgy and Bess.*

Amis, John. "Opera: Mozart to Gershwin: 'Porgy and Bess,'" *The Musical Times* (Nov 1952), 512–3.

Antheil, George. "The Foremost American Composer," in: Merle Armitage, ed, *George Gershwin*. NY: Longmans, Green, 1938; 115–9.

Antrim, Doran K. "Fortunes in Melody," *Etude* (Jan 1942), 11–2.

Ardoin, John. "Warfield Outstanding in 'Porgy and Bess,'" *Musical America* (July 1961), 45.

Arlen, Harold. "The Composer's Friend," in: Merle Armitage, ed, *George Gershwin*. NY: Longmans, Green, 1938; 121–2.

*Armitage, Merle, ed. *George Gershwin*. NY: Longmans, Green, 1938. A collection of 38 articles by friends and colleagues of Gershwin. Though there are inaccuracies in it, this collection is an important source of information about Gershwin.

———. "George Gershwin and His Time," in: Merle Armitage, ed, *George Gershwin*. NY: Longmans, Green, 1938; 5–15.

———. "George Gershwin," in his: *Accent on America*. NY: E. Weyhe, 1944; 289–98. Also a chapter on *Porgy and Bess*, 163–6; other citations, 312, 364.

———. *George Gershwin: Man and Legend*, with a note on the author by John Charles Thomas. NY: Duell, Sloan and Pearce, 1958.

*Arvey, Verna. "George Gershwin Through the Eyes of a Friend," *Opera and Concert* (Apr 1948), 10–11, 27–8. The author discusses Kay Swift's friendship with Gershwin.

———. "Afro-American Music Memo," *Music Journal* (Nov 1969), 36, 68–9.

*Astaire, Fred. *Steps in Time*. NY: Harper, 1959. Includes some reminiscences by Astaire about his association with Gershwin.

"Athens Applauds American Singers in 'Porgy and Bess,'" *Musical America* (Feb 1, 1955), 33.

Atkinson, Brooks. " 'Porgy and Bess,' Native Opera, Opens at the Alvin," *The New York Times* (Oct 11, 1935), 30. Review of premiere of *Porgy and Bess*.

———. " 'Of Thee I Sing:' Another Production from the Past Is Better Than Most of the New Ones," *The New York Times* (May 11, 1952), Sec II, 1.

———. "Negro Folk Drama: 'Porgy and Bess' Suitable for Production Before Audiences in European Capitals," *The New York Times* (Sep 7, 1952), Sec II, 1.

———. "Return of a Classic: 'Porgy and Bess' Comes Home from Europe," *The New York Times* (Mar 15, 1953), Sec II, 1.

"Auld Lang Syne," *Musical America* (Jan 1, 1955), 9. *Porgy and Bess* in Belgrade and Zagreb.

Austin, William W. *Music in the Twentieth Century*. NY: W. W. Norton, 1966; 48, 62, 89, 191–2, 291, 384–5, 441, 471, 502–4, 518.

"Austria," *Opera* (Dec 1952), 733. Review of *Porgy and Bess*.

Bagar, Robert C., and Louis Biancolli. *The Concert Companion*. NY/London: McGraw-Hill, 1947; 273–8. Program notes for *An American in Paris*, *Concerto in F*, selections from *Porgy and Bess*, and *Rhapsody in Blue*; originally written for the Philharmonic-Symphony Society of New York Programs.

"Barnet's 'Rhapsody' Arrangement Ordered Destroyed by Harms," *Variety* (Mar 9, 1949), 48.

Baskerville, David. *Jazz Influence on Art Music to Mid-Century*. Ph.D. Dissertation: University of California at Los Angeles, 1965. UM 65–15, 175.

BIBLIOGRAPHY

Dissertation Abstracts XXVI/8 (Feb 1966), 4710. Contains a chapter on *Porgy and Bess*.

Bauer, Marion. "The Gershwin Touch," *Rhapsody in Blue; the Jubilant Story of George Gershwin and His Music*. Hollywood: Warner Bros, 1945; 17.

Becker, Wolfgang. "Da Berlino," *Nuova Revista Musicale Italiana* (Mar–Apr 1970), 343–4. A review of a Berlin performance of *Porgy and Bess*.

*Behrman, Samuel Nathaniel. "Troubadour," *The New Yorker* (May 25, 1929), 27–29. Also in: Merle Armitage, ed, *George Gershwin*. NY: Longmans, Green, 1938; 211–8.

*————. *People in a Diary: A Memoir*. Boston; Little, Brown, 1972; 239–58. Gershwin's terminal illness is discussed with great insight.

"Belittling Gershwin," *Newsweek* (Aug 20, 1945), 79. A criticism of Gershwin.

Bellerby, L. "Second Thoughts on Porgy and Bess," *Jazz Journal* (Jan 1953), 6.

"Berlin," *Oper und Konzert* (June 1971), 5. Review of *Porgy and Bess*.

*Bernstein, Leonard. "A Nice Gershwin Tune," *The Atlantic Monthly* (Apr 1955), 39–42. Bernstein, in an imaginary conversation with a music-publishing executive, discusses Gershwin's *An American in Paris, Concerto in F, Porgy and Bess,* and *Rhapsody in Blue*.

*————. *The Joy of Music*. NY: Simon and Schuster, 1959. Bernstein's "A Nice Gershwin Tune" is reprinted here.

Blesh, Rudi, and Harriet Janis. *They All Played Ragtime: The True Story of an American Music*. NY: A. A. Knopf, 1950; 72, 204.

Blom, Eric. "George Gershwin," *Grove's Dictionary of Music and Musicians,* 5th ed, by Eric Blom, 10 vols. London: Macmillan, 1954–61; III, 607; X, 183.

*Bolton, Guy R., and Pelham Grenville Wodehouse. *Bring on the Girls!* NY: Simon and Schuster, 1953. Two authors of scripts for Gershwin musicals reminisce about the composer and their part in Gershwin productions.

Bonner, Eugene. "George Gershwin's Latest," *The Outlook and Independent* (Jan 2, 1929), 34. About *An American in Paris*.

Bookspan, Martin. "The Basic Repertoire: Gershwin's *An American in Paris,"* *HiFi/Stereo Review* (May 1965), 39–40.

*————. "The Basic Repertoire: Gershwin's *Rhapsody in Blue,"* *HiFi/Stereo Review* (Feb 1968), 55–6.

Borneman, Ernest. "Second Thoughts on Some Musical Sacrilege," *Melody Maker* (Nov 1, 1952), 8. Criticism of *Porgy and Bess*.

Rose, Fritz." 'Porgy and Bess:' die Negeroper erstmals auf Platten," *Musica Schallplatte* (May 1960), 58–9. Record review.

*Botkin, Henry. "Painter and Collector," in: Merle Armitage, ed, *George Gershwin*. NY: Longmans, Green, 1938; 137–43. Botkin discusses Gershwin's talents as a painter and art collector.

Bourgeois, Jacques. "Un disque d'extraits de Porgy and Bess," *Disques* (Feb-Mar 1953), 127. Record review of *Porgy and Bess*.

Bracker, Milton. " 'Of Thee I Sing' in Modern Dress," *The New York Times* (May 4, 1952), Sec II, 1, 3.

Braggiotti, Mario. "Gershwin Is Here to Stay," *Etude* (Feb 1953), 14, 63. Includes discussion of his works.

"Bregenzer Festspiele," *Oper und Konzert* (Sept 1971), 12. Review of *Porgy and Bess*.

Briggs, John. "George Gershwin: A Reappraisal," *Tomorrow* (July 1948), 20–4.

Buchanan, Charles L. "Gershwin and Musical Snobbery," *The Outlook* (Feb 2, 1927), 146–8.

Burke, Georgia. "The Porgy and Bess Story, 1952–53," *Equity* (May 1953), 13–5.

Burton, Jack. "George Gershwin, 1898–1937," *The Blue Book of Tin Pan Alley: A Human Interest Anthology of American Popular Music.* Watkins Glen, NY: Century House, 1950; 292–305. Cites works written by Gershwin, in chronological order, and lists recordings (mainly 78 rpm).

———. *The Blue Book of Broadway Musicals.* Watkins Glen, NY: Century House, 1952. Gershwin's scores are cited as follows: 110, 179–82, 249–50, 306.

———. *The Blue Book of Hollywood Musicals: Songs from the Sound Tracks and the Stars Who Sang Them Since the Birth of the Talkies a Quarter-Century Ago.* Watkins Glen, NY: Century House, 1953. Discusses these movies: *Delicious* (1931), 40; *A Damsel in Distress* (1937), 94; *Shall We Dance* (1937), 97, *The Goldwyn Follies* (1938), 109; *The Shocking Miss Pilgrim* (1947), 232; *An American in Paris* (1951), 263.

" 'Buying American' in Music," *The Literary Digest* (Dec 29, 1934), 24.

Calta, Louis. "Stage Folk to See Preview of 'Porgy,' " *The New York Times* (Mar 4, 1953), 21.

*Campbell, Frank C. "The Musical Scores of George Gershwin," *The Library of Congress Quarterly Journal of Current Acquisitions* (May 1954), 127–39. Discusses Gershwin's orchestral manuscripts at the Library of Congress; includes 22 musical examples.

*———. "Some Manuscripts of George Gershwin," *Manuscripts* (Winter 1954), 66–75. Another report of Gershwin's orchestral manuscripts at the Library of Congress.

Campbell-Watson, Frank. "Preamble" to "I Got Rhythm" Variations. NY: New World Music Corp, 1953.

*Capote, Truman. *The Muses are Heard: An Account.* NY: Random House, 1956. Capote's account of performances of *Porgy and Bess* in Russia.

Caruthers, Osgood. "Catfish Row à la Soviet," *The New York Times* (May 28, 1961), Sec II, 3. About an unauthorized Russian version of *Porgy and Bess*.

"Casting Woes for Prawy's 'Porgy'; Sells Out Every Rep Performance," *Variety* (Oct 29, 1969), 75.

"Catfish Row in an Encore," *Newsweek* (Feb 2, 1942), 55–7. Review of the revival of *Porgy and Bess* at New York's Majestic Theatre.

*Cerf, Bennett. "In Memory of George Gershwin," *Saturday Review of Literature* (July 17, 1943), 14–6. In his usual witty style, Cerf tells some anecdotes about Gershwin.

———. *Try and Stop Me.* NY: Simon & Schuster, 1944. Cerf's "In Memory of George Gershwin" is incorporated into this book of anecdotes.

Chalupt, René. *George Gershwin, le musicien de la "Rhapsody in Blue."* Paris: Amiot-Dumont, 1948. Italian translation by Robert Leydi as: *Gershwin.* Milan: Nuova Accademia, 1959.

BIBLIOGRAPHY

"Charleston (and Gershwin) Provide Folk-Opera," *The Literary Digest* (Oct 26, 1935), 18.

Chase, Gilbert, ed, *The American Composer Speaks: A Historical Anthology, 1770–1965*. Baton Rouge, La: Louisiana State University Press, 1966; 3, 5, 13, 26, 139–40, 260. Includes an introduction to Gershwin's article "The Composer in the Machine Age."

———. *American Music from the Pilgrims to the Present*, 2nd ed. NY: McGraw-Hill, 1966; 462, 488–95, 517, 518, 622, 630, 642–5. 1st ed, 1955. Includes discussion of *Porgy and Bess* and *Rhapsody in Blue*.

Chasins, Abram. "Paradox in Blue," *Saturday Review of Literature* (Feb 25, 1956), 37, 39, 64–6.

Clausen, Bernard C. "Strike Up the Band," *Christian Century* (July 8, 1931), 899–901.

Coeuroy, André. *Panorama de la musique Contemporaine*. Paris: Les Documentaires, 1928; 65, 70. Remarks on Gershwin and jazz.

"Composer's Pictures," *Arts and Decorations* (Jan 1934), 48–50.

"Congressman Attacks 'Porgy' Tour, Despite Show's Favorable Impact," *Variety* (Dec 14, 1955), 1f.

Copland, Aaron, *What to Listen for in Music*. NY/London: Whittlesey House, McGraw-Hill, 1939, 1953.

———. *Our New Music*. NY/London: Whittlesey House, McGraw-Hill, 1941, 85, 99. Rev ed as: *The New Music, 1900–1960*. NY: W. W. Norton, 1968, 61, 70.

Cowell, Henry. *American Composers on American Music*. Palo Alto: Stanford University Press, 1933. Reprint with a new introduction, NY: Frederick Ungar, 1962.

Croce, Arlene. *The Fred Astaire and Ginger Rogers Book*. NY: Outerbridge & Lazard (distributed by E. P. Dutton & Co.), 1972. Includes information about the movies *Shall We Dance* and *A Damsel in Distress*, both with Gershwin scores.

Cross, Milton, and David Ewen. *Milton Cross' Encyclopedia of the Great Composers and Their Music*, 2 vols, rev ed, Garden City, NY: Doubleday, 1962. 1st ed, 1953. Biographical section and program notes for *An American in Paris, Concerto in F, Porgy and Bess*, and *Rhapsody in Blue*.

Crowninshield, Frank. "Gershwin the Painter," in: *Rhapsody in Blue; the Jubilant Story of George Gershwin and His Music*. Hollywood: Warner Bros, 1945; 11–12.

Crowther, Bosley. "Americans in Paris: New Metro Film Affords a Fanciful Tour," *The New York Times* (Oct 14, 1951), Sec II, 1.

———. "Fitness of Folk Opera: A Rare Form in Films Is Exalted by Goldwyn's 'Porgy and Bess,' " *The New York Times* (June 28, 1959), Sec II, 1.

———. " 'Porgy and Bess' Again: Further Thoughts on a Second Look at the Filmed Folk Opera," *The New York Times* (Aug 2, 1959), Sec II, 1.

Daly, William. "George Gershwin as Orchestrator," in: Merle Armitage, ed, *George Gershwin*. NY: Longmans, Green, 1938; 30–1. Reissued from *The New York Times* (Jan 15, 1933), Sec X, 6. Daly's answer to a charge that he orchestrated Gershwin's symphonic works.

Damrosch, Walter. "Gershwin and the *Concerto in F*," in: Merle Armitage, ed, *George Gershwin*. NY: Longmans, Green, 1938; 32–3.

———. "Gershwin and His Music," in: *Rhapsody in Blue; the Jubilant Story of George Gershwin and His Music*. Hollywood: Warner Bros, 1945; 7–8.

Danz, Louis. "Gershwin and Schoenberg," in: Merle Armitage, ed, *George Gershwin*. NY: Longmans, Green, 1938; 99–101.

Dashiell, Alan. "Foreword and Discography," in: Isaac Goldberg, *George Gershwin: A Study in American Music*. NY: Frederick Ungar, 1958; xiii–xviii, 357–70.

Davenport, Marcia, and Ruth Sedgwick. "Rhapsody in Black," *Stage Magazine* (Nov 1935), 31–3.

David, Hubert W. "Gershwin, The Man We Love," *Melody Maker* (Dec 11, 1954), 8.

"Death of Gershwin," *Time* (July 19, 1937), 37–8. Obituary.

"Dick Nash's Word to [the] Worrisome: He's Not Rewriting 'Porgy and Bess,' " *Variety* (Jan 1, 1958), 7. About the screen adaptation of *Porgy and Bess*.

Doll, Bill. "Fan Mail, After Many Years," *Theatre Arts* (Oct 1959), 28–32, 84–5.

Donahue, Lester. "Gershwin and the Social Scene," in: Merle Armitage, ed, *George Gershwin*. NY: Longmans, Green, 1938; 170–7.

Dove, Ian. " 'Of Thee I Sing' Returned in Musical Style of the '30's," *Billboard* (Mar 22, 1969), 14.

Downes, Irene, ed. *Olin Downes on Music: A Selection from His Writings during the Half-Century*. NY: Simon & Schuster, 1957.

Downes, Olin. "A Concert of Jazz," *The New York Times* (Feb 13, 1924), 16. Also as: "*Rhapsody in Blue* Introduced in a Historic Whiteman Concert," in: Irene Downes, ed, *Olin Downes on Music: A Selection from His Writings during the Half-Century*. NY: Simon & Schuster, 1957; 83–5. Review of world premiere of the *Rhapsody in Blue*.

———. "A Piano Concerto in the Vernacular to Have Its Day with Damrosch," *The New York Times* (Nov 29, 1925), Sec VIII, 2. Article about the *Concerto in F* prior to its premiere, Dec 3, 1925.

———. "Gershwin's New Score Acclaimed," *The New York Times* (Dec 14, 1928), 37. Review of premiere of *An American in Paris*.

———. "George Gershwin Plays His Second Rhapsody for First Time Here with Koussevitsky and Boston Orchestra," *The New York Times* (Feb 6, 1932), 14.

———. " 'Porgy and Bess,' Native Opera, Opens at the Alvin" *The New York Times* (Oct 11, 1935), 30. Review of the opening of *Porgy and Bess*.

———. "When Critics Disagree: Amusing Dramatics and Musical Commentary Upon Gershwin's *Porgy and Bess*," *The New York Times* (Oct 20, 1935), Sec X, 7. Also as: "*Porgy and Bess* and the Future of American Opera," in: Irene Downes, ed, *Olin Downes on Music: A Selection from His Writings during the Half-Century*. NY: Simon & Schuster, 1957; 208–11.

———. "Hail & Farewell: Career & Position of George Gershwin in American Music," *The New York Times* (July 18, 1937), Sec X, 5. Also as: "Hail and Farewell," in: Merle Armitage, ed, *George Gershwin*. NY: Longmans, Greene, 1938; 219–24. Also as: "On the Passing of George Gershwin," in: Irene

Downes, ed, *Olin Downes on Music: A Selection From His Writings during the Half-Century.* NY: Simon & Schuster, 1957; 232–7.

———. "Gershwin Memorial: Retrospect of Rapid Rise of Composer and the Development of His Art," *The New York Times* (July 10, 1938), Sec IX, 5.

———. " 'Porgy' Fantasy: R[obert] R[ussell] Bennett Makes Symphonic Work from Gershwin Opera," *The New York Times* (Nov 15, 1942), Sec VIII, 7.

"Drama: Dissenting Opinion," *The Nation* (Oct 30, 1935), 518–9. About *Porgy and Bess.*

"Dubbing In the Voices, Also a Big Production," *Life* (June 15, 1959), 79–82. Discusses the dubbing of the singing voices in the film *Porgy and Bess.*

Duke, Vernon. "Gershwin, Schillinger, and Dukelsky," *The Musical Quarterly* (Jan 1947), 102–15. Duke discusses his and Gershwin's studies with Schillinger.

———. *Passport to Paris.* Boston: Little, Brown, 1955. Reminiscences about George and Ira Gershwin are included in this autobiography.

———. *Listen Here.* NY: Ivan Obolensky, 1963. A vitriolic assessment of music and musicians.

Duncan, Todd. "Memoirs of George Gershwin," in: Merle Armitage, ed, *George Gershwin.* NY: Longmans, Green, 1938; 58–64.

*Durham, Frank. *DuBose Heyward, the Man Who Wrote Porgy.* Columbia, SC: University of South Carolina Press, 1954.

Edens, Roger. "Labor Pains,"*Film and TV Music* (Spring 1957), 18–20. Discusses the motion picture *Funny Face.*

Edwards, Arthur C., and W. Thomas Marrocco. *Music in the United States.* Dubuque, Ia: Wm. C. Brown, 1968; 105–6, 107, 117, 154.

Eells, George. *The Life That Late He Led: A Biography of Cole Porter.* NY: G. P. Putnam's; London: W. H. Allen, 1967.

Ellsworth, Ray. "Americans on Microgroove: Part II," *High Fidelity* (Aug 1956), 60–6. Discusses recordings of Gershwin's works.

———. "The RCA Victor 'Porgy and Bess,' " *The American Record Guide* (Nov 1963), 196–9. Record review.

E[ngel], C[arl]. "Views and Reviews," *The Musical Quarterly* (Apr 1926), 299–314. Discusses Gershwin's *Concerto in F.*

———. "Views and Reviews," *The Musical Quarterly* (Oct 1932), 646–51. A review of *The George Gershwin Song-Book.*

Ewen, David. "A New Gilbert and Sullivan on Broadway," *The American Hebrew* (Sep 2, 1927), 517, 522–30. About George Gershwin and George S. Kaufman.

———."A Master of Symphonic Jazz," *The Jewish Tribune* (Oct 7, 1927), 16.

———. "New Harmonists," *The American Hebrew* (Aug 24, 1928), 435, 441. About Louis Gruenberg, Aaron Copland, Marion Bauer, and George Gershwin.

———. "The King of Tin-Pan Alley," *The Jewish Tribune* (Feb 15, 1929), 2, 11.

———, ed. *Composers of Today.* NY: H. W. Wilson, 1934; 85–6.

———. "Farewell to George Gershwin," in: Merle Armitage, ed, *George Gershwin.* NY: Longmans, Green, 1938; 203–8.

———. *The Story of George Gershwin,* illustrated by Graham Bernbach. NY:

Henry Holt, 1943. 211 pp. German translation by Gunther Martin, with a foreward by Friedrich Gulda, as: *George Gershwin: Leben und Werk.* Zürich: Amalthea-Verlag, 1954. Dutch translation as: *George Gershwin.* Haarlem: Gottmer, 1958.

———. "The Stature of George Gershwin," *The American Mercury* (June 1950), 716–24.

———, ed. *The Book of Modern Composers,* 2nd ed, rev & enlarged. NY: A. A. Knopf, 1950, 1st ed, 1942. Contains a brief biography, comments by Isaac Goldberg, an excerpt from an article by Gershwin discussing his aesthetic theories, and an essay by John Tasker Howard.

———. "The Mighty Five of American Popular Music," *Theatre Arts* (Dec 1951), 42, 74–6.

———. *Ewen's Musical Masterworks: The Encyclopedia of Musical Masterpieces,* 2nd ed. NY: Arco, 1954. Program notes for *An American in Paris, Concerto in F* and *Rhapsody in Blue.*

———. "Gershwin Would be Surprised," *Harper's Magazine* (May 1955), 68–70. About the growth of Gershwin's fame since his death.

———. "A Wartime 'Porgy,'" *The New York Times* (Oct 9, 1955), Sec II, 1, 3. First European performance in 1943 in Nazi-occupied Denmark of *Porgy and Bess.*

*———. *A Journey to Greatness.* NY: Henry Holt; London: W. H. Allen, 1956.

———, ed. *The Complete Book of 20th Century Music,* new & rev ed. Englewood Cliffs, N.J.: Prentice-Hall, 1959. 1st ed, 1952. Program notes for *An American in Paris, Concerto in F* and *Rhapsody in Blue.*

———. *The Story of America's Musical Theatre.* Philadelphia: Chilton, 1961; 89–93, 112–20, 141–7, 167–8, *passim.*

———. *The Life and Death of Tin Pan Alley.* NY: Funk & Wagnalls, 1964.

———. "There'll Always be a Gershwin," *Variety* (Jan 5, 1966), 207.

———. *George Gershwin: His Journey to Greatness.* Englewood Cliffs, NJ: Prentice-Hall, 1970. A revised, updated version of *A Journey to Greatness,* but with some factual errors retained and without the earlier book's discography and bibliography.

———. "Miami: A Festival of George Gershwin," *High Fidelity/Musical America* (Jan 1971), MA 24–5f. Works discussed include: *In a Mandarin's Orchid Garden, Lullaby, 135th Street* & *Promenade.*

"Exhibit of Gershwiniana at N.Y.C. Museum Pulls Int'l Show Biz Crowd," *Variety* (May 8, 1968), 241f.

Fabricant, Noah D., M.D. "George Gershwin's Fatal Headache," *The Eye, Ear, Nose and Throat Monthly* (May 1958), 332–4. A doctor's assessment of Gershwin's fatal illness.

Fiechtner, Helmut A. "Gershwin's 'Porgy and Bess,'" *Musica* (Jan 1966), 23–4. Review of the Vienna production of the opera.

"Filming 'Rhapsody in Blue,'" in: *Rhapsody in Blue; the Jubilant Story of George Gershwin and His Music.* Hollywood: Warner Bros, 1945; 19–20.

"First Gershwin Festival," *Music Educators Journal* (Sep 1970), 79. Notice of a Gershwin festival at the University of Miami.

"Folk Opera," *Time* (Oct 21, 1935), 48. About *Porgy and Bess.*

BIBLIOGRAPHY

Fossum, Knut. "Norway: Romantic 'Porgy,' " *Opera* (Jan 1968), 62–3. Review of *Porgy and Bess* at the Norwegian Opera.

Frankenstein, Alfred. *A Modern Guide to Symphonic Music*. NY: Meredith Press, 1966; 244–6. Discusses the *Concerto in F*.

Funke, Lewis, "News and Gossip of the Rialto: 'Porgy and Bess' Loses Official Support," *The New York Times* (Oct 2, 1955), Sec II, 1.

Garland, Robert. "Negroes are Critical of 'Porgy and Bess,' " *The New York World Telegram* (Jan 16, 1936), 14.

*Garson, Edith. "Supplements," in: Isaac Goldberg, *George Gershwin: A Study in American Music*. NY: Frederick Ungar, 1958; 297–356. Garson adds six chapters to the original Goldberg book of 1931.

*Gauthier, Eva. "Personal Appreciation," in: Merle Armitage, ed, *George Gershwin*. NY: Longmans, Green, 1938; 193–202.

————. "The Roaring Twenties," *Musical Courier* (Feb 1, 1955), 42–4. Miss Gauthier tells of Gershwin's first meeting with Ravel at a party in her home.

"[George and Ira] Gershwin Song Book," *Variety* (Oct 5, 1960), 59. A review of the book.

"George Gershwin," *Etude* (Sep 1937), 558. Obituary.

"George Gershwin," in: *The ASCAP Biographical Dictionary of Composers, Authors and Publishers*, 1966 ed, compiled and edited by The Lynn Farnol Group, Inc. NY: ASCAP, 1966; 256–7. Lists shows, songs, etc.

"German Orchestra in First West German Tour with All-Gershwin Program," *Variety* (Aug 31, 1955), 2f.

"Gershwin Concert Orchestra Filling 100 Dates on Tour," *Musical Courier* (Feb 15, 1953), 37.

"Gershwin Everywhere," *Time* (July 9, 1945), 67.

"Gershwin 50th Anniversary in ASCAP Celebrated in Miami Festival," *ASCAP Today* (Mar 1971), 20.

"Gershwin Memorabilia," *Variety* (June 14, 1967), 50.

"Gershwin Memorials," *Time* (July 25, 1938), 33–4.

"Gershwin Orchestra Tours 74 Cities," *Musical America* (Jan 15, 1954), 4.

"Gershwin Rhapsody Thirty Years Old," *Music Dealer* (Feb 1954), 11.

"Gershwin Service Here on Thursday," *The New York Times* (July 13, 1937), 20. About the funeral services for Gershwin.

"Gershwin: Talented Composer Gave *Porgy* Life and Rhythm," *News-Week* (Oct 12, 1935), 22.

Gershwin, Alan. "I Am George Gershwin's Illegitimate Son," *Confidential* (Feb 1959), 10–3, 45–6.

Gershwin, George. "Does Jazz Belong to Art?" *Second Line* (Sept-Oct 1965), 120–3. Reprinted from *Singing* (July 1926), 13–4.

————. "Mr. Gershwin Replies to Mr. Kramer," *Singing* (Oct 1926), 17–8. Gershwin answers a charge that he did not orchestrate the *Concerto in F*.

*————. "The Composer and the Machine Age," in: Merle Armitage, ed, *George Gershwin*. NY: Longmans, Green, 1938; 225–30. Originally appeared in: Oliver Sayler, ed, *Revolt in the Arts*. NY: Brentano's, 1930; (Rights turned over to Coward-McCann, 1933).

*————. "Introduction," in: Isaac Goldberg, *Tin Pan Alley: A Chronicle of the*

American Popular Music Racket. NY: John Day, 1930; vii-xi. Reprint, with supplement by Edward Jablonski, as: *Tin Pan Alley: A Chronicle of American Popular Music.* NY: Frederick Ungar, 1961. Gershwin discusses his composing habits.

*————. "The Relation of Jazz to American Music," in Henry Cowell, ed, *American Composers on American Music.* Palo Alto: Stanford University Press, 1933; reprint, NY: Frederick Ungar, 1962; 186–7.

*————. "Rhapsody in Catfish Row: Mr. Gershwin Tells the Origin and Scheme for His Music in That New Folk Opera Called 'Porgy and Bess,' " *The New York Times* (Oct 20, 1935), Sec X, 1–2. Also as: "Rhapsody in Catfish Row," in: Merle Armitage, ed, *George Gershwin.* NY: Longmans, Green, 1938; 72–7.

*Gershwin, Ira. "My Brother," in: Merle Armitage, ed, *George Gershwin.* NY: Longmans, Green, 1938; 16–23. Also in: Merle Armitage, *George Gershwin, Man and Legend.* NY: Duell, Sloan, & Pearce, 1958; 11–8.

————. "Gershwin on Gershwin," *Newsweek* (Oct 23, 1944), 14. Ira Gershwin voices objections to allegations that his brother had studied with Schillinger because his creative well had run dry.

————. "Twenty Years After," *The New Yorker* (May 17, 1952), 26–7.

————. "[New York is a Great Place to Be] . . . But I Wouldn't Want to Live There," *The Saturday Review* (Oct 18, 1958), 27, 48.

*————. *Lyrics on Several Occasions.* NY: A. A. Knopf, 1959.

————. "Which Came First?" *The Saturday Review* (Aug 29, 1959), 31–3, 45. Excerpts from his *Lyrics on Several Occasions.*

————. "That Inevitable Question: Which Comes First?" *Variety* (Jan 10, 1962), 187.

————. "Euterpe and the Lucky Lyricist," *Variety* (Jan 8, 1964), 198.

"Gershwin's American Opera Puts Audience on Its Feet," *News-Week* (Oct 19, 1935), 23–4.

"Gershwins Honored," *Variety* (June 1, 1966), 45.

" 'Gershwin's Music Subversive' Says Senator McCarthy," *Melody Maker* (June 13, 1953), 12.

Gilder, Rosamond. "Places and People: Broadway in Review," *Theatre Arts* (Apr 1942), 219–26. *Porgy and Bess* discussed on pp. 219–20.

Goldberg, Isaac. "George Gershwin and Jazz: A Critical Analysis of a Modern Composer," *Theatre Guild Magazine* (Mar 1930), 15–9, 55.

————. "Jazzo-Analysis," *Disques* [Philadelphia] (Nov 1930), 394–8.

*————. *Tin Pan Alley: A Chronicle of the American Popular Music Racket,* with an introduction by George Gershwin. NY: John Day, 1930. Reprint, with a supplement by Edward Jablonski, as: *Tin Pan Alley: A Chronicle of American Popular Music.* NY: Frederick Ungar, 1961.

*————. *George Gershwin: A Study in American Music.* NY: Simon & Schuster, 1931. Reprint edition supplemented by Edith Garson, with a foreword & discography by Alan Dashiell. NY: Frederick Ungar, 1958. The first Gershwin biography.

————. "Music by Gershwin," *Ladies Home Journal* (Feb 1931), 12–3; (Mar 1931), 20; (Apr 1931), 25.

————. "Gebrüder Gershwin," *Vanity Fair* (June 1932), 46–7, 62.

————. "Score by George Gershwin," *Stage Magazine* (Dec 1935), 37–8.

————. "What's Jewish in Gershwin's Music," *B'nai B'rith Magazine* (Apr 1936), 226–7, 247. Goldberg alludes to Jewish elements in Gershwin's music.

————. "In Memoriam: George Gershwin," *B'nai B'rith Magazine* (Aug-Sep 1937), 8–9, 26.

*————. "Homage to a Friend," in: Merle Armitage, ed, *George Gershwin*. NY: Longmans, Green, 1938; 161–7.

————. "Personal Note," in: David Ewen, ed, *The Book of Modern Composers*, 2nd ed rev and enlarged. NY: A. A. Knopf, 1950.

Gould, Jack. "Television in Review: '135th Street,' Written by Gershwin at 22, Is Offered by 'Omnibus' in Local Premiere," *The New York Times* (Mar 30, 1953), 18.

Grabbe, Paul. *The Story of One Hundred Symphonic Favorites*. NY: Grosset & Dunlap, 1940.

Graf, Max. " 'Porgy and Bess' Begins European Tour in Vienna," *Musical America* (Oct 1952), 9.

"The Great Songwriters and Records of Their Great Songs," *Billboard* (Oct 7, 1950), supplement, 79–81.

Green, Abel. "[George and Ira] Gershwin Song Book," *Variety* (Oct 5, 1960), 59.

Green, Benny. "Gershwin's *Porgy and Bess*," *Music and Musicians* (Oct 1962), 22–3.

Green, Stanley. "Catfish Row in a 'Near Original,' " *HiFi Review* (Aug 1959), 40. Review of the soundtrack of the film *Porgy and Bess*.

————. "A Songwriter by Any Other Name. . . ," *Variety* (Jan 8, 1964), 195.

————. *Ring Bells! Sing Songs!: Broadway Musicals of the 1930's*. New Rochelle, N.Y.: Arlington House. Touches on the scores Gershwin wrote for Broadway from *Strike Up the Band* of 1930 on.

Grigorev, Lev Grigorevic, and Jakov Michajlovic Platek. *Dzordz Gersvin*. Moscow: Gos. Muz. Izd, 1956.

Grofé, Ferde. "George Gershwin's Influence," in: Merle Armitage, ed, *George Gershwin*. NY: Longmans, Green, 1938; 27–9.

Grunfeld, Fred. "The Great American Opera," *Opera News* (Mar 19, 1960), 6–9. About *Porgy and Bess*.

Haggin, Bernard H. "Gershwin and Our Music," *The Nation* (Oct 5, 1932), 308–9.

————. "Music," *The Nation* (Aug 4, 1945), 115.

Hale, Philip. "Rhapsody, No. 2, for Orchestra," *Boston Symphony Orchestra Programmes* (Jan 29–30, 1932), 838–54. Program notes for world premiere of the work.

Hammerstein, Oscar, II. "To George Gershwin," in: Merle Armitage, ed, *George Gershwin*. NY: Longmans, Green, 1938; 1–4. Reissued from *The George Gershwin Memorial Concert Programme* (Hollywood Bowl, Sep 6, 1937).

Handy, William C. *Blues*. NY: A & C Boni, 1926.

Hangen, Welles. " 'Porgy and Bess' in the USSR," *The New York Times* (Jan 15, 1956), Sec II, 3.

Hanson, Howard. "Flowering of American Music," *The Saturday Review of Literature* 32 (Aug 6, 1949), 157–64. Discusses Gershwin on p. 160.

Harris, Sam H. "Gershwin and Gold," in: Merle Armitage, ed, *George Gershwin.* NY: Longmans, Green, 1938; 168–9.

Helm, Everett. "To Talk of Many Things," *Musical America* (July 1962), 46.

Heyward, Dorothy (Hartzell). "Porgy's Goat," *Harper's Magazine* (Dec 1957), 37–41.

*Heyward, Dorothy & Du Bose. *Porgy* [play]. NY: Doubleday, Page, 1927.

*Heyward, Du Bose. *Porgy.* NY: Doran, 1925.

————. "Porgy and Bess Return on Wings of Song," in: Merle Armitage, ed, *George Gershwin.* NY: Longmans, Green, 1938; 34–42. Reprinted from *Stage Magazine* (Oct 1935), 25–8. Heyward discusses his collaboration with Gershwin on *Porgy and Bess.*

Hill, Richard S. "Music," *The Library of Congress Quarterly Journal of Current Acquisitions* (Nov 1953), 15–26. Brief mention (p. 15) of Mrs. Rose Gershwin's bequest of scores and sketches of orchestral works.

Hitchcock, Hugh Wiley. *Music in the United States: A Historical Introduction.* Englewood Cliffs, NJ: Prentice-Hall, 1969; 178, 187–8, 218–9, 252.

Hogarth, Basil. "Strange Case of George Gershwin," *The Chesterian* (May-June 1934), 130–6.

Howard, John Tasker. *Our American Music: A Comprehensive History from 1620 to the Present,* 4th ed. NY: Thomas Y. Crowell, 1965; 424–9, 797–8, *passim.* 1st ed, 1931.

————. "George Gershwin," in: Oscar Thompson, *The International Cyclopedia of Music and Musicians,* 4th ed. NY: Dodd, Mead, 1964; 785–6. 1st ed, 1937.

————. *Our Contemporary Composers.* NY: Thomas Y. Crowell, 1941.

————. *This Modern Music: A Guide for the Bewildered Listener.* NY: Thomas Crowell, 1942; 123, 185, 190–1.

————. "George Gershwin," in: David Ewen, ed, *The Book of Modern Composers,* 2nd ed rev & enlarged. NY: A. A. Knopf, 1950.

Howard, John Tasker, and George Kent Bellows. "George Gershwin Symbolizes the Growth of Jazz," in their *A Short History of Music in America.* NY: Thomas Y. Crowell, 1957; 246–50, *passim.*

Idelsohn, A. Z. *Thesaurus of Hebrew-Oriental Melodies,* 10 Vols. (I, Yemen; II, Babylon; III, Persia, Bokhara, Daghestan; IV, Oriental Sephards: V, Morocco; VI-VII, Germany, VIII-X, East-Europe). Berlin and Leipzig: Breitkopf and Härtel, 1914–32.

————. "Synagog Music Past and Present," *Central Conference of American Rabbis, Yearbook,* XXXIII (1923).

————. "The Distinctive Elements of Jewish Folk-Song," *Music Teachers' National Association, Proceedings.* (1924). Unnumbered pages.

————. "Musical Characteristics of East-European Jewish Folk-Song," *The Musical Quarterly* (October 1932), 634–45.

————. *Jewish Music in its Historical Development.* NY: Henry Holt, 1929.

————. *Jewish Liturgy and its Development.* NY: Sacred Music Press, 1956.

"Inside stuff—Music," *Variety* (Apr 4, 1956), 49. Concerning Gershwin's debt to Joseph Schillinger.

BIBLIOGRAPHY

"Ira Gershwin Donates $1,500 Annually to School Named for Brother George," *Variety* (Sep 23, 1964), 83. An announcement that Ira Gershwin would contribute that amount yearly, to be divided among ten gifted students at Brooklyn's George Gershwin Junior High School.

"Ira Gershwin Opposes Filming 'Porgy' Now," *Variety* (Feb 8, 1956), 1f.

"Iron Curtain 'Agents' $1,000,000 Pic Deal on Gershwin's 'Porgy,'" *Variety* (Mar 14, 1956), 1f.

Isaacs, Edith J. R. "See America First: Broadway in Review," *Theatre Arts Monthly* (Dec 1935), 888–902. Review of *Porgy and Bess*, pp 893–4.

Israel, Robert A. "Great Man of Music," *The Southwestern Musician* (Jan 1953), 13f.

Iturbi, Jose. "Gershwin Abroad," in: *Rhapsody in Blue: the Jubilant Story of George Gershwin and His Music*. Hollywood: Warner Bros, 1945; 9–10.

Jablonski, Edward. "Gershwin After 20 Years," *Hi-Fi Music at Home* (July-Aug 1956), 22–3, 52, 54, 56–8. An evaluation of the composer twenty years after his death; includes discography.

———. "Unlikely Corners," *The American Record Guide* (May 1957), 131. Includes a record review of the soundtrack from the film *Funny Face* (Verve MGV–15001).

———. "Unlikely Corners," *The American Record Guide* (Sep 1957), 34–5. Record reviews of Gershwin albums by Sarah Vaughan and Chris Connor.

———. "The American Musical," *Hi-Fi Music at Home* (Oct 1958), 43–55. Brief history of the American musical (see particularly pp. 47–8); includes Gershwin discography.

———. "An Almost Completely New Work: Gershwin's Own Suite from 'Porgy and Bess,'" *The American Record Guide* (Aug 1959), 848–9. Record review of the suite.

———. "Gershwin Plays Gershwin—Enjoy, Enjoy,"*The American Record Guide* (Jan 1962), 365. Review of a recording (Distinguished Records 107) of Gershwin at the piano, taken from piano rolls.

———. "Gershwin on Music," *Musical America* (July 1962), 32–5. Gershwin is quoted speaking about himself and his work.

———. "Photo by George Gershwin: A Portfolio of Originals," *The American Record Guide* (July 1962), 844–8. Some photos by Gershwin of friends and associates.

———. "Ira Gershwin—Reluctant Celebrity," *Listen* (Mar-Apr 1964), 14–5.

———. "George Gershwin," *Hi Fi/Stereo Review* (May 1967), 49–61.

*Jablonski, Edward, and Lawrence D. Stewart. *The Gershwin Years,* with an introduction by Carl Van Vechten. Garden City, NY: Doubleday, 1958. Revised edition in preparation.

Jacobi, Frederick. "The Future of Gershwin," *Modern Music* (Nov-Dec 1937), 3–7. A critical evaluation of the composer.

Jacques, Henry. "Deux oeuvres de George Gershwin," *Disques* (Feb. 1952), 111. Record reviews of *An American in Paris* and *Rhapsody in Blue*.

"Jazz Concerto," *The Outlook* (Dec 16, 1925), 582–3. About the *Concerto in F*.

"Jazzed Homesickness in Paris," *The Literary Digest* (Jan 5, 1929), 22–3.

Jessel, George. *This Way, Miss,* with a forward by William Saroyan. NY: Henry Holt, 1955. Contains a tribute to the composer.

Johnson, Harold Earle. *Symphony Hall, Boston.* Boston: Little, Brown, 1950; 126–7, 339, 405. Touches on Gershwin's *Second Rhapsody.*

Johnson, J. Rosamond. "Emancipator of American Idioms," in: Merle Armitage, ed, *George Gershwin.* NY: Longmans, Green, 1938; 65–71.

Jones, LeRoi. "Movie Review," *Jazz Review* (Nov 1959), 50–1. Critical comments about Samuel Goldwyn's movie *Porgy and Bess* and of the opera itself.

Jones, Max. "Gershwin Could Not Have Had a Finer Monument," *Melody Maker* (Oct 18, 1952), 3. On *Porgy and Bess.*

Kahn, Henry. "Backstage with Porgy and Bess," *Melody Maker* (Oct 30, 1954).

*Kahn, Otto H. "George Gershwin and American Youth," in: Merle Armitage, ed, *George Gershwin.* NY: Longmans, Green, 1938; 126–8. Reissued from *The Musical Courier* (Jan 3, 1929), 31.

*Kaufman, George S., and Morrie Ryskind. *Of Thee I Sing.* NY: A. A. Knopf, 1932.

*Kaufman, George S., and Morrie Ryskind. *Let 'em Eat Cake.* NY: A. A. Knopf, 1933.

Keller, Hans. "Rhythm: Gershwin and Stravinsky," *Score and I.M.A. Magazine* (June 1957), 19–31.

———. "Gershwin's Genius," *The Musical Times* (Nov 1962), 763–4.

———. "Truth and Music," *Music and Musicians* (Oct 1967), 16.

Kennedy, J. B. "Words and Music," *Collier's* (Sep 22, 1928), 13.

Kern, Jerome. "Tribute," in: Merle Armitage, ed, *George Gershwin.* NY: Longmans, Green, 1938; 120.

Kernochan, Marshall. "Notable Music: Gershwin's 'Second Rhapsody' and 'Robin Hood,' " *The Outlook and Independent* (Mar 1932), 196.

Kertesz, Istvan. " 'Porgy es Bess'—Gershwin operájának bemutatója az Erkel Színházban," *Muzsika* (Apr 1970) ,13–7.

Khatchaturian, Aram. "George Gershwin," *Uj zenei szemle* (Dec 1955), 32–3.

Kilenyi, Edward, Sr. "George Gershwin As I Knew Him," *Etude* (Oct 1950), 11–2, 64. Reminiscences by one of Gershwin's teachers.

———. *Gershwiniana: Recollections and Reminiscences of Times Spent with My Student George Gershwin.* Typescript: n.p. 1962–63. A partisan account of Gershwin's studies with the author.

Kirby, Fred. " 'Do It Again' Is Excellent Gershwin—But Disappoints," *Billboard* (Mar 6, 1971), 28.

Knight, Arthur. "Catfish Row in Todd-AO," *The Saturday Review* (July 4, 1959), 24–5. Review of the motion picture *Porgy and Bess.*

———. "Musicals à la Mode," *The Saturday Review* (Apr 13, 1957), 26.

Kolodin, Irving. "*Porgy and Bess;* American Opera in the Theatre," *Theatre Arts Monthly* (Nov 1935), 853–65.

———. "Charleston Revisited," *Saturday Review of Literature* (Sep 29, 1951), 50–1. A record review of *Porgy and Bess.*

———. "Music to My Ears: 'Porgy,' " *Saturday Review of Literature* (Mar 28, 1953), 27–8. About *Porgy and Bess.*

———. "Paradox in Blue," *The Saturday Review* (Feb 25, 1956), 37, 60–1.

BIBLIOGRAPHY

————. "Catfish Row and Wilshire," *The Saturday Review* (June 13, 1959), 52. About the motion picture *Porgy and Bess*.

————. "Mid-Month Recordings: From George to George with Love," *The Saturday Review* (Oct 17, 1959), 78–9. Record review of songs.

————. "The Gershwins' Two Astaires," *The Saturday Review* (Oct 30, 1971), 70.

Kostelanetz, André. "George Gershwin—An American Composer," *Music Clubs Magazine* (May 1952), 4f.

*Koussevitsky, Serge. "Man and Musician," in: Merle Armitage, ed, *George Gershwin*. NY: Longmans, Green, 1938; 113–4.

Kovalyer, U. "The Russian Critic," *The Saturday Review* (Jan 14, 1956), 38. About *Porgy and Bess* in Leningrad.

Kramer, A. Walter. "I Do Not Think Jazz 'Belongs,' " *Singing* (Sep 1926), 13–4. Alleges Gershwin did not orchestrate the *Concerto in F*.

Kutner, Nanette. "Portrait in Our Time," in: Merle Armitage, ed, *George Gershwin*. NY: Longmans, Green, 1938; 235–47.

Kuznetsova, Irina. "Pyat'i odna," *Sovetskaya Muzyka* (Apr 1968), 46–51. About *Porgy and Bess*.

Kydrýnski, Lucjan. *Gershwin*, 2nd ed. Krakow: Polskie Wydawnictwo Muzyczne, 1967. 1st ed, 1962. A popular biography in Polish.

La Prade, Ernest. "Program Notes," *Symphony Society Bulletin* (Dec 2, 1925). Comments on *Concerto in F*.

Lancaster, Albert. "George Gershwin," *Keynote* (Autumn 1946), 21–2.

Langley, Allan Lincoln. "The Gershwin Myth," *The American Spectator* (Dec 1932), 1–2.

"Larry Adler to Unveil Gershwin String Quartet at Edinburgh Festival," *Variety* (June 5, 1963), 43. Announcement of the projected premiere of *Lullaby* (1919), as adapted by Adler.

Lawrence, Gertrude. *A Star Danced*. Garden City, NY: Doubleday, Doran, 1945. Some reminiscences about Gershwin.

Lawton, Dorothy. "Reading About Gershwin," in: *Rhapsody in Blue; the Jubilant Story of George Gershwin and His Music*. Hollywood: Warner Bros, 1945; 18.

Levant, Oscar. "Variations on a Gershwin Theme," *Town and Country* (Nov 1939), 58–61, 83–4. Typically Levant; witty and anecdotal.

————. "My Life; Or the Story of George Gershwin," in his: *A Smattering of Ignorance*. NY: Doubleday, Doran, 1940; 147–210. Levant's chapter on Gershwin is humorous and full of insight.

Levine, Henry. "Gershwin, Handy and the Blues," *Clavier* (Oct 1970), 10–20. Discusses various aspects of *Rhapsody in Blue*, including rhythm and piano fingering.

Levine, Irving R. "U.S.S.R. May Cite 'Porgy' as Evidence There's No Iron Curtain for Arts," *Variety* (Dec 1955), 1f.

Lewine, Richard. "An American in Paris," *Film Music* (Nov-Dec 1951), 14–6.

Leydi, Roberto. "George Gershwin e it 'Porgy and Bess,' " *Il Diapason* (Jan 1955), 15–23.

"L[ibrary] of C[ongress] Gets George Gershwin Manuscripts," *Billboard* (Mar 7, 1953), 18.

Lieberson, Goddard. *The Columbia Book of Musical Masterworks,* introduction by Edward Wallerstein. NY: Allen, Towne & Heath, 1947. Program notes for *An American in Paris, Concerto in F, Porgy and Bess,* and *Rhapsody in Blue;* formerly appeared in Columbia Masterwork albums.

Liebling, Leonard. "The George I Knew," in: Merle Armitage, ed, *George Gershwin.* NY: Longmans, Green, 1938; 123–5.

Lipsky, Leon. "George Gershwin, Jazz Glorified," *The American Hebrew* (Nov 20, 1925), 59, 67.

List, Kurt. "George Gershwin's Music," *Commentary* (Dec 1945), 27–34. A critical assessment of the composer's work.

"The Live Art of Music," *The Outlook* (Jan 13, 1926), 47–8.

Longolius, Christian. *George Gershwin.* Berlin/Halensee: Max Hesse Verlag, 1959.

Lucraft, Howard. "Behind Music USA," *Music USA* (Mar 1959), 9. Concerning the motion picture *Porgy and Bess.*

Lüttwitz, Heinrich von. "Armeleutedramen—In Schwarz und Weiss," *Musica* (Jan 1956), 82–3. Review of *Porgy and Bess* at Düsseldorf.

———. "Ein Musical von Gershwin," *Musica* (Nov-Dec 1963), 281–2. About two performances of *Girl Crazy* at Düsseldorf.

———. "Gelsenkirchen: 'Porgy and Bess' Ohne Negerlarven," *Neue Zeitschrift für Musik* (Aug 1971), 439–41.

Lyons, Leonard. "New York Is a Great Place to Be . . . ," *The Saturday Review* (Oct 18, 1958), 26, 46–7. (Answered by Ira Gershwin, ". . . But I Wouldn't Want to Live There.")

Maier, Guy. "Adventures of a Piano Teacher," *Etude* (Nov 1951), 26. Discusses publication of the *Rhapsody in Blue* for solo piano from pianist's standpoint.

Malipiero, Riccardo. "Porgy and Bess," *La Biennale di Venezia* (22, 1954), 36–8.

Malmberg, Helge. "George Gershwin," in: *Sohlmans Musiklexicon,* 4 vols (Stockholm: Sohlmans Förlag, 1951–52), II, 542–3.

Mamoulian, Rouben. "I Remember," in: Merle Armitage, ed, *George Gershwin.* NY: Longmans, Green, 1938; 47–57. Reminiscences about Gershwin by the director of the first production of *Porgy and Bess.*

"The Man I Love," *The New Republic* (July 21, 1937), 203f.

Marek, George. "Rapsody in Blue Twenty-Five Years After," *Good Housekeeping* (Feb 1949), 4f.

"Master of Jazz," *The Commonweal* (July 23, 1937), 316.

Mellers, Wilfrid. "Gershwin's Achievements," *The Monthly Musical Record* (Jan 1953), 13–6. Comments on Gershwin's flair for writing "commercial" music.

———. "Music, Theatre, and Commerce; a Note on Gershwin, Menotti and Marc Blitzstein," *The Score and I.M.A. Magazine* (June 1955), 70–1.

———. *Music in a New Found Land.* NY: A. A. Knopf, 1965. 1st ed, London: Barrie & Rockliff, 1964. Gives much attention to Gershwin's music.

Merman, Ethel. *Who Could Ask For Anything More,* as told to Pete Martin. NY: Doubleday, 1955. Includes a story of her audition with Gershwin for a role in *Girl Crazy* of 1930.

"Miami U's Gershwin Fest to Revue One-Act Opera '135th Street' & Other Works," *Variety* (Oct 14, 1970), 58. Announcement of a Gershwin festival.

Mila, Massimo. "Lettera da Venezia: 'Porgy and Bess' di Gershwin," *La Rassegna Musicale* (Oct-Dec 1954), 349–51.

Mingotti, Antonio. *Gershwin: Eine Bildbiographie.* Munich: Kindler, 1958. A pictorial biography.

Mitchell, Donald. "Concerts and Opera: (Some First Performances)," *The Musical Times* (July 1956), 374–5. Review of *Lady, Be Good.*

Montagu, George. "Musical Survey," *London Musical Events* (Dec 1952), 37–8. About *Porgy and Bess.*

Montgomery, Michael. "George Gershwin Piano-Rollography," *Record Research* (Mar-Apr 1962), 3–4. A compilation of 114 record rolls Gershwin made for different labels under various pseudonyms.

Montsalvatge, Xavier de. "Los Conciertos en Barcelona," *Musica* (Madrid) (Jan-Mar 1955), 107–8. Reviews *Porgy and Bess.*

Moor, Paul. " 'Porgy' Comes to Germany," *High Fidelity/Musical America* (Aug 1970), Sec II, 28–9.

Morgan, Alfred Lindsay. "New Musical Heights in Radio," *Etude* (Dec 1942), 806. About *Rhapsody in Blue.*

———. "A Famous Radio Debut," *Etude* (Apr 1944), 202, 252. Cites Arturo Toscanini's performance of *Concerto in F* with the NBC Symphony Orchestra, with Oscar Levant as soloist.

Morgenstern, Sam, ed. "George Gershwin, 1898–1937," in his: *Composers on Music: An Anthology of Composers' Writings from Palestrina to Copland.* NY: Pantheon, 1956; 510–3.

"The Most Potent Musical Forces of the First Half of the Twentieth Century," *Etude* (Jan 1951), 9–11, 47–8. Based on an opinion poll of prominent performers and composers, Gershwin ranks among the top musicians selected.

"Muenchen," *Oper und Konzert* (Apr 1971), 19–20. Review of *Porgy and Bess* in Munich.

Museum of the City of New York. *A Catalogue of the Exhibition Gershwin: George the Music, Ira the Words.* NY: Museum of the City of New York, 1968. Exhibition catalogue, May 6–Sep 2, 1968; lists memorabilia, manuscripts, letters, drawings, scenic designs, etc.

"—Music by Gershwin," *Music Clubs Magazine* (Feb 1968), 14–5.

"Music by Slide Rule," *Newsweek* (Sep 25, 1944), 80–2. Discusses Gershwin's studies with Schillinger.

"The New Etude Gallery of Musical Celebrities." *Etude* (Mar 1929), 193–4. Portrait and brief biography of Gershwin.

"New Gershwin Tunes Featured in Movie," *Down Beat* (Apr 23, 1964), 14–5. About three posthumous Gershwin songs in Billy Wilder's movie *Kiss Me Stupid.*

Newell, George. "George Gershwin and Jazz," *The Outlook* (Feb 29, 1928), 342–3, 351.

Nichols, Beverley. "George Gershwin," in: Merle Armitage, ed, *George Gershwin.* NY: Longmans, Green, 1938; 231–4. Reprinted from *Are They the Same at Home.* NY: Doubleday, Doran, 1927.

Niles, Abbe. "The Ewe Lamb of Widow Jazz," *The New Republic* (Dec 29, 1926), 164–6.

———. "A Note on Gershwin," *The Nation* (Feb 13, 1929), 193–4.

"No Credit," *Musical America* 8 (July 1959), 10. No singers given credit for dubbed voices in the film version of *Porgy and Bess.*

*Noguchi, Isamu. "Portrait," in Merle Armitage, ed, *George Gershwin*. NY: Longmans, Green, 1938; 209–10.

O'Connell, Charles. *The Victor Book of Overtures, Tone Poems, and Other Orchestral Works*. NY: Simon & Schuster, 1950.

"Odyssey with Gershwin," *Newsweek* (Jan 9, 1956), 43–4. Review of *Porgy and Bess.*

"Oh, Kay!" *Variety* (May 4, 1960), 60. Review of an off-Broadway production of the musical.

O'Hara, John. "An American in Memoriam," *Newsweek* (July 15, 1940), 34. Tribute to Gershwin.

*Osgood, Henry Osborne. *So This Is Jazz*. Boston: Little, Brown, 1926. Excellent source of information about the genesis and premiere of *Concerto in F* and *Rhaposdy in Blue.*

Parmenter, Ross. "'Porgy' Group Ends Its Recital Series," *The New York Times* (Aug 31, 1953), 22.

Pasi, Mario. *George Gershwin*. Parma: Guanda, 1958. Czech translation as: *George Gershwin*. Prague: Statni hudebni vyd, 1964.

Payne, Robert. *Gershwin*. NY: Pyramid Books, 1960. Emphasizes the Jewish quality in Gershwin's music; not always convincing.

Pironte, Alberto. "[Review of Rene Chalupt's] George Gershwin, le Musicien de la 'Rhapsody in Bleu,' " *La Rassegna Musicale* (Apr 1951), 178–9.

"Plush Gershwin Festival Set for '53 Longhair Tour with Blessing of Family," *Variety* (Jan 23, 1952), 1f. Announcement of an American tour by the Gershwin Concert Orchestra.

Pollak, Robert. "Gershwin," *The Magazine of Art* (Sep 1937), 531, 588. Claims that Gershwin is not an American Mozart.

Pool, Rosey E. *Een Nieuw lied voor America; het leven van George Gershwin (1838–1937)*. Amsterdam: Tilburg-Nederlands Boekhus, 1951.

———. "Een nieuw lied voor Amerika," *Mens en Melodie* (Jan 1953), 28.

Popov, I. "Russian Report: 'Porgy and Bess,' " *Musical Courier* (Mar 1, 1956). 7f.

"Porgy and Bess," *Opera* (Dec 1952), 710–18.

"Porgy and Bess," *Musica* [Madrid] (Jan-June 1953), 148–9.

"Porgy and Bess," *Mens en Melodie* (July 1955), 223–4.

"Porgy and Bess," *Music USA* (July 1959), 35.

"Porgy and Bess; Bethlehems nyinspelning," *Orkester Journal* (July-Aug 1957), 42–3.

"Porgy and Bess Hailed in Moscow," *Musical America* (Jan 15, 1956), 29.

" 'Porgy and Bess' in Moscow," *Etude* (Mar 1956), 14–5.

" 'Porgy and Bess' on Tour," *Theatre Arts* (Nov 1943), 677–8.

" 'Porgy and Bess' Praised in Spain," *The New York Times* (Feb 8, 1955), 19.

"Porgy and Bess Touring Europe," *Musical America* (Feb 15, 1956), 208.

"Porgy and Bess Tours Behind Iron Curtain," *Musical Courier* (Jan 15, 1955), 33.

" 'Porgy' Going Ahead with Russian Trip Plans Despite Lack of U.S. Coin Aid," *Variety* (Oct 26, 1955), 55f.

" 'Porgy' in Leningrad," *Time* (Jan 9, 1956), 51.

"Porgy Into Opera," *Time* (Sep 30, 1935), 49–50.

"Porgy Orgy," *Time* (Oct 20, 1952), 48.

"Porgy Orgy (contd.)," *Time* (Mar 7, 1955), 83.

" 'Porgy': the Play that Set a Pattern," *Theatre Arts* (Oct 1955), 33–64. Complete text, with numerous illustrations.

" ' Porgy Pix on Black Market as Musical Wows Vienna," *Variety* (Sep 17, 1952), 2f.

" 'Porgy' to TV for 112G; Two-Parter," *Variety* (Dec 26, 1956), 1f.

" 'Porgy' Trip to the USSR Delays 'Blues'; Will Tour Aussie and Later China," *Variety* (Sep 7, 1955), 65.

"Posthumous Exhibit Shows that Gershwin Knew Harmony on Canvas Also," *Newsweek* (Dec 20, 1937), 28. Comments on a one-man show of Gershwin's paintings at the Marie Harriman Gallery in New York.

Prawy, Marcel. "Made in U.S.A.," *Opera News* (Dec 15, 1952), 12–3. *Porgy and Bess* triumphs in Vienna.

"Proben zu Gershwins 'Porgy and Bess' in der Berliner Komischen Oper," *Opernwelt* (Mar 1970), 8. Six photographs.

Pryor, Thomas M. "Hollywood Dossier: 'Porgy and Bess' Heads for Films— Addenda," *The New York Times* (May 12, 1957), Sec II, 5.

———. "Hollywood 'Porgy' Strife: Switch of Directors of Folk Opera Makes 'the Livin' a Little Uneasy—Anamorphic Lenses Unveiled." *The New York Times* (Aug 3, 1958), Sec II, 5.

Pugliaro, Maria Vittoria. *Rapsodia in blue; l'arte e l'amore nella vita di George Gershwin*. Turin: S.A.S. 1952.

Raymond, Jack. "Berlin Acclaims Guests from Catfish Row," *The New York Times* (Sep 28, 1952), Sec II, 1,3. Review of *Porgy and Bess*.

———. " 'Porgy' Delights Belgrade Crowd," *The New York Times* (Dec 17, 1954), 36.

Reis, Clare. "George Gershwin," in her: *Composers in America: Biographical Sketches of Living Composers, with a Record of Their Works, 1912–1937*. NY: Macmillan, 1938; 112.

"Revive 'Porgy & Bess' in Estonia; Producer Studied African Lore," *Variety* (Feb 15, 1967), 22.

Reyna, Ferdinando. "Adesso anche a Parigi," *La Scala* No. 42 (May 1953), 38–42.

"Rhapsody in Blue," Screenplay by Howard Koch and Elliott Paul, Based on the Original Screen Story by Sonya Levien. Producer: Jesse L. Lasky. Hollywood, Calif: Warner Bros. Pictures, 1945. Shooting script of movie; includes cast.

"Rhapsody in Blue," *The New York Times Magazine* (June 3, 1945), 24–5.

"Rhapsody in Blue," *Musical Opinion* (June 1957), 537. Discusses the miniature score of Grofé's arrangement of the *Rhapsody* for symphony orchestra, published in England by Chappell.

"Rhapsody in Blue: Radio Broadcast," *Scholastic* (Apr 26, 1948), 14–6.

Rhapsody in Blue; The Jubilant Story of George Gershwin and His Music.

Hollywood: Warner Bros, 1945. A promotional pamphlet containing statements by Marion Bauer, Frank Crowninshield, Walter Damrosch, José Iturbi, Dorothy Lawton, Arthur Rodzinski, Mark A. Schubart, Deems Taylor, and Paul Whiteman.

Robinson, Edward. "George Gershwin: a Punster Turned Poet," *The Fortnightly Musical Revue* (Oct 31, 1928), 3–4.

Rodzinski, Artur. "George Gershwin," in: *Rhapsody in Blue; the Jubilant Story of Gershwin and His Music*. Hollywood: Warner Bros, 1945; 15.

Rolontz, Robert. "Gershwin Spec Misses Its Mark," *Billboard Music Week* (Jan 23, 1961), 8.

Rosenfeld, Paul. "No Chabrier," *The New Republic* (Jan 4, 1933), 217–8. Caustic assessment of Gershwin.

———. "Gershwin," in his: *Discoveries of a Music Critic*. NY: Harcourt, Brace, 1936; 264–72, 384. Critical evaluation of Gershwin's music.

Rosenfield, John. "A New 'Porgy' in Dallas," *The Saturday Review of Literature* (June 28, 1952), 44.

Rublowsky, John. "Gershwin and Ives: The Triumph of the Popular Spirit," in his: *Music in America*. NY: Macmillan, 1967; 146–55.

———. *Popular Music*. NY: Basic Books, 1967, 56–7, 150.

Rushmore, Robert. *The Life of George Gershwin*. NY: Crowell-Collier, 1966. A biography for young people, grades 7–9.

Sabin, Robert. "Current Production of 'Porgy and Bess' Justifies Its Success Here and Abroad," *Musical America* (Apr 15, 1953), 33.

Sablosky, Irving. *American Music*. Chicago: University of Chicago Press, 1969. 149–51, 154–5.

Saerchinger, Césare. "Jazz," *Musikblätter des Anbruch: Monatsschrift für moderne Musik* (Apr 1925), 205–10. The author discusses Paul Whiteman's contributions to jazz with special attention to *Rhapsody in Blue*.

Sandow, Hyman. "Gershwin to Write New Rhapsody," *Musical America* (Feb. 18, 1928), 5. Discusses Gershwin's plan to write *An American in Paris*.

———. "Gershwin Presents a New Work," *Musical America* (Aug 18, 1928), 5, 12. Gives information about *An American in Paris* prior to the premiere.

Sargeant, Winthrop. "Musical Events," *The New Yorker* (Apr 14, 1962), 174–6. Review of *Porgy and Bess*.

Schaefer, Hansjürgen. "*Porgy und Bess* in der Komischen Oper Berlin," *Musik und Gesellschaft* (May 1970), 325–8.

Schaefer, Theodore. "Gershwin Opera Heard in Capital," *Musical America* (Nov 15, 1952), 23.

Schillinger, Frances. *Joseph Schillinger: A Memoir by His Wife*. NY: Greenberg, 1949. Touches on Gershwin's study with her husband.

Schillinger, Joseph. *Kaleidophone*. NY: N. Witmark, 1940. Discusses Gershwin in his introduction to the book.

Schipke, Brigitte. *George Gershwin und die Welt seiner Musik*. Freiburg: Drei Ringe Musikverlag, 1955.

Schneerson, Grigoriy M. "Preface," in: *Porgy and Bess* (Moscow: State Publishers Music, 1965). Preface to a Russian edition of the score.

*Schoenberg, Arnold. "George Gershwin," in: Merle Armitage, ed, *George

Gershwin. NY: Longmans, Green, 1938; 97–8. Also in: Sam Morgenstern, ed, *Composers of Music: An Anthology of Composers' Writings from Palestrina to Copland.* NY: Pantheon, 1956; 384–6. Memorial tribute to Gershwin.

———. "A Self-Analysis," *Musical America* (Feb 1953), 14, 172. Includes Gershwin's portrait of Schoenberg.

Schoorl, Bob. *George Gershwin.* Amsterdam: A. J. G. Strengholt, 1952.

Schroeder, Jaun German. "Porgy and Bess: Musica de George Gershwin, Libreto du Bose Heyward," *Teatro; revista internacional de la escena* No. 15 (Mar-Apr 1955), 24–8.

Schubart, Mark A. "George Gershwin—Song Writer," in: *Rhapsody in Blue; the Jubilant Story of George Gershwin and His Music.* Hollywood: Warner Bros, 1945; 16.

Schumach, Murray. "Hollywood Recall: Ira Gershwin Provides Notes for 'Porgy,' " *The New York Times* (June 21, 1959), Sec II, 7.

Schwartz, Charles M. *Elements of Jewish Music in Gershwin's Melody,* M. A. Thesis: New York University, 1965. Examples given of Jewish style features in Gershwin's work.

———. *The Life and Orchestral Works of George Gershwin.* Ph.D. Dissertation: New York University, 1969. UM. 70–3105. *Dissertation Abstracts* XXX/9 (Mar 1970), 3977A.

———. "Gershwin," *The Dictionary of Contemporary Music.* NY: E. P. Dutton, 1973 (in preparation).

———."George Gershwin: A Bibliography," *Bibliographies in American Music.* The College Music Society Series. Detroit: Information Coordinators, 1973 (in preparation).

Schwarz, Boris. *Music and Musical Life in Soviet Russia, 1917–1970.* NY: W. W. Norton; London: Barrie & Jenkins, 1972; 188, 293, 357, 361, 443, 464.

Schwinger, Eckart. "Porgy and Bess," *Musica* (Mar-Apr 1970), 148–9. Review of a Berlin performance.

Schwinger, Wolfram. "Notizen über Gershwin," *Musik und Gesellschaft* (May 1960), 302–4.

———. *Er komponierte Amerika; George Gershwin, Mensch und Werk.* Berlin: Buchverlag Der Morgen, 1960.

Scully, Frank. "Scully's Scrapbook," *Variety* (Feb 15, 1956), 73. Claims that *Porgy and Bess* is a greater popular success than *The Marriage of Figaro.*

Seaman, Julian. *Great Orchestral Music: A Treasury of Program Notes.* NY: Rinehart, 1960. *(The Field of Music Series,* Vol 5) Program notes for *An American in Paris, Concerto in F,* and *Rhapsody in Blue;* cites numerous performances of Gershwin works.

Selden-Goth, Gisella. "Florence," *Musical Courier* (May 1955), 31. Review of *Porgy and Bess.*

Seldes, Gilbert. *The Seven Lively Arts.* NY: Harper, 1924. Discusses Gershwin favorably.

———. "The Gershwin Case," in: Merle Armitage, ed, *George Gershwin.* NY: Longmans, Green, 1938; 129–34. Reprinted from *Esquire* (Oct 1934).

Sendrey, Albert Heink. "Tennis Game," in: Merle Armitage, ed, *George Gershwin.* NY: Longmans, Green, 1938; 102–12.

Shaw, Arnold. "Gershwin, Arlen and the Blues," *Billboard* (June 24, 1967), supplement, 68–9.

Shawe-Taylor, Desmond. "Three Operas," *The New Statesman and Nation* (Oct 18, 1952), 448. Includes a review of *Porgy and Bess*.

———. "A Mini-Success," *American Musical Digest* I/5 (1970), 12. Reprinted from the *London Sunday Times* (Jan 4, 1970).

Siegmeister, Elie, ed. *The Music Lover's Handbook*. NY: William Morrow, 1943; 728–9, 753–7, *passim*.

Slonimsky, Nicolas. *Lexicon of Musical Invective*. NY: Coleman-Ross, 1953; 105. Includes derogatory reviews of *Concerto in F, Porgy and Bess,* and *Rhapsody in Blue*.

———. "Musical Oddities," *Etude* (Apr 1955). 4–5. Includes an anecdote about Gershwin and Ravel.

———. *Music Since 1900*. 4th ed. NY: Charles Scribner's 1971; 111, 294, 384–5, 395, 404, 422–3, 439, 462, 484, 487, 512, 515, 535, 541, 543, 549–50, 552, 558, 573, 578, 610, 651, 660, 699, 801, 1002, 1433, 1476, 1497. 1st, 2nd & 3rd ed published by Coleman-Ross. Documents numerous first performances of Gershwin works and quotes from several reviews.

———. *Bakers' Biographical Dictionary*, 5th ed. NY: G. Schirmer, 1968; 552–3. Excellent dictionary article.

Smith, Cecil M. *Musical Comedy in America*. NY: Theatre Arts Books, 1950. Discusses Gershwin's major musical comedies.

Smolian, Steven. *A Handbook of Film, Theatre, and Television Music on Record, 1948–1969*. NY: The Record Undertaker, 1970. Provides recording information about *An American in Paris, Funny Face, Girl Crazy, Of Thee I Sing, Oh, Kay* and *Porgy and Bess*.

Soria, Dorle J. "People and Places: Memorabilia to Go to Museum of the City of New York," *High Fidelity/Musical America* (Sep 1967), MA–5.

Spaeth, Sigmund, "Our New Folk-Music," in his: *They Still Sing of Love*. NY: Horace Liveright, 1929; 173–8. Speaks of Gershwin's role in infusing serious music with jazz.

———. "Two Contemporary Americans: Gershwin and Hadley," *Scholastic* (Apr 30, 1938), 23.

———. *A Guide to Great Orchestral Music*. NY: Modern Library, 1943. Program notes for *Concerto in F, Rhapsody in Blue,* and *Second Rhapsody*.

———. *A History of Popular Music in America*. NY: Random House, 1948. Discusses Gershwin songs and musical comedies.

———. "Theatre on the Disk," *Theatre Arts* (June 1954), 10.

Spingel, Hans Otto. "Die Leute von der Catfish Row," *Opernwelt* (Apr 1970), 14–5. Review of *Porgy and Bess* at Berlin Komische Oper, Jan 24, 1970.

Spitalny, Evelyn. "First Gershwin Festival Rocks Miami U. Campus with Music, not Mayhem," *Variety* (Nov 11, 1970), 46.

Stambler, Irwin. *Encyclopedia of Popular Music*. NY: St. Martin's Press, 1965; 87–90, 185, *passim*.

Steinert, Alexander. "Porgy and Bess and Gershwin," in: Merle Armitage, ed, *George Gershwin*. NY: Longmans, Green, 1938; 43–6.

BIBLIOGRAPHY

Stewart, Ollie. "American Opera Conquers Europe," *Theatre Arts* (Oct 1955), 30–2, 93–4.

"Stop the *Rhapsody,* Mab Told," *Down Beat* (Apr 8, 1949), 1. Discusses legal action by Gershwin's publisher (Harms) to prevent playing of an "unauthorized" arrangement of *Rhapsody in Blue* by Charlie Barnet's band.

Stravinsky, Igor, and Robert Craft. "Some Composers: by Igor Stravinsky with Robert Craft," *Musical America* (June 1962), 6, 8. Stravinsky discusses his impressions of Gershwin.

———. *Dialogues and a Diary.* Garden City, NY: Doubleday, 1963. Includes Stravinsky's comments in *Musical America* (June 1962).

"Student Production of 'Porgy and Bess,'" *USSR* (June 1961), 60–1. About the Russian production of *Porgy and Bess.*

Sutcliffe, James Helme. "East Berlin," *Opera News* (Mar 14, 1970), 32–4. Review of *Porgy and Bess.*

———. "West Berlin," *Opera* (June 1971), 535–7. Review of *Porgy and Bess.*

Sutton, Horace. "From Catfish Row to the Kremlin," *The Saturday Review* (Jan 14, 1956), 37–8. Review of *Porgy and Bess.*

Swift, Kay. *Who Could Ask for Anything More?,* illustrated by Julian Brazelton. NY: Simon & Schuster, 1943.

———. "Gershwin and the Universal Touch," *Music of the West Magazine* (Oct 1959), 7, 24. Comments favorably on Gershwin and *Porgy and Bess.*

"Talented Composer," *News-Week* (Oct 12, 1925), 22.

Tamussino, Ursula. "Gershwin Triumphiert über Mozart," *Phono: Internationale Schallplatten-Zeitschrift* (Mar-Apr 1965), 41f. About *Porgy and Bess.*

Taubman, Howard. "Why Gershwin's Tunes Live On: His Gift Was That Out of Popular Themes He Could Arrive at Something Memorable," *The New York Times* (Sep 28, 1952), Magazine Section-Sunday Edition, 20.

———. "After 20 Years: Gershwin Remains a Gifted Composer Who Cultivated a Specific Garden," *The New York Times* (July 7, 1957), Sec II, 7. Tribute to Gershwin twenty years after his death.

Taylor, Deems. *"An American in Paris,"* *Philharmonic-Symphony Society of New York Program* (Dec 13, 1928). Gives the program for the tone poem.

———. "Godfather to Polymnia," in his: *Of Men and Music.* NY: Simon & Schuster, 1937; 144–53. Primarily about Walter Damrosch; includes remarks about Damrosch's influence on Gershwin.

———. "Music and the Flag," in his: *Of Men and Music.* NY: Simon & Schuster, 1937; 123–30. Discusses the use of "national" style features, including jazz, in serious music; cites Gershwin.

———. "Gershwin as Pioneer," in: *Rhapsody in Blue; the Jubilant Story of George Gershwin and His Music.* Hollywood: Warner Bros, 1945; 13–4.

Taylor, Erma. "George Gershwin—A Lament," in: Merle Armitage, ed, *George Gershwin.* NY: Longmans, Green, 1938; 178–92. Reprinted from *Jones' Magazine* (Nov 1937).

Teichmann, Howard. *George S. Kaufman: An Intimate Portrait.* NY: Atheneum, 1972. Contains a number of humorous anecdotes relating to Kaufman's association with Gershwin.

Terry, Walter. "World of Dance: 'G[eorge] B[alanchine] Boo-Boo,'" *The Satur-*

day Review (Mar 7, 1970), 41. Review of Who Cares?, Balanchine-Gershwin ballet.

Teuteberg, Karin. "Gelsenkirchen," Oper und Konzert (Nov 1970), 9. About Porgy and Bess.

Thomas, Ernst. "America lebt in Strassen: Gershwin's 'Porgy and Bess' in Frankfurt," Neue Zeitschrift für Musik (Feb 1956), 90.

Thompson, Oscar. The International Cyclopedia of Music and Musicians, 9th ed. NY: Dodd, Mead, 1964, 785–6. (Article by John Tasker Howard.)

Thomson, Virgil. "George Gershwin," Modern Music (Nov-Dec 1935), 13–9. Critical comments on Porgy and Bess.

————. "Porgy in Maplewood," in his: The Musical Scene. NY: A. A. Knopf, 1945; 167–9. Reissue of a New York Herald Tribune review (Oct 19, 1941) of the Maplewood, N.J., revival of Porgy and Bess.

————. "It's About Time," in his: The Musical Scene. NY: A. A. Knopf, 1945; 17–9. Reissue of a New York Herald Tribune review (Nov 2, 1942) of the NBC Symphony Orchestra under Toscanini performing Rhapsody in Blue, with Earl Wild and Benny Goodman as soloists.

————. "Landscape with Music," in his: The Musical Scene. NY: A. A. Knopf, 1945; 25–8. Reissue of a New York Herald Tribune review (July 11, 1943) of a Hollywood Bowl performance of Rhapsody in Blue performed by Paul Whiteman, with Ray Turner as pianist.

————. "Gershwin Black and Blue," in his: The Art of Judging Music. NY: A. A. Knopf, 1948; 55–6. Reissue of a New York Herald Tribune review (Apr 19, 1946) of Rodzinski conducting the New York Philharmonic-Symphony Orchestra in performances of An American in Paris, Concerto in F, excerpts from Porgy and Bess, and Rhapsody in Blue, with Oscar Levant as soloist.

————. "Expert and Original," in his: Music Right and Left. NY: Henry Holt, 1951; 14–6. Reissue of a New York Herald Tribune review (Mar 9, 1950) of the St. Louis Symphony Orchestra concert. Manuel Rosenthal's Magic Manhattan is compared to Gershwin's An American in Paris.

————. "English Landscape," in his: Music Right and Left. NY: Henry Holt, 1951; 111–2. Reissue of a New York Herald Tribune review of Stokowski conducting the New York Philharmonic-Symphony Orchestra in a performance of the Concerto in F, with Byron Janis as pianist.

————. Virgil Thomson. NY: A. A. Knopf, 1967; 151, 240, 242, 279, 405. Numerous passing references to Gershwin.

————. American Music Since 1910, with an introduction by Nicolas Nabokov. NY: Holt, Rinehart & Winston, 1971; 62, 63, 146, passim. Numerous passing references to Gershwin.

Tippett, Michael. "The American Tradition," American Musical Digest (Oct 1969), 21. Abridged from The Listener (June 5, 1969), 804–5.

Todd, Arthur. "Theatre on the Disk: George Gershwin—American Rhapsodist," Theatre Arts (July 1952), 10, 93. Includes a discography.

"Toscanini, All-American," Newsweek XX/19 (Nov 9, 1942), 78. About Arturo Toscanini performing the Rhapsody in Blue on radio.

"Transition," News-Week (July 17, 1937), 20. Obituary.

Traube, Leonard. "Charleston Gets Itself Plenty of Somethin' in Bow of 'Porgy and Bess,'" *Variety* (July 1, 1970), 1f.

"Trunkful of Tunes," *Newsweek* (Mar 2, 1964), 48. Discusses unpublished tunes that Gershwin left behind.

"TV Packagers Want Gershwin Musical Rights," *Billboard* (Mar 31, 1951), 17.

"Twenty Years After," *The New Yorker* (May 17, 1952), 26–7. About Ira Gershwin.

"The Twenty-Fifth Anniversary of the Premiere Performance," *Southwestern Musician* (Apr 1949), 31f. About the *Rhapsody in Blue*.

Ulrich, Homer. *Symphonic Music: Its Evolution Since the Renaissance.* NY: Columbia University Press, 1952; 321–2. Brief general remarks on *An American in Paris, Concerto in F* and *Rhapsody in Blue*.

"Unpublished Gershwin Songs to be Released," *Variety* (Feb 19, 1964), 51. Claims that approximately fifty unpublished Gershwin tunes would be released.

Untermeyer, Louis. *Makers of the Modern World.* NY: Simon & Schuster, 1955. Considers Gershwin to be one of-the four most important composers of the past century.

Vallee, Rudy. "Troubadour's Tribute," in: Merle Armitage, ed, *George Gershwin.* NY: Longmans, Green, 1938; 135–6.

Van Vechten, Carl. "George Gershwin: An American Composer Who Is Writing Notable Music in the Jazz Idiom," *Vanity Fair* (Mar 1925), 40, 78, 84. Discusses Eva Gauthier's jazz concert and *Rhapsody in Blue*.

*———. "Introduction," in: Edward Jablonski and Lawrence D. Stewart, *The Gershwin Years.* Garden City, NY: Doubleday, 1958; 21–6.

Veinus, Abraham. *The Concerto.* NY: Dover, 1964; 289–91. Reprint of work first published by Doubleday, Doran, 1945. Discusses the *Concerto in F* and *Rhapsody in Blue*.

———. *Victor Book of Concertos.* NY: Simon & Schuster, 1948. Program notes for *Concerto in F* and *Rhapsody in Blue*.

Vernon, Grenville. "Porgy and Bess," *The Commonweal* (Oct 25, 1935), 642.

Waldo, Fullerton. "High Spots in American Music," *Etude* (Apr 1934), 23. Passing mention of Gershwin; portrait.

Walker, Raymond. "Down the Scale of Musical Memories," *Variety* (Oct 20, 1954), 50. Touches on the *Rhapsody in Blue*.

Wallgren, Olle. "Goteborg," *Opera News* (Apr 9, 1966), 33. Review of *Porgy and Bess*.

Waters, Edward N. "Gershwin's *Rhapsody in Blue*," *The Library of Congress Quarterly Journal of Acquisitions* (May 1947), 65–6. A report of Ferde Grofé's gift of his own orchestration of Gershwin's work; includes facsimile of two pages of music.

———. "Music," *The Library of Congress Quarterly Journal of Current Acquisitions* (Nov 1959), 19–50. Discusses the gift of Gershwin's manuscript of "*I Got Rhythm*" Variations, with facsimiles (pp. 23–4).

———. "Music," *The Library of Congress Quarterly Journal of Current Acquisitions* (Nov 1960), 13–39. Discusses gift of manuscript sketches for *Porgy and Bess* (p. 23).

————. "Harvest of the Year: Selected Acquisitions of the Music Division," *The Quarterly Journal of The Library of Congress* (Jan 1967), 47–82. Reports gifts of Gershwin commemorative medals and a Russian edition of *Porgy and Bess* (p. 79).

————. "Songs to Symphonies: Recent Acquisitions of the Music Division," *The Quarterly Journal of The Library of Congress* (Jan 1968), 50–91. Discusses gifts of three donors: Mrs. Kay Swift Galloway and the composer's two brothers, Ira and Arthur Gershwin. Gifts include the original manuscript of *The George Gershwin Song-Book,* manuscript fragments from the *Cuban Overture, "I Got Rhythm" Variations, Concerto in F,* a music sketchbook with Gershwin melodies, an exercise book from Gershwin's studies with Edward Kilenyi, a text outline of *"I Got Rhythm" Variations,* and three exercise books from Gershwin's study with Joseph Schillinger (pp. 53–5); also sundry letters and other documents (p. 75).

————. "Paean to a Year of Plenty: Recent Acquisitions of the Music Division," *The Quarterly Journal of The Library of Congress* (Jan 1969), 21–47. Reports gifts of a small sketchbook which Ira calls the "Red Tune Book" (p. 22); a collection of letters and personal papers with special emphasis on the musical play, *Lady in the Dark;* Ira Gershwin wrote the lyrics, Kurt Weill composed the music (pp. 37, 42).

————. "Variations on a Theme: Recent Acquisitions of the Music Division," *The Quarterly Journal of The Library of Congress* (Jan 1970), 51–83. Describes Gershwin's exercise book from his study with Edward Kilenyi (p. 53), an Ira Gershwin autograph note (p. 68), and a 560 page scrapbook from the period July 11–August 11, 1937, consisting of international articles and clippings related to Gershwin's terminal illness and death (p. 77).

————. "Notable Music Acquisitions," *The Quarterly Journal of The Library of Congress* (Jan 1971), 45–72. Describes the sketch for *Lullaby* for string quartet; also sketches for *Porgy and Bess* (p. 46); also drafts of Ira Gershwin's piece for *The Saturday Review,* ". . . But I Wouldn't Want to Live There."

————. "Notable Acquisitions of the Music Division," *The Quarterly Journal of The Library of Congress* (Jan 1972), 48–76. Describes gift of sketches for *Girl Crazy,* with Ira Gershwin's notes, sketches of *Porgy and Bess,* a notebook, titled "Themes," with material used in *Rhapsody in Blue* and *Concerto in F* (p. 49), and a manuscript score of *135th Street,* with notes by Ira Gershwin (p. 61). Also discussed is Ira Gershwin's gift of gold coins, including one of George Gershwin, the score of a suite derived from *Porgy and Bess* (called *Catfish Row*), and a script from an interview on March 13, 1933, over radio station WJZ (p. 64).

Watt, Douglas. "Popular Records: A Pair of Gershwins," *The New Yorker* (Dec 19, 1959), 132–7.

Wechsberg, Joseph. "Austria: 'Porgy' Makes a Hit," *Opera* (Dec 1965), 899–901.

————. "Vienna," *Opera News* (Dec 11, 1965), 32. Review of *Porgy and Bess.*

Westphal, Kurt. "Neue Musik in den Berliner Festwochen," *Melos* (Nov 1952), 322–4. About *Porgy and Bess.*

Whiteman, Paul. "George and the Rhapsody," in: Merle Armitage, ed, *George Gershwin.* NY: Longmans, Green, 1938; 24–6.

———. "Rhapsody in Blue," in: *Rhapsody in Blue; the Jubilant Story of George Gershwin and His Music*. Hollywood: Warner Bros, 1945; 5–6.

———. "The Gershwin I Knew," *Music Journal* (Apr 1955), 19, 21. Includes a discussion of *Rhapsody in Blue* .

Whiteman, Paul, and Mary Margaret McBride. *Jazz*. NY: J. H. Sears, 1926. Contains Whiteman's account of his role in the premiere of *Rhapsody in Blue*.

Whitman, Alden. "Paul Whiteman, 'the Jazz King' of the Jazz Age, Is Dead at 77," *The New York Times* (Dec 30, 1967), 24. Summarizes Whiteman's career.

Wiborg, M. "Three Emperors of Broadway," *Art and Decorations* (May 1925), 48.

Wier, Albert, ed. *The Macmillan Encyclopedia of Music and Musicians*. NY: Macmillan, 1938; 661.

Wilder, Alec. "George Gershwin (1898–1937)," in his: *American Popular Song*. NY: Oxford University Press, 1972; 121–62. An analytical study of Gershwin's songs.

Wilson, John S. "A Wide Variety of Porgys and Besses," *The New York Times* (May 24, 1959), Sec II, 15. Record review.

———. "Ella Does Right By George," *The New York Times* (Nov 29, 1959), Sec II, 19. Record review of Ella Fitzgerald singing Gershwin.

———. "Ella Meets the Gershwins, with an Assist from Nelson Riddle," *High Fidelity* (Jan 1960), 63–4. Review of recording, "Ella Fitzgerald Sings the George and Ira Gershwin Song-Book."

———. "A Plaque in Brooklyn to Mark George Gershwin's Birthplace," *The New York Times* (Sep 23, 1963), 31. Describes Gershwin's birthplace.

———. "Misunderstood Pioneer: Whiteman's 'King of Jazz' Misnomer Obscured His Genuine Contribution," *The New York Times* (Dec 30, 1967), Sec II, 24. An evaluation of Whiteman after his death.

Woollcott, Alexander. "George the Ingenuous," *Hearst's International-Cosmopolitan* (Nov 1933), 32–3, 122–3. Witty and anecdotal.

Worbs, Hans Christoph. *Welterfolge der modernen Oper*. Berlin: Rembrandt, 1967. Discusses 25 major 20th century operas, including *Porgy and Bess*.

Würz, Anton. "George Gershwin," in: Friedrich Blume, ed, *Die Musik in Geschichte und Gegenwart*, 14 vols (Kassel: Bärenreiter, 1949–), IV, col 1828–31.

Wyatt, Euphemia. "American Opera," *The Catholic World* (Mar 1942), 726–7. About *Porgy and Bess*.

Zepp, Arthur. "I Was There—A View from the Servant's Quarters," *Clavier* (Feb 1971), 12–8.

Zilboorg, Gregory. "The Psychology of the Creative Personality," in: Paul Smith, ed, *Creativity*. NY: Hastings House, 1959; 21–32.

Zimel, Heyman. "George Gershwin," *Young Israel* (June 1928), 10–1.

INDEX

401